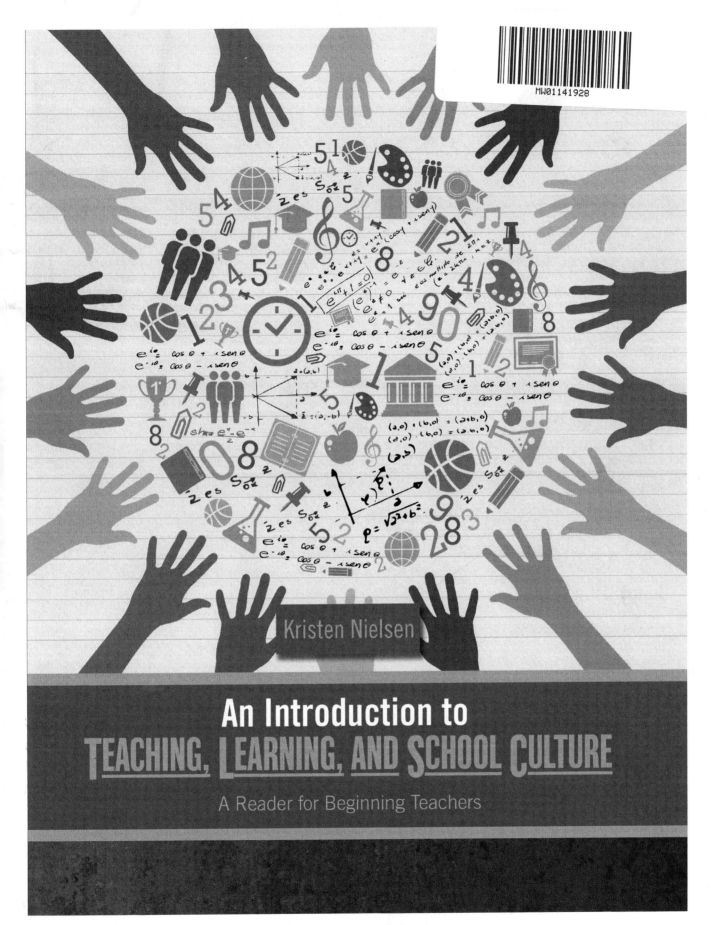

Kristen Nielsen

An Introduction to
TEACHING, LEARNING, AND SCHOOL CULTURE

A Reader for Beginning Teachers

Kendall Hunt
publishing company

MW01141928

Cover image © Shutterstock, Inc.

Kendall Hunt
publishing company

www.kendallhunt.com
Send all inquiries to:
4050 Westmark Drive
Dubuque, IA 52004-1840

Copyright © 2014 by Kristen Nielsen

ISBN 978-1-4652-5927-1

Printed in the United States of America

CONTENTS

About the Author   v
Introduction   vii

CHAPTER 1: **Understanding School Culture**...1

    1.1: Four Types of School Culture   1

CHAPTER 2: **Diversity in Schools** 9

    2.1: Citizenship, Education, and Diversity: Implications for Teacher Education   9
    2.2: Educating Everybody's Children: We Know What Works—And
        What Doesn't   22

CHAPTER 3: **Teaching and Inquiry** 57

    3.1: The Having of Wonderful Ideas   57

CHAPTER 4: **Classroom Communities** 67

    4.1: The Classroom as Community   67

CHAPTER 5: **Applying Learning Science in the Classroom** 77

    5.1: The Design of Learning Environments   77
    5.2: Learning: From Speculation to Science   93

CHAPTER 6: **Inclusive Practice and Learner Differentiation**.......................................117

    6.1: Differentiated Instruction: Inclusive Strategies For Standards-Based Learning
        That Benefit the Whole Class   117
    6.2: The Culturally Responsive Teacher   137

CHAPTER 7: **Teaching English Language Learners** 143

    7.1: What We Know—and Don't Yet Know—about Effective Instruction   143

CHAPTER 8: **Best Practices of Assessment** 153

    8.1: Types of Assessments   153
    8.2: Assessment as Learning   170
    8.3: Formative Assessment   174

CHAPTER 9: **Preparing for the Teaching Practicum and Field Observations**..............**181**
9.1: Bringing the World to Your Students   181
9.2: What to Look for in a Classroom   199
9.3: A Synthesis of Ethnographic Research   201

CHAPTER 10: **Preparing to Enter the Profession**..**209**
10.1: Beginning: The Challenge of Teaching   209

ABOUT THE AUTHOR

 Kristen Nielsen is a faculty member at the University of Calgary's Werklund School of Education, where she teaches courses in literacy and teacher education. She has worked in middle school through higher education for over fifteen years in the U.S. and Canada, and she has supported pre-service teacher experiences for the past seven years. She currently researches instructional methodology for writing and language, as well as pre-service and in-service teacher education.

INTRODUCTION

About twelve years ago, I first picked up a surfboard. It seemed like a perfect project for me, combining my love of the water with a physically challenging endorphin sport. There was also a certain artistry in the carving of both surfer and surfboard together into the shape of the wave that appealed to me, more like sculpting than dancing, as the body surged forward and then sideways at lightning speed and the surfer's shape formed an impression on the water. I already loved to snowboard, and I figured, as a long-time open water swimmer, that surfing would be a natural fit. It was on a trip to Costa Rica that surfing first piqued my interest. While in Dominical, a surf town in the south of the country with astonishing rip currents that made swimming without a surfboard a life-threatening pursuit, I made friends who had surfed their whole lives in California. Sitting under a palm tree, I watched them manipulate each wave with a power and precision of twisting and turning that seemed for one second as though they were in control, and at the next, at the complete mercy of the ocean. It was riveting to watch and impossible not to be inspired to imitation, and when I got home, I bought my first board and wetsuit in a surf shop in Belmar, NJ, without ever having set out on one in the ocean before.

I purchased a short board on the insistence of a surfer friend in New Jersey, whom I also had started dating: "Long boards are no fun. You can't turn them, and they just go straight, like riding on your living room sofa. Just get a short board and learn to surf on it from the start." I trusted his appraisal, but I would later learn that there are fairly solid reasons why most neophytes begin on a long board "from the start." It turns out that surfing is really, really hard. It's hard to catch a wave. It's hard to paddle out past the breakers on days when there are waves big enough to catch. It's hard to duck dive, the process of diving under incoming waves that allows a surfer to paddle out to where the waves can be caught. It's hard to keep from "going over the falls," the terrifying and spine mangling experience of being thrust mercilessly forward, down, and finally *under* a crashing wave, either a breaker that one is trying to surf but has possibly caught too late or one that is possibly not surfable (a "close out"). Oh, and standing up, yes that is hard too, but first a surfer has to arrive at the point where standing up is even possible by accomplishing all of the above, and so . . . back to the long board. As it turns out, beginners, and even many lifelong surfers take out long boards because it is easier to (1) force a long board through the surf rolling in to get past the inside small breakers to the "outside" where one can ride a larger breaking wave; (2) actually catch a wave, especially small waves on the living room sofa of surfboards; and (3) avoid the body mangling, skull jarring experience of going over the falls while on a living room sofa, which can hold its own within many powerful waves, rather than on a short board, which will drop the surfer directly to the bottom of the elevator shaft. Of course my mentor was right, short boarding was so much cooler, but he had been surfing *his entire life*, and I was only beginning. I was beginning, in fact, on a very short board, at 6 feet 4 inches, in the frustrating surf of the New Jersey tropical storm season. We went out several days a week that season, in either teeny tiny surf that was nearly impossible to catch with a short board or massive nine-foot-plus waves from a passing storm en route from the Caribbean, rollers that would send me slamming downward to the floor of the ocean, with time to think about my choice of hobby for what seemed like hours until I could finally resurface, sinuses newly flushed by salt water, and plans newly formed for enhanced health insurance. I did not know on my first few days that I probably should have started with a long board, though my error quickly became quite clear. No matter, I was already invested in my short board, and I was going to learn to surf with it.

I really struggled. For an entire summer of driving to the shore a few days a week, I struggled to learn to surf, and during this time, I followed all of the instructions of my new surfer friends closely. They gave me lots of details about what to do to master the ocean. They modeled what to do for me. I saw them catching ride after ride, and yet I could not get up on my board on an outside breaking wave. What was the secret? What was I doing wrong? I was an athletic, strong, determined individual with experienced surfer friends to teach me. Why could I not get up on a wave? Just once. And I mean, I did not get up and ride that board on a breaking wave even one single time all summer. I had near misses all the time. I could surf the small inside waves and whitewash to shore with no problem and stand up the whole time. Then out in the breaking surf, in the real waves, I would start to jump on the board, but I could not catch a breaking wave, failing to stand up on my board for one single actual ride. I spent a year on and off surfing the many beaches of New Jersey and returning to Costa Rica on a surf trip as well. I even went out in the frigid February water in Sandy Hook, New Jersey for a few days of winter storm waves, with a hood, booties, gloves, and Vaseline on my face. Resurfacing in the icy ocean from underwater, I felt the restarting of my heart each time, as I sucked in the frigid air. I was out there because I loved being in the ocean, even in winter. I often saw dolphins in the spring and summer. I skirted the floating glassy pink and purple jelly fish in August and collected bluefish eggs in my hands, like tapioca pearls, in September. For many days we started early for "Dawn Patrol" to watch the sun rise, and on others we surfed after dark when the moon was full. It was the most lovely of sports. And I was terrible at it.

After that year of frustration, I began putting my surfboard away and would only head to the beach occasionally. Perhaps it was the pressing demands of my graduate work or the end of my relationship with the surfer, or maybe it was the frustration of my lack of success riding waves, but I rarely mustered the enthusiasm to make the hour-long plus drive to the shore any longer. On hot days, I would swim in the pools closer to home, and my surfboard collected dust in the attic. Then, a few years later, while staying in California for a three-month-long research project, I decided to get back on a surfboard. Why not? I was staying right on the beach in the Mecca of surfing, and waves were just there for the taking. In New Jersey, we would have to drop everything and drive to the appropriate beach when the Internet told us the swells would arrive—and those waves were never reliable. In La Jolla there was surf every day.

My first day back on a board, I tugged and clawed at the rubber of my old wetsuit to get it over my shoulders. Stiff with dried salt and encrusted with sand after so many uses, followed by a few years in storage, it had lost its suppleness and was tough to manipulate. It would be a tiring paddle out. I headed out at La Jolla Shores in San Diego with my rental board, hoping for a miracle. I discovered, after two hours of beatings on a choppy day of high surf, that I was still terrible. I also rediscovered my love of the sport. In the first ten minutes I saw two seals, who nearly bumped the underside of my board as they popped their spotted puppy heads up next to me (oh, to be as at ease like them in the waves.) I felt the pleasurable ache in my arms, exhausted from paddling out past the breakers, ducking and jumping over the surf, fighting my way out. I caught rides on the white water of already broken waves, so big and powerful that I blasted forward as though shot from a cannon. I spent every day for the next three months surfing for at least an hour and a half at a time, and— I actually made progress. Within the first week, I rode a number of larger breaking waves. I could usually get on the board for three-to-eight seconds before being thrust off—an incredible achievement for me. I had purchased a board longer than a true short board, but not nearly long enough to classify as a sofa, at only 7 feet 2 inches. It was easier to push through the waves on my way out and a bit easier to catch waves with as well. Then, within the next month, I began to consistently catch and ride breaking waves. I still couldn't turn or manipulate the board with any sort of confidence or finesse, but I was up and running. By the end of three months I felt that I was a surfer, and though I knew I had years of surfing and learning and improving ahead of me before I could even begin to leave the novice phase, I had turned a corner and rarely found myself going over the falls. I had needed the consistency and the repetition of surfing every day to practice the concepts I had learned and to imitate examples my friends had set. Simply put, I needed to practice.

It occurred to me this year, on a return trip to San Diego for a few weeks, and after finishing a teacher education course in the spring term, that I had been trying to teach my students to surf. Like surfing, teaching is incredibly, unfathomably difficult, and it presents the learner with multiple complex demands and challenges all at once that can only be managed with practice and with expertise. Like surfing, teaching has high rates of attrition, as novices become frustrated by repeated difficulties in the classroom and beyond, far more complex than those they had imagined in Ed school, and they simply give up. Also like surfing, teaching can be explained, theorized, and modeled, but it cannot be mastered without practice, application, and dedication. Finally, like being out on the water, teaching is a lovely profession, with incredible moments of beauty and joy. Even the small success can be enough to sustain the teacher through the challenges. So when my students struggle with their first tastes of teaching in their field experiences, I know that some of this struggle is simply part of the learning process, a process that will include some moments of beauty and a few crashes as well, and there will be years of practice and repetition before beginning teachers leave the novice phase. I see my job as a teacher educator, as one that includes sharing the reality of the most difficult and lovely of professions with my students.

IN SEARCH OF A FAST TRACK TO EXPERIENCED TEACHING

Pre-service teachers come to the profession from a wide range of backgrounds and are motivated to succeed as educators for a variety of different reasons: love of subject matter, love of students, love of the sharing and co-creating of knowledge, appreciation for a previous teacher and his or her expertise, a wish to help learners who struggle or to support social justice. Whatever the motivation, all pre-service teachers approach the teacher education experiences with a sense of urgency, a wish to become, as quickly as possible, skillful and talented educators who can successfully obtain a job, manage a classroom, plan and share content, and lead their students to high achievement. There is also a desperate scramble for a sense of safety and security around the prospect of entering a classroom for the first time as teachers. These first classroom experiences are unsettling, and my students are often in search of ways to feel more secure and confident. They are looking for shortcuts to success.

On many occasions, pre-service teachers in my education classes will jump in with a question or two at the end of each class, and after a lengthy discussion and analysis of problems in teaching, along the lines of: "But what can we actually *do* to manage a classroom of so many diverse learners? Could you give us a few *specific* strategies?" or: "How do we help our students become motivated to learn? What are some *specific* steps we can take?" As everyone leans in for the important tips and strategies, I struggle to provide the nutshell answers they are looking for, sort of a top-ten list of teacher behaviors that can solve their classroom problems. But I know that offering them their top ten list will be inauthentic and unrealistic. My students are always looking for a handbag of tricks that will fast track them to experienced and successful teaching, and I am always having to explain to them that no such fast track exists. While we, as teacher educators, can support our students, encourage their learning, engage their understanding of the actualities of the classroom, we cannot provide a substitute for experience, and it is experience alone that builds expertise and achievement.

So what then is the purpose of teacher education and what would we hope to accomplish during courses and fieldwork for pre-service teachers? As soon as we can acknowledge that education programs, courses, field experiences, and the readings and materials that accompany them cannot replace the experience teachers will need to succeed in the classroom over time, we can focus on the deep thinking and problem posing that will help pre-service teachers make their first transitions to teaching and support their future professional growth. This problem posing should prompt them to ask and answer the most critical questions for future educators. We can help students work through authentic problems and scenarios in education and grapple with difficult dilemmas through engaged thinking, both individually and collaboratively. The hard work in education classes takes places within the classroom through discussion and sharing of views and ideas, and the readings in this text are chosen to foster the kind of inquiry that supports teacher knowledge. Again, the goal is not to fast track a pre-service teacher to becoming an expert, but rather to begin the habits of inquiry and deep analysis that will support beginning teachers and lead to further knowledge growth through practice, and still more practice.

The readings in this text are organized by topic and are designed to support a foundational understanding of teaching in a contemporary context. These introductory level readings provide an overview of essential topics in education and prompt readers to dig more deeply into each area through research and by making connections to practical classroom examples and field experiences. Each topic was chosen because of its critical contribution to teacher knowledge. Each topic should also be introduced in the beginning of a teacher education program and then reinforced/revisited throughout to allow time for understanding. It is recommended that the readings be accompanied by case studies, inquiry projects, pair and group discussion, classroom videos, teaching observations, and field experiences and that students have the opportunity to lead these exercises as much as— possible. It is also highly recommended that classes engage in storytelling.

Personal stories and anecdotes also complement the readings in this text. Stories from the classroom and beyond have the power to transport beginning teachers to real contexts and situations and to engage their interest and critical thinking through lively experience. Storytelling marks a second moment of my classes where students really lean in to listen. They strive to catch the details of a story and to learn about the real experiences and problems teachers face through anecdotes. My stories are often told through a comical lens, intended to entertain and to put a humorous spin on a challenging classroom moment, rendering it less painful in retrospect and emphasizing what I learned from it. I also encourage my students to share, in return, their stories from the field and to respond to each others' narratives. Frequently, I plan just a portion of class time to be dedicated to such sharing and end up with an entire class or two on narrating and responding to tales from the classroom because the level of student engagement extends the sharing period.

The critical goals for this text are to provide the core ideas and problems in education, at a beginning level, to engage students in dialogue and questioning, and to lead them toward deeper learning in their future studies and professional lives. As they leave their education courses and experiences, I encourage all beginning teachers to continue learning, to practice, and to persevere. This is the most challenging of professions, and expertise will develop over time.

CHAPTER 1

Understanding School Culture

Four Types of School Culture

— by Cletus R. Bulach, Fred C. Lunenburg, and Les Potter

Phase One (Change the existing culture of control)

In this chapter, four distinct types of school cultures and the leadership style that creates that type are described. How to implement Phase 1 of the high performing school culture will also be described. The four types are:

1. the laissez-faire school culture is an underperforming school (2 percent–5 percent)
2. the traditional school culture is a low-performing school (60 percent–75 percent)
3. the enlightened traditional school culture is an above average performing school (10 percent–15 percent)
4. the high-performing school culture (2 percent–5 percent)

These four types of school cultures were observed while making on-site visits and conducting interviews with faculty and students at 65 individual schools in West Virginia.* All schools, because of the values and beliefs of the school community, have an established culture. As a result of this underlying culture, various rules and expectations are in place. A key component of any school's climate is the control culture. How faculty and students are controlled determines the type of school culture and climate. In addition to the control culture, the leadership style of the principal often plays a key role in shaping a school's culture. Keep in mind that a school can be a blend between two or more cultures.

---

*Cletus R. Bulach was serving as the external evaluator for the West Virginia character education grant while conducting these interviews and on-site visits in (2002–2005). He logged 5000 miles and spent 5 months in every school district in the State. One school in each district was visited. Two sets of students were interviewed. One was the student leadership team and the other set was a randomly selected set of classroom students. The teachers at each school were interviewed using a "force field analysis" technique (described in chapter 2).

In this chapter, the authors also describe the role of control for implementing Phase 1 of the reform process for creating a high-performing school. Prior to implementing the "high-performing" school culture (Phase 1), school officials must first identify the type of school culture that exists at their school. Describing the four types of school cultures assists with that process.

The Laissez-Faire, Low-Performing School

A laissez-faire school is a low-performing school and it is characterized by a lack of control. There are not many schools with this type of culture, but they do exist. Based on our collective experience, we estimate that the number of schools with this type of culture is around 2–5 percent. The morning that I (Bulach) entered the office of a school of this type, the front office was noisy, and there were a number of people waiting for the secretary to admit them to school. The principal, who could have been assisting with the overflow, was in her office. I patiently waited until the secretary had time for me. When told that I was the evaluator of their character education program, she rang the principal, and I was ushered into her office. Before I could enter, someone came in from the hall and said there was a bunch of students in the hallway. The principal went to the hall and said to the students, "What is going on?" A student said that "Coach is not here to let us in our room!"

The principal at this school did not have a procedure in place to make sure that all teachers had arrived and were at their posts to supervise students. Later that day, I asked to meet with the teacher who was responsible for student council, as I wanted to interview the student leadership team about their perceptions of the school and their character education program. The teacher was not in his room. Instead he was supervising the class of another teacher, who was out sick. I found that teacher in the teachers' lounge. The principal of the school was totally unaware of this incident.

In walking through the school to check for evidence of a character education program, I noticed a number of students in the hallway. I personally escorted one student to his room only to find him sitting in a locker on another floor 10 minutes later. As I walked into classrooms and observed what teachers were doing, some were teaching, and others were sitting at their desks while the students talked and were off task. In a laissez-faire school, the principal does not have procedures in place to control the faculty, and the teachers do not have procedures in place to control the students.

A variation of this type is a school where procedures are in place, but teachers do not follow them, and the principal does not follow through to make sure the procedure is carried out. The leadership style tends to be nondirective, and the principal tends to ask people to do things, However, there tends to be little follow-through to make sure the request is acted on. Faculty and students tend to be self-serving, and there is an absence of servant leadership. Servant leadership will be described in detail in chapter 2.

In interviewing students and teachers at this school, some of the negative comments were as follows:

- Some teachers punish the whole class when one student is the problem.
- Teachers and the principal have favorites. They will punish some kids and the same thing goes unpunished for the ones they like—particularly the dress code.
- The dress code and other rules are not enforced. Some teachers look other way.
- The punishment does not always fit the crime.
- New students are not accepted.
- There is a lack of organization.
- People here are judgmental.

The Traditional, Underperforming School

A second type of school culture is a traditional school, and it is characterized by a heavy emphasis on control. It is an underperforming school, and in our opinion 60–75 percent of schools have this type of culture. The principal and the administrative team are very much in control. Teachers are subordinate to the leadership team and are not involved in the decision-making process. There is a faculty handbook, and there are procedures established for everything that is supposed to happen at that school. Lesson plans are submitted on a daily basis, and everything is checked to make sure everyone is following procedures. The same is true for students. Teachers are very much in control of what happens in each classroom.

Students are not involved in what happens at the school. There is no student council or student leadership team. If one does exist, it has no decision-making power. It is a rubber stamp for the administration. The leadership style is directive and position, reward, and coercion are three forms of power used to control students and faculty. Coercion power in the form of punishment, however, is the most frequently used form of power. There are six other forms of power in addition to these three. The nine forms of power, and their use and misuse are described in chapter 4 (Phase 3).

In one such school, when I asked the students what they liked about their school, they had little to say. Several comments about what they liked were, "When school is out!" and "When I get off the bus!" When asked what they did not like, they were hesitant to talk. One student asked, "Will we get in trouble if we tell you things?" When I assured them that all comments were anonymous, and no one would know who said what, it was difficult to keep them quiet. Everyone wanted to talk. Their frustrated and angry comments were as follows:

- Some teachers are nice but a lot of them are not nice.
- Some teachers cuss and call students names.
- Teachers have favorites. They will punish some kids, and the same thing goes unpunished for the ones they like.
- The teachers have double standards. They won't let us do things, but they do them. (Eating and drinking in their room was an example given.)
- The principal is mean.
- I do not like anything about it.
- The teachers put us down and ignore us.
- The teachers do not help us when we need it.

In this type of school, faculty and the administration use grades and punishment to motivate the students. If students do not study, they receive an F. If they do not obey rules, they are punished. These are forms of extrinsic motivation and one of the major reasons why the schools are under-performing. Students tend to do what they have to do to stay out of trouble and get the grade they want. In talking with a teacher in one of these schools, she commented that, "If you give the students any freedom, they get out of control." The administration and teachers in this type of school have to constantly be on watch to make sure students do what they are supposed to do.

The majority of schools in the United States fall into this category. Silva and Mackin (2002) wrote:

Next to prisons, high schools are the least democratic institutions in our American society. They are cursed by a tradition of hypocrisy—teaching and espousing democratic doctrine within the classroom, but doing it in a highly controlled authoritarian manner that makes the actual practice of democratic principles largely nonexistent anywhere in the school. (p. 1)

Their opinion is supported by Kohn (2006, 2004), who stated that there is an over-reliance on punishment as a way of disciplining students who do not follow rules. He wrote that school officials' response to discipline with ever-harsher measures is counterproductive. The next type of school culture attempts to address this over-reliance on punishment.

The Enlightened Traditional, Above Average—Performing School

A third type of school culture is an enlightened traditional school, and it is an above average—performing school. We estimate that approximately 10 percent—15 percent of schools have some variation of this type of culture. The principal and administrative teams are also very much in control; however, they have created incentives or reinforcers for faculty and students to control themselves. Instead of relying on position and coercion to control faculty and students, they have an established system of rewards to encourage faculty and students to control themselves. This is an attempt to shift control from the leaders to subordinates. Some examples of incentives or rewards are:

- Teacher of the year: Teachers are recognized at a board meeting and given a parking spot close to the school entrance as a way to encourage teachers to go the extra mile.
- Leadership team: teachers are chosen by the principal to provide advice and assist with the communication process when needed.
- Student of the month: Each teacher has a student of the month, or sometimes only one is chosen for the entire school as a way to recognize attendance, character behavior, citizenship, and so forth. Other variations can be students who are recognized at the end of a grading period, the end of the semester, or the end of the year.
- Points system: Students who do what they are supposed to do regarding homework, attendance, and behavior earn points. These points can be cashed in at the student store for pencils, paper, or other school-related items or for treats in the cafeteria.
- Redirects, reminders, or violations: Students who do not do what they are supposed to do are given a redirect. The redirect can be for any rule infraction or failure to exhibit a behavior related to a character trait. If a student receives three redirects in one day, a punishment is incurred. At the end of a grading period, all students who have incurred no punishments in the form of office referrals or less than three redirects are rewarded with a field trip or something else that the students have requested. One school has a "movie madness" afternoon where students select a movie they want to watch, and business partners provide food and drinks.
- Caught doing good: A certificate is given to students who do good deeds. This can be related to the character word for the month or any other deed that a teacher deems worthy of recognition. Some schools provide treats or rewards for each certificate and recognize students during morning announcements.

In the enlightened traditional school, both punishment and reward are used to motivate and/or control students. The motivation is still extrinsic, but there is an improvement in student behavior. According to the research of Marzano, Marzano, and Pickering (2003), there is a 24 percent increase in student misbehavior where there are no consequences, a 28 percent decrease where there are consequences, a 31 percent decrease if there are rewards for positive behavior, and a 33 percent decrease if punishment and rewards are both used.

Marzano and colleagues (2003) stated that, "The guiding principle for disciplinary interventions is that they should include a healthy balance between negative consequences for inappropriate behavior and positive consequences for appropriate behavior" (p. 40). Kohn (2006), however, stated that this type of discipline does not help students to grow to be responsible students. He believes that students should control their behavior because it is the right thing to do and not because of a reward.

The controversy over the use of rewards has been ongoing. According to Sergiovanni and Starratt (2002), the use of rewards is not a good practice because student behavior is motivated for external reasons, that is, the desired behavior occurs because of the reward and not because it is the right thing to do. They believe that students should not be rewarded (external motivation) for a behavior that they are supposed to do because it is the right thing to do (internal motivation). Giving a reward (external) for something they are supposed to do (internal) extinguishes the internal motivation. Intermittent reward, however, according to these theorists does not extinguish internal motivation.

Several schools were observed using intermittent rewards for students "caught doing good." They received a "caught doing good" certificate and personal recognition. The certificate was put in a box, and at the end of the week, several names were drawn from the box. Those students received a prize from the school's business partners. One school drew two names and their business partner, a bank, gave each student a $50 savings bond.

Another variation of "caught doing good" is the ability of students to trade in a number of "caught doing good" certificates to remove a redirect or reminder. In some schools, students who have more than three redirects, reminders, or violations are excluded from the end-of-grading-period reward. The intent here is to present students with the opportunity to get back into the good graces of school officials. Supposedly, once a student knows they are excluded from the end-of-grading-period reward, there is no incentive for them to behave other than traditional discipline procedures.

The ability to trade "caught doing good" certificates for rule infractions is an incentive for the so-called "bad actors" to continue trying to improve their behavior. In schools that use point systems instead of certificates, students can use points to buy back a violation or redirect. This practice encourages desirable behavior by rewarding it while continuing to punish undesirable behavior.

Many enlightened traditional schools do not have a plan in place to motivate students who have lost the chance to take part in the end-of-report-period reward. This is a mistake as there is no motivation for these students to behave once they have lost the opportunity to take part in the reward. A system should be put in place so they can earn back the right to take part. One of the comments frequently heard during the student interviews when asked about their character education program was that it had no effect on the bad actors. These bad actors are typically 5 percent to 7 percent of the students, and they are the students who make it difficult for teachers to teach and other students to learn. A plan has to be developed to encourage these students to control their disruptive behavior.

An interesting variation of "caught doing good" was observed at a middle school, and it involved the use of a character bulletin board. Teachers who saw a student doing something representative of the character trait being taught would put a post-it note with the student's name on the bulletin board. In the morning, before classes started, students looked at the bulletin board to see if their name was there. If it was, they took it to the teacher who put it there, and then three things happened.

1. The teacher verbally reinforced the student's positive behavior.
2. The student was given a treat.
3. The post-it note was put in a jar in the office.

A post-it was periodically drawn from the jar, and that student and the teacher were given a prize. The teacher's reward was a free period while the principal taught the class. The students' treat or prize can be as small as a pencil or an ice cream at lunch or a McDonald's meal or something larger from another business partner.

The intriguing part was the interest and excitement created by not rewarding the behavior when it happened. Instead the students had to check the bulletin board each morning to see who was caught being good. When students at this school were interviewed, they said they really liked the character bulletin board and the excitement it generated when they took their name off the board and went to the teacher, cook, or other person who put their name there to find out what they had done. And teachers liked having the principal take their class for a period.

Marzano and colleagues (2003) stated that behavior limits need to be established, and a record-keeping system must be in place. In some schools it means having a pencil, finishing homework, having textbooks, raising hands, not getting out of seats unless permitted, walking on the right side of the hall, following the dress code, and so forth. Students with too many violations lose their freedom at lunch. Too many violations can be as few as one to as many as five. Instead of going to lunch and perhaps recess with the other students, misbehaving students get their lunch and report to a separate room where they are counseled on what they have to do to earn back the right to eat lunch with the other students.

In an enlightened traditional school, a system is in place to encourage students and others to control their own behavior. The burden of controlling what people are supposed to do is shared with everyone in the school. Students and faculty are given the freedom to control their own behavior, and incentives are in place to encourage desirable behavior. If students and faculty do not control their own behavior and undesirable behavior is the result, then someone controls them and does something to extinguish the undesirable behavior.

This is in contrast to the traditional school where students and faculty have little freedom—students are controlled by teachers, and teachers are controlled by the administration. They must do what they are supposed to or they will receive admonishment or punishment. The leadership style in an enlightened traditional school tends to be collaborative. The forms of power used are information, personality, ego, and moral power. Position and coercion power are used when the preceding forms of power do not work. Servant leadership can take place in this type of school, but the focus on getting a reward tends to be self-serving. The forms of power and servant leadership will be discussed in detail in chapter 4.

The High-Performing School

A fourth type of school culture is the high-performing school. We estimate that there have to be some schools (2 percent—5 percent) with this type of culture. We do know of the one observed in West Virginia and of several in Indiana that have implemented this reform. The school in West Virginia was the impetus for this chapter and the book. The high-performing school has many of the same features as the enlightened traditional school, but it has added an additional reward for desirable behavior.

While the enlightened traditional school relies on individuals to control their own behavior, the high-performing school creates an incentive or reward for the peer group to help control other students. For example, if there are no redirects, reminders, or violations or less than a prescribed number, the peer group gets a reward. This can take many forms. The peer group can be a class of students, a team, an advisory group, a homeroom, a grade level, or the entire school. The larger the peer group, the more students are involved in controlling the other students.

Ideally, the entire school should be involved, but it has been successful in a single classroom as well. This system requires setting a benchmark for the students to try to reach or stay under. For example, if office referrals for the entire school for a week totaled 100, the benchmark can be set at 50. If the number of office referrals for the next week were under that benchmark, all the students are given a reward. The reward can be a recess, board games, or some other compensation that is a motivator.

In a high-performing school all students receive the reward, whereas in an enlightened traditional school only those students who have behaved responsibly are compensated. In a high-performing school peer pressure on those students who are disruptive does occur. There is also an additional incentive for disruptive students to do what they are supposed to do because they will also enjoy the reward, whereas in the enlightened traditional setting, they are excluded.

Office referrals can be used to establish benchmarks, but a better system uses redirects, reminders, or pink slips. There is a lot of student behavior that does not warrant punishment, but it does interfere with creating a caring learning environment. Responsible student behavior must be encouraged. The redirects, reminders, or pink slips are one way to encourage responsible student behavior without punishing students every time they forget to do what they are supposed to do.

Only one high-performing school was observed during the on-site visits and interviews in West Virginia. School officials at this middle school set a benchmark and reward for each day, as well as an end-of-report-period reward for students with fewer than three redirects during the period. Their benchmark was 25 or fewer redirects for a day. If that benchmark were met, the reward was 10 extra minutes of locker time the next day. This particular school had approximately 350 students, and they met their benchmark on an average of four times per week. On the day of the visit, they had fewer than 10 redirects, and the reward was an extra 10 minutes of free time before dismissal.

When asked to describe a redirect, the principal stated that any time a teacher had to reprimand a student for not raising their hand, running, wearing a cap, talking, and so forth, it was considered a redirect. When asked how state guidelines for time requirements were addressed, the principal stated that students have more "time on task" at his school because teachers had fewer interruptions of the instructional process. He stated that when they started this system 10 years ago, the benchmark was 100 redirects and each year they have lowered the benchmark to the current 25.

While there was only one high-performing school observed, a number of teachers were seen in other schools who used some variation of the high-performing school at the classroom level. Some teachers used movies and popcorn, but this was not a strong motivator because students had often already seen the movie. Some used field trips, which tend to be strong motivators.

The strongest motivator is free time. Students want time to interact with their friends. If the reward is a weekly event, a strong motivator is extra time on Friday to go to the gym or playground and hang out or play games. If the reward for reducing the number redirects is a daily event, five minutes of extra time at recess is a very strong motivator. At the elementary level, the ability to delay gratification is difficult for students. Extra recess is a very strong motivator because they know at the end of the day whether they have met their target. Choosing a reward that will motivate the peer group to become active in controlling each other is extremely important.

An elementary school that was visited had a banner displayed outside the classroom with the fewest redirects for the month. A classroom was visited where a teacher had two jars of marbles. She told her students if they had a good day, she would take a handful of marbles from jar one and put it into jar two. When the jar one was empty and jar two full, the entire class could go to McDonald's for ice cream. She had some other rules regarding the marbles:

1. If they had a bad day, she would remove a handful of marbles from jar two and place them back in jar one or vice versa if they had a good day.
2. If a student did something good, she might take a marble from jar one and place it in jar two.
3. If a student did something bad, she might take a marble out of jar two and place it back in jar one.

Through use of the marbles and the jars, this teacher created a high-performing classroom and an incentive for the students to help each other to behave responsibly. Another variation of this class-room control/incentive technique involved the use of a paper chain. The teacher added a link to the chain when the class did what they were supposed to do. When it reached a certain length, the entire class got a reward. When there were only a few marbles left in jar one or only a few more links to add to the chain, student behavior was wonderful. They worked together because they knew the reward was soon to come.

One interesting observation about the high-performing school or classroom is that it teaches a very important character trait—citizenship. It creates a community within a classroom, grade level, team, or school where students are encouraged to be responsible citizens. They follow rules, obey authority, help each other, intervene when something wrong is about to happen or is happening, and so forth. They learn to recognize undesirable behavior and model desirable behavior.

This type of school creates an environment where students can become responsible citizens. The leadership style, as in an enlightened traditional school, tends to be collaborative. The interesting transformation, however, is that control has been shifted to students. They are being asked to help control each other whereas in the past, it was the teachers and other faculty members' responsibility to control students.

This shift in control changes the peer group from a negative force to a positive force. Berger (2003) wrote: "I was raised with the message that peer pressure was something terrible, something to avoid, something negative. Peer pressure meant kids trying to talk you into smoking cigarettes or taking drugs. I realized after 10 years of teaching that positive peer pressure was the primary reason my classroom was a safe, supportive environment for student learning. Peer pressure wasn't something to be afraid of, to be avoided, but rather to be cultivated in a positive direction." (p. 36) In most classrooms, peer pressure is still a negative force. Changing the existing control culture is a common sense approach to give control to the peer group and make it a positive force.

The Role of Control in a High Performing School

A culture has been created in most schools where control issues are a major factor. Boards control superintendents, who control central office, who control principals, who control teachers, who control students. It is all about control. They believe they have to have control and in fact **they do have to control**. Losing control is one of the greatest fears of any educator, whether teacher, administrator, or board member. Control has to be there! **Learning cannot occur in a school where there is not a highly controlled environment.**

CHAPTER 2

Diversity in Schools

Citizenship Education and Diversity: Implications for Teacher Education

In the first part of this article, the author argues that teachers should help students to develop a delicate balance of cultural, national, and global identifications because of the rich diversity in the United States and throughout the world. To help students become effective citizens, teachers need to acquire reflective cultural, national, and global identifications. In the second part of this article, the author describes how he tries to help the students in one of his teacher education courses to challenge and critically examine their cultural and national identifications.

Because of the increasing racial, ethnic, cultural, and language diversity in the United States, effective teachers in the new century must help students become reflective citizens in pluralistic democratic nation-states. In this article, I argue that citizenship education needs to be reconceptualized because of the increased salience of diversity issues throughout the world. A new kind of citizenship education, called *multicultural citizenship*, will enable students to acquire a delicate balance of cultural, national, and global identifications and to understand the ways in which knowledge is constructed; to become knowledge producers; and to participate in civic action to create a more humane nation and world (J. A. Banks, 1997a). Teachers must develop reflective cultural, national, and global identifications themselves if they are to help students become thoughtful, caring, and reflective citizens in a multicultural world society.

This article consists of two major parts. In the first, I describe the theoretical and conceptual goals for citizenship education in a pluralistic democratic society. In the second, I describe how I implement these goals in one of my teacher education courses. The tone and style of the second part of the article are more personalized than those of the first part because I describe how the theory that I have developed is implemented in my own classroom.

Banks, James A. Citizenship Education and Diversity: Implications for Teacher Education. *Journal of Teacher Education*, 52(1), 5-16, Copyright © 2001 by Sage Publications. Reprinted by permission of Sage Publications, Inc.

Balancing Diversity and Unity

Most nation-states and societies throughout the world are characterized by cultural, ethnic, language, and religious diversity. One of the challenges to pluralistic democratic nation-states is to provide opportunities for cultural and ethnic groups to maintain components of their community cultures while at the same time constructing a nation-state in which diverse groups are structurally included and to which they feel allegiance. A delicate balance of unity and diversity should be an essential goal of democratic nation-states.

The challenge of balancing diversity and unity is intensifying as democratic nation-states such as the United States, Canada, Australia, and the United Kingdom become more diversified and as racial and ethnic groups within these nations become involved in cultural and ethnic revitalization movements. The democratic ideologies institutionalized within the major democratic Western nations and the wide gap between these ideals and realities were major factors that resulted in the rise of ethnic revitalization movements in nation-states such as the United States, Canada, and the United Kingdom during the 1960s and 1970s.

These nations share a democratic ideal, a major tenet of which is that the state should protect human rights and promote equality and the structural inclusion of diverse groups into the fabric of society. These societies are also characterized by widespread inequality and by racial, ethnic, and class stratification. The discrepancy between democratic ideals and societal realities and the rising expectations of structurally excluded racial, ethnic, and social-class groups created protest and revival movements within the Western democratic nations.

THE NEED FOR A NEW CONCEPTION OF CITIZENSHIP EDUCATION

Because of growing ethnic, cultural, racial, and religious diversity throughout the world, citizenship education needs to be changed in substantial ways to prepare students to function effectively in the 21st century. Citizens in the new century need the knowledge, attitudes, and skills required to function in their ethnic and cultural communities and beyond their cultural borders and to participate in the construction of a national civic culture that is a moral and just community that embodies democratic ideals and values, such as those embodied in the Universal Declaration of Human Rights. Students also need to acquire the knowledge and skills needed to become effective citizens in the global community.

Citizenship education in the past, in the United States as well as in many other nations, embraced an assimilationist ideology. In the United States, its aim was to educate students so they would fit into a mythical Anglo-Saxon Protestant conception of the "good citizen." Anglo conformity was the goal of citizenship education. One of its aims was to eradicate the community cultures and languages of students from diverse ethnic, cultural, racial, and language groups. One consequence of this assimilationist conception of citizenship education was that many students lost their first cultures, languages, and ethnic identities. Some students also became alienated from family and community. Another consequence was that many students became socially and politically alienated within the national civic culture.

Ethnic minorities of color often became marginalized in both their community cultures and in the national civic culture because they could function effectively in neither. When they acquired the language and culture of the Anglo mainstream, they were denied structural inclusion and full participation into the civic culture because of their racial characteristics.

Citizenship education must be transformed in this new century because of the large influx of immigrants who are now settling in nations throughout the world, because of the continuing existence of institutional racism and discrimination throughout the world, and because of the widening gap between the rich and the poor.

The U.S. Census (U.S. Bureau of the Census, 1998) projects that 47% of the U.S. population will consist of ethnic minorities of color by 2050. The percentage of ethnic minorities in nation-states throughout the world has increased significantly within the past 30 years. In many Western nations, the ethnic minority population is growing at significantly greater rates than is the majority population. Institutionalized discrimination and racism are manifest by the significant gaps in the incomes, education, and health of minority and majority groups in many nation-states. Ethnic, racial, and religious minorities are also the victims of violence in many nation-states.

In the United States, the share of the nation's wealth held by the wealthiest households (0.5%) rose sharply in the 1980s after declining for 40 years. In 1976, this segment of the population held 14% of the nation's wealth. In 1983, it held 26.9% (Phillips, 1990). In 1997, 12.7% of Americans, which included a higher percentage of African Americans and Hispanics (8.6% of non-Hispanic Whites, 26.0% of African Americans, 27.1% of Hispanics), were living in poverty (U.S. Bureau of the Census, 1998).

Cultural Communities and Multicultural Citizenship

Citizens should be able to maintain attachments to their cultural communities as well as participate effectively in the shared national culture. Cultural and ethnic communities need to be respected and given legitimacy not only because they provide safe spaces for ethnic, cultural, and language groups on the margins of society, but also because they serve as a conscience for the nation-state. These communities take action to force the nation to live up to its democratic ideals when they are most seriously violated. It was the abolitionists and not the founding fathers in the United States who argued that freedom and equality should be extended to all Americans. African Americans led the civil rights movement of the 1960s and 1970s that forced the United States to eradicate its system of racial apartheid.

Okihiro (1994) points out that people and groups in the margins have been the conscience of the United States throughout its history. They have kept the United States committed to its democratic ideals as stated in its founding documents: the Declaration of Independence, the Constitution, and the Bill of Rights. He argues that the margins have been the main sites for keeping democracy and freedom alive in the United States. It was the groups in the margins that reminded and forced America to live up to its democratic ideals when they were most severely tested. Examples include (a) slavery and the middle passage, (b) Indian removal in the 1830s, (c) the internment of Japanese Americans during World War II, and (d) segregation and apartheid in the South that crumbled during the 1960s and 1970s in response to the African American-led civil rights movement. In *The Story of American Freedom*, Foner (1998) makes an argument similar to Okihiro's:

> The authors of the notion of freedom as a universal birthright, a truly human ideal, were not so much the founding fathers who created a nation dedicated to liberty but resting in large measure on slavery, but abolitionists . . . and women. (p. xx)

A new kind of citizenship is needed for the 21st century, which Kymlicka (1995) calls "multicultural citizenship." It recognizes and legitimizes the right and need of citizens to maintain commitments both to their ethnic and cultural communities and to the national civic culture. Only when the national civic culture is transformed in ways that reflect and give voice to the diverse ethnic, racial, language, and religious communities that constitute it will it be viewed as legitimate by all of its citizens. Only then can they develop clarified commitments to the commonwealth and its ideals.

The Assimilationist Fallacy and Citizenship Education

An assimilationist conception of citizenship will not be effective in the 21st century because it is based on a serious fallacy. The assimilationist assumes that the most effective way to reduce strong ethnic boundaries, attachments, and affiliations within a nation-state is to provide marginalized and excluded ethnic and racial groups opportunities to experience equality in the nation's social, economic, and political institutions. As they begin to participate more fully in the mainstream society and institutions, argues the assimilationist, marginalized cultural and ethnic groups will focus less on their specific concerns and more on national issues and priorities (Patterson, 1977).

When ethnic groups experience equality, argues the assimilationist, ethnic attachments die of their own weight. The assimilationist views the ideal society as one in which there are no traces of ethnic or racial attachments. All groups will share one dominant national and overarching culture; people will forsake their ethnic cultures when they are structurally included in the national civic culture and community.

Apter (1977) calls the assimilationist position the "assimilationist fallacy." This position holds that as modernization occurs, ethnic groups experience social, political, and economic equality, and commitments to ethnic and community attachments weaken and disappear. Ethnicity, argues the assimilationist, promotes division, exhumes ethnic conflicts, and leads to divisions within society. It also promotes group rights over the rights of the individual.

As Apter (1977) keenly observes, the assimilationist conception is not so much wrong as it is an incomplete and inadequate explanation of ethnic realities in modernized, pluralistic, and democratic nation-states. Ethnicity and assimilationism coexist in modernized democratic nation-states. As Apter suggests, "The two tendencies, toward and against [ethnicity], can go on at the same time. Indeed, the more development and growth that takes place, the more some [ethnic] groupings have to gain by their parochialism" (p. 65).

Ethnicity and modernity coexist in part because of what assimilationists call the "pathological condition"; that is, ethnic groups such as Mexicans in the United States and Afro-Caribbeans in the United Kingdom maintain attachments to their ethnic groups and cultures in part because they have been excluded from full participation in the social, economic, and political institutions of their nation-states.

However, members of marginalized ethnic groups, as well as more privileged ethnic and cultural groups such as Greeks and Jews in the United States, maintain ethnic affiliations and ethnic attachments for more fundamental psychological and sociological reasons. Ethnicity helps them to fulfill some basic psychological and sociological needs that the "thin" culture of modernization leaves starving. Apter (1977) comments insightfully on this point:

> [Ethnic revival] is a response to the thinning out of enlightenment culture, the deterioration of which is a part of the process of democratization and pluralization. . . . Assimilation itself then vitiates the enlightenment culture. As it does, it leaves what might be called a *primordial space* [italics added], a space people try to fill when they believe they have lost something fundamental and try to recreate it. (p. 75)

Multicultural citizenship education allows students to maintain attachments to their cultural and ethnic communities while at the same time helping them to attain the knowledge and skills needed to participate in the wider civic culture and community.

Helping Students to Develop Cultural, National, and Global Identifications

Citizenship education should help students to develop thoughtful and clarified identifications with their cultural communities and their nation-states. It should also help students to develop clarified global identifications and deep understandings of their roles in the world community (Diaz, Massialas, & Xanthopoulos, 1999). Students need to understand how life in their cultural communities and nations influences other nations and the cogent influence that international events have on their daily lives. Global education should have as major goals helping students to develop understandings of the interdependence among nations in the world today, clarified attitudes toward other nations, and reflective identifications with the world community.

Developing a Delicate Balance of Identifications

Nonreflective and unexamined cultural attachments may prevent the development of a cohesive nation with clearly defined national goals and policies. Although we need to help students to develop reflective and clarified cultural identifications, they must also be helped to clarify and strengthen their identifications with their nation-states. However, blind nationalism will prevent students from developing reflective and positive global identifications. Nationalism and national attachments in most nations of the world are strong and tenacious. An important aim of citizenship education should be to help students develop global identifications and a deep understanding of the need to take action as citizens of the global community to help solve the world's difficult global problems.

Cultural, national, and global experiences and identifications are interactive and interrelated in a dynamic way. Writes Arnove (1999),

> There is a dialect at work by which . . . global processes interact with national and local actors and contexts to be modified, and in some cases transformed. There is a process of give-and-take, an exchange by which international trends are reshaped to local ends. (pp. 2–3)

Students should develop a delicate balance of cultural, national, and global identifications (see Figure 1). However, educators often try to help students develop strong national identifications by eradicating their ethnic and community cultures and making students ashamed of their families, community beliefs, languages, and behaviors.

I believe that cultural, national, and global identifications are developmental in nature, that individuals can attain healthy and reflective national identifications only when they have acquired healthy and reflective cultural identifications, and that individuals can develop reflective and positive global identifications only after they have realistic, reflective, and positive national identifications (J. A. Banks, 2001). These identifications are dynamic and interactive; they are not discrete.

Individuals can develop a clarified commitment to and identification with a nation-state and the national culture only when they believe that they are a meaningful part of the nation-state and

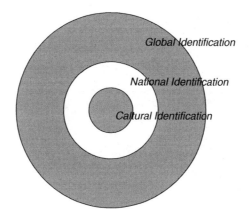

A major goal of multicultural citizenship education should be to help students acquire a delicate balance of cultural, national and global identifications.

Figure 2.1 *Cultural, National, and Global Identifications*

that it acknowledges, reflects, and values their culture and them as individuals. A nation-state that alienates and does not structurally include all cultural groups into the national culture runs the risk of creating alienation and causing groups to focus on specific concerns and issues rather than on the overarching goals and policies of the nation-state.

Multicultural Citizenship Education, Knowledge, and Action

To help students acquire reflective and clarified cultural, national, and global identifications, citizenship education must teach them to know, to care, and to act. As Paulo Freire (1985) points out, students must be taught to read the word and the world. In other words, they must acquire higher levels of knowledge, understand the relationship between knowledge and action, develop a commitment to act to improve the world, and acquire the skills needed to participate in civic action. Multicultural citizens take actions within their communities and nations to make the world more humane. Multicultural citizenship education helps students learn how to act to change the world.

To become thoughtful and effective citizen actors, students must understand the ways in which knowledge is constructed and how knowledge production is related to the location of knowledge producers in the social, political, and economic contexts of society. Multicultural citizenship education must also help students to become knowledge producers themselves and to use the knowledge they have acquired and constructed to take democratic social and civic action.

I have conceptualized five types of knowledge that can help educators to conceptualize and teach about knowledge construction (J. A. Banks, 1996): (a) personal/cultural knowledge, (b) popular knowledge, (c) mainstream academic knowledge, (d) transformative academic knowledge, and (e) school knowledge. Although the categories of this ideal-type typology can be conceptually distinguished, in reality they overlap and are interrelated in a dynamic way. *Mainstream academic knowledge* and *transformative academic knowledge* are briefly defined below because these concepts are used in the discussion in the second part of this article.

Mainstream academic knowledge consists of the concepts, paradigms, theories, and explanations that constitute traditional and established knowledge in the behavioral and social sciences. An important assumption within main-stream knowledge is that objective truths can be verified through rigorous and objective research procedures that are uninfluenced by human interests, values, and perspectives (Homans, 1967).

Transformative academic knowledge consists of the concepts, paradigms, themes, and explanations that challenge mainstream academic knowledge and that expand the historical and literary canon (J. A. Banks, 1996, 1998; Limerick, 1987). Transformative scholars assume that knowledge is influenced by personal values, the social context, and factors such as race, class, and gender. Whereas the primary goal of mainstream academic knowledge is to build theory and explanations, an important goal of transformative knowledge is to use knowledge to change society to make it more just and humane.

The Knowledge Construction Process and Student Identifications

The knowledge construction process describes the ways in which teachers help students to understand, investigate, and determine how the implicit cultural assumptions, frames of reference, perspectives, and biases within a discipline influence the ways in which knowledge is constructed. When the knowledge construction process is implemented in the classroom, teachers help students to understand how knowledge is created and how it is influenced by the racial, ethnic, social-class, and gender positions of individuals and groups.

When students participate in knowledge construction, they challenge the mainstream academic metanarrative and construct liberatory and transformative ways of conceptualizing the U.S. and the world experience. Understanding the knowledge construction process and participating in it themselves help students to construct clarified cultural, national, and global identifications and to become knowledgeable, caring, and active citizens in democratic societies.

IMPLICATIONS FOR TEACHER EDUCATION

Helping Teachers to Develop Clarified Cultural and National Identifications

Teachers need to develop reflective cultural and national identifications if they are to function effectively in diverse classrooms and help students from different cultures and groups to construct clarified identifications. Several characteristics of U.S. teachers and teacher education students make it difficult and problematic for them to develop reflective cultural and national identifications.

Most of the nation's teacher education students are middle-class White females who have little experience with other racial, ethnic, or social-class groups. Even when they come from working-class backgrounds, teacher education students tend to distance themselves from their class origins and to view themselves as middle class in values, perspectives, and behaviors. This occurs in part because White students who come from lower- and working-class communities and cultures—like students of color—must distance themselves from their primordial cultures to experience academic and social success in educational institutions. This is true not only in the United States but in other nations, as is epitomized in this statement by a Canadian Ukrainian who recalls his school experiences (Diakiw, 1994):

> This [school] was not an environment in which I was able to talk proudly about my heritage. I retreated and assimilated as fast as I could. I was ashamed of my background. I was particularly embarrassed about my parents. Compared to my friends' parents, mine seemed ignorant and crude . . . . I visited in their homes but not until the end of grade thirteen did I invite any friends to mine. Only then did I realize that despite the differences in culture and wealth, my parents were among the best. (p. 54)

When teacher education students from working-class backgrounds distance themselves from their class origins, they become less able to connect their childhood experiences with those of low income and working-class students of color. Consequently, they are less likely to develop an empathetic understanding of students whose behaviors and values conflict with those of the school's mainstream culture (Erickson, 2001).

One of the consequences of the monocultural experiences and the privileged racial and class status of many White college students in teacher education programs is their tendency to view themselves as noncultural and nonethnic beings who are colorblind and raceless. Consequently, they often view race and culture as something possessed by outsiders and others and view themselves as "just Americans." These kinds of perceptions and perspectives often lead majority group students to ask these kinds of question during class discussions: "Why do we have to focus on race and other kinds of differences? Why can't we all be just Americans?"

The culturally isolated experiences of most of my teacher education students, reinforced by their assimilationist high school education and the popular culture, result in their accepting without question the metanarrative of U.S. history that has dominated the nation's curriculum since the late 1800s. The metanarrative that is institutionalized within the nation's schools, colleges, and universities is called "American exceptionalism" by historians such as Appleby (1992) and Kammen (1997).

The institutionalized metanarrative conceptualizes the development of U.S. history as a linear movement of Europeans from the east to the west coast of the United States, a movement that was ordained by God to bring civilization to the West, which was a *wilderness* and a *frontier*. These words connote that the lands on which the Native Americans lived were uninhabited until the Europeans arrived in the West.

Frederick Jackson Turner (1894/1989), in a paper presented at the 1893 meeting of the American Historical Association that was destined to become a classic, characterized the frontier as "the meeting point between savagery and civilization" (p. 3). Turner's characterization of the West epitomizes the metanarrative that is institutionalized in the nation's schools, colleges, and universities. However, the established metanarrative, which I call "mainstream academic knowledge" (J. A. Banks, 1996) and Apple (1993) describes as "official knowledge," has been strongly challenged by transformative scholars within the past 30 years (C.A.M. Banks, 1996; Limerick, 1987). The use of concepts such as wilderness, frontier, and westward movement are legacies of Turner's frontier thesis and the times in which he lived and worked. Cherry McGee Banks (1996) describes the serious limitations of the mainstream metanarrative:

> By telling part of the story and leaving other parts of the story out, meta-narratives suggest not only that some parts of the story don't count, but that some parts don't even exist. The exclusive nature of meta-narratives, their canonized place in formal school curricula, and the extent to which they are woven into the societal curriculum result in meta-narratives producing a feeling of well-being and comfort within mainstream society and their validity rarely being questioned. (p. 49)

The strong and persistent challenge that transformative scholars of color and women have directed toward mainstream academic knowledge since the mid-1960s has resulted in significant curriculum changes in the nation's schools, colleges, and universities and in textbooks. However, despite these substantial changes, many of the concepts, perspectives, and periodizations of the mainstream meta- narrative are still deeply embedded in the curriculum, in textbooks, and in the popular culture.

Helping Teacher Education Students Rethink Race, Culture, and Ethnicity

To develop clarified cultural and national identifications, teacher education students must be helped to critically analyze and rethink their notions of race, culture, and ethnicity and to view themselves as cultural and racial beings. They also need to reconstruct race, culture, and ethnicity in ways that are inclusive and that reveal the ways in which these concepts are related to the social, economic, and political structures in U.S. society (Nieto, 1999; Omi & Winant, 1994).

Teacher education students need to understand, for example, the ways in which the statement, "I am not ethnic; I am just American," reveals the privileged position of an individual who is proclaiming his or her own unique culture as American and other cultures as non-American. A statement such as "I don't see color" reveals a privileged position that refuses to legitimize racial identifications that are very important to people of color and that are often used to justify inaction and perpetuation of the status quo. If educators do not "see" color and the ways in which institutionalized racism privileges some groups and disadvantages others, they will be unable to take action to eliminate racial inequality in schools.

In an important ethnographic study of a school, Schofield (2001) found that teachers who said they were colorblind suspended African American males at highly disproportionate rates and failed to integrate content about African Americans into the curriculum. Color-blindness was used to justify inaction and the perpetuation of institutionalized discrimination within the school. Colorblindness is part of the "racial text" of teacher education which, as Cochran-Smith (2000) points out, teachers and teacher educators must "unlearn."

In the first course I teach for teacher education students, I incorporate readings, activities, lectures, and discussions designed to help students construct new concepts of race, culture, and ethnicity. Most students in the course are White women. These activities are designed, in part, to help the students "unlearn racism" and to read the "racial text" of U.S. society and popular culture (Cochran-Smith, 2000). Assignments include a personal reflection paper on the book *We Can't Teach What We Don't Know: White Teachers, Multicultural Schools* (Howard, 1999) as well as a family history project.

In his book, Howard (1999) describes his personal journey as a White person to come to grips with racial issues and to become an effective educator. He speaks in a personal and engaging way to White teachers. In their reflection papers, my students describe their powerful reactions to Howard's book and how it helps them to rethink their personal journey related to race and their ideas about race. Howard makes racism explicit for most of my students for the first time in their lives.

In their family history project, the students are asked not only to provide a brief account of their family's historical journey but also to give explicit attention to the ways in which race, class, and gender have influenced their family and personal histories. Although the family history project is a popular assignment, most of the students have to struggle to describe ways in which race has influenced their family and personal histories because race is largely invisible to them (McIntosh, 1997). Gender is much more visible to my women students. More of the female than male students are able to relate gender to their family and personal stories in meaningful ways.

Challenging the Metanarrative

A series of activities in the course is designed to help students examine the U.S. metanarrative, to construct new conceptions and narratives that describe the development of U.S. history and culture (which I call transformative knowledge), and to think of creative and effective ways to teach new conceptions of the American experience to students. These activities include historical readings, discussions, and role-playing events about U.S. ethnic and racial groups (J. A. Banks, 1997b), with the emphasis on the history of ethnic groups of color. The perspectives in these historical accounts are primarily those of the groups being studied rather than those of outsiders.

The perspectives of both insiders and outsiders are needed to give students a comprehensive understanding of U.S. history and culture. However, I emphasize the perspectives of insiders in this course because my students have been exposed to outsider perspectives for most of their education prior to my course. I also focus on insider perspectives because one of the most important goals of the course is to help students learn how to challenge and critically analyze the mainstream metanarrative they have learned during their high school and college years.

The historical readings in my course are supplemented by videotapes that powerfully depict the perspectives of ethnic groups of color on historical and contemporary events. These videotapes include *The Shadow of Hate: A History of Intolerance in America* (Guggenheim, 1995), which chronicles how various groups within the United States, including the Irish, Jews, and African Americans, have been victimized by discrimination. One of the most trenchant examples of discrimination in the videotape is the description of the way Leo Frank, a Jewish northerner living in Atlanta, became a victim of anti-Semitism and racial hostility when he was accused of murdering a White girl who worked in a pencil factory he co-owned.

The Leo Frank case provides the students an opportunity to understand the ways in which race is a social construction, is contextual, and how the meaning of race has changed historically and continues to change today (Jacobson, 1998). Leo Frank was considered Jewish and not White in 1915 Atlanta. In a lecture, I provide the students an overview of Karen Brodkin's (1998) book that describes the process by which Jews became White in America and what the experiences of Jews and other White ethnics, such as the Irish and Italians, reveal about the characteristics of race in the United States.

Brodkin (1998) argues that Jews had to assimilate mainstream American behaviors, ideologies, attitudes, and perspectives to become White. Among the important attitudes they had to acquire, she argues, were the institutionalized attitudes and perceptions that mainstream Whites held toward groups of color. Brodkin argues, as does Toni Morrison (1992), that Whites defined themselves in opposition to African Americans, and that this oppositional definition was one important way in which disparate groups of White ethnics were able to form a collectivity in the United States and to construct themselves as one cultural and identity group.

Ignatiev (1995) describes the ways in which the Irish, like other White ethnic groups, became White by acquiring mainstream White values and behaviors directed against ethnic groups of color. My students are always surprised to learn how the meaning of race has changed through time and that the idea that Whites are one racial group is a rather recent historical development.

I use a videotape that deals with a contemporary Native American issue to relate historical events to current issues and to help the students understand the ways in which our nation's past and present are connected. *In Whose Honor?* (Rosenstein, 1997) chronicles the struggle of Charlene Teters, a Native American graduate student, to end the use of a Native American chief as a football team mascot at the University of Illinois in Champaign-Urbana. The team is called The Fighting Illini, after Chief Illiniwek. During halftime, a student dresses up as Chief Illiniwek and dances. Teters considers the chief and the dance sacrilegious and demeaning to Native Americans. The videotape describes the social action taken by Teters to end the tradition, as well as the strong opposition by the board of trustees and alumni who want to maintain a tradition that is deeply beloved by vocal and influential alumni and board members. The people who defend the 70-year-old tradition cannot understand how anyone can find it offensive.

In Whose Honor? (Rosenstein, 1997) helps the students understand how the construction of *Indian* in U.S. society is controlled by mainstream institutions, including the mainstream media. Through questioning and discussion, I help the students relate Columbus's construction of the Native people of the Caribbean as Indians, Cortés's construction of the Aztecs as savages, Turner's construction of the West as a wilderness, and the selection of Chief Illiniwek as a mascot. We discuss the following questions to uncover ways in which these events are connected (J. A. Banks, 2000):

1. Which groups have the power to define and institutionalize their conceptions within the schools, colleges, and universities?
2. What is the relationship between knowledge and power? Who exercises the most power in this case study?
3. Who benefits from the ways in which Native Americans have been and are often defined in U.S. society? Who loses?
4. How can views of Native Americans be reconstructed in ways that will help empower Native American groups and create more justice in society?

An Unfinished Journey

My project to help teacher education students develop reflective cultural and national identifications is a work in progress that has rewards, challenges, unrealized possibilities, conflicts, and—at times—frustrations for my students and me. My work on global identifications and issues is incomplete and episodic. Each time I teach the course, I feel that I do not have enough time to deal with cultural and national issues. Global issues remain mostly an unrealized and hoped-for goal. Making links when discussing cultural and national issues is the extent to which I deal with global issues in the course.

The class is an unfinished journey for the students and me in several important ways. It is a beginning of what I hope will be a lifelong journey for my students. I realize that one course with a transformative goal can have only a limited influence on the knowledge, beliefs, and values of students who have been exposed to mainstream knowledge and perspectives for most of their prior education. Students are required to take a second multicultural education course in our teacher education program. Also, other members of the teacher education faculty are trying to integrate ethnic, cultural, and racial content into the foundations and methods courses.

My course is also an unfinished journey because I am still trying to figure out how to achieve the delicate balance of showing respect for my students while at the same time encouraging them to seriously challenge their deeply held beliefs, attitudes, values, and knowledge claims. I am also trying to conceptualize effective ways to determine the short-term and long-term effectiveness of the course. The opinions of most of my students when the course ends are encouraging. However, I do not know the relationship between these opinions and the behavior of the students when they become teachers.

When I taught the class in fall 1999, 21 of 25 students wrote positive and detailed responses to the following question on the University of Washington's standardized course evaluation form: "Was this class intellectually stimulating? Did it stretch your thinking? Yes No Why or why not?"

However, I worry about the 4 students in this class of 25 who merely checked Yes in answer to the question and made no further comments. The responses of these 4 students evoke these questions: What are the meanings of their terse responses? In what ways might these 4 students differ from the other students who wrote detailed comments? Do they need a different kind of course and a different set of experiences? How will these 4 students, as well as the other 21 students, view the experience in my course a year after they have been teaching? Will the course make a difference in the ways in which they teach and deal with multicultural content? I was heartened to read in a study reported by Ladson-Billings (1999) that some of the students in a teacher education program who had been "the most resistant to the program's emphasis on equity and diversity issues feel that it has been most beneficial to them in their teaching" (p. 116).

My observations of my students during this 10-week course, reading of their reflection papers and other papers, listening to their class discussions, having conversations with them, and studying their end-of-class course evaluations indicate that most of my students attain some of the important course objectives. They develop an understanding of how knowledge is constructed, how it relates to power, and how the mainstream metanarrative privileges some groups and marginalizes others. They also develop a better understanding of race, culture, and ethnicity and begin the process of questioning some of their assumptions about these concepts. Perhaps most important, most of my students begin to view their own cultural and racial journeys from different and more critical perspectives. I believe that these critical perspectives will help them to develop more reflective cultural, national, and global identifications.

Teachers with the knowledge and skills I teach in my course are better able to interrogate the assumptions of official school knowledge, less likely to be victimized by knowledge that protects hegemony and inequality, and better able to help students acquire the knowledge and skills needed to take citizen action that will make the world more just and humane.

ACKNOWLEDGMENT

Different versions of this article were presented at several conferences as keynote addresses in 2000, including the 44th Annual Meeting of the Comparative and International Education Society, San Antonio, Texas, March 8 to 11; the 20th Anniversary Conference of the Intercultural Education Society, Sophia University, Tokyo, Japan, May 26 to 28; and the Fifth International Conference of the National Council for the Social Studies, University of Calgary, Canada, June 28 to July 1. I wish to acknowledge the helpful and thoughtful feedback I received from the participants at these conferences. I am grateful to Cherry A. McGee Banks, Geneva Gay, Walter C. Parker (colleagues at the University of Washington), and Marilyn Cochran-Smith for their thoughtful comments on an earlier draft of this article.

REFERENCES

Apple, M. W. (1993). *Official knowledge: Democratic education in a conservative age*. New York: Routledge.

Appleby, J. (1992). Recovering America's historic diversity: Beyond exceptionalism. *Journal of American History, 79*(2), 419–431.

Apter, D. E. (1977). Political life and cultural pluralism. In M. M. Tumin & W. Plotch (Eds.), *Pluralism in a democratic society* (pp. 58–91). New York: Praeger.

Arnove, R. F. (1999). Reframing comparative education: The dialectic of the global and the local. In R. F. Arnove & C. A. Torres (Eds.), *Comparative education: The dialectic of the global and the local* (pp. 1–23). New York: Rowman & Littlefield.

Banks, C.A.M. (1996). Intellectual leadership and African American challenges to meta-narratives. In J. A. Banks (Ed.), *Multicultural education, transformative knowledge, and action: Historical and contemporary perspectives* (pp. 46–63). New York: Teachers College Press.

Banks, J. A. (1996). The canon debate, knowledge construction, and multicultural education. In J. A. Banks (Ed.), *Multicultural education, transformative knowledge, and action* (pp. 3–29). New York: Teachers College Press.

Banks, J. A. (1997a). *Educating citizens in a multicultural society*. New York: Teachers College Press.

Banks, J. A. (1997b). *Teaching strategies for ethnic studies* (6th ed.). Boston: Allyn & Bacon.

Banks, J. A. (1998). The lives and values of researchers: Implications for educating citizens in a multicultural society. *Educational Researcher, 27*(7), 4–17.

Banks, J. A. (2000). The social construction of difference and the quest for educational equality. In R. S. Brandt (Ed.), *Education in a new era* (pp. 21–45). Alexandria, VA: Association for Supervision and Curriculum Development.

Banks, J. A. (2001). *Cultural diversity and education: Foundations, curriculum and teaching* (4th ed.). Boston: Allyn & Bacon.

Brodkin, K. (1998). *How Jews became White folks and what that says about race in America*. New Brunswick, NJ: Rutgers University Press.

Cochran-Smith, M. (2000). Blind vision: Unlearning racism in teacher education. *Harvard Educational Review, 72*(2), 157–190.

Diakiw, J. (1994). Growing up Ukrainian in Toronto. In C. E. James & A. Shadd (Eds.), *Talking about difference: Encounters in culture, language and identity* (pp. 49–55). Toronto, Canada: Between the Lines.

Diaz, C. F., Massialas, B. G., & Xanthopoulos, J. A. (1999). *Global perspectives for educators*. Boston: Allyn & Bacon.

Erickson, F. (2001). Culture in society and in educational practices. In J. A. Banks & C.A.M. Banks (Eds.), *Multicultural education: Issues and perspectives* (4th ed., pp. 31–58). New York: John Wiley.

Foner, E. (1998). *The story of American freedom*. New York: Norton.

Freire, P. (1985). *The politics of education: Culture, power, and liberation*. New York: Bergin & Garvey.

Guggenheim, C. (1995). *The shadow of hate: A history of intolerance in America* [Videotape]. (Available from: Teaching Tolerance, 400 Washington Avenue, Montgomery, AL 36104)

Homans, G. C. (1967). *The nature of social science*. New York: Harcourt Brace.

Howard, G. (1999). *We can't teach what we don't know: White teachers, multiracial schools*. New York: Teachers College Press.

Ignatiev, I. (1995). *How the Irish became White*. New York: Routledge.

Jacobson, M. F. (1998). *Whiteness of a different color: European immigrants and the alchemy of race*. Cambridge, MA: Harvard University Press.

Kammen, M. (1997). *In the past lane: Historical perspectives on American culture*. New York: Oxford University Press.

Kymlicka, W. (1995). *Multicultural citizenship: A liberal theory of minority rights*. New York: Oxford University Press.

Ladson-Billings, G. (1999). Preparing teachers for diversity: Historical perspectives, current trends, and future directions. In L. Darling-Hammond & G. Sykes (Eds.), *Teaching as the learning profession* (pp. 86–123). San Francisco: Jossey-Bass.

Limerick, P. N. (1987). *The legacy of conquest: The unbroken past of the American West.* New York: Norton.

McIntosh, P. (1997). White privilege: Unpacking the invisible knapsack. In V. Cyrus (Ed.), *Experiencing race, class, and gender* (2nd ed., pp. 194–198). Mountain View, CA: Mayfield.

Morrison, T. (1992). *Playing in the dark: Whiteness and the literary imagination.* Cambridge: Harvard University Press.

Nieto, S. (1999). *The light in their eyes: Creating multicultural learning communities.* New York: Teachers College Press.

Okihiro, G. (1994). *Margins and mainstreams: Asians in American history and culture.* Seattle: University of Washington Press.

Omi, M., & Winant, H. (1994). *Racial formation in the United States* (2nd ed.). New York: Routledge.

Patterson, O. (1977). *Ethnic chauvinism: The reactionary impulse.* New York: Stein and Day.

Phillips, K. (1990). *The politics of rich and poor.* New York: Random House.

Rosenstein, J. (Writer, Producer, Ed.). (1997). *In whose honor? American Indian mascots in sports* [Videotape]. (Available from New Day Films, 22D Hollywood Avenue, Ho-ho-kus, NJ 07423; 888-367-9154)

Schofield, J. W. (2001). The colorblind perspective in school: Causes and consequences. In J. A. Banks & C.A.M. Banks (Eds.), *Multicultural education: Issues and perspectives* (4th ed., pp. 327–352). New York: John Wiley.

Turner, F. J. (1894/1989). The significance of the frontier in American history. In C. A. Milner II (Ed.), *Major problems in the history of the American West* (pp. 2–21). Lexington, MA: Heath.

U.S. Bureau of the Census. (1998). *Statistical abstract of the United States* (118th ed.). Washington, DC: Government Printing Office.

Educating Everybody's Children: We Know What Works—And What Doesn't

— by Robert W. Cole

Children know how to learn in more ways than we know how to teach them.
—Ronald Edmonds (1991)

Good instruction is good instruction, regardless of students' racial, ethnic, or socioeconomic backgrounds. To a large extent, good teaching—teaching that is engaging, relevant, multicultural, and appealing to a variety of modalities and learning styles—works well with all children.

The instructional strategies outlined in this chapter reflect a sampling of the most exciting and determined efforts to change the way the United States educates its citizens. These "ideas at work" range in complexity and magnitude. They represent concepts that cut across content areas. They overlap so comfortably that they sometimes look like separate facets of a single gem. They are as much about attitude and general approach as about specific pedagogical techniques and classroom application. They have a few characteristics in common:

- They tend to be inclusive, not exclusive.
- They work best in context with other ideas and concepts, not in isolation.
- They often focus on students working within social situations rather than alone.
- Their activities, techniques, and goals are interactive and interdisciplinary, realistic rather than esoteric.
- Possibly most important, they empower students to be actively involved in the processes of their own learning, rather than passively receptive.

None of the ideas in this chapter is new. Although some of them tend to be identified with specific programs, individuals, or locations, they are presented here as generic—that is, as applicable in virtually any classroom, in any subject area. All are adaptable.

Why ideas *at* work rather than ideas *that* work? Because "ideas that work" implies a kind of guarantee of effectiveness. In the real world of the schools, however, nothing works every time, everywhere, for everyone. No single strategy, approach, or technique works with all students. But the concepts in this chapter have proven themselves over time, with a multitude of students of diverse backgrounds and widely ranging abilities.

Unfortunately, numerous barriers can prevent poor and minority students from receiving good instruction. Some of these barriers are caused by educators' attitudes and beliefs; others are the result of institutional practices. The intent of the listing that follows is not to provide a thorough cataloguing of every barrier to sound instruction, but rather to place educators on alert.

ATTITUDES AND BELIEFS

Racism and Prejudice

Despite much progress during the past few decades, racism and prejudice are still ugly realities in all sectors of life in the United States, including education. Today, racism may be less overt and virulent than in the past, but its effects can still greatly harm minority students. In fact, subtle, insidious forms of racism may be even more harmful to young people than more blatant forms.

Prejudice against the poor, of whatever race or ethnicity, is another force that works against the academic achievement of disadvantaged students. For example, some teachers of poor students don't let them take materials home, out of fear that the materials will never be returned. Yet these same students tend to be proud to have the responsibility for taking materials home and are generally exceedingly careful to return them.

Obviously teachers must avoid discriminating, consciously or unconsciously, against students because of their racial, ethnic, or socioeconomic backgrounds. Such discrimination can be as blatant as imposing harsher discipline on minority students or as subtle as lowering expectations for poor children because they have "difficult" home lives. Teachers must be aware that they see students' behavior through the lens of their own culture. They must carefully examine their own attitudes and behaviors to be sure that they are not imposing a double standard. Most important, they must believe sincerely and completely that all children can learn.

Expectations

Educators must hold equally high expectations for affluent white students and poor and minority students—despite the disparity in students' backgrounds. Under the right conditions, low-income and minority students can learn just as well as any other children. One necessary condition, of course, is that the teacher hold expectations of high performance for *all* students.

Both high and low expectations can create self-fulfilling prophecies. Students must believe that they can achieve before they will risk trying, and young people are astute at sensing whether their teachers believe they can succeed. By the same token, teachers must truly believe their students can achieve before they will put forth their best effort to teach them. The teacher's beliefs must be translated into instructional practices if students are to benefit: actions speak louder than attitudes.

Teachers must also be sensitive to the subtle ways in which low expectations can be conveyed. According to researcher Sandra Graham of the University of California–Los Angeles, when a teacher expresses sympathy over failure, students typically infer that the teacher thinks they are incapable of succeeding, not that they simply may not have tried hard enough. Similarly, when a teacher gives students lavish praise for completing a simple task or offers help before being asked for it, students infer that the teacher thinks they are stupid. In other words, holding high expectations is not simply a matter of cheerleading; it requires insight into how students may interpret a teacher's words and behaviors.

Teachers must also resist the temptation to attribute student failure to lack of ability ("I've taught this concept and they didn't understand it; they must not be smart enough"). Failure to learn can stem from many other causes, such as inadequate prior knowledge, insufficient effort or motivation, lack of the right learning strategy, or inappropriate teaching. The bottom line is this: if students are not learning, the teacher needs to change the approach to teaching them.

Teachers are not the only ones who need to examine their expectations for students, however. Administrators who decide what courses their schools offer should ask themselves whether they are providing too few challenging courses. And counselors must consider whether they are steering students into undemanding courses because the students are poor, minority, or female. The expectation that all students can achieve at high levels, under the right circumstances, should be the guiding principle of every school.

Lack of Understanding of Cultural Differences

Teachers sometimes misinterpret the behaviors of poor and minority students because they do not understand the cultures they come from. White teachers can easily misread the behaviors of black students, for example. In *Black Students and School Failure*, Jacqueline Jordan Irvine (1990) writes:

> Because the culture of black children is different and often misunderstood, ignored, or discounted, black students are likely to experience cultural discontinuity in schools. . . . This lack of cultural sync becomes evident in instructional situations in which teachers misinterpret, denigrate, and dismiss black students' language, nonverbal cues, physical movements, learning styles, cognitive approaches, and worldview. When teachers and students are out of sync, they clash and confront each other, both consciously and unconsciously. . . . (p. xix)

Only when teachers understand their students' cultural backgrounds can they avoid this kind of culture clash. In the meantime, the ways in which teachers comprehend and react to students' culture, language, and behaviors may create problems (Erickson, 1987). In too many schools, students are, in effect, required to leave their family and cultural backgrounds at the schoolhouse door and live in a kind of "hybrid culture" composed of the community of fellow learners (Au & Kawakami, 1991).

Especially in the early grades, teachers and students may differ in their expectations for the classroom setting; each may act in ways that the other misinterprets. In addition, those teachers (and they are legion) who insist on a single pedagogical style and who see other styles as being out of step, may be refusing to allow students to work to their strengths.

As Knapp and Shields (1990a) suggest, the so-called "deficit" or "disadvantage" model has two serious problems: (1) teachers are likely to set low standards for certain children "because their patterns of behavior, language use, and values do not match those required in the school setting"; and (2) over time a cycle of failure and despair is created that culminates "in students' turning their backs on school and dropping out . . . because teachers and administrators fail to adapt to and take advantage of the strengths that these students do possess" (p. 755).

INSTITUTIONAL PRACTICES

Tracking

The most notorious of the harmful institutional practices is tracking, which dooms children in the low tracks to a second-rate education by failing to provide them with the support they need to move to a higher track. As a result, they fall further and further behind their peers. Students in low tracks are stigmatized and lose self-esteem and motivation, while expectations for their performance plummet.

In *Keeping Track*, researcher Jeannie Oakes (1985) says, "We can be quite certain that the deficiencies of slower students are not more easily remediated when they are grouped together" (p. 12). Yet even now the practice of tracking persists, despite the negative effects on students documented by Oakes and many other researchers. Tracking is especially harmful to poor and minority students because these students are more likely to end up in the low tracks.

Effective alternatives to tracking have included the Accelerated Schools Project, developed by Henry Levin of Stanford University, which includes accelerated programs to bring at-risk students into the mainstream by the end of elementary school and results in faster learning because students receive engaging, active, interdisciplinary instruction; and the Higher Order Thinking Skills (HOTS) program, developed by Stanley Pogrow of the University of Arizona– Tucson, which works to enhance the general thinking skills of remedial students by showing them how to work with ideas. These programs and others are aimed at helping students get up to speed, rather than permanently segregating them and feeding them a dumbed-down curriculum.

Inappropriate Instruction

Inappropriate instruction harms poor and minority students. Instead of being presented in a variety of modes, instruction in too many U.S. schools tends to be abstract, devoid of application, overly sequential, and redundant. Bits of knowledge are emphasized, not the big picture, thus handicapping global thinkers. Moreover, the largely Eurocentric curriculum downplays the experiences and contributions of minorities.

For teachers of diverse students, it is especially important to use a broad repertoire of strategies. Some children may be global thinkers; others, more analytical. Some children may learn best from lecture and reading; others, through manipulatives and other hands-on experiences. Some children may thrive on competition; others may achieve far more in cooperative groups.

Differential Access

Poor and minority students are often denied access to challenging coursework. Counselors place them in remedial or undemanding courses, and because more challenging courses often require students to have taken specific introductory courses, students can never switch to a more demanding track. Irvine (1990) cites data showing that "black students, particularly black male students, are three times as likely to be in a class for the educable mentally retarded as are white students, but only one-half as likely to be in a class for the gifted and talented" (p. xiv). In addition, the pull-out programs intended to help many of these students end up fragmenting their school day. And after pull-out programs end, students are given little support for reentering the regular classroom, so they tend to backslide when they rejoin their peers.

Lack of Consequences

Unfortunately, there are few consequences for students and teachers if poor and minority students do not learn. So long as students put in the required seat time, they will receive a diploma; so long as teachers go through the motions, they will have a job. In many cases, nobody—not the education establishment, not the parents or guardians, not the politicians—protests a status quo that is woefully deficient.

Schools that have had success in teaching poor and minority students do not keep ineffective teachers on the faculty; in these schools, teachers are held responsible if their students do not learn. These schools also collaborate with parents or guardians to ensure that students who come to school and strive to achieve are rewarded.

Disciplinary Practices

Teachers sometimes punish poor and minority children more harshly than they do other children for the same offenses. Moreover, suspension is often the punishment of choice, causing students to miss valuable class time. According to Irvine (1990), "one factor related to the nonachievement of black students is the disproportionate use of severe disciplinary practices, which leads to black students' exclusion from classes, their perceptions of mistreatment, and feelings of alienation and rejection, which result ultimately in their misbehaving more and/or leaving school" (p. 16).

On the other hand, some teachers are more lenient with poor or minority students, because they believe these children have been socialized differently than mainstream children. For example, teachers might overlook boisterous or aggressive behavior among poor or minority students while chastising mainstream students for similar behavior. Teachers need to establish a clear, reasonable discipline policy and require all students to abide by it.

Involvement of Parents or Guardians

Poor and minority parents or guardians often have no opportunities to create an ongoing relationship with their children's schools; in fact, they often have no communication with the schools at all. In turn, schools tend to make few efforts to develop a relationship with poor and minority parents or guardians, who may be too intimidated or hard-pressed to initiate contact themselves. For parents who don't speak English, the language barrier can pose another formidable obstacle.

James Comer of the Yale Child Study Center has developed a process to foster good relationships among children, teachers, and parents or guardians. Parents or guardians are encouraged to be an active presence in the school. Social activities bring families and school staff together, helping parents or guardians gain trust in the school. The program has reportedly helped to lower dropout rates, among other benefits.

Unequal Access to Resources

Unequal access to resources further reduces poor and minority students' chances of receiving equal opportunities to learn. Poor and minority students typically attend schools that receive less funding than those attended by mainstream students. As a result, they are taught with inferior materials and equipment and have fewer manipulatives, laboratories, and facilities. Teachers in such schools receive less staff-development, must cope with larger classes, and have less free time.

The Negative Impact of Testing

Standardized tests can be seen as one way in which a meritocratic society reorders a widely disparate populace into hierarchies of abilities, achievement, and opportunity. In fact, the power of tests to translate difference into disadvantage is felt at many points in the world of education, most notably in the decision to place low-income and language-minority students into compensatory or bilingual education classes, where a watered-down, fragmented, and rote curriculum reinforces the disadvantages presumably diagnosed by the tests.

More than ever before, it would seem, multiple-choice tests are being used inappropriately as the ultimate measure of students' learning and capabilities—despite a wealth of evidence that undermines the wisdom of using them in this manner. Decisions that significantly affect students' academic destinies are often made on the basis of a single test score. Moreover, norm-referenced tests reinforce the attitude that some students should be *expected* to do poorly. To be fair to all students, assessment should be primarily criterion-referenced and, as far as possible, based on actual performances. Perhaps most important, a variety of measures should be used to assess student learning.

Lack of Bilingual Instruction

Not surprisingly, many students who do not speak English fall behind in their studies early, because they are not taught content in their native language. When they eventually learn English, they have lost so much ground in their schoolwork that they find it difficult (and sometimes impossible) to catch up with their peers. In far too many cases, these students become discouraged and drop out of school.

Overall, there is the too-common problem of organizational inertia and resistance to change: reluctance to accept bilingual programs, to hire bilingual personnel, to upgrade the status of teachers of English as a second language (ESL), to support the acquisition and development of primary-language materials, to monitor and assess the progress of language-minority students, and to deal with the unique problems facing newcomers, including their need for counseling.

The number of bilingual teachers in U.S. schools is woefully insufficient, and the use of existing bilingual teachers is far from satisfactory. Schools do not use bilingual teachers to the best advantage—that is, to take maximum advantage of their dual-language abilities. The training and staffing of ESL and "sheltered English" classes remain inadequate. Beyond staffing, there is a dearth of primary-language materials, especially for languages other than Spanish, and bilingual educators regard even those materials as inadequate.

Students who speak a language other than English need to be taught content, for a time, in their native language, while they are also given intensive training in English. When they rejoin their English-speaking peers, they will be up to speed in their studies.

UNIVERSAL TEACHING STRATEGIES

Naming the barriers to the kind of schooling we want for all of our children is at least a beginning. Naming the problem allows the challenging process of treating it to begin. The next section of this chapter will outline 16 generic instructional strategies that are intended to provide assistance in treatment.

STRATEGY 1.1

Provide opportunities for students to work in a variety of social configurations and settings

Susie, Ron, Tasha, Jamal, and Juan have a lot in common. They are roughly the same age, sit in the same classroom, have the same teacher, and enjoy many of the same foods, games, and interests. As learners, however, they differ in critical ways. Susie is one of the 13 percent of youngsters in grades K–12 who learn best working alone; Ron, one of the 28 percent strongly oriented to working with a peer; and Tasha and Jamal, two of the 28 percent who learn best with adults (Tasha, by the way, with a collegial adult; Jamal, with an authoritative adult).

Of the five children, only Juan seems to learn reasonably well in any or all of those social configurations. In that respect, he represents fewer than one-third of the youngsters in a typical K–12 classroom. Of the five, only Susie and Juan are reasonably well served in the traditional teacher-oriented, teacher-directed classroom. Most of the time, the other three would be much better off in a different kind of learning situation—one far more diverse in its activities, curricular organization, and social configurations.

Few individuals in today's work world think of trying to solve a problem or launch a product or service without massive and persistent teamwork, including open discussion, fact gathering, consideration and argument, trial-and-error experimentation, research, and development. Typically, they not only depend on working with other individuals in their place of business, but also frequently call on outside consultants. Only in U.S. classrooms are individuals expected to find every answer, solve every problem, complete every task, and pass every test by relying solely on their own efforts and abilities.

The concept of cooperative/collaborative learning seeks to tap the potential that group interaction offers for learning and development. In its most formal manifestation, it places students—usually of varying levels of performance—into small groups in which they work together toward common goals. At the other end of the continuum is the more informal arrangement of peer tutoring, which has gained legitimacy as an effective form of cooperative/collaborative learning.

Those who advocate attending to students' varying learning styles note that some young people work best alone; others work most successfully with authority figures such as parents or teachers. In planning the use of various teaching strategies, teachers must be prepared to make adjustments according to the needs and learning styles of their students (Carbo, Dunn, & Dunn, 1986).

"So often teachers tell students to 'get along' or 'cooperate' but spend little time on skill practice and discussion of this basic human need," writes Robert Slavin (1986, p. 24). "Cooperative learning provides the teacher with a model to improve academic performance and socialization skills, and to instill democratic values. A wealth of research supports the idea that the consistent use of this technique improves students' academic performance and helps them become more caring." Slavin cites positive effects in such diverse areas as student achievement at various grade levels and subjects, intergroup relations, relationships between mainstreamed and normal-progress students, and student self-esteem.

David Johnson and Roger Johnson (1990), two veteran advocates of cooperation and collaboration in the classroom, note that people in general do not know instinctively how to interact effectively with others. If cooperative efforts in the classroom are to succeed, students must get to know and trust one another, communicate accurately and unambiguously, accept and support one another, and resolve conflicts constructively.

Some advocates of cooperative/collaborative learning suggest that students be periodically regrouped within heterogeneous classes. They also recognize the value of flexible grouping—that is, regrouping at various times by varying criteria for varying purposes, based on immediate needs. Their reasoning is as follows:

- Small-group participation in various contexts for various purposes helps students recognize and learn to function effectively in a variety of social configurations.
- Forming teams of students who perform at different levels of achievement not only encourages self-esteem and group pride, but also engenders general appreciation and understanding of how individuals differ from each other in attitudes, abilities, points of view, and approaches to problem solving.

Cooperative/collaborative learning has been incorporated in a variety of classrooms for a variety of purposes. Those applications have involved student-selected activities, apportioning specific elements of classroom projects or lessons, brainstorming, role playing, problem solving, developing awareness of thinking strategies used by oneself or by one's peers, common interests, group analyses, and team learning.

To implement a technique known as a circle of knowledge, for instance, a teacher organizes a class into small groups (circles) of four or five students each, appoints a recorder/reporter in each, poses to all a single question to which there are many possible answers, sets a time limit, expects each group member to contribute at least one answer, and then, after facilitating whole-class sharing and challenges, announces a winning group.

Another technique, the jigsaw, allows a teacher to assign specific components of a major learning project to small task-oriented groups; each group has only a piece of the larger picture under consideration. When all the groups have reported their findings to the entire class, every student has the opportunity to grasp the entire picture.

Peer conferencing and peer collaboration are two techniques that are particularly useful for teaching writing. They offer student writers the critical response of firsthand, face-to-face comments, help them discover what it is to write for an audience, and provide them with opportunities to improve their writing ability as they work on assignments and interact with their peers (Herrmann, 1989).

Cross-age and peer tutoring are other forms of student-to-student interaction. The age-old idea of tutoring has helped countless students. Many students identify with peers more easily than with adults, especially adult authority figures, and find it easier to model the behaviors of their peers than of their adult teachers. Finally, the one-to-one nature of peer tutoring offers immediate feedback, clarification, extension, and modification—usually in a nonthreatening social relationship (Webb, 1988).

Resources

Adams, 1990; Carbo, Dunn, & Dunn, 1986; Dunn & Dunn, 1993; Edmonds, 1991; Herrmann, 1989; Johnson & Johnson, 1986, 1990; Kilman & Richards, 1990; Knapp & Shields, 1990a, 1990b; Lehr & Harris, 1988; Slavin, 1986, 1987; Stevens, Madden, Slavin, & Farnish, 1987; Stover, 1993; Webb, 1988.

STRATEGY 1.2

Use reality-based learning approaches

Jim had trouble writing effectively. To be sure, his sentences were complete and grammatical, the words in them spelled correctly, the syntax straightforward if prosaic. There was one overriding problem with Jim's writing: what he wrote didn't say much of anything. His content and purpose were not specific, precise, or clear. That fact led to a more personal problem for Jim: he had ceased to trust his teacher's judgments of his work. When the teacher observed that his writing wasn't clear, Jim balked. "You're just saying that," he blurted out. "What have you got against me?"

"I'll tell you what, Jim," said the teacher. "Write to me about something you know that I don't know anything about."

After considering two or three possibilities, Jim named a card game his teacher had never heard of.

"OK," the teacher agreed. "Write step-by-step instructions on how to play the game and bring them to me. I'll follow the instructions, and you can tell me whenever I make a mistake."

"Fair enough!" Jim said.

Jim wrote in his typical style, and his teacher followed the instructions as earnestly as possible. Step by frustrated step, Jim saw the game fall to pieces. He stopped the exercise midway through.

"Give me time for a rewrite," he said, determined as ever. This time, however, he was convinced that he had a problem with his writing, and he was armed with a clearer perception of what to do about it.

Provide students with real purposes and real audiences for their speaking and writing, and you offer them valuable feedback as well as increased motivation. Writing an essay on a topic assigned by the teacher to every member of the entire class lacks the punch and the credibility of writing a personal letter to an editor, a local politician, or a community activist to express a heartfelt compliment, complain about an injustice, or inquire about an important issue. Students derive no satisfaction from succeeding with a mindless, silly activity such as circling the silent *E* in a list of words. Such an activity has no relation to real reading and no link to real life.

Communicating with real people about real issues, feelings, and beliefs is further enhanced when the content and style of that writing are grounded in the outside reality that the student brings to school. No matter how gilded or gutted its location—in city, suburb, or countryside—the student's community and personal experiences are valuable resources to be explored. They are grounds for inquiry and learning—things that count most in any classroom!

Schema theory firmly undergirds the strategy of reality-based learning. It outlines the belief that individual facts and phenomena are best perceived, learned, and understood within the larger contexts of structure or process. The value of reality-based learning has been firmly documented in the language arts—in reading and writing as well as in the understanding and appreciation of literature. It bridges school and home, classroom and clubhouse, hallway and street.

Extending the recognition and use of authentic purposes, materials, and content into any subject area helps ensure that learning experiences are meaningful and satisfying. Thus maps, directions, brochures, and directories find a comfortable home in English classes, and community surveys in math classes.

Ideas proliferate in every school—real problems to solve, real issues to resolve: how to manage recycling in the school cafeteria; how to make hallways safer and more hospitable; what to do about truancy or dropouts; whether to lock school doors and when. Problems awaiting study lie just outside the walls of virtually any school in the United States: traffic patterns; paths for bicyclists, joggers, or rollerbladers; recreational needs and resources for young people; the needs of and services for an aging population.

The combined processes of analyzing real problems and then suggesting solutions to them not only motivate learners, but also enable them to range in their thinking processes from recognizing information they need in the resources available to them, to gathering relevant information, to summarizing ideas, to generating potential solutions, and finally to analyzing the consequences and effectiveness of their solutions.

Reality-based learning counters the common notion that many students suffer from "cultural deprivation" and bring no educationally worthwhile experiences to school. "A more worthwhile approach . . . might be to examine the relationship between what particular groups of children know or how they learn and pedagogical practices," suggests Etta Ruth Hollins (1993, p. 93). "An improvement in teachers' understanding of how to build on and extend the knowledge and skills these children bring to school, rather than attempting to force the children to fit existing school practices, might get better results."

Resources

Bloome, 1976, 1985; Danehower, 1993; Hall, 1989; Hollins, 1993; Knapp & Turnbull, 1990; Lozanov & Gateva, 1988; Marzano et al., 1988; Marzano et al., 1992; Palincsar & Klenk, 1991; Palincsar, Ransom, & Derber, 1989/1990; Resnick, 1987; Richardson, 1988; Rowan, Guthrie, Lee, & Guthrie, 1986; U.S. Department of Labor, 1992; Walmsley & Walp, 1990.

STRATEGY 1.3

Encourage interdisciplinary teaching

Lynn Cherkasky-Davis (1993) described a collaborative project at the Foundations School (part of the Chicago Public Schools): an original version of the opera *Aida*, written, produced, costumed, rehearsed, and staged by students. What did that culminating event represent?

It represented what the students had learned about the history, geography, sociology, culture, and drama of ancient Egypt, topics that over preceding weeks both nourished and fed on every subject area in the curriculum.

How useful might it be for a student to know something about the economics and the technology of 19th century New England whaling before reading *Moby-Dick*—and what better opportunity to merge the talents and interests inherent in the respective teachers of social studies, science, and language arts?

How might a thoughtful reading of Aldous Huxley's *Brave New World* illuminate issues, arguments, and ideas as diverse as eugenics, Malthusian economics, and the perceived amorality of modern mores and technology—again using convergent elements of separate disciplines?

Rarely, if ever, do we live our lives outside of school according to academic pigeonholes. We don't switch to a different frame of reference or way of doing things every 20 or 40 or 60 minutes. Even a well-executed shopping trip to the supermarket is an interdisciplinary experience! Scheduling, timing, planning, measuring, counting, reading, identifying, describing, comparing, assessing, affording, budgeting—not to mention spatial orientation, nutrition, and considerations of quality of life—all come into play within a single trip. Consciously or unconsciously, by the time we have negotiated our way from home through traffic to parking lot, then aisle to aisle to the checkout lane and home again, we have routinely called on the skills and content of every basic academic discipline that schools have to offer.

Most interdisciplinary teaching is not nearly so eclectic nor so involved. Just the same, such teaching does cross traditional subject-area lines and typically involves professional teamwork. It can incorporate into a social studies unit samples of literature and art produced during a given period or by a particular society. Ask students to interpret the samples in light of a specific social context, or to infer specific characteristics of the society from their observations and interpretations. Then let them compare their interpretations with those of their peers, and finally with written records from that period or society.

As another example, how about having students study the social impact of a given scientific or technological development at the same time they are becoming acquainted with the science or technology itself? Mathematics is a natural for interdisciplinary learning. Solving its problems can depend heavily on reading skills. Not only is math an integral component in scientific processes; it also plays an appealing role in creating puzzles, music, and architecture.

Interdisciplinary projects promote thinking strategies that cross content areas and transfer solidly into real-life applications—analytical observation, for instance, or critical thinking, comparison and contrast, evaluation, perspective, and judgment. The teacher's role includes supporting those processes and helping students, through practice, to become aware of them and comfortable in using them.

Probably no other interdisciplinary approach has won greater acceptance, especially in the earlier grades, than that which has integrated five "basic skills"—reading, writing, listening, speaking, and mathematics—into one holistic classroom enterprise. Dorothy Strickland (1985) has itemized how simply and obviously such integration can be attained. Reading, for instance, can serve as model and motivation for writing that classmates can share by listening to such spoken activities as storytelling, reporting, oral composition, poetry, and dramatic readings. Reading skills also give a student access to information required in solving mathematical problems, and they play a major role in the interpretation of tables, charts, and graphs.

The "whole language" approach to instruction in reading and the language arts is a salutary example of how "disciplines" once viewed and taught as essentially discrete and separate from each other—that is, reading, writing, speaking, and listening—can easily be explored as interwoven threads in a single, unified tapestry of individual development.

Resources

Cherkasky-Davis, 1993; Jacobs, 1991; Marzano et al., 1988; Paris, Wasik, & Turner, 1991; Strickland, 1985; U.S. Department of Labor, 1992.

STRATEGY 1.4

Involve students actively

In collecting lunch money, the 1st grade teacher discovered that 8 of her 20 students had apparently brought their lunches to school with them. Rather than simply filing that observation mentally under "classroom administrivia," she posed a question to her class: "Twelve of you brought lunch money today. Knowing that, how many of you apparently brought your own lunches to school with you?"

"Some got out blocks," Mary Lindquist reported. "Some got out toy figures, some used number lines, some used their fingers, and some just thought through it. There were 10 or 12 different solutions, and each child wanted to explain his or her own way."

Students passively memorizing a single arithmetic procedure? Not at all. Instead, students actively involved in problem solving, whether or not they agreed on their methods and results.

"Most of us can remember sitting in a math class at one time or another thinking, 'When in the world am I ever going to use this?'" Lindquist commented. Mary Lindquist, then president of the National Council of Teachers of Mathematics, recounted the anecdote during an interview for an article that appeared in *Better Homes and Gardens* (Atkins, 1993). "Rote memorization is not preparing our children for the future. Kids need to use and understand math."

"By far, the highest percentage of students are tactile/kinesthetic," writes Angela Bruno (1982), "and when these youngsters manipulate hands-on materials they tend to remember more of the required information than through the use of any other sense."

There are several other reasons why students should be allowed to construct their own understandings, generate their own analyses, and create their own solutions to problems:

- It is neither engaging nor authentic to understand a fact or a situation exactly as someone else understands it. In real life, we build our own understandings to supplement, change, or confirm for ourselves what we already think we know or what others offer us in knowledge or ideas.
- Teachers promote interest and engagement when they let students address problems for which answers do not exist or are not readily apparent. Students then have real purposes for discovering and applying information and for using all the strategies that might possibly apply and that are available to them.
- Students who are intrinsically motivated and substantially engaged because of interest in meaningful learning activities are more likely to achieve high levels of performance than those for whom the completion of learning activities is simply a means of avoiding punishment.

Integrated throughout the school day and in every area of the curriculum, the range of active learning experiences includes games, simulations, role playing, creative dramatics, pantomime, storytelling, drawing, and contests that demonstrate integration of concepts and allow students to experience the ways in which concepts relate to each other in the world outside school. Other hands-on, tactile materials and activities include Cuisenaire rods, measuring cups, blocks and cubes, task cards, flip charts, field trips, and laboratory experiences. Many advocates suggest strongly that students be allowed to select for themselves those activities in which they will become involved.

Resources

Atkins, 1993; Brown, 1990; Bruno, 1982; Cohen, 1992; Hartshorn & Boren, 1990; Hodges, 1994; Joyner, 1990; National Council of Teachers of Mathematics, 1989; Roser, 1987; Strickland & Morrow, 1989.

STRATEGY 1.5

Analyze students' learning and reading styles

Everyone knows that there are all kinds of people: thinkers and doers, audiences and actors, readers and viewers, athletes and couch potatoes. (At least one venerated 6th grade music teacher routinely divided her class into singers and listeners.) Probably no other approach attempts to accommodate differences among individual students in greater detail than does that body of thought given the general rubric of learning styles.

David Kolb (Boyatzis & Kolb, 1991) identifies four predominant learning styles. *Imaginative* learners, he says, excel in watching, sensing, and feeling; *analytic* learners, in watching and thinking; *common-sense* learners, in thinking and doing; and *dynamic* learners, in doing, sensing, and feeling.

Anthony Gregorc (1982, 1985a, 1985b) identifies four basic processes by which individuals differ in their learning patterns: (1) a *concrete-sequential* process characterized as structured, practical, predictable, and thorough; (2) an *abstract-sequential* process—logical, analytical, conceptual, and studious; (3) an *abstract-random* process—sensitive, sociable, imaginative, and expressive; and (4) a *concrete-random* process—intuitive, original, investigative, and able to solve problems.

In his highly regarded theory of multiple intelligences, Howard Gardner (1999) outlined eight different aspects by which individuals can come to know the world: linguistic, logical/mathematical, musical, spatial, bodily/kinesthetic, interpersonal, intrapersonal, and naturalist.

Addressing perennial debates about the best approach to teaching reading—phonics, whole language, sight vocabulary, and so forth—Marie Carbo (1987) writes that "any one of a dozen reading methods is 'best' if it enables a child to learn to read with facility and enjoyment" (p. 56).

No matter how much they echo or differ from each other, all descriptions of learning styles are simply attempts to define and accommodate the manner in which a given student learns most readily. The theory holds that learning styles develop through the unique interactions of biology, experience, personal interests, talents, and energy. A task force commissioned by the National Association of Secondary School Principals considered the many factors that can significantly shape an individual's learning style and selected 24 for further study; these range from "perceptual responses," "field dependence/independence," and "successive/simultaneous processing" to "persistence," "environmental elements," and "need for mobility."

Whatever the ultimate taxonomy of learning styles, it seems obvious that although all children can learn, each concentrates, processes, absorbs, and remembers new and difficult information differently. According to Rita and Kenneth Dunn (1993), the factors involved include the following:

- **Immediate environment**—for example, noise level, temperature, amount of light, furniture type, and room design.
- Emotional profile—for example, degree of motivation, persistence, responsibility, and need for structure and feedback.
- Sociological needs—for example, learning alone or with peers, learning with adults present, learning in groups.
- Physical characteristics—for example, perceptual strengths (auditory, visual, tactile, kinesthetic), best time of day for learning, potential need for periodic nourishment and mobility.
- Psychological inclination—for example, global and analytic strengths.

In the most formal model of matching instruction to learning style, teachers first identify each individual student's style through observation, interview, or questionnaire. They share their observations individually with students and parents, and then plan and carry out an appropriate learning program for that child. The program includes compatible instructional practices and management strategies appropriate to what has been observed about the child's learning style. A less formal approach is to emphasize strategies that capitalize on the styles of most students, while accommodating those whose style differs markedly from the group.

Thus, instruction that attends to learning or reading styles capitalizes on an individual student's strengths and preferences while simultaneously removing barriers to learning. Instructional planning extends to such complementary methods, materials, and techniques as floor games, choices among reading materials and ways of receiving or presenting information, and participation in given activities (that is, with the entire class, in a small group, or alone). No one learning style is considered better or worse than any other (Carbo & Hodges, 1988; Hodges, 1994).

Research in learning styles and reading styles indicates that teaching academic underachievers in ways that complement their strengths in style has significantly increased their standardized test scores in reading and across subject areas.

Resources

Andrews, 1990, 1991; Bauer, 1991; Boyatzis & Kolb, 1991; Brunner & Majewski, 1990; Butler, 1984; Carbo, 1987; Carbo & Hodges, 1988; Dunn & Dunn, 1993; Gardner, 1999; Gardner & Hatch, 1989; Garrett, 1991; Gregorc, 1982, 1985a, 1985b; Hodges, 1994; Lewis & Steinberger, 1991; Orsak, 1990; Perrin, 1990.

STRATEGY 1.6

Actively model behaviors

Dorothy had tried for weeks to get her 6th graders to open up in class discussions. After years of traditional teaching, however (that is, the teacher asking the questions and one or two students offering "right" or "wrong" answers), her students were predictably passive. They consistently resisted all her attempts to open up her classroom. On the rare occasions when an intrepid student asked a question in return or dared to offer a comment, the eyes of every student in the room swung immediately and automatically to Dorothy for her verdict: right or wrong?

Then, quite by chance, Dorothy happened on a life-sized human figure made of cardboard. She realized at once that it was the very thing she needed to make her point. The following day, she launched a classroom discussion and popped a direct question to see if any of her students would volunteer a response.

Kathy did volunteer—tentatively, of course, and with just a word or two—but her response seemed to the class to merit a judgment from the teacher. All eyes fell in silence on Dorothy. Without saying a word, Dorothy walked to her closet, pulled out the cardboard figure, and set it in the chair behind her desk. With every eye following her in amazement, she sat down beside Kathy and stared silently at the cardboard figure, waiting like her students for its response.

Dorothy was modeling the behavior she saw in her students—behavior she was hoping they would overcome. They got the point! The humor in the situation engaged their trust, demonstrated Dorothy's sincerity as a teacher, and dramatized their responsibility as participants in their own learning. Class discussions began to pick up, and Dorothy found fewer and fewer occasions to pull her cardboard counterpart out of the closet.

Most modeling, of course, is intended to work the other way around—that is, teachers usually behave as they would have their students behave. Learners gain when teachers practice what they preach, try out ideas in front of the class, or even participate actively in projects or tasks with the class.

When modeling, teachers—regardless of their subject area—follow the same assignments or suggestions that they give their students: they write on the same topics, figure out the same problems, play the same games, and ask themselves the same questions. And they do so in full view and hearing of their students, often as coparticipants in small-group activities, or one-to-one with a student.

The practice is neither demeaning nor condescending. Instead, it dramatizes desired behavior, one of the surest means available to demonstrate process, motivate and guide students, and help develop perspective on a given task or concept. As a teacher, let your students hear you think aloud. Teachers who share thoughts on how they have completed a certain task or arrived at a particular conclusion help students become aware of their own thinking strategies.

Modeling enables teachers to furnish appropriate cues and reminders that help students apply particular problem-solving processes or complete specific tasks—in storytelling, for instance, or inquiry, or evaluation. Among such techniques, scaffolding is one of the most generic and useful approaches. Scaffolding is a device by which the teacher builds on the point of reference at which a student hesitates or leaves off—in telling a story, in explaining a process, in seeking an answer, in any moment of discourse, analysis, or explanation. In scaffolding, the teacher simply suggests the next step, both reinforcing what the student has already achieved and guiding the student to greater understanding or accomplishment.

More generally, Costa and Marzano (1987) identify seven starting points by which teachers can create a classroom "language of cognition":

- Using precise vocabulary.
- Posing critical and interpretive questions, rather than simple recall.
- Providing data, not solutions.
- Giving directions.
- Probing for specificity.
- Modeling metacognitive processes.
- Analyzing the logic of language.

"Most teachers put too much emphasis on facts and right answers and too little attention on how to interpret those facts," writes school administrator Robert Burroughs (1993), commenting specifically on the teaching of literature. "The result has been growth in basic literacy at the expense of thoughtfulness. . . . "

Burroughs outlines specific preferred techniques among those he has seen teachers use to guide learning processes and thus structure growth in understanding and appreciation. The techniques are adaptable to discourse, inquiry, or discussion in any subject area:

- Focusing—refocusing students' efforts at refining their own responses if, for instance, they begin wandering from the specific content at hand.
- Modifying or shaping—rephrasing a student's idea in slightly different language; for instance, if a student suggests that a character in a novel is resisting change, the teacher might add a word or two to encourage consideration of other explanations for the character's behavior.
- Hinting—calling attention to a passage in the text that challenges a student's view.
- Summarizing—restating ideas to bring them to everyone's attention and to spur discussion, or summarizing various positions students have taken along the way (1993, pp. 27–29).

Resources

Burroughs, 1993; Costa & Marzano, 1987; Langer, 1991; Marzano et al., 1988; Paris, Wasik, & Turner, 1991; Rosenshine & Meister, 1992; Vygotsky, 1962, 1978.

STRATEGY 1.7

Explore the fullest dimensions of thought

"What a beautiful horse!" said the city-bred dude. "How much is it worth?"

"Depends if you're buyin' or sellin'," answered the cowhand.

"Thinking cannot be divorced from content," writes Carr (1988). "In fact, thinking is a way of learning content. In every course, and especially in content subjects, students should be taught to think logically, analyze and compare, question and evaluate. Skills taught in isolation do little more than prepare students for tests of isolated skills."

If any of the ideas at work described in this chapter challenges the conventional wisdom of classroom practice, it is this notion: students, regardless of their performance levels, are capable of using higher-order thinking skills. This concept contrasts sharply with the attitude and practice of the high school English teacher who, on the first day of school, gave all 125 of her seniors a writing assignment. She collected and corrected their papers; pointed out the various lapses in spelling, grammar, and punctuation; and then used those errors to justify an unproductive, unchallenging year spent reviewing the same sterile exercises in spelling, grammar, and punctuation that her students had seen countless times before.

No one condones faulty grammar and inaccurate spelling, of course. At the same time, however (and far more important), teachers need not wait until students have mastered basic skills before they introduce the more complex skills of analysis, synthesis, criticism, and metacognition into their classroom routines. The process of gathering information, evaluating it critically, drawing inferences, and arriving at logical conclusions is based on evidence, and evidence can be expressed and recognized by many different means and in many different formats.

Yes, every student should learn to spell accurately, but it is not necessary to know that *I* comes before *E* except after *C* in order to test fairness or bias in an editorial statement or to detect straightforwardness or ambiguity in a politician's promise.

Wiggins (1992) notes that tests typically overassess students' knowledge and underassess their know-how. Onosko (1992) reports measurable "climates of thoughtfulness" in the classrooms of social studies teachers who reflect on their own practices, who value thinking, and who emphasize depth over breadth in content coverage.

Carr (1988) and others suggest various ways by which to introduce and pursue higher-order thinking skills in the classroom. For example, using all major news media—newspapers, magazines, television, and radio—motivates students, and comparing different accounts of the same story helps them develop questioning attitudes. "In the process," writes Carr, "they become more discriminating consumers of news media, advertising, and entertainment."

"All classification tasks," she notes, "require identification of attributes and sorting into categories according to some rule. While sorting concrete objects is an appropriate activity for the young child, verbal analogies (for example, 'How are a diamond and an egg alike?') are appropriate for learners of any age. . . . Applications to mathematics and science, especially the inquiry approach to science, are readily apparent."

"Schema theory," she continues, "holds that information, if it is to be retained, must be categorized with something already stored in memory. Brainstorming techniques that aid comprehension . . . help students to access their prior knowledge about a topic to be introduced, and thus to classify and retain the new information."

Children's literature becomes its own powerful tool, Carr concludes, citing Somers and Worthington (1979): "Literature offers children more opportunities than any other area of the curriculum to consider ideas, values, and ethical questions."

Just how seriously should Chicken Little's neighbors have taken her complaint that the sky was falling? Why? Why not? Was it fair for the Little Red Hen to keep all the bread she had baked for herself? How true is it that sticks and stones can break your bones, but names will never hurt you? Why does a rolling stone gather no moss? If water is heavier than air, how do raindrops get up in the sky? How does science differ from art, music from noise, wisdom from fact?

What is truth?

Resources

Adams, 1986; Bransford, Sherwood, Vye, & Rieser, 1986; Carr, 1988; Chi, Bassok, Lewis, Reimann, & Glaser, 1989; Lambert, 1990; Onosko, 1992; Paul, 1984; Rosenshine & Meister, 1992; Somers & Worthington, 1979; Wiggins, 1992.

STRATEGY 1.8

Use a multicultural teaching approach

Multiculturalism doesn't mean what it used to mean in education in the United States. Adding a speech by Martin Luther King Jr. to the literature anthology and offering parental instructions in Spanish—both good ideas in their own right—simply do not go far enough anymore. Teaching multiculturally throughout the curriculum is more than simply an attempt to combat racism. The more important aim of studying human cultures in all their diversity is to understand what it is to be human.

Unfortunately, such study has too often been skewed to a single perspective while more inclusive perspectives have been labeled as somehow disloyal to the American tradition. The fact that racism is so prevalent in American society has until recently led many theorists to concentrate primarily on the study of specific ethnic groups, on their characteristics and unique contributions to the more general culture—usually described from a Euro-American or Anglo-American point of view.

By contrast, the history of the United States is actually the history of all the cultures that it comprises. Until recently, multicultural education has focused mostly on minority groups, even though Euro-Americans and Anglo-Americans also spring from a culture that was not originally and purely "American." Such skewing sets up the fallacy that Euro- and Anglo-American descendants are the "real" Americans while all others, particularly people of color, are culturally "different."

Classroom instruction in a multicultural context is enhanced when it involves students in learning about *themselves* first—through oral history projects, for example, in which children involve their parents, grandparents, and other older, living adults who can relate information about family backgrounds and histories. Shared in the classroom, such information becomes a powerful tool both for identifying similarities among students and for highlighting how they differ from one another in positive rather than negative ways.

In short, teaching multiculturally cultivates a school culture that celebrates diversity; supports mutual acceptance of, respect for, and understanding of all human differences; and provides a balanced viewpoint on key issues involved in such teaching. It provides students with a global, international perspective on the world in which they live. It seeks to eliminate racial, ethnic, cultural, and gender stereotypes and to resolve or ameliorate problems associated with racism and prejudice. And it underscores the importance of teaching ethics, values, and citizenship in promoting the democratic heritage of the United States.

Resources

Au & Kawakami, 1985; Banks, 1990; Bennett, 1986; Bloom, 1985; Collins, 1988; Dillon, 1989; Fullinwider, 1993; Hall, 1989; Hollins, 1993; Kendall, 1983; Quellmalz & Hoskyn, 1988; Taylor & Dorsey-Gaines, 1988; Tiedt & Tiedt, 1986.

STRATEGY 1.9

Use alternative assessments

The student report card is no longer the primary measure of success in schooling. The general vocabulary of education in the United States now includes a whole range of assessment terms: adequate yearly progress, SAT, standardized tests, norms, criterion references, outcomes, portfolios, and on and on. Little wonder that teachers and administrators feel pressured by the demands of "assessment" and harried by the clamor and misunderstanding that surround the term today.

Various modes of assessment yield critical and useful information to inform and shape tools and methods that promise to improve academic achievement. "Why do we evaluate students?" ask Rasbow and Hernandez (1988). Among the answers are to determine the following:

- If objectives have been achieved.
- The knowledge and skills that students have acquired.

- Areas in which the curriculum needs improvement.
- The effectiveness of a teaching process or methodology.
- Student responses to specific aspects of the curriculum.
- Students' ability to use knowledge and skills.

Evaluations are also used to do the following:

- Design instruction for individuals, groups, or entire classes.
- Diagnose a student's level of understanding before recommending further instruction on a given topic.
- Gather information on the quality of the learning environment.
- Guide the direction of future study.
- Summarize an activity, topic, or unit of work.
- Provide a basis for extra help where needed.
- Identify the most useful information to communicate to students and parents.

Traditional assessment techniques and instruments for filling one or another of those roles are as familiar to most teachers as they are widespread in use: the National Assessment of Educational Progress, the SAT, norm- and criterion-referenced tests (some mandated by state legislatures, and even by the federal government), standardized tests in specific subject areas (the Stanford, the California, and the Metropolitan, among others), performance scales, and checklists. And, of course, among teacher-made instruments, examples include the essay exam and the ubiquitous multiple-choice test.

Researchers and curriculum specialists have emphasized the power of various alternative methods of assessment, such as the following:

- Exhibitions or demonstrations that serve as culminating activities in a student's learning experience.
- Observation and analysis of hands-on or open-ended experiences.
- Portfolios (collections of records, letters of reference, samples of work, sometimes even including videotapes of student performance or task accomplishment—in fact, any evidence that appropriately documents a student's skills, capabilities, and past experiences).

If two of the primary purposes of assessment are to determine whether the goals of education are being met and to inform various stakeholders of the progress of education, then assessment techniques should be sufficiently varied to perform these functions as appropriately and accurately as possible. Those goals vary, after all, from broad national goals to the individual teacher's lesson plan. They encompass diagnoses of ability or style in teaching and learning, measurements of proficiency and achievement of individual students or entire classes, and the effectiveness of entire schools, districts, state systems, or national programs. The audiences for assessments may include students, teachers, parents, policymakers, colleges, and businesses. Some assessments serve gatekeeping roles—college admission tests, for instance.

Some assessment methods reflect some of what we have come to realize are preferred teaching practices; consequently, they contain activities that are congruent with and that support good instruction. They tend to invite diverse responses and to promote a range of thinking—hands-on science and mathematics problem-solving activities, for example. In some cases, assessment tasks may extend over several days, allowing students to reflect on their work, to polish and revise it. Some assessments give students the opportunity to respond in any of several ways, including writing, drawing, and making charts or graphic organizers.

In general, trends indicate that alternative assessment tends to do the following:

- Use a variety of progress indicators, such as projects, writing samples, interviews, and observations.
- **Focus on an individual's progress over time rather than on one-time performance within a group.**
- Bring teachers into conference with students about their work and progress, helping students to evaluate themselves by perceiving the results of their own work.

Resources

Association for Supervision and Curriculum Development, 1992; Buechler, 1992; Grace, 1992; Hewitt, 1993; Johnson, 1993; Lockwood, 1991; Marzano et al., 1992; Marzano, Pickering, & McTighe, 1993; Perrone, 1991; Rasbow & Hernandez, 1988; Schnitzer, 1993; Sweet & Zimmerman, 1992; Worthen, 1993.

STRATEGY 1.10

Promote home/school partnerships

Years ago, the professionals at Harlem Park Middle School in Baltimore realized the vital importance of taking parental involvement seriously. They added three parent coordinators to their staff and located them full-time in the neighborhoods the school serves rather than in the school building itself. Living and working in those neighborhoods, the coordinators helped to fight a steady rise in the school's dropout rate by teaching parents how to keep their children in school, help with homework, keep track of progress, and work with school representatives before a crisis develops.

In Mesa, Arizona, school officials recognized that parenthood is 18 years of on-the-job training. So they organized a "Parent University," filling a Saturday schedule with 40 workshops ranging from creative art activities for preschoolers, to helping young people survive junior high, to financing a college education. More than 800 people attended (Education Leaders Consortium, 1989).

The list of ways in which school people have come to grips with the need to bring home and school together for the good of the children varies widely across the United States, limited only by the resourcefulness and imagination of the people in each school and district.

Epstein (1989) outlines several broad avenues by which parents and schools can share in a child's development. Parents have the basic obligation to provide food, clothing, and shelter; to ensure a child's general health and safety; and to provide child rearing and home training. But parents can also provide school supplies, a place for schoolwork at home, and positive home conditions for learning. The school, in turn, is obliged to communicate to the home such important information as school calendars; schedules; notices of special events, school goals, programs, and services; school rules, codes, and policies; report cards, grades, test scores, and informal evaluations; and the availability of parent/teacher conferences.

Parents can be directly involved in the work of the school: assisting teachers and students with lessons; chaperoning class trips; participating in classroom activities; aiding administrators, teachers, and school staff in the school cafeteria, library, laboratories, and workshops; organizing parent groups in fund-raising, community relations, political awareness, and program development; attending student assemblies, sports events, and special presentations; and participating in workshops, discussion groups, and training sessions. Parents can involve themselves in learning activities at home by developing a child's social and personal skills and by contributing to basic-skills education, development of advanced skills, and enrichment.

In governance and advocacy, parents can assume decision-making roles in parent-teacher organizations, on advisory councils, or through other committees and groups at the school, district, or state levels. They can become activists in monitoring schools and by working for school improvement.

Among private philanthropic organizations, the Rockefeller Foundation funded a $3 million effort to launch a project that incorporated the pioneering practices of James Comer, a child psychiatrist at Yale University. The Comer Model is based on the belief that parental involvement is the cornerstone of effective and responsible school change. Comer maintains that one cannot separate academic development from the child's social and cultural background. Thus one of several programs within the project has emphasized a school's obligation to work cooperatively with parents and mental health professionals in meeting the needs of children.

Williams and Chavkin (1989) report that successful home/school programs tend to share seven characteristics: (1) they are guided by written policies; (2) they enjoy administrative support; (3) they include training of staff, parents, or both; (4) they take a partnership approach; (5) they maintain two-way communications; (6) they encourage networking; and (7) they are constantly informed and reshaped by project evaluation.

Having abstracted and reviewed nearly 50 studies of home/school cooperation, Henderson (1987) reached the following conclusions:

- The family provides the primary educational environment.
- Involving parents in their children's formal education improves student achievement.
- Parent involvement is most effective when it is comprehensive, long-lasting, and well planned.

The benefits of family involvement are not confined to early childhood or the elementary levels of schooling; strong effects result from involving parents continuously throughout high school. Henderson also concluded that involving parents in their own children's education at home is not enough. To ensure the quality of schools as institutions serving the community, parents must be involved at all levels of schooling. Moreover, children from low-income and minority families have the most to gain when schools involve parents. Parents can help, regardless of their level of formal education.

We cannot look at the school and the home in isolation from one another. We must see how they interconnect with each other and with the world at large.

Resources

Becher, 1984; Comer, 1980; Education Leaders Consortium, 1989; Epstein, 1987, 1989; Epstein & Dauber, 1991; Goodson & Hess, 1975; Henderson, 1987; Leler, 1983; Steinberg, 1988; U.S. Department of Education, 1990; Williams & Chavkin, 1989.

STRATEGY 1.11

Use accelerated learning techniques

In *Empowering the Spectrum of Your Mind*, Colin Rose (1985) declares that most of us are probably using only 4 percent of the enormous potential of our brains. "The more you use your brain," he maintains, "and the more facts and experience you store, the more associations and connections you make. Therefore, the easier it is to remember and learn yet more new material."

Once considered appropriate for use almost exclusively with students identified as gifted and talented, accelerated learning has come to be regarded as effective with students of any level of performance or ability. How does one "accelerate learning"? What is the theory behind the phrase? Rose (1985) begins with a seemingly obvious fact: no learning can take place without memory. How does one best encode things into memory? By creating concrete images of sights, sounds, and feelings, and by the strong association of one image with another. The stronger the original encoding, the better the ultimate recall. "To achieve good memory," Rose writes, "you need to link a series of facts or ideas together, so that when one is remembered, it triggers recall for a whole series of others."

Thus, an ideal learning pattern involves the following steps:

- Immediate rehearsal of new facts in the short term.
- Repetition or testing of the facts a few minutes later.
- Review of the facts an hour later.
- A short recap of them after a night's rest. (Sleep appears to help memorization; new information is reviewed during REM—rapid eye movement—sleep.)
- Short review a week later.
- Short review a month later.

Rose claims that such a schedule of learning can enable the recall of up to 88 percent of the new information an individual receives—four times better than the usual rate of recall.

Among techniques recommended by advocates of accelerated learning are the following:

- Chunking, that is, reducing new information to manageable bits—a chunk no longer than seven words or seven digits, for instance.
- Use of music and rhyme as aids to memory.
- Peripheral learning and the use of memory maps to encourage association, and thus recall.
- Encoding as specifically as possible by principles rather than through isolated examples by rote.
- Psychiatrist Georgi Lozanov (Lozanov & Gateva, 1988) urges maintaining an upbeat classroom presentation at all times, with constant attention to physical surroundings, self-esteem, goals and outcomes, competition, right and wrong answers, and individual learning styles, expectations, and outcomes.

Resources

Galyean, 1983; Levin, 1988a, 1988b, 1991a, 1991b; Lozanov & Gateva, 1988; Means & Knapp, 1991; Pritchard & Taylor, 1980; Richardson, 1988; Rose, 1985; Russell, 1975; Schuster, 1985.

STRATEGY 1.12

Foster strategies in questioning

The classroom "discussion" dragged on. Predictably, the teacher asked one factual-recall question after another about the short story at hand. Each question invariably elicited a right-or-wrong answer from one, and sometimes two, student volunteers. Then the teacher reached that point in the story where the main character faced what seemed like a life-or-death personal dilemma. "I wonder how many of you have ever faced such a situation," the teacher remarked offhandedly. Hands shot up all around the room, some flapping in urgency. "Oh, my! I'm afraid I've touched some raw nerves," the teacher exclaimed. "Let me withdraw the question." All the raised hands dropped. So did the students' attention to the topic.

That teacher couldn't have read Lehr and Harris's *At-Risk, Low-Achieving Students in the Classroom* (1988). The authors suggest (and their suggestions are well supported by research) how even the timeless classroom practice of questions from the teacher can be adapted to elicit individual involvement rather than passive response. They also show how to follow through for even greater student participation and response. Their advice, in part, includes the following suggestions (pp. 43–44):

- Structure questions so that students can succeed.
- Encourage students to respond. (Most teachers answer two-thirds of their own questions.)
- Ask questions in all modes. (Most questions are asked at the level of basic recall or recognition. Questioning that is more complex increases student achievement.)
- Pause. The number and quality of student answers increase when teachers provide wait time of three to five seconds after asking a question. Appropriate wait time is particularly important in teaching low achievers. Some higher-level questions might require as much as 15 to 20 seconds of wait time.
- Call on students randomly, but be sure not to forget the low achiever.
- If a student's response is vague, call for clarification or elaboration—for example, "Tell me more." Probe students to encourage higher levels of thinking.
- Encourage students to develop and ask their own questions, thus increasing their opportunities for thinking.
- Use techniques that require students to pose their own questions and to make discoveries on their own. For example, ask students in a science class to make predictions, based on their own experiences, before a demonstration or an experiment. The processes of observing, comparing, and describing are as important as the product.

Other studies of questioning techniques suggest that teachers break the total content of their questioning into bits small enough so that students are assured of being able to answer at least three-quarters of the questions correctly. They urge a high proportion of questions that are well beyond mere factual recall—questions that encourage interpretation or that challenge critical thinking.

Questioning need not simply follow a lesson or an assignment as a means of checking to see if students have completed or understood it. Reading specialists, for instance, have long advocated the use of prereading questioning techniques, using teacher- or student-generated questions to develop background knowledge, to preview key concepts, and to set purposes for the reading. Questioning after reading should provide students with opportunities to practice or rehearse what they have learned from the text, as well as increase associations between textual information and their own background knowledge ("Questioning Promotes," 1987).

To stimulate student discussions, Dillon (1984) suggests a three-step process:

- Carefully formulate one or two questions to get the discussion going.
- From then on, ask questions only when perplexed and genuinely in need of more information.
- Then make more statements that present facts or opinions, reflect students' opinions to them, register confusion, or invite elaboration and student-to-student exchanges.

Student-generated questions and student-led discussions give students a higher stake and interest in their classroom activities and learning. Framing their own questions requires young people to interact with the meaning of content or text from a variety of perspectives. Generating their own questions, they support and challenge each other and recognize the social aspects of exploring the meaning of what they encounter in reading or in other learning activities.

Teachers need to model effective questioning and discussion strategies, including how to interact with others as well as how to think about and discuss text or content. Touch a raw nerve now and then—not to aggravate, but to stimulate!

Resources

Adams, 1986; Carlsen, 1991; Dillon, 1984; Goatley & Raphael, 1992; Lehr & Harris, 1988; "Questioning Promotes," 1987; Roberts & Zody, 1989; "Teachers' Questions," 1987.

STRATEGY 1.13

Emphasize brain-compatible instruction

Think of your most recent drink of water. Exactly what steps did you follow in taking it? What facts, what prior experiences, what understandings did you call on? It's been estimated that you performed 50 or so actions while taking that drink of water. Did you think of all 50—that is, did you bring any of them, in isolation, to the forefront of your consciousness while drinking?

Probably not. Your brain handled all the necessary steps for you! At the same time, your brain was probably helping you consider your plans for the weekend, reminding you of the slight soreness in your left thumb, telling you it was a warm afternoon, and juggling countless other "programs"—chains of thought needed to accomplish some foreseen goal, whether soaking your thumb or quenching your thirst (Della Neve et al., 1986).

Brain-compatible instruction builds on the notion that the human brain operates as an incredibly powerful parallel processor, always doing many different things simultaneously (Caine & Caine, 1991). The brain is capable of such a vast number and array of functions that its functioning can be visualized most easily only in terms of programs and patterns—one program, perhaps, for getting a glass of water at the kitchen sink, a different program for sipping from the water fountain outside your classroom door.

How does the brain differentiate among the vast array of programs it stores? By recognizing an apparently endless number and variety of patterns among them. Thus "brain-compatible instruction defines learning as the acquisition of useful programs," write Della Neve and her colleagues (1986). "The human brain is exceedingly intricate. For educational purposes, however, what counts is a broad, holistic understanding of what the brain is for (it did not evolve to pass tests or fill in worksheets), its principal architecture, its main drives, and its way of relating to the real world."

Carnine (1990) describes some of the misunderstandings that can result in teachers, students, or both after "brain-antagonistic" instruction:

Very young children know that the name of an object stays the same even after the orientation of the object has changed. For example, when a chair is turned to face the opposite direction, it remains a chair.

Consequently, in preschool, when a *b* is flipped to face the opposite direction, children often assume that it still goes by the name of *b*. Making this error doesn't necessarily imply that a student's visual brain function is weak or that the student would benefit from a kinesthetic approach to learning lowercase letters. Extensive research has shown that students are more likely to confuse objects and symbols that share visual or auditory sameness, such as *b* and *d*.

In solving simple computation problems, such as 24 + 13, 1st graders learn that they can start with the bottom number in the units column or with the top number: 4 + 3 equals 7, and so does 3 + 4. The sameness they note is that these problems can be worked in either direction, from top to bottom or the reverse.

Soon thereafter come subtraction problems, such as 24–13. Students can still apply the sameness learned in addition, thinking of the difference between 4 and 3 or between 3 and 4 and always subtracting the smaller number from the larger. However, when students encounter a problem such as 74 – 15, applying the sameness noted earlier leads them to subtract the smaller from the larger number and come up with the answer 61. Such a mistake is a sensible application of a mislearned sameness. . . .

"The brain's search for samenesses," Carnine concludes, "has little regard for the intentions of educators." At the same time, he notes that although the brain's relentless search for patterns helps explain certain common student misconceptions, it can also help educators develop more effective classroom activities.

Della Neve and her colleagues at Drew Elementary School developed their own seven principles, which serve as focal points to guide teachers in designing and implementing brain-compatible instruction:

1. Create a nonthreatening climate.
2. Input lots of raw material from which students can extract patterns—a vast array of activities, aided by an ample supply of materials, equipment, and print and audiovisual resources.
3. Emphasize genuine communication in talking, listening, writing, and reading as ways to interact with other people.
4. Encourage lots of manipulation of materials. Students need to be in command and able to push things around, encouraging them to work toward goals and explore a range of means.
5. Emphasize reality. By using problems, examples, and contacts drawn from the "real world" rather than contrived exercises, texts, worksheets, and basal readers, students can see the real value of their own learning.
6. Address learning activities to actual, productive uses.
7. Respect natural thinking, including intuitive leaps, a grasp of patterns (as in number tables or good writing), and aesthetic and nonverbal interests and activities.

"Brain-based instruction," Caine and Caine (1991) warn us, "stems from recognizing that the brain does not take logical steps down one path like an analog computer, but can go down a hundred different paths simultaneously like an enormously powerful digital computer."

They add, "Each brain is unique. Teaching should be multifaceted to allow all students to express visual, tactile, emotional, and auditory preferences. Providing choices that are variable enough to attract individual interests may require the reshaping of schools so that they exhibit the complexity found in life."

Resources

Bateson, 1980; Caine & Caine, 1991; Campbell, 1989; Carnine, 1990; Cousins, 1989; Della Neve, Hart, & Thomas, 1986; Hart, 1983, 1986; Vygotsky, 1962, 1978.

STRATEGY 1.14

Activate students' prior knowledge

Activating students' prior knowledge—through the use of schema theory, for example—helps youngsters integrate new knowledge and skills with their own experiences. By doing so, teachers acknowledge that all students, regardless of their background, bring a wealth of knowledge to learning. The kind and amount "of knowledge one has before encountering a given topic in a discipline affects how one constructs meaning," writes Gaea Leinhardt (1992). "The impact of prior knowledge is not a matter of 'readiness,' component skills, or exhaustiveness; it is an issue of depth, interconnectedness, and access. Outcomes are determined jointly by what was known before and by the content of the instruction" (pp. 51–56).

Consequently, it just makes sense for teachers to begin by learning what students already know about a topic, thus preventing youngsters from having to repeat what they already know or trying to build on knowledge they do not yet possess. Connecting new knowledge to previous learning builds a strong foundation for future learning; it also gives teachers valuable opportunities to correct misperceptions. Modifying activities to suit learners' preferences helps them construct new understandings.

When tapping into students' prior knowledge, teachers recognize that the most effective means of learning is discovery, and the most effective means of teaching is modeling. Modeling by the teacher is one of many powerful tools for activating prior knowledge. Depending on the task, the teacher decides what prior knowledge needs to be activated and asks students to develop and answer questions that cause them to activate it. The teacher then proceeds to model appropriate questioning processes. Activating students' prior knowledge engages them more actively in learning, in generating their own questions, and in leading their own discussions.

Another strategy that effectively activates students' prior knowledge, allowing them to explore what they already know about a topic, is the K-W-L activity, first developed by Donna Ogle. This strategy asks students to identify what they already *know* about a topic, *what* they would like to learn, and, at the conclusion of the unit, what they actually did *learn*.

Teachers can encourage students to develop a list of questions they would like to answer. (Teacher modeling helps students form these questions.) Teachers can then assist students in clustering similar questions and in deciding which questions to answer by further explaining the content to be learned. The teacher and students design a plan to find the answer for each question. Allowing students to work in cooperative and collaborative groups is effective because such groups encourage students to share their answers and the rationale behind the answers. During the sharing, the teacher has an opportunity to correct student misunderstandings.

In exploring new topics, students can experience a variety of active, experiential, or authentic assignments. Such assignments—for example, manipulating objects or concepts, engaging in product-oriented activities, and participating in real-life experiences that actively construct knowledge—allow youngsters to explore concepts in some depth and to make discoveries on their own. The opportunity to apply new learnings to real-life contexts that reflect the students' world helps them retain and effectively use new concepts and skills.

STRATEGY 1.15

Use a constructivist approach to teaching

Many of the approaches to teaching and learning that appear in this book challenge the traditional model of schooling, which demands that students receive knowledge solely from the teacher. In explaining the nature of the "pedagogy of poverty," Martin Haberman (1991) notes that teachers and students are engaged in fundamentally different activities: teachers teach and students learn. But what if teachers join students as fellow learners searching for answers to real-life problems or for ways to describe and generalize scientific phenomena?

Another means of creating what might be called a pedagogy of plenty is to embrace a constructivist approach to teaching. Constructivism emphasizes an understanding of how and why students (and adults) learn; it provides a way to combine good teaching and learning practices. These practices include activating students' prior knowledge; providing a variety of active learning resources; using a variety of hands-on, minds-on activities; engaging youngsters in a variety of cooperative learning experiences; allowing students to formulate questions and discover concepts that can guide future learnings; asking students to think aloud while approaching a task; modeling powerful thinking strategies; and providing students with opportunities to apply new learnings within the context of real-life activities.

Such an instructional setting honors the importance of hands-on and "heads-on" experiences in learning. For students to learn to reason about their world, they must be constantly encouraged to ask questions and to solve problems that have meaning to them. Teachers can provide a wide variety of activities to help students construct—and reconstruct—their new learning in their own terms, as they begin to realize that knowledge is created out of life experiences.

Constructivist theory suggests that the goal of schooling is not simply acquiring specific knowledge and expertise, but rather *building understanding*. Learning how to learn becomes the goal. Considered from a constructivist viewpoint, the learning environment is a laboratory that provides the tools to support learners in their quest for understanding. In this approach, teachers facilitate learning by providing appropriate activities such as modeling and questioning techniques in well-designed, well-organized, well-managed classroom environments that allow students to construct their own understandings of concepts.

Constructivist teaching is best facilitated though the use of varied learning configurations. Providing students with opportunities to work in collaborative or small-group learning activities helps them to construct their own knowledge. Students have the opportunity to listen to other points of view, debate, discuss, and form insights into new ideas while working collaboratively with their peers. Such activities must also activate students' prior knowledge to help them develop questioning skills.

STRATEGY 1.16

Organize instructionally effective classroom environments

When the classroom environment encourages growth and development, students will respond. Instructionally effective environments offer youngsters a wide variety of powerful experiences, which include ways of interacting with and learning from one another in instructional areas that support experiential, problem-based, active learning. Creating such environments calls for the teacher to construct and allow cooperative, collaborative strategies.

Classroom design simply means arranging the room to make the best use of space and to create a comfortable learning climate—both physically and psychologically. Classroom management reflects the ways in which the teacher orchestrates high-quality instructional activities that help children take charge of their learning and eliminate unwanted behavioral and discipline problems.

Classroom Design

Our school system was invented to provide a sit-and-learn process of education. In 1915, for instance, John Dewey reportedly described the difficulties he encountered during an exhaustive search for furniture "suitable from all points of view—artistic . . . and educational—to the needs of children." According to the account, Dewey finally met one school-supply dealer who admitted, "I'm afraid we do not have what you want. You want something at which children may work; these are for listening."

Amazingly, little has changed in U.S. classrooms since Dewey's time. Regardless of individual differences, many, many children are still expected to sit on a hard seat, not move, and not speak—just listen and answer questions.

Research strongly supports the important role of environmental preferences in students' motivation and their ability to learn. The *quality* of the environment in which we live and work is vitally important. Individuals tend to respond to their physical environment first in terms of personal comfort. Harmony makes it easier to concentrate and remember information.

The proper use of space within a classroom generates student activity and learning. Room arrangement, for example, allows students to work at computer stations, engage in small-group work, engage in project-based learning, and use multimedia equipment for individual or group activities. Appropriate classroom design empowers teachers to create instructional areas, such as learning and interest centers and media centers, that offer students varied learning opportunities and accommodate individual learning needs and interests.

Well-designed classrooms display high levels of student cooperation, academic success, and task involvement. Teachers work to develop intrinsic motivation in students, which is essential to creating lifelong learners. Thus effective classroom environments create multiple learning situations capable of addressing students' diverse characteristics to enhance their satisfaction and academic performance. Such classes are child centered; they meet young people's instructional needs by exposing them to a variety of highly motivating, stimulating, multilevel instructional activities.

Current research in the functioning of the brain confirms that we learn best in a rich, multisensory environment. We learn more about people by interacting with them in real-life contexts. We learn more meaningfully when we are fully immersed in the learning experience. Therefore, we should provide students with active learning experiences that incorporate a wide variety of materials, including high-quality, well-written literature.

Powerful learning activities are most likely to occur in a highly organized learning environment. When orchestrating such a setting, it is important to keep in mind how instruction will be reinforced, reviewed, and enriched to extend youngsters' learning potential; how procedures for completing assignments, working, locating instructional resources, and acquiring assistance will be facilitated; and how students will evaluate their own performance and that of others.

CLASSROOM MANAGEMENT

Making a classroom an effective educational tool depends on creating not only a physically comfortable environment that supports instructional goals but also one that is emotionally, socially, psychologically, and physically safe. Classrooms should be places where a child can think, discover, grow, and ultimately learn to work independently and cooperatively in a group setting, developing self-discipline and self-esteem. At the heart of an emotionally safe learning environment is cooperation—among staff, students, and other stakeholders.

Cooperation leads to ownership, involvement, and great opportunities for student self-discipline, says Jerome Freiberg (1996)—but first must come *trust*. Students learn to trust through opportunities to take ownership of and responsibility for their own actions and those of others. Strategies to promote cooperation include establishing rules and regulations (with the assistance of students) for codes of behavior and conduct; talking about consequences of behavior; offering youngsters training in peer mediation and conflict resolution; creating rotating classroom management positions, with clearly outlined responsibilities; and helping youngsters develop norms of collaboration and social skills to enable them to work effectively in groups.

When children are truly engaged in learning and the approach to discipline is an active one, teachers do not have to waste valuable time dealing with disciplinary issues. When learning becomes less meaningful to students' lives, less interactive, or less stimulating, teachers increasingly need to control their students; in the process, they unwittingly create opportunities for undesirable student behaviors.

Teachers who try to impose too many rules, too much rigidity, and too many uniform activities quickly lose control. Teachers who can bring themselves to share power and confidence with their students gain more control. That is exactly why teachers should concentrate on creating conditions in which students can and will manage themselves.

Author's note: I would like to acknowledge the ASCD Advisory Panel on Improving Student Achievement and Lloyd W. Kline for their contributions to this chapter.

BIBLIOGRAPHY

Adams, M. J. (1986, June 17–18). Teaching thinking to Chapter 1 students. In B. I. Williams et al. (Eds.), *Designs for compensatory education: Conference proceedings and papers.* Chapel Hill, NC: Research and Evaluation Associates, Inc.

Adams, M. J. (1990). *Beginning to read: Thinking and learning about print.* Cambridge, MA: Bradford Books/MIT Press.

Andrews, R. H. (1990, July–September). The development of a learning styles program in a low socioeconomic, underachieving, North Carolina elementary school. *Journal of Reading, Writing, and Learning Disability International, 6*(3), 307–314.

Andrews, R. H. (1991). Insights into education: An elementary principal's perspective. In R. S. Dunn (Ed.), *Hands-on approaches to learning styles: Practical approaches to successful schooling* (pp. 50–52). New Wilmington, PA: Association for the Advancement of International Education.

Ascher, C. (1990, March). *Testing students in urban schools: Current problems and new directions* (Urban Diversity Series No. 100). New York: ERIC Clearinghouse on Urban Education/Institute for Urban and Minority Education.

Association for Supervision and Curriculum Development. (1992). *Redesigning assessment*[Videotape]. Alexandria, VA: Author.

Atkins, A. (1993, February). New ways to learn. *Better Homes and Gardens, 71*(2), 35–36.

Au, K., & Kawakami, A. J. (1985). Research currents: Talk story and learning to read. *Language Arts, 62*(4), 406–411.

Au, K., & Kawakami, A. J. (1991). Culture and ownership: Schooling of minority students. *Childhood Education, 67*(5), 280–284.

Banks, J. A. (1990). *Preparing teachers and administrators in a multicultural society.* Austin, TX: Southwest Educational Development Laboratory.

Bateson, G. (1980). *Mind and nature: A necessary unity.* New York: Bantam.

Bauer, E. (1991). The relationships between and among learning styles, perceptual preferences, instructional strategies, mathematics achievement and attitude toward mathematics of learning disabled and emotionally handicapped students in a suburban junior high school. *Dissertation Abstracts International, 53*(6), 1378.

Becher, R. M. (1984). *Parent involvement: A review of research and principles of successful practice.* Washington, DC: National Institute of Education.

Bempechat, J., & Ginsberg, H. P. (1989, November). *Underachievement and educational disadvantage: The home and school experience of at-risk youth* (Urban Diversity Series No. 99). New York: ERIC Clearinghouse on Urban Education/Institute for Urban and Minority Education.

Benard, B. (1991, April). *Moving toward a "just and vital culture": Multiculturalism in our schools.* Portland, OR: Western Regional Center for Drug-Free Schools and Communities, Northwest Regional Educational Laboratory. (ERIC Document Reproduction Service No. ED336439)

Bennett, C. I. (1986). *Comprehensive multicultural education: Theory and practice.* Newton, MA: Allyn and Bacon.

Bloom, B. S. (1976). *Human characteristics and school learning.* New York: McGraw-Hill.

Bloome, D. (1985). Reading as a social process. *Language Arts, 62*(2), 134–142.

Boyatzis, R. E., & Kolb, D. A. (1991). Assessing individuality in learning: The learning skills profile. *Educational Psychology: An International Journal of Experimental Educational Psychology, 11*(34), 279–295.

Bransford, J. D., Sherwood, R. S., Vye, N. J., & Rieser, J. (1986, October). Teaching thinking and problem solving: Research foundations. *American Psychologist, 41*(10), 1078–1089.

Brown, S. (1990, October). Integrating manipulatives and computers in problem-solving experiences. *Arithmetic Teacher, 38*(2), 8–10.

Brunner, C. E., & Majewski, W. S. (1990, October). Mildly handicapped students can succeed with learning styles. *Educational Leadership, 48*(2), 21–23.

Bruno, A. (1982, October). Hands-on wins hands down. *Early Years, 13*(2), 60–67.

Buechler, M. (1992, April). *Performance assessment.* Policy Bulletin. Bloomington, IN: Indiana Education Policy Center.

Burroughs, R. (1993, July). The uses of literature. *Executive Educator, 15*(7), 27–29.

Butler, K. A. (1984). *Learning and teaching styles: In theory and practice.* Maynard, MA: Gabriel Systems.

Caine, R. N., & Caine, G. (1991). *Teaching and the human brain.* Alexandria, VA: Association for Supervision and Curriculum Development.

Campbell, J. (1989). *The improbable machine.* New York: Simon & Schuster.

Carbo, M. (1987, October). Matching reading styles: Correcting ineffective instruction. *Educational Leadership, 45*(2), 55–62.

Carbo, M., Dunn, R., & Dunn, K. (1986). *Teaching students to read through their individual learning styles.* Englewood Cliffs, NJ: Prentice-Hall.

Carbo, M., & Hodges, H. (1988, Summer). Learning styles strategies can help students at risk.*Teaching Exceptional Children, 20*(4), 55–58.

Carlsen, W. S. (1991, Summer). Questioning in classrooms: A sociolinguistic perspective. *Review of Educational Research, 61*(2), 157–178.

Carnine, D. (1990, January). New research on the brain: Implications for instruction. *Phi Delta Kappan, 71*(5), 372–377.

Carr, K. S. (1988, Winter). How can we teach critical thinking? *Childhood Education, 65*(2), 69–73.

Cherkasky-Davis, L. (1993, June 11). Presentation at the annual conference of the Educational Press Association of America, Philadelphia.

Chi, M. T. H., Bassok, M., Lewis, M. W., Reimann, P., & Glaser, R. (1989). Self-explanations: How students study and use examples in learning to solve problems. *Cognitive Science, 13*(2), 145–182.

Cohen, H. G. (1992, March). Two teaching strategies: Their effectiveness with students of varying cognitive abilities. *School, Science and Mathematics, 92*(3), 126–132.

Cole, M., & Griffin, P. (Eds.). (1987). *Improving science and mathematics education for minorities and women: Contextual factors in education.* Madison, WI: University of Wisconsin.

Collins, J. (1988, December). Language and class in minority education. *Anthropology in Education, 19*(4), 299–326.

Comer, J. P. (1980). *School power.* New York: Macmillan, The Free Press.

Connolly, L. H., & Tucker, S. M. (1982, March). *Motivating the Mexican American student.* Las Cruces, NM: ERIC Clearinghouse on Rural Education and Small Schools. (ERIC Document Reproduction Service No. ED287657)

Costa, A. L., & Marzano, R. (1987, October). Teaching the language of thinking. *Educational Leadership, 45*(2), 29–33.

Cousins, N. (1989). *Head first: The biology of hope.* New York: E. P. Dutton.

Danehower, V. F. (1993, Summer). Implementing whole language: Understanding the change process. *Schools in the Middle, 2*(4), 45–46.

Darling-Hammond, L., & Ascher, C. (1991, March). *Creating accountability in big city schools* (Urban Diversity Series No. 102). New York: ERIC Clearinghouse on Urban Education/Institute on Urban and Minority Education, and the National Center for Restructuring Education, Schools and Teaching. (ERIC Document Reproduction Service No. ED334339)

Dash, R. (Ed.). (1988, September). *The challenge—Preparing teachers for diverse student populations* (Roundtable Report). San Francisco: Far West Laboratory for Educational Research and Development. (ERIC Document Reproduction Service No. ED334191)

Della Neve, C., Hart, L. A., & Thomas, E. C. (1986, October). Huge learning jumps show potency of brain-based instruction. *Phi Delta Kappan, 68*(2), 143–148.

Dillon, D. R. (1989). Showing them that I want them to learn and that I care about who they are: A micro-ethnography of the social organization of a secondary low-track English-reading classroom.*American Educational Research Journal, 26*(2), 227–259.

Dillon, J. T. (1984, November). Research on questioning and discussion. *Educational Leadership, 42*(3), 50–56.

Dunn, R., & Dunn, K. (1993). *Teaching secondary students through their individual learning styles: Practical approaches for grades 7–12.* Boston: Allyn and Bacon.

Edmonds, R. (Program Consultant). (1991). *Effective schools for children at risk* [Videotape]. Alexandria, VA: Association for Supervision and Curriculum Development.

Education Leaders Consortium. (1989). *Schools, parents work best when they work together.* Washington, DC: Education Leaders Consortium.

Epstein, J. L. (1987). Toward a theory of family-school connections: Teacher practices and parent involvement. In K. Hurrelmann, F. X. Kaufmann, & F. Lösel (Eds.), *Social intervention: Potential and constraints.* New York: Walter de Gruyter.

Epstein, J. L. (1989). Effects on student achievement of teachers' practices of parental involvement. In S. Silvern (Ed.), *Literacy through family, community, and school.* Greenwich, CT: JAI Press.

Epstein, J. L., & Dauber, S. L. (1991, January). School programs and teacher practices of parent involvement in inner-city elementary and middle schools. *Elementary School Journal, 91*(3), 289–305.

Erickson, F. (1987). Transformation and school success: The politics and culture of educational attainment. *Anthropology and Education Quarterly, 18*(4), 335–356.

ETS Policy Information Center. (1990). *The education reform decade.* Princeton, NJ: Educational Testing Service.

Farr, M., & Daniels, H. (1986). *Language diversity and writing instruction.* New York: ERIC Clearinghouse on Urban Education/Institute for Urban and Minority Education, the ERIC Clearinghouse on Reading and Communication Skills, and the NCTE.

Flaxman, E., Ascher, C., & Harrington, C. (1988, December). *Youth mentoring: Programs and practices* (Urban Diversity Series No. 97). New York: ERIC Clearinghouse on Urban Education/Institute for Urban and Minority Education.

Freiberg, J. (1996, September). From tourists to citizens in the classroom. *Educational Leadership, 54*(1), 32–36.

Fullinwider, R. K. (1993, Spring). Multiculturalism: Themes and variations. *Perspective, 5*(2).

Galyean, B. C. (1983). *Mind sight: Learning through imaging.* Long Beach, CA: Center for Integrative Learning.

Gardner, H. (1999). *Intelligence reframed: Multiple intelligences for the 21st century.* New York: BasicBooks.

Gardner, H., & Hatch, T. (1989, November). Multiple intelligences go to school. *Educational Researcher, 18*(8), 4–9.

Garrett, S. L. (1991). The effects of perceptual preference and motivation on vocabulary and test scores among high school students. Unpublished doctoral dissertation, University of La Verne, California.

Goatley, V. J., & Raphael, T. E. (1992). Non-traditional learners' written and dialogic response to literature. In C. K. Kinzer & D. K. Leu (Eds.), *Literacy research, theory, and practice: Views from many perspectives.* Chicago: National Reading Conference.

Goodson, B. D., & Hess, R. D. (1975). *Parents as teachers of young children: An evaluative review of some contemporary concepts and programs.* Washington, DC: Bureau of Educational Personnel Development, DHEW, Office of Education.

Grace, C. (1992). *The portfolio and its use: Developmentally appropriate assessment of young children.* Urbana, IL: ERIC Clearinghouse on Elementary and Early Childhood Education.

Gregorc, A. E. (1982). *An adult's guide to style.* Columbia, CT: Gregorc Associates, Inc.

Gregorc, A. E. (1985a). *Inside styles: Beyond the basics.* Columbia, CT: Gregorc Associates, Inc.

Gregorc, A. E. (1985b). *Gregorc style delineator.* Columbia, CT: Gregorc Associates, Inc.

Haberman, M. (1987, November). *Recruiting and selecting teachers for urban schools.* New York: ERIC Clearinghouse on Urban Education/Institute for Urban and Minority Education and Association of Teacher Educators.

Haberman, M. (1991). The pedagogy of poverty versus good teaching. *Phi Delta Kappan, 73*(4), 290–294.

Hall, E. T. (1989, Fall). Unstated features of the cultural context of learning. *Educational Forum, 54*(1), 21–34.

Hart, L. (1983, January). A quick tour of the brain. *School Administrator, 40*(1), 13–15.

Hart, L. (1986, May). All "thinking" paths lead to the brain. *Educational Leadership, 43*(8), 45–48.

Hartshorn, R., & Boren, S. (1990, June). *Experiential learning of mathematics: Using manipulatives.* Charleston, WV: ERIC Clearinghouse on Rural Education and Small Schools. (ERIC Document Reproduction Service No. ED321967)

Henderson, A. T. (1987). *The evidence continues to grow: Parent involvement improves students' achievement.* Columbia, MD: National Committee for Citizens in Education.

Herrmann, A. W. (1989, May). *Teaching writing with peer response groups.* Bloomington, IN: ERIC Clearinghouse on Reading and Communication Skills. (ERIC Document Reproduction Service No. ED307616)

Hewitt, G. (1993, May/June). Vermont's portfolio-based writing assessment program: A brief history. *Teachers & Writers, 24*(5), 1–6.

Hodges, H. (1994, January). A consumer's guide to learning styles programs: An expert's advice on selecting and implementing various models in the classroom. *School Administrator, 51*(1), 14–18.

Hollins, E. R. (1993, Spring). Assessing teacher competence for diverse populations. *Theory into Practice, 32*(1), 93–99.

Irvine, J. J. (1990). *Black students and school failure: Policies, practices, and prescriptions.* New York: Greenwood Press.

Jacobs, H. H. (1991, October). Planning for curriculum integration. *Educational Leadership, 49*(2), 27–28.

Johnson, D. W., & Johnson, R. T. (1986). *Learning together and alone* (2nd ed.). Englewood Cliffs, NJ: Prentice-Hall.

Johnson, D. W., & Johnson, R. T. (1990, December/January). Social skills for successful group work. *Educational Leadership, 47*(4), 29–33.

Johnson, N. J. (1993). *Celebrating growth over time: Classroom-based assessment in language arts* (Literacy Improvement Series for Elementary Educators). Washington, DC: Office of Educational Research and Improvement.

Joyner, J. M. (1990, October). Using manipulatives successfully. *Arithmetic Teacher, 38*(2), 6–7.

Kendall, F. E. (1983). *Diversity in the classroom: A multicultural approach to the education of young children.* New York: Teachers College Press.

Kilman, M., & Richards, J. (1990). *Now that we've done the calculation, how do we solve the problem? Writing, sharing, and discussing arithmetic stories.* Newton, MA: The Literacies Institute, Education Development Center, Inc.

Knapp, M. S., & Shields, P. M. (1990a, June). Reconceiving academic instruction for the children of poverty. *Phi Delta Kappan, 71*(10), 753–758.

Knapp, M. S., & Shields, P. M. (Eds.). (1990b, January). *Better schooling for the children of poverty: Alternatives to conventional wisdom.* Study of Academic Instruction for Disadvantaged Students. Volume II: Commissioned Papers and Literature Review. Washington, DC, and Menlo Park, CA: Policy Studies Associates and SRI International.

Knapp, M. S., & Turnbull, B. J. (1990, January). *Better schooling for the children of poverty: Alternatives to conventional wisdom.* Study of Academic Instruction for Disadvantaged Students. Volume I: Summary. Washington, DC, and Menlo Park, CA: Policy Studies Associates and SRI International.

Lambert, M. (1990). When the problem is not the question and the solution is not the answer: Mathematical knowing and teaching. *American Educational Research Journal, 27*(1), 29–63.

Langer, J. A. (1991). *Literary understanding and literature instruction* (Report Series 2.11). Albany, NY: National Research Center on Literature Teaching and Learning.

Lehr, J. B., & Harris, H. W. (1988). *At-risk, low-achieving students in the classroom.* Washington, DC: National Education Association.

Leinhardt, G. (1992, April). What research on learning tells us about teaching. *Educational Leadership, 49*(7), 51–56.

Leler, H. (1983). Parent education and involvement in relation to the schools and to parents of school-aged children. In R. Haskins & D. Adams (Eds.), *Parent education and public policy.* Norwood, NJ: Ablex.

Levin, H. M. (1988a). *Structuring schools for greater effectiveness with educationally disadvantaged or at-risk students.* Paper presented at the annual meeting of the American Educational Research Association, New Orleans.

Levin, H. M. (1988b, September). *Accelerated schools for at-risk students.* (CPRE Research Report Series RR-010). New Brunswick, NJ: Center for Policy Research in Education, Eagleton Institute of Politics, Rutgers, State University of New Jersey.

Levin, H. M. (1991a, January). Don't remediate: Accelerate. *Principal, 70*(3), 11–13.

Levin, H. M. (1991b). *Accelerating the progress of ALL students* (Rockefeller Institute Special Report, Number 31). Albany: State University of New York, Nelson A. Rockefeller Institute of Government.

Lewis, A., & Steinberger, E. (1991). *Learning styles: Putting research and common sense into practice.* Arlington, VA: American Association of School Administrators.

Lockwood, A. T. (1991, March). Authentic assessment. *Focus in Change, 3*(1). (Available from the National Center for Effective Schools, Madison, WI.)

Lozanov, G., & Gateva, E. (1988). *The foreign language teacher's suggestopedic manual.* New York: Gordon and Breach Science Publishers.

Maehr, M. L. (1980, April). *Cultural differences do not have to mean motivational inequality.* Paper presented at the annual meeting of the American Educational Research Association, Boston. (ERIC Document Reproduction Service No. ED199353)

Marzano, R. J., Brandt, R. S., Hughes, C. S., Jones, B. F., Presseisen, B. Z., Rankin, S. C., & Suhor, C. (1988). *Dimensions of thinking.* Alexandria, VA: Association for Supervision and Curriculum Development.

Marzano, R. J., Pickering, D., & McTighe, J. (1993). *Assessing student outcomes: Performance assessment using the Dimensions of Learning model.* Alexandria, VA: Association for Supervision and Curriculum Development.

Marzano, R. J., Pickering, D. J., Whisler, J., Kendall, J. S., Mayeski, F., & Paynter, D. E. (1992).*Toward a comprehensive model of assessment.* Aurora, CO: Mid-continent Regional Educational Laboratory.

Mathematical Sciences Education Board. (1993). *Making mathematics work for minorities: Framework for a national action plan.* Washington, DC: National Academy Press. (ERIC Document Reproduction Service No. ED373961)

Means, B., & Knapp, M. S. (1991). *Teaching advanced skills to educationally disadvantaged students.* (Final Report). Washington, DC: Prepared under contract by SRI International and Policy Studies Associates for the U.S. Department of Education, Office of Planning, Budget, and Evaluation.

Miller, S. K., & Crano, W. D. (1980, April). *Raising low-income/minority achievement by reducing student sense of academic futility: The underlying theoretical commonalities of suggested strategies.* Paper presented at the annual meeting of the American Educational Research Association, Boston. (ERIC Document Reproduction Service No. ED186575)

National Council of Teachers of Mathematics. (1989). *Curriculum and evaluation standards for school mathematics.* Reston, VA: Author.

Oakes, J. (1985). *Keeping track: How schools structure inequality.* New Haven, CT: Yale University Press.

Onosko, J. J. (1992, April). Exploring the thinking of thoughtful teachers. *Educational Leadership, 49*(7), 40–43.

Orsak, L. (1990, October). Learning styles versus the Rip Van Winkle syndrome. *Educational Leadership, 48*(2), 19–20.

Palincsar, A. S., Englert, C. S., Raphael, T. E., & Gavalek, J. R. (1991, May/June). Examining the context of strategy instruction. *Remedial and Special Education (RASE), 12*(3), 43–53.

Palincsar, A. S., & Klenk, L. J. (1991). Learning dialogues to promote text comprehension. In B. Means & M. S. Knapp (Eds.), *Teaching advanced skills to educationally disadvantaged students.* Washington, DC: U.S. Department of Education.

Palincsar, A. S., Ransom, K., & Derber, S. (1989/1990, December/January). Collaborative research and development of reciprocal teaching. *Educational Leadership, 46*(4), 37–40.

Paris, S. G., Wasik, B. A., & Turner, J. C. (1991). The development of strategic readers. In R. Barr, M. L. Kamil, P. B. Mosenthal, & P. D. Pearson (Eds.), *Handbook of reading research* (Vol. 2, pp. 609–640). New York: Longman.

Paul, R. W. (1984, September). Critical thinking: Fundamental to education for a free society.*Educational Leadership, 42*(1), 4–14.

Perrin, J. (1990, October). The learning styles project for potential dropouts. *Educational Leadership, 48*(2), 23–24.

Perrone, V. (1991). *Expanding student assessment.* Alexandria, VA: Association for Supervision and Curriculum Development.

Pritchard, A., & Taylor, J. (1980). *Accelerated learning: The use of suggestion in the classroom.* Novato, CA: Academic Therapy.

Quality Education for Minorities Project. (1990, January). *Education that works: An action plan for the education of minorities.* Cambridge: Massachusetts Institute of Technology.

Quellmalz, E. S., & Hoskyn, J. (1988, April). Making a difference in Arkansas: The multicultural reading and thinking project. *Educational Leadership, 46*(7), 52–55.

Questioning promotes active reader/text interaction. (1987, Spring). *IRT Communication Quarterly.*

Rasbow, J., & Hernandez, A. C. R. (1988, June). The price of the "GPA perspective": An empirical study of "making the grade." *Youth and Society, 19*(4), 363–377.

Resnick, L. B. (1987). Learning in school and out. *Educational Researcher, 16*(9), 13–20.

Richardson, R. B. (1988, March). *Active affective learning for accelerated schools.* Stanford, CA: Center for Educational Research at Stanford University.

Roberts, J., & Zody, M. (1989, March). Using the research for effective supervision: Measuring a teacher's questioning techniques. *NASSP Bulletin, 73*(515), 8–14.

Rose, C. (1985). *Empowering the spectrum of your mind.* Flushing, NY: Spectrum Educational Services, Inc.

Rosenshine, B., & Meister, C. (1992, April). The use of scaffolds for teaching higher-level cognitive strategies. *Educational Leadership, 49*(7), 26–33.

Roser, N. L. (1987). Research currents: Returning literature and literacy. *Language Arts, 64*, 90–97.

Rowan, B., Guthrie, L. F., Lee, G. V., & Guthrie, G. P. (1986). *The design and implementation of Chapter 1 instructional services: A study of 24 schools.* San Francisco: Far West Laboratory for Educational Research and Development.

Russell, A. (1990, Summer/Fall). In *Carnegie Quarterly 25*, 3–4. New York: Carnegie Corporation of New York.

Russell, P. (1975). *The brain book.* New York: E. P. Dutton.

Schnitzer, S. (1993, April). Designing an authentic assessment. *Educational Leadership, 50*(7), 32–35.

Schuster, D. H. (1985). *Suggestive accelerated learning and teaching: A manual of classroom procedures based on the Lozanov method.* Ames, IA: Society for Accelerated Learning and Teaching.

Secada, W. G., & Carey, D. A. (1990, October). *Teaching mathematics with understanding to limited English proficient students* (Urban Diversity Series, No. 101). New York: ERIC Clearinghouse on Urban Education/Institute on Urban and Minority Education.

Shulman, J. H., & Mesa-Bains, A. (Eds.). (1990, November). *Teaching diverse students: Cases and commentaries.* San Francisco: Far West Laboratory for Educational Research and Development.

Sinatra, R. (1983, May). Brain research sheds light on language learning. *Educational Leadership, 40*(8), 9–12.

Slavin, R. E. (1986). *Using student team learning* (3rd ed.). Baltimore: Johns Hopkins University Press.

Slavin, R. E. (1987, October). Making Chapter 1 make a difference. *Phi Delta Kappan, 69*(2), 110–119.

Somers, A. B., & Worthington, J. E. (1979). *Response guides for teaching children's books.* Urbana, IL: National Council of Teachers of English.

Steinberg, A. (1988, November/December). School-parent relationships that work: An interview with Dr. James Comer. *Harvard Education Letter, 4*(6), 4–6.

Stevens, R. J., Madden, N. A., Slavin, R. E., & Farnish, A. M. (1987). Cooperative integrated reading and composition: Two field experiments. *Reading Research Quarterly, 22*(4), 433–454.

Stover, D. (1993, May 25). School boards caught up in debate over tracking. *School Board News, 13*(9), 1, 8.

Strickland, D. S. (1985). *Integrating the basic skills through the content areas.* Workshop materials. New York: Teachers College, Columbia University.

Strickland, D. S., & Morrow, L. M. (1989). *Emerging literacy: Young children learn to read and write.* Newark, DE: International Reading Association.

Sweet, D., & Zimmerman, J. (Eds.). (1992, November). *Performance assessment.* Education Research Consumer Guide. Washington, DC: Office of Educational Research and Improvement. (ERIC Document Reproduction Service No. ED353329)

Taylor, D., & Dorsey-Gaines, C. (1988). *Growing up literate: Learning from inner-city families.* Portsmouth, NH: Heinemann.

Teachers' questions: Why do you ask? (May, 1987). *Harvard Education Letter, 3*(3), 1.

Tiedt, P. L., & Tiedt, I. M. (1986). *Multicultural teaching.* Newton, MA: Allyn and Bacon.

U.S. Department of Education, Office of Educational Research and Improvement. (1990, August). Parental involvement in education. *Issues in Education* (0-861-983). Washington, DC: Author.

U.S. Department of Labor. (1992). *Learning a living: A blueprint for high performance.* (A SCANS Report for America 2000). Washington, DC: Secretary's Commission on Achieving Necessary Skills, U.S. Department of Labor.

Vygotsky, L. S. (1962). *Thought and language* (E. Hanfmann, Ed., & G. Vakar, Trans.). Cambridge, MA: MIT Press.

Vygotsky, L. S. (1978). *Mind in society: The development of higher psychological processes.* Cambridge, MA: Harvard University Press.

Walmsley, S. A., & Walp, T. P. (1990). Integrating literature and composing into the language arts curriculum: Philosophy and practice. *Elementary School Journal, 90*(3), 251–274.

Webb, M. (1988, Spring). Peer helping relationships in urban schools. *Equity and Choice, 4*(3), 35–48.

Wiggins, G. (1992, May). Creating tests worth taking. *Educational Leadership, 49*(8), 26–33.

Williams, D. I., Jr., & Chavkin, N. F. (1989, October). Essential elements of strong parent involvement programs. *Educational Leadership, 47*(2), 19–20.

Willis, S. (1991, June). Forging new paths to success: Promising programs for teaching disadvantaged students. *ASCD Curriculum Update.*

Worthen, B. R. (1993, February). Critical issues that will determine the future of alternative assessment. *Phi Delta Kappan, 74*(6), 444–454.

CHAPTER 3

Teaching and Inquiry

The Having of Wonderful Ideas

— Eleanor Duckworth

Kevin, Stephanie, and the Mathematician

With a friend, I reviewed some classic Piagetian interviews with a few children. One involved the ordering of lengths. I had cut 10 cellophane drinking straws into different lengths and asked the children to put them in order, from smallest to biggest. The first two 7-year-olds did it with no difficulty and little interest. Then came Kevin. Before I said a word about the straws, he picked them up and said to me, "I know what I'm going to do," and proceeded, on his own, to order them by length. He didn't mean, "I know what you're going to ask me to do." He meant, "I have a wonderful idea about what to do with these straws. You'll be surprised by my wonderful idea."

It wasn't easy for him. He needed a good deal of trial and error as he set about developing his system. But he was so pleased with himself when he accomplished his self-set task that when I decided to offer them to him to keep (10 whole drinking straws!), he glowed with joy, showed them to one or two select friends, and stored them away with other treasures in a shoe box.

The having of wonderful ideas is what I consider the essence of intellectual development. And I consider it the essence of pedagogy to give Kevin the occasion to have his wonderful ideas and to let him feel good about himself for having them. To develop this point of view and to indicate where Piaget fits in for me, I need to start with some autobiography, and I apologize for that, but it was a struggle of some years' duration for me to see how Piaget was relevant to schools at all.

I had never heard of Piaget when I first sat in a class of his. It was as a philosopher that Piaget won me, and I went on to spend two years in Geneva as a graduate student and research assistant. Then, some years later, I began to pay attention to schools, when, as a Ph. D. dropout, I accepted a job developing elementary science curriculum, and found myself in the midst of an exciting circle of educators.

The colleagues I admired most got along very well without any special knowledge of psychology. They trusted their own insights about when and how children were learning, and they were right to: Their insights were excellent. Moreover, they were especially distrustful of Piaget. He had not yet appeared on the cover of Saturday Review or the New York Times Magazine, and they had their own picture of him: a severe, humorless intellectual confronting a small child with questions that were surely incomprehensible, while the child tried to tell from the look in his eyes what the answer was supposed to be. No wonder the child couldn't think straight. (More than one of these colleagues first started to pay attention to Piaget when they saw a photo of him. He may be Swiss, but he doesn't look like Calvin! Maybe he can talk to children after all.)

I myself didn't know what to think. My colleagues did not seem to be any the worse for not taking Piaget seriously. Nor, I had to admit, did I seem to be any the better. Schools were such complicated places compared with psychology labs that I couldn't find a way to be of any special help. Not only did Piaget seem irrelevant, I was no longer sure that he was right. For a couple of years, I scarcely mentioned him and simply went about the business of trying to be helpful, with no single instance, as I recall, of drawing directly on any of his specific findings.

> The lowest point came when one of my colleagues gleefully showed me an essay written in a first grade by 6-year-old Stephanie. The children had been investigating capillary tubes, and were looking at the differences in the height of the water as a function of the diameter of the tube. Stephanie's essay read as follows: "I know why it looks like there's more in the skinny tube. Because it's higher. But the other is fatter, so there's the same."

My colleague triumphantly took this statement as proof that 6-year-olds can reason about the compensation of two dimensions. I didn't know what to say. Of course, it should have been simple. Some 6-year-olds can reason about compensation. The ages that Piaget mentions are only norms, not universals. Children develop at a variety of speeds, some more slowly and some more quickly. But I was so unsure of myself at that point that this incident shook me badly, and all of that only sounded like a lame excuse.

I do have something else to say about that incident later. For now, I shall simply try to describe my struggle.

Even if I did believe that Piaget was right, how could he be helpful? If the main thing that we take from Piaget is that before certain ages children are unable to understand certain things—conservation, transitivity, spatial coordinates-what do we do about it? Do we try to teach the children these things? Probably not, because on the one hand Piaget leads us to believe that we probably won't be very successful at it; and on the other hand, if there is one thing we have learned from Piaget it is that children can probably be left to their own devices in coming to understand these notions. We don't have to try to furnish them. It took a few months before that was clear to me, but I did conclude that this was not a very good way to make use of Piaget.

An alternative might be to keep in mind the limits on children's abilities to classify, conserve, order, and so forth, when deciding what to teach them at certain ages. However, I found this an inadequate criterion. There was so much else to keep in mind. The most obvious reason, of course, was that any class of children has a great diversity of levels. Tailoring to an average level of development is sure to miss a large proportion of the children. In addition, a Piaget psychologist has no monopoly here. When trying to approximate the abilities of a group of children of a given age, able teachers like my colleagues could make as good approximations as 1.

What I found most appealing was that the people with whom I was working judged the merits of any suggestion by how well it worked in classrooms. That is, instead of deciding on a priori grounds what children ought to know, or what they ought to be able to do at a certain age, they found activities, lessons, points of departure, that would engage children in real classrooms, with real teachers. In their view, it was easy to devise all-embracing schemes of how science (as it was in this instance) could be organized for children, but to make things work pedagogically in classrooms was the difficult part. They started with the difficult part. A theory of intellectual development might have been the basis of a theoretical framework of a curriculum. But in making things work in a classroom, it was but a small part compared with finding ways to interest children, to take into account different children's interests and abilities, to help teachers with no special training in the subject, and so forth. So, the burden of this curriculum effort was classroom trials. The criterion was whether they worked, and their working depended only in part on their being at the right intellectual level for the children. They might be perfectly all right, from the point of view of intellectual demands, and yet fall short in other ways. Most often, it was a complex combination.

As I was struggling to find some framework within which my knowledge of Piaget would be useful, I found, more or less incidentally, that I was starting to be useful myself. As an observer for some of the pilot teaching of this program, and later as a pilot teacher myself, I found that I had a certain skill in being able to watch and listen to children and that I did have some good insights about how they were really seeing the problem. This led to a certain ability to raise questions that made sense to the children or to think of new orientations for the whole activity that might correspond better to their way of seeing things. I don't want to suggest that I was unique in this. Many of the teachers with whom I was working had similar insights, as did many of the mathematicians and scientists among my colleagues, who, from their points of view, could tell when children were seeing things differently from the ways they did. But the question of whether I was unique is not really pertinent. For me, through my experience with Piaget of working closely with one child at a time and trying to figure out what was really in that child's mind, I had gained a wonderful background for being sensitive to children in classrooms. I think that a certain amount of this kind of background would be similarly useful for every teacher.

This sensitivity to children in classrooms continued to be central in my own development. As a framework for thinking about learning, my understanding of Piaget has been invaluable. This understanding, however, has also been deepened by working with teachers and children. I may be able to shed some light on that mutual relationship by referring again to 6-year-old Stephanie's essay on compensation. Few of us, looking at water rise in capillary tubes of different diameters, would bother to wonder whether the quantities are the same. Nobody asked Stephanie to make that comparison and, in fact, it is impossible to tell just by looking. On her own, she felt it was a significant thing to comment upon. I take that as an indication that for her it was a wonderful idea. Not long before, she believed that there was more water in the tube in which the water was higher. She had recently won her own intellectual struggle on that issue, and she wanted to point out her finding to the world for the benefit of those who might be taken in by preliminary appearances.

This incident, once I had figured it out, helped me think about a point that bothered me in one of Piaget's anecdotes. You may recall Piaget's account of a mathematician friend who inspired his studies of the conservation of number. This man told Piaget about an incident from his childhood, where he counted a number of pebbles he had set out in a line. Having counted them from left to right and found there were 10, he decided to see how many there would be if he counted them from right to left. Intrigued to find that there were still 10, he put them in a different arrangement and counted them again. He kept rearranging and counting them until he decided that, no matter what the arrangement, he was always going to find that there were 10. Number is independent of the order of counting.

My problem was this: In Piaget's accounts, if 10 eggs are spread out so they take more space than 10 eggcups, a classic non-conserver will maintain that there are more eggs than eggcups, even if he counts and finds that he comes to 10 in both cases. Counting is not sufficient to convince him that there are enough eggcups for all the eggs. How is it, then, that for the mathematician, counting was sufficient? If he was a non-conserver at the time, counting should not have made any differ- ence. If he was a conserver, he should have known from the start that it would always come out the same.

I think it must be that the whole enterprise was his own wonderful idea. He raised the question for himself and figured out for himself how to try to answer it. In essence, I am saying that he was in a transitional moment, and that Stephanie and Kevin were, too. He was at a point where a certain experience fit into certain thoughts and took him a step forward. A powerful pedagogical point can be made from this. These three instances dramatize it because they deal with children moving ahead with Piaget notions, which are usually difficult to advance on the basis of anyone experience. The point has two aspects: First, the right question at the right time can move children to peaks in their thinking that result in significant steps forward and real intellectual excitement; and, second, although it is almost impossible for an adult to know exactly the right time to ask a specific question of a specific child-especially for a teacher who is concerned with 30 or more children-children can raise the right question for themselves if the setting is right. Once the right question is raised, they are moved to tax themselves to the fullest to find an answer. The answers did not come easily in any of these three cases, but the children were prepared to work them through. Having confidence in one's ideas does not mean "I know my ideas are right"; it means "I am willing to try out my ideas."

As I put together experiences like these and continued to think about them, I started developing some ideas about what education could be and about the relationships between education and intellectual development.

Hank

It is a truism that all children in their first and second years make incredible intellectual advances. Piaget has documented these advances from his own point of view, but every parent and every psychologist knows this to be the case. One recurring question is, why does the intellectual development of vast numbers of children then slow down? What happens to children's curiosity and resourcefulness later in their childhood? Why do so few continue to have their own wonderful ideas? I think part of the answer is that intellectual breakthroughs come to be less and less valued. Either they are dismissed as being trivial-as Kevin's or Stephanie's or the mathematician's might have been by some adults-or else they are discouraged as being unacceptable—like discovering how it feels to wear shoes on the wrong feet, or asking questions that are socially embarrassing, or destroying something to see what it's like inside. The effect is to discourage children from exploring their own ideas and to make them feel that they have no important ideas of their own, only silly or evil ones.

But I think there is at least one other part of the answer, too. Wonderful ideas do not spring out of nothing. They build on a foundation of other ideas. The following incident may help to clarify what I mean.

Hank was an energetic and not very scholarly fifth grader. His class had been learning about electric circuits with flashlight batteries, bulbs, and various wires. After the children had developed considerable familiarity with these materials, the teacher made a number of mystery boxesi[i]. Two wires protruded from each box, but inside, unseen, each box had a different way of making contact between the wires. In one box the wires were attached to a battery; in another they were attached to a bulb; in a third, to a certain length of resistance wire; in a fourth box they were not attached at all; and so forth. By trying to complete the circuit on the outside of a box, the children were able to figure out what made the connection inside the box. Like many other children, Hank attached a battery and a bulb to the wire outside the box. Because the bulb lit, he knew at least that the wires inside the box were connected in some way. But, because it was somewhat dimmer than usual, he also knew that the wires inside were not connected directly to each other and that they were not connected by a piece of ordinary copper wire. Along with many of the children, he knew that the degree of dimness of the bulb meant that the wires inside were connected either by another bulb of the same kind or by a certain length of resistance wire.

The teacher expected them to go only this far. However, in order to push the children to think a little further, she asked them if they could tell whether it was a bulb or a piece of wire inside the box. She herself thought there was no way to tell. After some thought, Hank had an idea. He undid the battery and bulb that he had already attached on the outside of the box. In their place, using additional copper wire, he attached six batteries in a series. He had already experimented enough to know that six batteries would burn out a bulb, if it was a bulb inside the box. He also knew that once a bulb is burned out, it no longer completes the circuit. He then attached the original battery and bulb again. This time he found that the bulb on the outside of the box did not light. So he reasoned, rightly, that there had been a bulb inside the box and that now it was burned out. If there had been a wire inside, it would not have burned through and the bulb on the outside would still light.

Note that to carry out that idea, Hank had to take the risk of destroying a light bulb. In fact, he did destroy one. In accepting this idea, the teacher had to accept not only the fact that Hank had a good idea that even she did not have, but also that it was worthwhile to destroy a small piece of property for the sake of following through an idea. These features almost turn the incident into a parable. Without these kinds of acceptance, Hank would not have been able to pursue his idea. Think of how many times this acceptance is not forthcoming in the life of anyone child.

> But the main point to be made here is that in order to have his idea, Hank had to know a lot about batteries, bulbs, and wires. His previous work and familiarity with those materials were a necessary aspect of this occasion for him to have a wonderful idea. David Hawkins has said of curriculum development, "You don't want to cover a subject; you want to uncover it." That, it seems to me, is what schools should be about. They can help to uncover parts of the world that children would not otherwise know how to tackle. Wonderful ideas are built on other wonderful ideas. In Piaget's terms, you must reach out to the world with your own intellectual tools and grasp it, assimilate it, yourself. All kinds of things are hidden from us-even though they surround us-unless we know how to reach out for them. Schools and teachers can provide materials and questions in ways that suggest things to be done with them; and children, in the doing, cannot help being inventive.

There are two aspects to providing occasions for wonderful ideas. One is being willing to accept children's ideas. The other is providing a setting that suggests wonderful ideas to children-different ideas to different children-as they are caught up in intellectual problems that are real to them.

What Schools Can Do

I had the chance to evaluate an elementary science program in Africa. For the purposes of this discussion it might have been set anywhere.

Although the program was by no means a deliberate attempt to apply Piaget's ideas, it was, to my mind, such an application in the best sense. The assumptions that lay behind the work are consistent with the ideas I have just been developing. The program set out to reveal the world to children. The developers sought to familiarize the children with the material world-that is, with biological phenomena, physical phenomena, and technological phenomena: flashlights, mosquito larvae, clouds, clay. When I speak of familiarity, I mean feeling at home with these things: knowing what to expect of them, what can be done with them, how they react to various circumstances, what you like about them and what you don't like about them, and how they can be changed, avoided, preserved, destroyed, or enhanced.

Certainly the material world is too diverse and too complex for a child to become familiar with all of it in the course of an elementary school career. The best one can do is to make such knowledge, such familiarity, seem interesting and accessible to the child. That is, one can familiarize children with a few phenomena in such a way as to catch their interest, to let them raise and answer their own questions, to let them realize that their ideas are significant-so that they have the interest, the ability, and the self-confidence to go on by themselves.

Such a program is a curriculum, so to speak, but a curriculum with a difference. The difference can best be characterized by saying that the unexpected is valued. Instead of expecting teachers and children to do only what was specified in the booklets, it was the intention of the program that children and teachers would have so many unanticipated ideas of their own about the materials that they would never even use the booklets. The purpose of developing booklets at all is that teachers and children start producing and following through their own ideas, if possible getting beyond needing anybody else's suggestions. Although it is unlikely to be completely realized, this represents the ideal orientation of the program. It is a rather radical view of curriculum development.

It is just as necessary for teachers as for children to feel confidence in their own ideas. It is important for them as people and it is important in order for them to feel free to acknowledge the children's ideas. If teachers feel that their class must do things just as the book says and that their excellence as teachers depends on this, they cannot possibly accept the children's divergence and creations. A teachers' guide must give enough indications, enough suggestions, so that the teacher has ideas to start with and to pursue. But it must also enable the teacher to feel free to move in her own directions when she has other ideas.

> For instance, the teachers' guides for this program include many examples of things children are likely to do. The risk is that teachers may see these as things that the children in their classes must do. Whether or not the children do them becomes a measure of successful or unsuccessful teaching. Sometimes the writers of the teachers' guides intentionally omit mention of some of the most exciting activities because they almost always happen even if they are not arranged. If the teacher expects them, she will often force them, and they no longer happen with the excitement of wonderful ideas. Often the writers include extreme examples, so extreme that a teacher cannot really expect them to happen in her class. These examples are meant to convey the message that "even if the children do that it's OK! Look, in one class they even did this!" This approach often is more fruitful than the use of more common examples whose message is likely to be "this is what ought to happen in your class."

The teachers' guides dealt with materials that were readily available in or out of schools, and suggested activities that could be done with these materials so that children became interested in them and started asking their own questions. For instance, there are common substances all around us that provide the essential basis of chemistry knowledge. They interact in all sorts of interesting ways, accessible to all of us if only we know how to reach out for them. This is a good instance of a part of the world that is waiting to be uncovered. How can it be uncovered for children in a way that gives them an interest in continuing to find out about it, a way that gives them the occasion to take their own initiatives, and to feel at home in this part of the world?

The teachers' guide suggests starting with salt, ashes, sugar, cassava starch, alum, lemon juice, and water. When mixed together, some of these cause bubbles. Which combinations cause bubbles? How long does the bubbling last? How can it be kept going longer? What other substances cause bubbles? If a combination bubbles, what can be added that will stop the bubbling? Other things change color when they are mixed together, and similar questions can be asked of them.

Written teachers' guides, however, cannot bear the burden alone, if this kind of teaching is totally new. To get such a program started, a great deal of teacher education is necessary as well. Although I shall not try to go into this in any detail, there seem to be three major aspects to such teacher education. First, teachers themselves must learn in the way that the children in their classes will be learning. Almost anyone of the units developed in this program is as effective with adults as it is with children.

The teachers themselves learn through some of the units and feel what it is like to learn in this way. Second, the teachers work with one or two children at a time so that they can observe them closely enough to realize what is involved for the children. Last, it seems valuable for teachers to see films or live demonstrations of a class of children learning in this way, so that they can begin to think that it really is possible to run their class in such a way. A fourth aspect is of a slightly different nature. Except for the rare teacher who will take this leap all on his or her own on the basis of a single course and some written teachers' guides, most teachers need the support of at least some nearby co-workers who are trying to do the same thing, and with whom they can share notes. An even better help is the presence of an experienced teacher to whom they can go with questions and problems.

An Evaluation Study

What the children are doing in one of these classrooms may be lively and interesting, but it would be helpful to know what difference the approach makes to them in the long run, to compare in some way the children who were in this program with children who were not, and to see whether in some standard situation they now act differently.

One of my thoughts about ways in which these children might be different was based on the fact that many teachers in this program had told us that their children improved at having ideas of what to do, at raising questions, and at answering their own questions; that is, at having their own ideas and being confident about their own ideas. I wanted to see whether this indeed was the case.

My second thought was more ambitious. If these children had really become more intellectually alert, so that their minds were alive and working not only in school but outside school, they might, over a long enough period of time, make significant headway in their intellectual development, as compared with other children.

In sum, these two aspects would put to the test my notions that the development of intelligence is a matter of having wonderful ideas and feeling confident enough to try them out, and that schools can have an effect on the continuing development of wonderful ideas. The study has been written up elsewhere (Duckworth, 1978), but let me give a summary of it here.

The evaluation had two phases. The procedure developed for the first phase was inspired in part by a physics examination given to students at Cornell University by Philip Morrison. His examination was held in the laboratory. The students were given sets of materials, the same set of materials for each student, but they were given no specific problem. Their problem was to find a problem and then to work on it. For Morrison, the crucial thing is finding the question, just as it was for Kevin, Stephanie, and the mathematician. In this examination, clear differences in the degree of both knowledge and inventiveness were revealed in the problems the students set themselves, and the work they did was only as good as their problems.

In our evaluation study, we had to modify this procedure somewhat to make it appropriate for children as young as 6 years of age. Our general question was what children with a year or more of experience in this program would do with materials when they were left to their own resources without any teacher at all. We wanted to know whether children who had been in the program had more ideas about what to do with materials than did other children.

The materials we chose were not, of course, the same as those that children in the program had studied. We chose materials of two sorts: on the one hand, imported materials that none of the children had ever seen before-plastic color filters, geometric pattern blocks, folding mirrors, commercial building sets, for example. On the other hand, we chose some materials that were familiar to all the children whether or not they had been in the program-cigarette foil, match boxes, rubber rings from inner tubes, scraps of wire, wood, and metal, empty spools, and so forth.

From each class we chose a dozen children at random and told them-in their own vernacular-to go into the room and do whatever they wanted with the materials they would find there. We told them that they could move around the room, talk to each other, and work with their friends.

We studied 15 experimental classes and 13 control classes from first to seventh grades. Briefly, and inadequately, summarizing the results of this phase, we found that the children who had been in the program did indeed have more ideas about how to work with the materials. Typically, the children in these classes would take a first look at what was offered, try a few things, and then settle down to work with involvement and concentration. Children sometimes worked alone and sometimes collaborated. They carried materials from table to table, using them in ways we had not anticipated. As time went on, there was no sign that they were running out of ideas. On the contrary, their work became so interesting that we were always disappointed to have to stop them after 40 minutes.

By contrast, the other children had a much smaller range of ideas about what to do with the materials. On the one hand, they tended to copy a few leaders. On the other hand, they tended to leave one piece of work fairly soon and to switch to something else. There were few instances of elaborate work in which a child spent a lot of time and effort to overcome difficulties in what he was trying to do. In some of these classes, after 30 to 35 minutes, all the children had run out of ideas and were doing nothing.

We had assessed two things in our evaluation: diversity of ideas in a class, and depth to which the ideas were pursued. The experimental classes were overwhelmingly ahead in each of the two dimensions. This first phase of assessment was actually a substitute for what we really wanted to do. Ideally, we wanted to know whether the experience of these children in the program had the effect of making them more alert, more aware of the possibilities in ordinary things around them, and more questioning and exploring during the time they spent outside school. This would be an intriguing question to try to answer, but we did not have the time to tackle it. The procedure that we did develop, as just described, may have been too close to the school setting to give rise to any valid conclusions about what children are like in the world outside school. However, if you can accept with me, tentatively, the thought that our results might indicate a greater intellectual alertness in general a tendency to have wonderful ideas—then the next phase takes on a considerable interest.

I am hypothesizing that this alertness is the motor of intellectual development (in Piaget's terms, operational thinking). No doubt there is a continuum: No normal child is completely un-alert. But some are far more alert than others. I am also hypothesizing that a child's alertness is not fixed. I believe that, by opening up to children the many fascinating aspects of the ordinary world and by enabling them to feel that their ideas are worthwhile having and following through, their tendency to have wonderful ideas can be affected in significant ways. This program seemed to be doing both those things, and by the time I evaluated it, some children had been in the classes for up to three years. It seemed to me that we might-just might-find that the two or three years of increased alertness that this program fostered had made some difference to the intellectual development of the children.

In the second phase, then, we examined the same children individually, using Piaget problems administered by a trained assistant who spoke the language of the children. A statistical analysis revealed that on five of the six problems we studied, the children in the experimental classes did significantly better than the children in the comparison classes.

I find this a pretty stunning result on the whole. But I want to insist on one particular view of the result. I do not, in any way, want to suggest that the important thing for education to be about is acceleration of Piaget stages (see chapter 3). I want to make a theoretical point. My thesis at the outset of this chapter was that the development of intelligence is a matter of having wonderful ideas. In other words, it is a creative affair. When children are afforded the occasions to be intellectually creative-by being offered matter to be concerned about intellectually and by having their ideas accepted-then not only do they learn about the world, but as a happy side effect their general intellectual ability is stimulated as well.

Another way of putting this is that I think the distinction made between "divergent" and "convergent" thinking is oversimplified. Even to think a problem through to its most appropriate end point (convergent) one must create various hypotheses to check out (divergent). When Hank came up with a closed end point to the problem, it was the result of a brilliantly imaginative-that is, divergent-thought. We must conceive of the possibilities before we can check them out.

Conclusion

I am suggesting that children do not have a built-in pace of intellectual development. I would temper that suggestion by saying that the built-in aspect of the pace is minimal. The having of wonderful ideas, which I consider the essence of intellectual development, would depend instead to an overwhelming extent on the occasions for having them. I have dwelt at some length on how important it is to allow children to accept their own ideas and to work them through. I would like now to consider the intellectual basis for new ideas.

I react strongly against the thought that we need to provide children with only a set of intellectual processes- a dry, content-less set of tools that they can go about applying. I believe that the tools cannot help developing once children have something real to think about; and if they don't have anything real to think about, they won't be applying tools anyway. That is, there really is no such thing as a contentless intellectual tool. If a person has some knowledge at his disposal, he can try to make sense of new experiences and new information related to it. He fits it into what he has. By knowledge I do not mean verbal summaries of somebody else's knowledge. I am not urging textbooks and lectures. I mean a person's own repertoire of thoughts, actions, connections, predictions, and feelings. Some of these may have as their source something read or heard. But the individual has done the work of putting them together for himself or herself, and they give rise to new ways to put them together.

The greater the child's repertoire of actions and thoughts-in Piaget's terms, schemes-the more material he or she has for trying to put things together in his or her own mind. The essence of the African program I described is that children increase the repertoires of actions that they carry out on ordinary things, which in turn gives rise to the need to make more intellectual connections.

Let us consider a child who has had the world of common substances opened to him, as described earlier. He now has a vastly increased repertoire of actions to carry out and of connections to make. He has seen that when you boil away sea water, a salt residue remains. Would some residue remain if he boiled away beer? If he dissolved this residue in water again, would he have beer again-flat beer? He has seen that he can get a colored liquid from flower petals if he crushes them. Could he get that liquid to go into water and make colored water? Could he make colored coconut oil this way? All these questions and the actions they lead to are based on the familiarity the child has gained with the possibilities contained in this world of common substances.

Intelligence cannot develop without matter to think about. Making new connections depends on knowing enough about something in the first place to provide a basis for thinking of other things to do—of other questions to ask-that demand more complex connections in order to make sense. The more ideas about something people already have at their disposal, the more new ideas occur and the more they can coordinate to build up still more complicated schemes.

Piaget has speculated that some people reach the level of formal operations in some specific area that they know well-auto mechanics, for example—without reaching formal levels in other areas. That fits into what I am trying to say. In an area you know well, you can think of many possibilities, and working them through demands formal operations. If there is no area in which you are familiar enough with the complexities to work through them, then you are not likely to develop formal operations. Knowing enough about things is one prerequisite for wonderful ideas.

I shall make one closing remark. The wonderful ideas that I refer to need not necessarily look wonderful to the outside world. I see no difference in kind between wonderful ideas that many other people have already had, and wonderful ideas that nobody has yet happened upon. That is, the nature of creative intellectual acts remains the same, whether it is an infant who for the first time makes the connection between seeing things and reaching for them, or Kevin who had the idea of putting straws in order of their length, or a musician who invents a harmonic sequence, or an astronomer who develops a new theory of the creation of the universe. In each case, new connections are being made among things already mastered. The more we help children to have their wonderful ideas and to feel good about themselves for having them, the more likely it is that they will some day happen upon wonderful ideas that no one else has happened upon before.

CHAPTER 4

Classroom Communities

The Classroom as Community

— *by Alfie Kohn*

The evident weakness in American schools has much to do with the weakening of their community context. . . . Education can never merely be for the sake of individual self—enhancement. It pulls us into the common world or it fails altogether.

—Robert Bellah et al., *The Good Society*

WHY COMMUNITY?

For all the talk one hears in certain educational circles about the importance of creating "communities," few people indicate precisely what that term means. Perhaps they find it difficult to nail down the concept; like Justice Powell struggling to define *pornography*, they may resort to saying that they know it when they see it.

But I think we can do better. Indeed, we have an obligation to specify what this idea means if we are proposing that it should guide our work. In saying that a classroom or school is a "community," then, I mean that it is a place in which students feel cared about and are encouraged to care about each other. They experience a sense of being valued and respected; the children matter to one another and to the teacher. They have come to think in the plural: they feel connected to each other; they are part of an "us." And, as a result of all this, they feel safe in their classes, not only physically but emotionally.

To say that a classroom is a community, in other words, is to say that it is a place where

care and trust are emphasized above restrictions and threats, where unity and pride (of accomplishment and in purpose) replace winning and losing, and where each person is asked, helped, and inspired to live up to such ideals and values as kindness, fairness, and responsibility. [Such] a classroom community seeks to meet each student's need to feel competent connected to others, and autonomous. . . . Students are not only exposed to basic human values, they also have many opportunities to think about, discuss, and act on those values, while gaining experiences that promote empathy and understanding of others (Child Development Project 1991).

In recent years, more educators have begun to pay attention to these dimensions of schooling. Thomas J. Sergiovanni (1994, p. xi) has gone so far as to declare that "community building must become the heart of any school improvement effort." After all, how many children can grow— intellectually, emotionally, or any other way— without a supportive environment? Virtually any meaningful long-term goal we might have for students requires us to attend to the climate of the school and, specifically, the extent to which children feel related, as opposed to isolated.

Some of the most important work on formulating, researching, and implementing the idea of caring communities has been done in connection with an elementary school program called the Child Development Project (Battistich et al. 1989; Watson et al. 1989; Kohn 1990c; Solomon et al. 1992). The staff of the CDP, based in Oakland, California, has worked in eight school districts both within and beyond California to promote students' social, moral, and intellectual development.[1] The definition of community cited just above comes from the CDP, and in fact the whole of this book reflects the impact of this group's work: it has profoundly shaped my thinking about what ought to happen in schools, about how a caring community can be constructed as well as why it is so important to do so.

The rationale for promoting community is powerfully evident from a recent CDP study of two dozen elementary schools around the country. Students in the upper grades were asked about the extent to which they experienced their classroom and school as supportive communities. It turned out that the stronger that community feeling was, the more the students reported liking school and the more they saw learning as something valuable in its own right. These students also tended to be more concerned about others and more skilled at resolving conflict than those who didn't feel part of a community. What's more, these positive effects were particularly pronounced in schools that had more low-income students (Battistich et al. 1995).

The CDP study suggests that taking the time to help children care about each other might just affect their enthusiasm about academic learning. That is an insight with the potential to reshape the whole enterprise of school reform, but it really shouldn't be surprising. Students need to feel safe in order to take intellectual risks; they must be comfortable before they can venture into the realm of discomfort. Few things stifle creativity like the fear of being judged or humiliated. Thus, a supportive environment will allow people of any age to play with possibilities and challenge themselves to stretch their thinking. The moral is: if you want academic excellence, you have to attend to how children feel about school and about each other.

Note that the CDP study also supports the idea that students in communities are better at conflict resolution and more likely to care about others. This finding is consistent with the work of Piaget (1965) and other researchers who have argued that cooperative relationships among children are the key to moral development. Each member of a community has the opportunity to see things as they appear to others, and in so doing to think in a way that is deeper and less self-centered.

Another way of emphasizing the importance of community is to point out how difficult it is to do other things of value without it.

Three examples should illustrate the point.

- "When a spirit of cooperative community is missing, 'democratic' [class] meetings can become merely a forum for pressing and defending one's narrow self–interest" (Lickona and Paradise 1980, p. 334). Of course, these meetings can themselves help to build and support that cooperative spirit, but it is important that they are construed from the beginning as activities by and for *us*. A meeting should be experienced as one important way that our community shares and decides, plans and reflects. Otherwise, it may come to resemble something closer to a courtroom, where individuals press their case against one another: a meeting of the "mines."

- Multi-age classrooms and cross-age activities are enormously useful; they have the potential to promote generosity as well as better thinking skills for both the older and younger children involved (Foot et al. 1990; Pavan 1992; Child Development Project 1996b). How, then, do we explain the complaints that in some of these classrooms the younger children are teased or excluded? The likely culprit is a failure to create a community, to promote a sense of connection and caring. Unfortunately, some teachers or parents may be inclined to reject the whole idea of multi-age education rather than embracing the idea of community to make it work.

- I visited a well-known free school in Massachusetts not long ago, a place where students not only direct their own learning but decide when and whether to have a lesson. Yet discipline in this stunningly unconventional school is suspiciously familiar: it consists of an intricate welter of bylaws, along with a Justice Committee to enforce them by meting out punishments to those found guilty of wrongdoing. To be sure, the process here is distinctive by virtue of the fact that power rests in the hands of students. But one is led to wonder why the school is still stuck on the traditional arrangement of threats and punishments to deal with conflicts.

After some reflection, I concluded that a move from "doing to" to "working with" is impossible unless there has been an effort to create and sustain relationships among the people involved. The alternative to discipline is to treat an inappropriate act as a problem to be solved together—but that is predicated on the experience of *being* together. With nothing more than a loosely confederated bunch of free individuals, one is left with the same old rules-and-penalties model. The pursuit of laissez-faire liberty condemns us to a system of control, even though different people may be doing the controlling.

Autonomy is not enough; we need community, too.

OBJECTIONS TO COMMUNITY

The idea of community at first seems so bland and unobjectionable that support for it might almost be dismissed as hollow rhetoric. On closer inspection, though, it represents a radical and disconcerting challenge to much of what we take for granted. This is true because it calls into question several overlapping aspects of the status quo.

When we talk about "discipline," for example, we are talking about how the adult intervenes with this student or that one. Moreover, the intervention—like the usual view of teaching itself—is often conceived as instilling something in, or transmitting something to, each student. Even people committed to cooperative learning often see their mission as changing each participant into someone who can listen, make eye contact, encourage others, and so forth.

The community approach goes beyond teacher-student interaction and asks us to consider the broader question of how everyone gets along together. It also suggests that the way students turn out is a function not only of what each has been taught, but of how their environment has been set up. If we want to help children grow into compassionate people, we have to help them change the way the classroom works and feels, not just the way each separate member of that class acts. We have to transform not just individuals but educational *structures*.

The structural approach has another interesting implication: caring is more than just a characteristic of teachers. Obviously it's very important that the adults in a school be generous, warm people. But it's just as vital to attend to how the classroom or school is arranged. When administrators proudly tell me how caring their teachers are, I am apt to reply, "That's great. But do you have awards assemblies?" If things have been set up so that one student can succeed only if another fails, if the school sets children against each other in a race for artificially scarce recognition, then nice teachers can accomplish only so much. Similarly, the personal qualities of the staff may not be able to mitigate the harm of practices like posting lists of consequences on the wall or singling children out for public praise. While it's important that the teacher is sympathetic, this does not a community make.

The questions we ought to be asking, in other words, go well beyond "Does this teacher want the best for her students?" We need to ask as well: How does the classroom system work (Alschuler 1980; Bowers and Flinders 1990)? Are students helped to develop a sense of responsibility for each other? By what means? What happens if a child is reduced to tears by cruel taunts, or by deliberate exclusion? What expectations, norms, and structures have been established to deal with such an incident—and to make it less likely to happen in the first place?

Here's a paradoxical exercise worth trying out at a faculty meeting: Start by talking about the meaning of community in a school context. Invite participants to come up with some concrete markers for the concept, some indications of what an observer would see and hear and feel in a place that truly deserved to be called a community. Then ask everyone to think of the most effective ways by which a community can be *destroyed*. If, for some perverse reason, we were determined to eliminate that sense of community, what practices would be most likely to have that effect?

Don't be surprised if participants nominate competition as the number one community destroyer—not only awards assemblies but spelling bees, charts that rank students against each other, grading on a curve, and other things that teach each person to regard everyone else as obstacles to his or her own success (Kohn 1992).

Certain broader educational practices are likely to be mentioned, too. It would be hard to think of a more effective way to snuff out a sense of community than grouping students by putative ability. The most extreme versions of this practice—segregation of students with special needs or of those lucky enough to be deemed "gifted" (Sapon-Shevin 1994)— are likely to have the most extreme effects.

Finally, traditional discipline, or some aspect thereof, may round out the list. That's another reason that this emphasis on community is more controversial than it first appears. (It also explains what a chapter on this topic is doing in a book with a critical perspective on discipline.) The creation of caring communities clashes with the theory and practice of classroom management. It's not just that students who truly feel part of a community are less likely to do the things that bring down the weight of discipline on their heads. It's that a serious commitment to building community offers an invitation to move beyond discipline.

PSEUDOCOMMUNITY

Talk about turning classrooms and schools into communities may make some people nervous for another, very basic reason: anything that smacks of a social orientation can raise suspicions in a culture like that of the United States. Some see any emphasis on community as a potential threat to the rights of the individual.

Is there reason to be concerned? It is certainly true that some sort of balance needs to be struck between the rights or needs of the group and those of each person in the group. But the United States in general, and U.S. schools in particular, are tilted so far toward an individualist ethic that we have a long way to go before we have to worry about excess in the opposite direction. (This may not be true in places like Japan.) Here, students are given solitary seatwork assignments followed by solitary homework assignments followed by solitary tests. At best, they are exhorted to take responsibility only for their own behavior.

But we can go further than that. The individual is not likely to be swallowed up in a true community because a community is quite different from a collective. This distinction, vividly drawn by the philosopher Martin Buber, is as relevant to education as to political theory. A community not only preserves and nourishes the individuals who compose it but also underscores the relationships among these individuals. These functions are missing in a collective, whose members must simply overcome their private preferences in order to serve the group. (Interestingly, the latter model calls to mind the emphasis on obedience and loyalty to the social order that defines the work of conservative proponents of character education.)

The distinction between a community and a collective may seem awfully abstract, but it springs to life in real classrooms. There are some places where children develop a genuine commitment to each other and to the "us" composed of these real people. There are other places where children are exhorted to silence their own needs in the name of an abstraction called "the group" or "others"[2]— or are roused to jingoistic fervor in the name of something called "school spirit." The point in a collective is conformity, which pretty well excludes the conflict that is essential from a constructivist perspective (see Chapter 5). "Real community is forged out of struggle," observes one educator. "Students won't always agree on issues, and the fights, arguments, tears, and anger are the crucible from which a real community grows" (Christensen 1994, p. 14).

It may help to think of conformity to a collective as a sort of "pseudocommunity," analogous to what I have called pseudochoice. This is what critics sometimes have in mind when they warn about the dangers of community, which means their criticism might be misplaced. A second version of pseudocommunity is peer pressure. It is discouraging to find thoughtful educators endorsing an arrangement whereby students are essentially bullied by their peers into doing the right thing. Because the pressure comes from other students rather than from an adult, some people confuse this behavior with the dynamics of community. Of course, it is nothing of the kind. The goal is compliance (rather than learning), the focus is on behavior (rather than the students' underlying motives and values), and the climate of the class is characterized by the very opposite of safety, warmth, and trust.

One more variant of pseudocommunity might be identified before we move on to some thoughts about how to establish the real thing. I remember participating in a teacher workshop one summer that featured a rather self-conscious bit of community-building. The participants were divided into colors, and I watched the members of the red group try to carry out their assignment, which was to invent a logo and a slogan. This activity was supposed to model the process of creating "commonality," and these teachers would presumably go back and do something similar with their students.

But why *should* any of these strangers have felt part of the group to which they were assigned? They didn't know each other yet, and there was nothing of substance—no honest commonality— around which to create community. The earnest attempt to get consensus about whether they would henceforth be known as the Red Hot Chili Peppers led me to wonder why anyone should care. Indeed, the participants were not particularly responsive during the exercise, leading the facilitator to assume they were just shy or tired and in need of some artificial inducement to participate more energetically. But the problem was not with the attitudes of the individuals; it was with the forced attempt to create a community out of thin air.

BUILDING A COMMUNITY: PREREQUISITES

A real or authentic community doesn't feel empty. It is constructed over time by people with a common purpose who come to know and trust each other. Of course, it is precisely the commitment to make a community that helps these things happen. But a bunch of strangers cannot be tossed into a room and expected to emerge in a matter of hours as anything more than a bunch of acquaintances.

If the strangers are students and the room is in a school, there are three essential prerequisites for helping them build a community. First, they need time. A schedule that limits them to 45 minutes a day together, like "pull-out" programs that regularly remove some of their members, makes it much harder to succeed. By contrast, the chance for a teacher to work with the same group of students for more than one year makes it easier to succeed (Burke 1996).

Second, they need to be relatively few in number. Lost in the debate about whether excessive class size interferes with academic achievement is its unequivocal effect on a sense of community. Things become even more problematic when the whole school is too large (see Meier 1995).

Finally, they need a teacher who is herself part of a community of adults in the school. Just as teachers who are controlled from above tend to control those below, so teachers who are not part of a collaborative network of educators find it difficult to help students work together. What's more, research has found that shallow, unimaginative instruction—as well as a cynical set of beliefs about children—tends to be associated with teachers who are left to their own devices and wind up valuing their privacy more than anything else. To put this positively, teachers who do exemplary work in helping students engage deeply with what they are learning are invariably part of collegial communities of educators (McLaughlin 1993).

Where those communities do exist, teachers always seem to be in and out of each other's rooms—not as part of a formal (and intimidating) observation process but in order to give and receive feedback voluntarily. Teachers feel safe enough to acknowledge they need help with a problem instead of pretending they have everything under control. They have frequent opportunities to discuss their work—general pedagogical issues or the status of a particular student—with their colleagues. A real effort is made to address threats to community such as cliques or rivalry between teachers. Besides improving the quality of life for the educators themselves, such a school provides the skills and support that will help them replicate this community in their own classrooms.

BUILDING A COMMUNITY: STRATEGIES

Someone more interested in constructing a community than destroying it might well begin by thinking about how to promote a feeling of *safety*. What can be done in a classroom or school to help every student feel at ease? What can be done to minimize the chance of being ridiculed—by children or adults?

As is so often the case, the best way to proceed is to ask the students these very questions. Early in the year, a teacher might say, "Look, it's really important to me that you feel free to say things, to come up with ideas that may sound weird, to make mistakes—and not to be afraid that other people are going to laugh at you. In fact, I want everyone in here to feel that way. What do you think we can do to make sure that happens?" (Notice that this is another example of meaningful student choice within a teacher-devised framework.)

The ideas that students come up with, perhaps after a few moments of quiet reflection or conversation with a partner, ought to be written down, discussed, and posted. They also ought to be amended later, as needed, when new situations present themselves. For example, imagine that the teacher asks a question of the whole class one morning, and someone waves his hand while exclaiming with boastful disdain, "That's easy!" It might occur to another student that this is a perfect example of how *not* to foster safety or trust. Without humiliating the first student, the teacher might ask everyone to think about how it feels to hear someone else say that a question you are struggling with is supposed to be easy to answer. (Of course, the teacher may need to consider that the underlying problem rests with the whole instructional model that calls for students to race to answer factual questions posed by the teacher.)

The pursuit of safety in particular, or community more generally, is a project best pursued on four levels at once: strengthening the adult's relationship with each student; building students' connections with each other, one dyad at a time; providing for numerous classwide and schoolwide activities in which students work together toward a common end; and weaving the goal of community through academic instruction. Let us take each in turn.

Relationship With the Adults

Children are more likely to be respectful when important adults in their lives respect *them*. They are more likely to care about others if they know *they* are cared about. If their emotional needs are met, they have the luxury of being able to meet other people's needs—rather than spending their lives preoccupied with themselves.

To be a *caring* person, though, an educator must first be a person. Many of us are inclined instead to hide behind the mannerisms of a constantly competent, smoothly controlling, crisply authoritative Teacher (or Principal). To do so is to play a role, and even if the script calls for nurturance, this is not the same as being fully human with children. A real person sometimes gets flustered or distracted or tired, says things without thinking and later regrets them, maintains interests outside of teaching and doesn't mind discussing them. Also, a real person avoids distancing maneuvers such as referring to him-or herself in the third person (as in: "Mr. Kohn has a special surprise for you today, boys and girls").

Here, again, what initially looks like a commonsense prescription reveals itself as challenging and even controversial. To be a person in front of kids is to be vulnerable, and vulnerability is not an easy posture for adults who themselves had to strike a self-protective pose when they were growing up. Moreover, to reach out to children and develop genuine, warm relationships with them may compromise one's ability to control them. Much of what is wrong with our schools can be traced back to the fact that when these two objectives clash, connection frequently gives way to control.

Beyond being a real person, what does it mean for an adult to be caring in a school context? It means remembering details about students' lives ("Hey, George! Did your mom end up taking you to the museum over the weekend?"). It means writing notes to students and calling them up and even visiting them at home. It means being available, as time permits, for private conversations about nothing in particular.

Caring teachers converse with students in a distinctive way: they think about how what they say sounds from the students' point of view. They respond authentically and respectfully rather than giving patronizing pats on the head (or otherwise slathering them with "positive reinforcement"). They explain what they are up to and give reasons for their requests. They ask students what *they* think, and then care about the answers.

Once again, behaviors are less important than the purposes to which they are put. Rule enforcers may indeed be observant—they may, in fact, "continually monitor the class" (Canter and Canter 1992, p. 147)— but not out of any real concern for who their students are and what they need. The vigilance is more about "withitness" (see p. 55) than connection. Similarly, in an article entitled "Prepare to Take Effective Control," teachers are advised "to learn as many names as possible. Your discipline will be far more effective when you can issue a quiet rebuke to a pupil by name" (Wilson 1995, p. A6). The question is not whether a teacher watches or knows his students, but why.

Educators who form truly caring relationships with students are not only meeting emotional needs; they are also setting a powerful example. Whenever an adult listens patiently, or shows concern for someone he doesn't know, or apologizes for something he regrets having said, he is modeling for students, teaching them how they might be with each other.

Connections Between Students

Many elementary school teachers like to have children create their personal "shields," decorated with words or icons that say something about who each child is. But why should students draw their own shields when they could pair up and draw their partners'? From this simple exercise, every student might learn about someone else, disclose something about herself, and figure out how to represent the information about the other child to his satisfaction. In fact, any number of familiar activities, which subtly perpetuate an ideology of independence, could be transformed into a lesson in *inter* dependence.

In some classrooms, students experience cooperation only when the teacher announces that it is time for cooperative learning. This is not enough, however: communities are built upon a foundation of cooperating throughout the day, with students continually being invited to work, play, and reflect with someone else. Of course, solitary activity has its place, too, but doing things together ought to be, as a computer programmer might put it, the "default setting" in class. Students should have the chance to interact with virtually every other student at some point. This can include getting-to-know-you activities (for example, interviewing someone and then introducing him or her to the class) as well as periodic opportunities to find a partner and check in about whatever is being discussed at the moment.

A community rests on the knowledge of, and connections among, the individuals who are part of it. This knowledge, in turn, is deepened by helping students imagine how things appear from other people's points of view. What psychologists call "perspective taking" plays a critical role in helping children become generous, caring people (Kohn 1990a), and activities designed to promote an understanding of how others think and feel (Feshbach et al. 1983) have the added advantage of creating the basis for community.

Classwide and Schoolwide Activities

While it is important to cultivate the teacher's relationship with each student, and each student's relationship with others, the recipe for community also calls for plenty of opportunity for the whole class to collaborate on common endeavors. Thus, a teacher might have all her students work together to produce a class mural, or collage, or quilt; to choose or even compose a class song; to decide on a name or image that captures the spirit of the class[3]; to write a book, stage a play, or publish a newspaper together; or to do some community service activity as a class (see Child Development Project 1996a, pp. 20–23).

The single most significant and multifaceted activity for the class as a whole is the class meeting, described at length in the previous chapter. Such a meeting at the beginning of the year can be particularly effective at helping students experience themselves as part of a community. Rather than asking students to simply create a list of rules, though—or worse, getting them to think up consequences for individuals who break the rules—the teacher might propose some broader questions for discussion: "What makes school awful sometimes? Try to remember an experience during a previous year when you hated school, when you felt bad about yourself, or about everyone else, and you couldn't wait for it to be over. What exactly was going on when you were feeling that way? How was the class set up?"

Not enough teachers encourage this sort of rumination. Particularly in elementary schools, one often finds an aggressively sunny outlook, such that space is made only for happy feelings. (In a 3rd grade classroom in Minnesota, I once saw a poster near the door that read: ONLY POSITIVE ATTITUDES ALLOWED BEYOND THIS POINT. The message here might be restated as "Have a nice day—or else.") Alas, feelings of anger or self-doubt do not vanish when their expression is forbidden.

We can put such feelings to good use by inviting students to consider carefully why some of their previous school experiences provoked negative reactions. And, of course, the crucial follow-up question is this: "What can we do this year to make sure things go better?" It may make sense to ask students to recall some good memories, too—memories of when school was exciting and appealing, and real learning was taking place—and then puzzle out the common denominators of *those* experiences so they might be re-created this year.

Here is a second way to help students think past the confines of discipline—and to use an early class meeting to begin fostering a sense of community.[4] Begin by asking this question (adapting it as necessary to the students' developmental level): "What if, some time this year, you found yourself acting in a way you weren't proud of? Suppose you hurt someone's feelings, or did something even worse. How would you want us, the rest of the community, to help you then?" After everyone has reflected privately on this question, and perhaps discussed it, pose the follow-up question: "What if *someone else* acted that way? How could we help that person?"

This thought experiment represents nothing short of a revolution in thinking about classroom problems. Actions that would normally be defined as misbehavior—and therefore as requiring discipline—are reconstrued as signs that somebody needs help. If a student had trouble with long division, after all, we would naturally want to help him understand the procedure (and its rationale), rather than seeking to punish him. So if a student instead had trouble, say, controlling her temper, our response again ought to be "How can we help?"— not "What consequence should you suffer?" We should ask, in other words, "What can we do for you?"— not "What can we do *to* you?"

It works both ways, really: The best choice for dealing with problems, or for preventing their occurrence in the first place, is to invoke the support and ideas of the community. And the best choice for building a community may be to take on this sort of challenge together.

Now let's take that idea one step further. If activities and discussions involving the whole class can help to turn that class into a community, then activities and discussions involving the whole school might help to turn the entire student body into a community. The fact that few schools have tried schoolwide discussions may suggest that few schools are small enough to allow everyone to gather and do anything other than listen passively. Fortunately, some creative educators are finding ways around the barrier of size. Each solution amounts to a different way of setting up mini-communities school.

- An elementary school in Minnesota reserves an afternoon every week for what might be called advisory groups (more commonly found in cutting-edge secondary schools). Each cluster consists of two kindergartners, two 1st graders, and so on—as well as two adults, one of whom is typically a staff member who doesn't teach. (Office assistants, custodians, cafeteria workers, and others are, after all, part of the school community, too.) People spend their time together getting to know each other, learning conflict resolution skills, and doing service projects.
- An elementary school in Florida divides its entire student body into four parts, with each grade represented in proportion to its total numbers—in effect, creating four small schools. Every day begins with a morning meeting for each community.
- A number of schools have begun to pair classrooms of older and younger students—say, a 5th grade with a 1st grade—for a block of time every week or two, with each child assigned a "buddy" from the other class. Wildly popular wherever it is tried, this activity creates focused cross-age interactions that can improve the feel of the whole school.

When children are given opportunities to develop caring, trusting friendships across grade levels, when these friendships center around shared learning experiences that are engaging for both older and younger students, and when students see that their teachers have buddies, too, the concept of community is experienced, not just idealized (Child Development Project 1996b, p. 1).

The Child Development Project has developed a series of other schoolwide programs toward the same end, many of which involve families. These include a film night (with the movie selected for its potential for generating thoughtful discussion), a science display (in place of the usual science fair, where parents are not supposed to help with the projects and students are forced to compete against each other), and a read-aloud activity (Child Development Project 1994).

Using Academic Instruction

The quest for community is not— indeed, cannot be—separate from what students are learning. Teachers can deliberately use one to promote the other in any of several ways.

First, community-building activities can be devoted to academic issues. If a class meeting can be used to talk about the best way to make sure that materials are put back where they belong, then why can't one be devoted to talking about how to approach the next unit in history—or how confusing last night's homework was? In fact, even when meetings are not explicitly devoted to curricular questions, they often provide intellectual benefits as students learn to think clearly about problems.

Second, skillful teachers can often find a way to work academic lessons into other tasks and discussions. I visited a kindergarten in New Jersey where students had complained about "too many floods in the bathroom." The problem became a science lesson, as the class generated hypotheses about why the floods were happening, and also a lesson in reading and writing, as the teacher helped students record various proposals for solving the problem. In Japanese elementary schools, academic skills are similarly woven through community-building activities (Lewis 1995).

Third, academic study is pursued cooperatively: students learn from each other and, in the process, form connections with each other. Cooperative learning is likely to provide these benefits, however, only if it is not based on incentives—a process I have called "group grade grubbing" (Kohn 1991)—and if teams are never set against each other in a competition.

Finally, elements of the curriculum may be selected with an eye to supporting social and moral growth and, indirectly, the construction of community. This can be done most readily in language arts units, with works of literature chosen and taught in such a way as to promote reflection about things like fairness and compassion, along with topics such as narrative construction and character development.

ALL OF THE ABOVE

This last example of how academic instruction can support social learning gives us a chance to pull back and reflect on the larger question of how building community may have certain academic prerequisites. Recall that this chapter began with the argument that a classroom devoid of community, one where children's need for connection is thwarted, has an adverse impact on learning. So it is that the absence of a learner-centered curriculum makes it difficult to create a real community:

> How could we create a caring community in the classroom when children's own needs—to make sense of the world, to be known and liked by others, to influence the environment— were being ignored by a skill-and-drill curriculum? A curriculum that holds little intrinsic interest for children forces teachers to use "motivators," "consequences," and competition to keep children on-task, thereby undermining community and demonstrating that some children are more valued than others (Lewis, Schaps, and Watson 1995, p. 552).

Another teacher describes the problem even more bluntly: "I can sit students in a circle, play getting-to-know-you games until the cows come home, but if what I am teaching in the class holds no interest for the students, I'm just holding them hostage until the bell rings" (Christensen 1994, p. 15).

If we are committed to moving beyond discipline, we need an engaging curriculum *and* a caring community. But we need something else as well: the chance for students to make meaningful decisions about their schooling. That, of course, was the subject of the last chapter, but it is worth reiterating here that a community without choices is just as incomplete as choices without community.

This incompleteness is painfully obvious when we visit "schools with a 'community' emphasis where children memorize 'correct' answers to moral questions and issues" (Goodman 1992, pp. 156–157). It is obvious when we read manuals for teachers filled with practical advice on how to design a safe, caring classroom—except that the students have little to say about how or why this happens: the teacher is essentially advised to *impose* a community, using praise, time-outs, and other mechanisms of control (e.g., Charney 1991).

And let's add one more piece of evidence to the case against such an approach: in the course of its research, the Child Development Project discovered that elementary school students who reported feeling a sense of community in their classrooms were also apt to exhibit *low* levels of moral reasoning if they lacked an active role in decision making. More sophisticated, principled ways of thinking about ethical questions went hand in hand with community only in those classrooms where students were involved in choosing how to design that community (Battistich et al. 1994).

Community is not enough; we need autonomy, too. In fact, when both of these features are present, there is another way to describe the arrangement that results: it is called democracy.

CHAPTER 5

Applying Learning Science in the Classroom

The Design of Learning Environments

— Edited by J.D Bransford, A.L. Brown and R.R.Cocking

In this chapter we discuss implications of new knowledge about learning for the design of learning environments, especially schools. Learning theory does not provide a simple recipe for designing effective learning environments; similarly, physics constrains but does not dictate how to build a bridge (e.g., Simon, 1969). Nevertheless, new developments in the science of learning raise important questions about the design of learning environments—questions that suggest the value of rethinking what is taught, how it is taught, and how it is assessed. The focus in this chapter is on general characteristics of learning environments that need to be examined in light of new developments in the science of learning; Chapter 7 provides specific examples of instruction in the areas of mathematics, science, and history—examples that make the arguments in the present chapter more concrete.

We begin our discussion of learning environments by revisiting a point made in Chapter 1—that the learning goals for schools have undergone major changes during the past century. Everyone expects much more from today's schools than was expected 100 years ago. A fundamental tenet of modern learning theory is that different kinds of learning goals require different approaches to instruction (Chapter 3); new goals for education require changes in opportunities to learn. After discussing changes in goals, we explore the design of learning environments from four perspectives that appear to be particularly important given current data about human learning, namely, the degree to which learning environments are learner centered, knowledge centered, assessment centered, and community centered. Later, we define these perspectives and explain how they relate to the preceding discussions in Chapters 1–4.

Changes in Educational Goals

As discussed in Chapter 1, educational goals for the twenty-first century are very different from the goals of earlier times. This shift is important to keep in mind when considering claims that schools are "getting worse." In many cases, schools seem to be functioning as well as ever, but the challenges and expectations have changed quite dramatically (e.g., Bruer, 1993; Resnick, 1987).

Consider the goals of schooling in the early 1800s. Instruction in writing focused on the mechanics of making notation as dictated by the teacher, transforming oral messages into written ones. It was not until the mid to late 1800s that writing began to be taught on a mass level in most European countries, and school children began to be asked to compose their own written texts. Even then, writing instruction was largely aimed at giving children the capacity to closely imitate very simple text forms. It was not until the 1930s that the idea emerged of primary school students expressing themselves in writing (Alcorta, 1994; Schneuwly, 1994). As in writing, it was not until relatively recently that analysis and interpretation of what is read became an expectation of skilled reading by all school children. Overall, the definition of functional literacy changed from being able to sign one's name to word decoding to reading for new information (Resnick and Resnick, 1977).

In the early 1900s, the challenge of providing mass education was seen by many as analogous to mass production in factories. School administrators were eager to make use of the "scientific" organization of factories to structure efficient classrooms. Children were regarded as raw materials to be efficiently processed by technical workers (the teachers) to reach the end product (Bennett and LeCompte, 1990; Callahan, 1962; Kliebard, 1975). This approach attempted to sort the raw materials (the children) so that they could be treated somewhat as an assembly line. Teachers were viewed as workers whose job was to carry out directives from their superiors—the efficiency experts of schooling (administrators and researchers).

The emulation of factory efficiency fostered the development of standardized tests for measurement of the "product," of clerical work by teachers to keep records of costs and progress (often at the expense of teaching), and of "management" of teaching by central district authorities who had little knowledge of educational practice or philosophy (Callahan, 1962). In short, the factory model affected the design of curriculum, instruction, and assessment in schools.

Today, students need to understand the current state of their knowledge and to build on it, improve it, and make decisions in the face of uncertainty (Talbert and McLaughlin, 1993). These two notions of knowledge were identified by John Dewey (1916) as "records" of previous cultural accomplishments and engagement in active processes as represented by the phrase "to do." For example, doing mathematics involves solving problems, abstracting, inventing, proving (see, e.g., Romberg, 1983). Doing history involves the construction and evaluation of historical documents (see, e.g., Wineberg, 1996). Doing science includes such activities as testing theories through experimentation and observation (e.g., Lehrer and Schauble, 1996a, b; Linn, 1992, 1994; Schwab, 1978). Society envisions graduates of school systems who can identify and solve problems and make contributions to society throughout their lifetime—who display the qualities of "adaptive expertise". To achieve this vision requires rethinking what is taught, how teachers teach, and how what students learn is assessed.

BOX 5.1 LITERACY: THEN AND NOW

Colonists were literate enough if they could sign their name, or even an X, on deeds. When immigrants arrived in large numbers in the 1800s, educators urged schools to deliver "recitation literacy" to the foreign children who filled the school-rooms. That literacy was the ability to hold a book and reel off memorized portions of basic American texts such as the opening paragraph of the Declaration of Independence, a part of the Gettysburg address, or some Bryant or Longfellow. With the coming of World War I, and the prospect of large numbers of men handling new equipment in foreign countries, Army testers redefined reading. Suddenly, to the dismay of men used to reading familiar passages, passing the army reading test meant being able to make sense, on the spot, of never-before-seen text. Currently, that kind of "extraction literacy," revolutionary in 1914, looks meager. Finding out who, what, when, where or how simply does not yield the inferences, questions, or ideas we now think of as defining full or "higher literacy." The idea of a classroom where young women, poor and minority students, and learning disabled students *all* read (not recite) and write about (not copy) Shakespeare or Steinbeck is a radical and hopeful departure from the long-running conception of literacy as serviceable skills for the many and generative, reflective reading and writing for the few (Wolf, 1988:1).

The remainder of this chapter is organized around Figure 5.1, which illustrates four perspectives on learning environments that seem particularly important given the principles of learning discussed in earlier chapters. Although we discuss these perspectives separately, they need to be conceptualized as a system of interconnected components that mutually support one another (e.g., Brown and Campione, 1996); we first discuss each perspective separately and then describe how they interrelate.

Learner-Centered Environments

We use the term "learner centered" to refer to environments that pay careful attention to the knowledge, skills, attitudes, and beliefs that learners bring to the educational setting. This term includes teaching practices that have been called "culturally responsive," "culturally appropriate," "culturally compatible," and "culturally relevant" (Ladson-Billings, 1995). The term also fits the concept of "diagnostic teaching" (Bell et al., 1980): attempting to discover what students think in relation to the problems on hand, discussing their misconceptions sensitively, and giving them situations to go on thinking about which will enable them to readjust their ideas (Bell, 1982a:7). Teachers who are learner centered recognize the importance of building on the conceptual and cultural knowledge that students bring with them to the classroom.

Diagnostic teaching provides an example of starting from the structure of a child's knowledge. The information on which to base a diagnosis may be acquired through observation, questioning and conversation, and reflection on the products of student activity. A key strategy is to prompt children to explain and develop their knowledge structures by asking them to make predictions about various situations and explain the reasons for their predictions. By selecting critical tasks that embody known misconceptions, teachers can help students test their thinking and see how and why various ideas might need to change (Bell, 1982a, b, 1985; Bell et al., 1986; Bell and Purdy, 1985). The

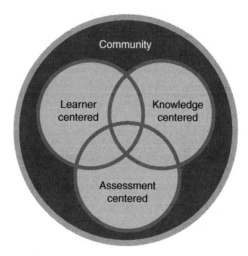

FIGURE 5.1 Perspectives on learning environments.

Source: Cognition and Technology at Vanderbilt (in press).

model is one of engaging students in cognitive conflict and then having discussions about conflicting viewpoints (see Piaget, 1973; Festinger, 1957). "To promote learning, it is important to focus on controlled changes of structure in a fixed context . . . or on deliberate transfer of a structure from one context to another" (Bell, 1985:72).

Learner-centered instruction also includes a sensitivity to the cultural practices of students and the effect of those practices on classroom learning. In a study of the Kamehameha School in Hawaii, teachers were deliberate in learning about students' home and community cultural practices and language use and incorporated them in classroom literacy instruction (Au and Jordan, 1981). After using the native Hawaiian "talk-story" (jointly produced student narratives), shifting the focus of instruction from decoding to comprehending, and including students' home experiences as a part of the discussion of reading materials, students demonstrated significant improvement in standardized test performance in reading.

Learner-centered teachers also respect the language practices of their students because they provide a basis for further learning. In science, one standard way of talking in both school and professional science is impersonal and expository, without any reference to personal or social intentions or experiences (Lemke, 1990; Wertsch, 1991). This way, which predominates in schools, privileges middle-class, mainstream ways of knowing and constitutes a barrier for students from other backgrounds who do not come to school already practiced in "school talk" (Heath, 1983). Everyday and scientific discourses need to be coordinated to assist students' scientific understanding.

In science discourse as it develops in most classrooms, students' talk frequently expresses multiple intentions or voices (see Ballenger, 1997; Bakhtin, 1984; Warren and Rosebery, 1996; Wertsch, 1991). In their narratives and arguments, students express both scientific and social intentions: scientific in that the students present evidence in support of a scientific argument; social in that they also talk about themselves as certain types of people (e.g., virtuous, honest, trustworthy). If the responses of other students and the teacher to these multivoiced narratives are always keyed to the scientific point, it helps to shape the meaning that is taken from them and relates them back to the context of the unfolding scientific argument (Ballenger, 1997). In standard science lessons, the scientific point in the talk of many students, particularly those whose discourse is not mainstream, is often missed, and the social intention is often devalued (Lemke, 1990; Michaels and Bruce, 1989; Wertsch, 1991).

In another example of connecting everyday talk and school talk, African American high school students were shown that many of their forms of everyday speech were examples of a very high form of literacy that was taught in school, but never before connected with their everyday experience (Lee, 1991, 1992). Like Proust who discovered he had been speaking prose all of his life, the students discovered that they were fluent in a set of competencies that were considered academically advanced.

Overall, learner-centered environments include teachers who are aware that learners construct their own meanings, beginning with the beliefs, understandings, and cultural practices they bring to the classroom. If teaching is conceived as constructing a bridge between the subject matter and the student, learner-centered teachers keep a constant eye on both ends of the bridge. The teachers attempt to get a sense of what students know and can do as well as their interests and passions—what each student knows, cares about, is able to do, and wants to do. Accomplished teachers "give learners reason," by respecting and understanding learners' prior experiences and understandings, assuming that these can serve as a foundation on which to build bridges to new understandings (Duckworth, 1987).

Knowledge-Centered Environments

Environments that are solely learner centered would not necessarily help students acquire the knowledge and skills necessary to function effectively in society. As noted in Chapter 2, the ability of experts to think and solve problems is not simply due to a generic set of "thinking skills" or strategies but, instead, requires well-organized bodies of knowledge that support planning and strategic thinking. Knowledge-centered environments take seriously the need to help students become knowledgeable (Bruner, 1981) by learning in ways that lead to understanding and subsequent transfer. Current knowledge on learning and transfer (Chapter 3) and development (Chapter 4) provide important guidelines for achieving these goals. Standards in areas such as mathematics and science help define the knowledge and competencies that students need to acquire (e.g., American Association for the Advancement of Science, 1989; National Council of Teachers of Mathematics, 1989; National Research Council, 1996).

Knowledge-centered environments intersect with learner-centered environments when instruction begins with a concern for students' initial preconceptions about the subject matter. The story *Fish Is Fish* illustrates how people construct new knowledge based on their current knowledge. Without carefully considering the knowledge that students' bring to the learning situation, it is difficult to predict what they will understand about new information that is presented to them.

Knowledge-centered environments also focus on the kinds of information and activities that help students develop an understanding of disciplines (e.g., Prawat et al., 1992). This focus requires a critical examination of existing curricula. In history, a widely used history text on the American Revolution left out crucial information necessary to understand rather than merely memorize (Beck et al., 1989, 1991). In science, existing curricula tend to overemphasize facts and underemphasize "doing science" to explore and test big ideas (American Association for the Advancement of Science, 1989; National Research Council, 1996). The Third International Mathematics and Science Study (Schmidt et al., 1997) characterized American curricula in mathematics and science as being "a mile wide and an inch deep."

As discussed in the first part of this book, knowledge-centered environments also include an emphasis on sense-making—on helping students become metacognitive by expecting new information to make sense and asking for clarification when it doesn't (e.g., Palincsar and Brown, 1984; Schoenfeld, 1983, 1985, 1991). A concern with sense-making raises questions about many existing curricula. For example, it has been argued that many mathematics curricula emphasize

> . . . not so much a form of thinking as a substitute for thinking. The process of calculation or computation only involves the deployment of a set routine with no room for ingenuity or flair, no place for guess work or surprise, no chance for discovery, no need for the human being, in fact (Scheffler, 1975:184).

The argument here is not that students should never learn to compute, but that they should also learn other things about mathematics, especially the fact that it is possible for them to make sense of mathematics and to think mathematically (e.g., Cobb et al., 1992).

There are interesting new approaches to the development of curricula that support learning with understanding and encourage sense making. One is "progressive formalization," which begins with the informal ideas that students bring to school and gradually helps them see how these ideas can be transformed and formalized. Instructional units encourage students to build on their informal ideas in a gradual but structured manner so that they acquire the concepts and procedures of a discipline.

The idea of progressive formalization is exemplified by the algebra strand for middle school students using *Mathematics in Context* (National Center for Research in Mathematical Sciences Education and Freudenthal Institute, 1997). It begins by having students use their own words, pictures, or diagrams to describe mathematical situations to organize their own knowledge and work and to explain their strategies. In later units, students gradually begin to use symbols to describe situations, organize their mathematical work, or express their strategies. At this level, students devise their own symbols or learn some nonconventional notation. Their representations of problem situations and explanations of their work are a mixture of words and symbols. Later, students learn and use standard conventional algebraic notation for writing expressions and equations, for manipulating algebraic expressions and solving equations, and for graphing equations. Movement along this continuum is not necessarily smooth, nor all in one direction. Although students are actually doing algebra less formally in the earlier grades, they are not forced to generalize their knowledge to a more formal level, nor to operate at a more formal level, before they have had sufficient experience with the underlying concepts. Thus, students may move back and forth among levels of formality depending on the problem situation or on the mathematics involved.

Central to curriculum frameworks such as "progressive formalization" are questions about what is developmentally appropriate to teach at various ages. Such questions represent another example of overlap between learner-centered and knowledge-centered perspectives. Older views that young children are incapable of complex reasoning have been replaced by evidence that children are capable of sophisticated levels of thinking and reasoning when they have the knowledge necessary to support these activities (see Chapter 4). An impressive body of research shows the potential benefit of early access by students to important conceptual ideas. In classrooms using a form of "cognitively guided" instruction in geometry, second-grade children's skills for representing and visualizing three-dimensional forms exceeded those of comparison groups of undergraduate students at a leading university (Lehrer and Chazan, 1998). Young children have also demonstrated powerful forms of early algebraic generalization (Lehrer and Chazan, 1998). Forms of generalization in science, such as experimentation, can be introduced before the secondary school years through a developmental approach to important mathematical and scientific ideas (Schauble et al., 1995; Warren and Rosebery, 1996). Such an approach entails becoming cognizant of the early origins of students' thinking and then identifying how those ideas can be fostered and elaborated (Brown and Campione, 1994).

Attempts to create environments that are knowledge centered also raise important questions about how to foster an integrated understanding of a discipline. Many models of curriculum design seem to produce knowledge and skills that are disconnected rather than organized into coherent wholes. The National Research Council (1990:4) notes that "To the Romans, a curriculum was a rutted course that guided the path of two-wheeled chariots." This rutted path metaphor is an appropriate description of the curriculum for many school subjects:

> Vast numbers of learning objectives, each associated with pedagogical strategies, serve as mile posts along the trail mapped by texts from kindergarten to twelfth grade. . . . Problems are solved not by observing and responding to the natural landscape through which the mathematics curriculum passes, but by mastering time tested routines, conveniently placed along the path (National Research Council, 1990:4).

An alternative to a "rutted path" curriculum is one of "learning the landscape" (Greeno, 1991). In this metaphor, learning is analogous to learning to live in an environment: learning your way around, learning what resources are available, and learning how to use those resources in conducting your activities productively and enjoyably (Greeno, 1991:175). The progressive formalization framework discussed above is consistent with this metaphor. Knowing where one is in a landscape requires a network of connections that link one's present location to the larger space.

Traditional curricula often fail to help students "learn their way around" a discipline. The curricula include the familiar scope and sequence charts that specify procedural objectives to be mastered by students at each grade: though an individual objective might be reasonable, it is not seen as part of a larger network. Yet it is the network, the connections among objectives, that is important. This is the kind of knowledge that characterizes expertise. Stress on isolated parts can train students in a series of routines without educating them to understand an overall picture that will ensure the development of integrated knowledge structures and information about conditions of applicability.

An alternative to simply progressing through a series of exercises that derive from a scope and sequence chart is to expose students to the major features of a subject domain as they arise naturally in problem situations. Activities can be structured so that students are able to explore, explain, extend, and evaluate their progress. Ideas are best introduced when students see a need or a reason for their use—this helps them see relevant uses of knowledge to make sense of what they are learning. Problem situations used to engage students may include the historic reasons for the development of the domain, the relationship of that domain to other domains, or the uses of ideas in that domain (see Webb and Romberg, 1992). We present examples from history, science, and mathematics instruction that emphasize the importance of introducing ideas and concepts in ways that promote deep understanding.

A challenge for the design of knowledge-centered environments is to strike the appropriate balance between activities designed to promote understanding and those designed to promote the automaticity of skills necessary to function effectively without being overwhelmed by attentional requirements. Students for whom it is effortful to read, write, and calculate can encounter serious difficulties learning. The importance of automaticity has been demonstrated in a number of areas (e.g., Beck et al., 1989, 1991; Hasselbring et al., 1987; LaBerge and Samuels, 1974;).

Assessment-Centered Environments

In addition to being learner centered and knowledge centered, effectively designed learning environments must also be assessment centered. The key principles of assessment are that they should provide opportunities for feedback and revision and that what is assessed must be congruent with one's learning goals.

It is important to distinguish between two major uses of assessment. The first, formative assessment, involves the use of assessments (usually administered in the context of the classroom) as sources of feedback to improve teaching and learning. The second, summative assessment, measures what students have learned at the end of some set of learning activities. Examples of formative assessments include teachers' comments on work in progress, such as drafts of papers or preparations for presentations. Examples of summative assessments include teacher-made tests given at the end of a unit of study and state and national achievement tests that students take at the end of a year. Ideally, teachers' formative and summative assessments are aligned with the state and national assessments that students take at the end of the year; often, however, this is not the case. Issues of summative assessment for purposes of national, state, and district accountability are beyond the scope of this report; our discussion focuses on classroom-based formative and summative assessments.

Formative Assessments and Feedback

Studies of adaptive expertise, learning, transfer, and early development show that feedback is extremely important. Students' thinking must be made visible (through discussions, papers, or tests), and feedback must be provided. Given the goal of learning with understanding, assessments and feedback must focus on understanding, and not only on memory for procedures or facts (although these can be valuable, too). Assessments that emphasize understanding do not necessarily require elaborate or complicated assessment procedures. Even multiple-choice tests can be organized in ways that assess understanding (see below).

Opportunities for feedback should occur continuously, but not intrusively, as a part of instruction. Effective teachers continually attempt to learn about their students' thinking and understanding. They do a great deal of on-line monitoring of both group work and individual performances, and they attempt to assess students' abilities to link their current activities to other parts of the curriculum and their lives. The feedback they give to students can be formal or informal. Effective teachers also help students build skills of self-assessment. Students learn to assess their own work, as well as the work of their peers, in order to help everyone learn more effectively (see, e.g., Vye et al., 1998, in press). Such self-assessment is an important part of the metacognitive approach to instruction.

In many classrooms, opportunities for feedback appear to occur relatively infrequently. Most teacher feedback—grades on tests, papers, worksheets, homework, and on report cards—represent summative assessments that are intended to measure the results of learning. After receiving grades, students typically move on to a new topic and work for another set of grades. Feedback is most valuable when students have the opportunity to use it to revise their thinking as they are working on a unit or project. The addition of opportunities for formative assessment increases students' learning and transfer, and they learn to value opportunities to revise (Barron et al., 1998; Black and William, 1998; Vye et al., 1998b). Opportunities to work collaboratively in groups can also increase the quality of the feedback available to students (Barron, 1991; Bereiter and Scardamalia, 1989; Fuchs et al., 1992; Johnson and Johnson, 1975; Slavin, 1987; Vye et al., 1998a), although many students must be helped to learn how to work collaboratively. New technologies provide opportunities to increase feedback by allowing students, teachers, and content experts to interact both synchronously and asynchronously.

A challenge of implementing good assessment practices involves the need to change many teachers', parents', and students' models of what effective learning looks like. Many assessments developed by teachers overly emphasize memory for procedures and facts (Porter et al., 1993). In addition, many standardized tests that are used for accountability still overemphasize memory for isolated facts and procedures, yet teachers are often judged by how well their students do on such tests. One mathematics teacher consistently produced students who scored high on statewide examinations by helping students memorize a number of mathematical procedures (e.g., proofs) that typically appeared on the examinations, but the students did not really understand what they were doing, and often could not answer questions that required an understanding of mathematics (Schoenfeld, 1988).

Appropriately designed assessments can help teachers realize the need to rethink their teaching practices. Many physics teachers have been surprised at their students' inabilities to answer seemingly obvious (to the expert) questions that assessed their students' understanding, and this outcome has motivated them to revise their instructional practices (Redish, 1996). Similarly, visually based assessments of "number sense" (see Case and Moss, 1996) have helped teachers discover the need to help their students develop important aspects of mathematical understanding (Cognition and Technology Group at Vanderbilt, in press b). Innovative assessments that reveal students' understanding of important concepts in science and mathematics have also been developed (Lehrer and Schauble, 1996a,b).

Formats for Assessing Understanding

Teachers have limited time to assess students' performances and provide feedback, but new advances in technology can help solve this problem. Even without technology, however, advances have been made in devising simple assessments that measure understanding rather than memorization. In the area of physics, assessments like those used in Chapter 2 to compare experts and novices have been revised for use in classrooms. One task presents students with two problems and asks them to state whether both would be solved using a similar approach and state the reason for the decision:

1. A 2.5-kilogram ball with a radius of 4 centimeters is traveling at 7 meters/second on a rough horizontal surface, but not spinning. At some later time, the ball is rolling without slipping 5 meters/second. How much work was done by friction?
2. A 0.5-kilogram ball with a radius of 15 centimeters is initially sliding at 10 meters/second without spinning. The ball travels on a horizontal surface and eventually rolls without slipping. Find the ball's final velocity.

Novices typically state that these two problems are solved similarly because they match on surface features—both involve a ball sliding and rolling on a horizontal surface. Students who are learning with understanding state that the problems are solved differently: the first can be solved by applying the work-energy theorem; the second can be solved by applying conservation of angular momentum (Hardiman et al., 1989); These kinds of assessment items can be used during the course of instruction to monitor the depth of conceptual understanding.

Portfolio assessments are another method of formative assessment. They provide a format for keeping records of students' work as they progress throughout the year and, most importantly, for allowing students to discuss their achievements and difficulties with their teachers, parents, and fellow students (e.g., Wiske, 1997; Wolf, 1988). They take time to implement and they are often implemented poorly—portfolios often become simply another place to store student work but no discussion of the work takes place— but used properly, they provide students and others with valuable information about their learning progress over time.

Theoretical Frameworks for Assessment

A challenge for the learning sciences is to provide a theoretical framework that links assessment practices to learning theory. An important step in this direction is represented by the work of Baxter and Glaser (1997), who provide a framework for integrating cognition and context in assessing achievement in science. In their report, performance is described in terms of the content and process task demands of the subject matter and the nature and extent of cognitive activity likely to be observed in a particular assessment situation. The framework provides a basis for examining how developers' intentions are realized in performance assessments that purport to measure reasoning, understanding, and complex problem solving.

BOX 5.2 HOW DO YOU KNOW?

A 1-kilogram stick that is 2 meters long is placed on a frictionless surface and is free to rotate about a vertical pivot through one end. A 50-gram lump of putty is attached 80 centimeters from the pivot. Which of the following principles would allow you to determine the magnitude of the net force between the stick and the putty when the angular velocity of the system is 3 radians/second?

A. Newton's second law, $\vec{F}_{net} = M\vec{a}$
B. Angular momentum or conservation of angular momentum
C. Linear momentum or conservation of linear momentum
D. Work-energy theorem or conservation of mechanical energy
E. Conservation of linear momentum followed by conservation of mechanical energy

Performance on this item was near random for students finishing an introductory calculus-based physics course. The temptation is to match the "rotation" surface feature of the problem with "angular momentum," when in fact the problem is solved by a simple application of Newton's second law. Data such as these are important for helping teachers guide students toward the development of fluid, transferable knowledge (Leonard et al., 1996).

Characterizing assessments in terms of components of competence and the content-process demands of the subject matter brings specificity to generic assessment objectives such as "higher level thinking and deep understanding." Characterizing student performance in terms of cognitive activities focuses attention on the differences in competence and subject-matter achievement that can be observed in learning and assessment situations. The kind and quality of cognitive activities in an assessment is a function of the content and process demands of the task involved. For example, consider the content-process framework for science assessment shown in Figure 5.2 (Baxter and Glaser, 1997). In this figure, task demands for content knowledge are conceptualized on a continuum from rich to lean (y axis). At one extreme are knowledge-rich tasks, tasks that require in-depth understanding of

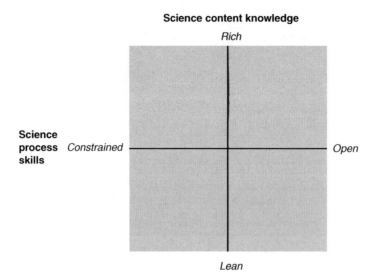

Figure 5.2 Content-process space of science assessments.

subject matter for their completion. At the other extreme are tasks that are not dependent on prior knowledge or related experiences; rather, performance is primarily dependent on the information given in the assessment situation. The task demands for process skills are conceptualized as a continuum from constrained to open (x axis). In open situations, explicit directions are minimized; students are expected to generate and carry out appropriate process skills for problem solution. In process-constrained situations, directions can be of two types: step-by-step, subject-specific procedures given as part of the task, or directions to explain the process skills that are necessary for task completion. In this situation, students are asked to generate explanations, an activity that does not require using the process skills. Assessment tasks can involve many possible combinations of content knowledge and process skills; Table 5.1 illustrates the relationship between the structure of knowledge and the organized cognitive activities.

Community-Centered Environments

New developments in the science of learning suggest that the degree to which environments are community centered is also important for learning. Especially important are norms for people learning from one another and continually attempting to improve. We use the term community centered

Table 5.1 Cognitive Activity and Structure of Knowledge

Organized Cognitive Activity	Structure of Knowledge	
	Fragmented	**Meaningful**
Problem Representation	Surface features and shallow understanding	Underlying principles and relevant concepts
Strategy Use	Undirected trial-and-error problem solving	Efficient, informative, and goal oriented
Self-Monitoring	Minimal and sporadic	Ongoing and flexible
Explanation	Single statement of fact of description of superficial factors	Principled and coherent

to refer to several aspects of community, including the classroom as a community, the school as a community, and the degree to which students, teachers, and administers feel connected to the larger community of homes, businesses, states, the nation, and even the world.

Classroom and School Communities

At the level of classrooms and schools, learning seems to be enhanced by social norms that value the search for understanding and allow students (and teachers) the freedom to make mistakes in order to learn (e.g., Brown and Campione, 1994; Cobb et al., 1992). Different classrooms and schools reflect different sets of norms and expectations. For example, an unwritten norm that operates in some classrooms is never to get caught making a mistake or not knowing an answer (see, e.g., Holt, 1964). This norm can hinder students' willingness to ask questions when they do not understand the material or to explore new questions and hypotheses. Some norms and expectations are more subject specific. For example, the norms in a mathematics class may be that mathematics is knowing how to compute answers; a much better norm would be that the goal of inquiry is mathematical understanding. Different norms and practices have major effects on what is taught and how it is assessed (e.g., Cobb et al., 1992). Sometimes there are different sets of expectations for different students. Teachers may convey expectations for school success to some students and expectations for school failure to others (MacCorquodale, 1988). For example, girls are sometimes discouraged from participating in higher level mathematics and science. Students, too, may share and convey cultural expectations that proscribe the participation of girls in some classes (Schofield et al., 1990).

BOX 5.3 TALKING IN CLASS

A speech-language pathologist working in an Inuit school (in northern Canada) asked a principal—who was not an Inuit—to compile a list of children who had speech and language problems in the school. The list contained a third of the students in the school, and next to several names the principal wrote, "Does not talk in class." The speech-language pathologist consulted a local Inuit teacher for help determining how each child functioned in his or her native language. She looked at the names and said, "Well-raised Inuit children should not talk in class. They should be learning by looking and listening."

When the speech-language pathologist asked that teacher about one toddler she was studying who was very talkative and seemed to the non-Inuit researcher to be very bright, the teacher said: "Do you think he might have a learning problem? Some of these children who don't have such high intelligence have trouble stopping themselves. They don't know when to stop talking" (Crago, 1988:219).

Classroom norms can also encourage modes of participation that may be unfamiliar to some students. For example, some groups rely on learning by observation and listening and then becoming involved in ongoing activities; school-like forms of talking may be unfamiliar for the children whose community has only recently included schools (Rogoff et al., 1993); see Box 5.3.

The sense of community in classrooms is also affected by grading practices, and these can have positive or negative effects depending on the students. For example, Navajo high school students do not treat tests and grades as competitive events the way that Anglo students do (Deyhle and Margonis, 1995). An Anglo high school counselor reported that Navajo parents complained about their children being singled out when the counselor started a "high achiever" bulletin board and wanted to put up the pictures of students with B averages or better. The counselor "compromised" by putting up happy stickers with the students' names on them. A Navajo student, staring at the board, said "The board embarrasses us, to be stuck out like that" (Deyhle and Margonis, 1995:28).

More broadly, competition among students for teacher attention, approval, and grades is a commonly used motivator in U.S. schools. And in some situations, competition may create situations that impede learning. This is especially so if individual competition is at odds with a community ethic of individuals' contributing their strengths to the community (Suina and Smolkin, 1994).

An emphasis on community is also imortant when attempting to borrow successful educational practices from other countries. For example, Japanese teachers spend considerable time working with the whole class, and they frequently ask students who have made errors to share their thinking with the rest of the class. This can be very valuable because it leads to discussions that deepen the understanding of everyone in the class. However, this practice works only because Japanese teachers have developed a classroom culture in which students are skilled at learning from one another and respect the fact that an analysis of errors is fruitful for learning (Hatano and Inagaki, 1996). Japanese students value listening, so they learn from large class discussions even if they do not have many chances to participate. The culture of American classrooms is often very different—many emphasize the importance of being right and contributing by talking. Teaching and learning must be viewed from the perspective of the overall culture of the society and its relationship to the norms of the classrooms. To simply attempt to import one or two Japanese teaching techniques into American classrooms may not produce the desired results.

The sense of community in a school also appears to be strongly affected by the adults who work in that environment. As Barth (1988) states:

> The relationship among adults who live in a school has more to do with the character and quality of the school and with the accomplishments of the students than any other factor.

Studies by Bray (1998) and Talbert and McLaughlin (1993) emphasize the importance of teacher learning communities. We say more about this in Chapter 8.

Connections to the Broader Community

An analysis of learning environments from the perspective of community also includes a concern for connections between the school environment and the broader community, including homes, community centers, after-school programs, and businesses. As John Dewey (1916) noted long ago:

> From the standpoint of the child, the great waste in school comes from his inability to utilize the experience he gets outside . . . while on the other hand, he is unable to apply in daily life what he is learning in school. That is the isolation of the school—its isolation from life.

The importance of connecting the school with outside learning activities can be appreciated by considering Figure 5.3, which shows the percentage of time during a typical school year that students spend in school, sleeping, and engaged in other activities (see Cognition and Technology Group at Vanderbilt, in press a). The percentage of time spent in school is comparatively small. If students spend one-third of their nonsleeping time outside of school watching television, this means that they spend more time watching television in a year than they spend in school. (We say more about television and learning in the next section.)

A key environment for learning is the family. Even when family members do not focus consciously on instructional roles, they provide resources for children's learning, activities in which learning occurs, and connections to community (Moll, 1986a, b, 1990). Children also learn from the attitudes of family members toward skills and values of schooling.

The success of the family as a learning environment, especially in children's early years (see Chapter 4), has provided inspiration and guidance for some of the changes recommended in schools.

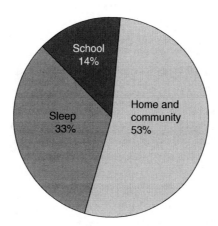

FIGURE 5.3 Comparison of time spent in school, home and community, and sleep. Percentages were calculated using 180 school days each year, and each school day was estimated to be 6.5 hours in length.

The phenomenal development of children from birth to age 4 or 5 is generally supported by family interactions in which children learn by engaging with and observing others in shared endeavors. Conversations and other interactions that occur around events of interest with trusted and skilled adult and child companions are especially powerful environments for children's learning. Many of the recommendations for changes in schools can be seen as extensions of the learning activities that occur within families. In addition, recommendations to include families in classroom activities and planning hold promise of bringing together two powerful systems for supporting children's learning.

Children participate in many other institutions outside their homes that can foster learning. Some of these institutions have learning as part of their goals, including many after-school programs, organizations such as Boy and Girl Scouts and 4-H Clubs, museums, and religious groups. Others make learning more incidental, but learning takes place nevertheless (see McLaughlin, 1990, on youth clubs; Griffin and Cole, 1984, on the Fifth Dimension Program).

Connections to experts outside of school can also have a positive influence on in-school learning because they provide opportunities for students to interact with parents and other people who take an interest in what students are doing. It can be very motivating both to students and teachers to have opportunities to share their work with others. Opportunities to prepare for these events helps teachers raise standards because the consequences go beyond mere scores on a test (e.g., Brown and Campione, 1994, 1996; Cognition and Technology Group at Vanderbilt, in press b).

The idea of outside audiences who present challenges (complete with deadlines) has been incorporated into a number of instructional programs (e.g., Cognition and Technology Group at Vanderbilt, 1997; Wiske, 1997). Working to prepare for outsiders provides motivation that helps teachers maintain student interest. In addition, teachers and students develop a better sense of community as they prepare to face a common challenge. Students are also motivated to prepare for outside audiences who do not come to the classroom but will see their projects. Preparing exhibits for museums represents an excellent example (see Collins et al., 1991).

Television

For better or for worse, most children spent a considerable amount of time watching television; it has played an increasingly prominent role in children's development over the past 50 years. Children watch a great deal of television before entering school, and television viewing continues throughout life. In fact, many students spend more hours watching television than attending school. Parents want their children to learn from television; at the same time they are concerned about what they are learning from the programs they watch (Greenfield, 1984).

Watching Different Kinds of Programs

Television programming for children ranges from educational to purely entertaining (see Wright and Huston, 1995). And there are different ways of watching programs—a child may watch in isolation or with an adult. Furthermore, just as in domains like chess, physics, or teaching (see Chapter 2), people's existing knowledge and beliefs affect what they notice, understand, and remember from viewing television (Newcomb and Collins, 1979). The same program can have different effects depending on who is watching and whether the viewing is a solo activity or part of an interactive group. An important distinction is whether the program is intended to be educational or not.

One group of preschoolers aged 2-4 and first-grade students aged 6-7 watched about 7-8 hours of noneducational programming per week; the preschool children also watched an average of 2 hours of educational programming per week, and the older students watched 1 hour. Despite the low ratio of educational to noneducational viewing, the educational programs seemed to have positive benefits. The 2- to 4-year-old preschoolers performed better than non-viewers of educational programs on tests of school readiness, reading, mathematics, and vocabulary as much as 3 years later (Wright and Huston, 1995). Specifically, viewing educational programs was a positive predictor of letter-word knowledge, vocabulary size, and school readiness on standardized achievement tests. For the older students, the viewing of educational programs was related to better performance on tests of reading comprehension and teachers' judgments of school adjustment in first and second grades, compared with children who were infrequent viewers. Overall, the effects of television viewing were not as widespread for the older students, and there were fewer significant effects for the older children than for the preschoolers. It is important to note that the effects of watching educational programs were evident "even when initial language skills, family education, income, and the quality of the home environment are taken into account" (Wright and Huston, 1995:22).

Effects on Beliefs and Attitudes

Television also provides images and role models that can affect how children view themselves, how they see others, attitudes about what academic subjects they should be interested in, and other topics related to person perception. These images can have both positive and negative effects. For example, when 8- to 14-year-olds watched programs designed to show positive attributes of children around the world, they were less likely to say that children from their own country were more interesting or more intelligent (O'Brien, 1981), and they began to see more similarities among people around the world (Greenfield, 1984). And children who watched episodes of Sesame Street featuring handicapped children had more positive feelings toward children with disabilities.

However, children can also misinterpret programs about people from different cultures, depending on what they already know (Newcomb and Collins, 1979). Stereotyping represents a powerful effect of watching television that is potentially negative. Children bring sex role stereotypes with them to school that derive from television programs and commercials (Dorr, 1982).

As a powerful visual medium, television creates stereotypes even when there is no intent to sell an image. But experimental studies indicate that such stereotyping effects decrease with children as young as 5 if adults offer critiques of the stereotypic portrayals as the children watch programs (Dorr, 1982). Thus, entertainment programs can educate in positive ways and learned information can be extended through adult guidance and commentary.

In sum, television has an impact on children's learning that must be taken seriously. But the medium is neither inherently beneficial nor harmful. The content that students watch, and how they watch it, has important effects on what they learn. Especially significant is the fact that informative or educational programming has been shown to have beneficial effects on school achievement and that a preponderance of non-educational, entertainment viewing can have negative effects. Furthermore, the benefits of informative viewing occur despite the fact that the ratio of young children's viewing tends to be 7:1 in favor of entertainment television. These findings support the wisdom of continued attempts to develop and study television programs that can help students acquire the kinds of knowledge, skills, and attitudes that support their learning in school.

The Importance of Alignment

In the beginning of this chapter we noted that the four perspectives on learning environments (the degree to which they are learner, knowledge, assessment, and community centered) would be discussed separately but ultimately needed to be aligned in ways that mutually support one another. Alignment is as important for schools as for organizations in general (e.g., Covey, 1990). A key aspect of task analysis is the idea of aligning goals for learning with what is taught, how it is taught, and how it is assessed (both formatively and summatively). Without this alignment, it is difficult to know what is being learned. Students may be learning valuable information, but one cannot tell unless there is alignment between what they are learning and the assessment of that learning. Similarly, students may be learning things that others don't value unless curricula and assessments are aligned with the broad learning goals of communities (Lehrer and Shumow, 1997).

A systems approach to promote coordination among activities is needed to design effective learning environments (Brown and Campione, 1996). Many schools have checklists of innovative practices, such as the use of collaborative learning, teaching for understanding and problem solving, and using formative assessment. Often, however, these activities are not coordinated with one another. Teaching for understanding and problem solving may be "what we do on Fridays"; collaborative learning may be used to promote memorization of fact-based tests; and formative assessments may focus on skills that are totally disconnected from the rest of the students' curriculum. In addition, students may be given opportunities to study collaboratively for tests yet be graded on a curve so that they compete with one another rather than trying to meet particular performance standards. In these situations, activities in the classroom are not aligned.

Activities *within* a particular classroom may be aligned yet fail to fit with the rest of the school. And a school as a whole needs to have a consistent alignment. Some schools communicate a consistent policy about norms and expectations for conduct and achievement. Others send mixed messages. For example, teachers may send behavior problems to the principal, who may inadvertently undermine the teacher by making light of the students' behavior. Similarly, schedules may or may not be made flexible in order to accommodate in-depth inquiry, and schools may or may not be adjusted to minimize disruptions, including nonacademic "pullout" programs and even the number of classroom interruptions made by a principal's overzealous use of the classroom intercom. Overall, different activities within a school may or may not compete with one another and impede overall progress. When principals and teachers work together to define a common vision for their entire school, learning can improve (e.g., Barth, 1988, 1991; Peterson et al., 1995).

Activities within schools must also be aligned with the goals and assessment practices of the community. Ideally, teachers' goals for learning fit with the curriculum they teach and the school's goals, which in turn fit the goals implicit in the tests of accountability used by the school system. Often these factors are out of alignment. Effective change requires a simultaneous consideration of all these factors (e.g., Cognition and Technology Group at Vanderbilt, in press b). The new scientific findings about learning provide a framework for guiding systemic change.

Conclusion

The goals and expectations for schooling have changed quite dramatically during the past century, and new goals suggest the need to rethink such questions as what is taught, how it is taught, and how students are assessed. We emphasized that research on learning does not provide a recipe for designing effective learning environments, but it does support the value of asking certain kinds of questions about the design of learning environments.

Four perspectives on the design of learning environments—the degree to which they are student centered, knowledge centered, assessment centered, and community centered—are important in designing these environments.

A focus on the degree to which environments are learner centered is consistent with the strong body of evidence suggesting that learners' use their current knowledge to construct new knowledge and that what they know and believe at the moment affects how they interpret new information. Sometimes learners' current knowledge supports new learning, sometimes it hampers learning: effective instruction begins with what learners bring to the setting; this includes cultural practices and beliefs as well as knowledge of academic content.

Learner-centered environments attempt to help students make connections between their previous knowledge and their current academic tasks. Parents are especially good at helping their children make connections. Teachers have a harder time because they do not share the life experiences of each of their students. Nevertheless, there are ways to systematically become familiar with each student's special interests and strengths.

Effective environments must also be knowledge centered. It is not sufficient only to attempt to teach general problem solving and thinking skills; the ability to think and solve problems requires well-organized knowledge that is accessible in appropriate contexts. An emphasis on being knowledge centered raises a number of questions, such as the degree to which instruction begins with students' current knowledge and skills, rather than simply presents new facts about the subject matter. While young students are capable of grasping more complex concepts than was believed previously, those concepts must be presented in ways that are developmentally appropriate. A knowledge-centered perspective on learning environments also highlights the importance of thinking about designs for curricula. To what extent do they help students learn with understanding versus promote the acquisition of disconnected sets of facts and skills? Curricula that emphasize an excessively broad range of subjects run the risk of developing disconnected rather than connected knowledge; they fit well with the idea of a curriculum as being a well-worn path in a road. An alternative metaphor for curriculum is to help students develop interconnected pathways within a discipline so that they "learn their away around in it" and not lose sight of where they are.

Issues of assessment also represent an important perspective for viewing the design of learning environments. Feedback is fundamental to learning, but opportunities to receive it are often scarce in classrooms. Students may receive grades on tests and essays, but these are summative assessments that occur at the end of projects; also needed are formative assessments that provide students opportunities to revise and hence improve the quality of their thinking and learning. Assessments must reflect the learning goals that define various environments. If the goal is to enhance understanding, it is not sufficient to provide assessments that focus primarily on memory for facts and formulas. Many instructors have changed their approach to teaching after seeing how their students failed to understand seemingly obvious (to the expert) ideas.

The fourth perspective on learning environments involves the degree to which they promote a sense of community. Ideally, students, teachers, and other interested participants share norms that value learning and high standards. Norms such as these increase people's opportunities to interact, receive feedback, and learn. There are several aspects of community, including the community of the classroom, the school, and the connections between the school and the larger community, including the home. The importance of connected communities becomes clear when one examines the relatively small amount of time spent in school compared to other settings. Activities in homes, community centers, and after-school clubs can have important effects on students' academic achievement.

Finally, there needs to be alignment among the four perspectives of learning environments. They all have the potential to overlap and mutually influence one another. Issues of alignment appear to be very important for accelerating learning both within and outside of schools.

Learning: From Speculation to Science

The essence of matter, the origins of the universe, the nature of the human mind—these are the profound questions that have engaged thinkers through the centuries. Until quite recently, understanding the mind—and the thinking and learning that the mind makes possible—has remained an elusive quest, in part because of a lack of powerful research tools. Today, the world is in the midst of an extraordinary outpouring of scientific work on the mind and brain, on the processes of thinking and learning, on the neural processes that occur during thought and learning, and on the development of competence.

The revolution in the study of the mind that has occurred in the last three or four decades has important implications for education. As we illustrate, a new theory of learning is coming into focus that leads to very different approaches to the design of curriculum, teaching, and assessment than those often found in schools today. Equally important, the growth of inter-disciplinary inquiries and new kinds of scientific collaborations have begun to make the path from basic research to educational practice somewhat more visible, if not yet easy to travel. Thirty years ago, educators paid little attention to the work of cognitive scientists, and researchers in the nascent field of cognitive science worked far removed from classrooms. Today, cognitive researchers are spending more time working with teachers, testing and refining their theories in real classrooms where they can see how different settings and classroom interactions influence applications of their theories.

What is perhaps currently most striking is the variety of research approaches and techniques that have been developed and ways in which evidence from many different branches of science are beginning to converge. The story we can now tell about learning is far richer than ever before, and it promises to evolve dramatically in the next generation. For example:

- Research from cognitive psychology has increased understanding of the nature of competent performance and the principles of knowledge organization that underlie people's abilities to solve problems in a wide variety of areas, including mathematics, science, literature, social studies, and history.
- Developmental researchers have shown that young children understand a great deal about basic principles of biology and physical causality, about number, narrative, and personal intent, and that these capabilities make it possible to create innovative curricula that introduce important concepts for advanced reasoning at early ages.
- Research on learning and transfer has uncovered important principles for structuring learning experiences that enable people to use what they have learned in new settings.
- Work in social psychology, cognitive psychology, and anthropology is making clear that all learning takes place in settings that have particular sets of cultural and social norms and expectations and that these settings influence learning and transfer in powerful ways.
- Neuroscience is beginning to provide evidence for many principles of learning that have emerged from laboratory research, and it is showing how learning changes the physical structure of the brain and, with it, the functional organization of the brain.
- Collaborative studies of the design and evaluation of learning environments, among cognitive and developmental psychologists and educators, are yielding new knowledge about the nature of learning and teaching as it takes place in a variety of settings. In addition, researchers are discovering ways to learn from the "wisdom of practice" that comes from successful teachers who can share their expertise.

- Emerging technologies are leading to the development of many new opportunities to guide and enhance learning that were unimagined even a few years ago.

All of these developments in the study of learning have led to an era of new relevance of science to practice. In short, investment in basic research is paying off in practical applications. These developments in understanding of how humans learn have particular significance in light of changes in what is expected of the nation's educational systems.

In the early part of the twentieth century, education focused on the acquisition of literacy skills: simple reading, writing, and calculating. It was not the general rule for educational systems to train people to think and read critically, to express themselves clearly and persuasively, to solve complex problems in science and mathematics. Now, at the end of the century, these aspects of high literacy are required of almost everyone in order to successfully negotiate the complexities of contemporary life. The skill demands for work have increased dramatically, as has the need for organizations and workers to change in response to competitive workplace pressures. Thoughtful participation in the democratic process has also become increasingly complicated as the locus of attention has shifted from local to national and global concerns.

Above all, information and knowledge are growing at a far more rapid rate than ever before in the history of humankind. As Nobel laureate Herbert Simon wisely stated, the meaning of "knowing" has shifted from being able to remember and repeat information to being able to find and use it (Simon, 1996). More than ever, the sheer magnitude of human knowledge renders its coverage by education an impossibility; rather, the goal of education is better conceived as helping students develop the intellectual tools and learning strategies needed to acquire the knowledge that allows people to think productively about history, science and technology, social phenomena, mathematics, and the arts. Fundamental understanding about subjects, including how to frame and ask meaningful questions about various subject areas, contributes to individuals' more basic understanding of principles of learning that can assist them in becoming self-sustaining, lifelong learners.

Focus: People, Schools, and the Potential to Learn

The scientific literatures on cognition, learning, development, culture, and brain are voluminous. Three organizing decisions, made fairly early in the work of the committee, provided the framework for our study and are reflected in the contents of this book.

- First, we focus primarily on research on human learning (though the study of animal learning provides important collateral information), including new developments from neuroscience.
- Second, we focus especially on learning research that has implications for the design of formal instructional environments, primarily preschools, kindergarten through high schools (K-12), and colleges.
- Third, and related to the second point, we focus on research that helps explore the possibility of helping all individuals achieve their fullest potential.

New ideas about ways to facilitate learning—and about who is most capable of learning—can powerfully affect the quality of people's lives. At different points in history, scholars have worried that formal educational environments have been better at selecting talent than developing it (see, e.g., Bloom, 1964). Many people who had difficulty in school might have prospered if the new ideas about effective instructional practices had been available. Furthermore, given new instructional practices, even those who did well in traditional educational environments might have developed skills, knowledge, and attitudes that would have significantly enhanced their achievements.

Learning research suggests that there are new ways to introduce students to traditional subjects, such as mathematics, science, history and literature, and that these new approaches make it possible for the majority of individuals to develop a deep understanding of important subject matter. This committee is especially interested in theories and data that are relevant to the development of new ways to introduce students to such traditional subjects as mathematics, science, history, and literature. There is hope that new approaches can make it possible for a majority of individuals to develop a moderate to deep understanding of important subjects.

Development of the Science of Learning

This report builds on research that began in the latter part of the nineteenth century—the time in history at which systematic attempts were made to study the human mind through scientific methods. Before then, such study was the province of philosophy and theology. Some of the most influential early work was done in Leipzig in the laboratory of Wilhelm Wundt, who with his colleagues tried to subject human consciousness to precise analysis—mainly by asking subjects to reflect on their thought processes through introspection.

By the turn of the century, a new school of behaviorism was emerging. In reaction to the subjectivity inherent in introspection, behaviorists held that the scientific study of psychology must restrict itself to the study of observable behaviors and the stimulus conditions that control them. An extremely influential article, published by John B. Watson in 1913, provides a glimpse of the behaviorist credo:

> . . . all schools of psychology except that of behaviorism claim that "consciousness" is the subject-matter of psychology. Behaviorism, on the contrary, holds that the subject matter of human psychology is the behavior or activities of the human being. Behaviorism claims that "consciousness" is neither a definable nor a useable concept; that it is merely another word for the "soul" of more ancient times. The old psychology is thus dominated by a kind of subtle religious philosophy.

Drawing on the empiricist tradition, behaviorists conceptualized learning as a process of forming connections between stimuli and responses. Motivation to learn was assumed to be driven primarily by drives, such as hunger, and the availability of external forces, such as rewards and punishments (e.g., Thorndike, 1913; Skinner, 1950).

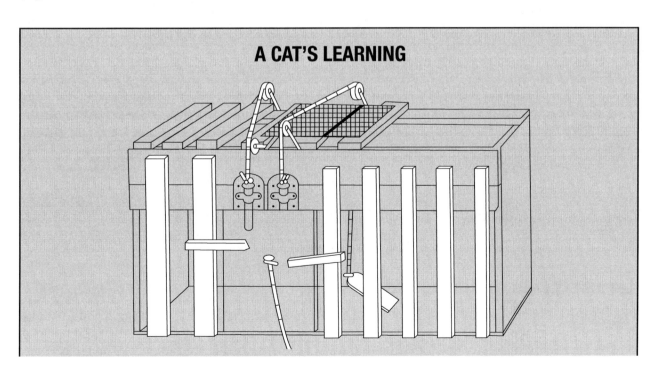

A CAT'S LEARNING

"When put into the box, the cat would show evident signs of discomfort and impulse to escape from confinement. It tries to squeeze through any opening; it claws and bites at the wire; it thrusts its paws out through any opening and claws at everything it reaches . . . . It does not pay very much attention to the food outside but seems simply to strive instinctively to escape from confinement . . . . The cat that is clawing all over the box in her impulsive struggle will probably claw the string or loop or button so as to open the door. And gradually all the other unsuccessful impulses will be stamped out and the particular impulse leading to the successful act will be stamped in by the resulting pleasure, until, after many trials, the cat will, when put in the box, immediately claw the button or loop in a definite way" (Thorndike, 1913:13).

In a classic behaviorist study by Edward L. Thorndike (1913), hungry cats had to learn to pull a string hanging in a "puzzle box" in order for a door to open that let them escape and get food. What was involved in learning to escape in this manner? Thorndike concluded that the cats did not think about how to escape and then do it; instead, they engaged in trial-and-error behavior; Sometimes a cat in the puzzle box accidentally pulled the strings while playing and the door opened, allowing the cat to escape. But this event did not appear to produce an insight on the part of the cat because, when placed in the puzzle box again, the cat did not immediately pull the string to escape. Instead, it took a number of trials for the cats to learn through trial and error. Thorndike argued that rewards (e.g., food) increased the strength of connections between stimuli and responses. The explanation of what appeared to be complex problem-solving phenomena as escaping from a complicated puzzle box could thus be explained without recourse to unobservable mental events, such as thinking.

A limitation of early behaviorism stemmed from its focus on observable stimulus conditions and the behaviors associated with those conditions. This orientation made it difficult to study such phenomena as understanding, reasoning, and thinking—phenomena that are of paramount importance for education. Over time, radical behaviorism (often called "Behaviorism with a Capital B") gave way to a more moderate form of behaviorism ("behaviorism with a small b") that preserved the scientific rigor of using behavior as data, but also allowed hypotheses about internal "mental" states when these became necessary to explain various phenomena (e.g., Hull, 1943; Spence, 1942).

In the late 1950s, the complexity of understanding humans and their environments became increasingly apparent, and a new field emerged— cognitive science. From its inception, cognitive science approached learning from a multidisciplinary perspective that included anthropology, linguistics, philosophy, developmental psychology, computer science, neuroscience, and several branches of psychology (Norman, 1980,1993; Newell and Simon, 1972). New experimental tools, methodologies, and ways of postulating theories made it possible for scientists to begin serious study of mental functioning: to test their theories rather than simply speculate about thinking and learning (see, e.g., Anderson, 1982, 1987; deGroot, 1965,1969; Newell and Simon, 1972; Ericsson and Charness, 1994), and, in recent years, to develop insights into the importance of the social and cultural contexts of learning (e.g., Cole, 1996; Lave, 1988; Lave and Wenger, 1991; Rogoff, 1990; Rogoff et al., 1993). The introduction of rigorous qualitative research methodologies have provided perspectives on learning that complement and enrich the experimental research traditions (Erickson, 1986; Hammersly and Atkinson, 1983; Heath, 1982; Lincoln and Guba, 1985; Marshall and Rossman, 1955; Miles and Huberman, 1984; Spradley, 1979).

Learning with Understanding

One of the hallmarks of the new science of learning is its emphasis on learning with understanding. Intuitively, understanding is good, but it has been difficult to study from a scientific perspective. At the same time, students often have limited opportunities to understand or make sense of topics because many curricula have emphasized memory rather than understanding. Textbooks are filled with facts that students are expected to memorize, and most tests assess students' abilities to remember the facts. When studying about veins and arteries, for example, students may be expected to remember that arteries are thicker than veins, more elastic, and carry blood from the heart; veins carry blood back to the heart. A test item for this information may look like the following:

1. Arteries
   a. Are more elastic than veins
   b. Carry blood that is pumped from the heart
   c. Are less elastic than veins
   d. Both a and b
   e. Both b and c

The new science of learning does not deny that facts are important for thinking and problem solving. Research on expertise in areas such as chess, history, science, and mathematics demonstrate that experts' abilities to think and solve problems depend strongly on a rich body of knowledge about subject matter (e.g., Chase and Simon, 1973; Chi et al., 1981; deGroot, 1965). However, the research also shows clearly that "usable knowledge" is not the same as a mere list of disconnected facts. Experts' knowledge is connected and organized around important concepts (e.g., Newton's second law of motion); it is "conditionalized" to specify the contexts in which it is applicable; it supports understanding and transfer (to other contexts) rather than only the ability to remember.

For example, people who are knowledgeable about veins and arteries know more than the facts noted above: they also understand why veins and arteries have particular properties. They know that blood pumped from the heart exits in spurts and that the elasticity of the arteries helps accommodate pressure changes. They know that blood from the heart needs to move upward (to the brain) as well as downward and that the elasticity of an artery permits it to function as a one-way valve that closes at the end of each spurt and prevents the blood from flowing backward. Because they understand relationships between the structure and function of veins and arteries, knowledgeable individuals are more likely to be able to use what they have learned to solve novel problems—to show evidence of transfer. For example, imagine being asked to design an artificial artery—would it have to be elastic? Why or why not? An understanding of reasons for the properties of arteries suggests that elasticity may not be necessary—perhaps the problem can be solved by creating a conduit that is strong enough to handle the pressure of spurts from the heart and also function as a one-way valve. An understanding of veins and arteries does not guarantee an answer to this design question, but it does support thinking about alternatives that are not readily available if one only memorizes facts (Bransford and Stein, 1993).

Pre-Existing Knowledge

An emphasis on understanding leads to one of the primary characteristics of the new science of learning: its focus on the processes of knowing (e.g., Piaget, 1978; Vygotsky, 1978). Humans are viewed as goal-directed agents who actively seek information. They come to formal education with a range of prior knowledge, skills, beliefs, and concepts that significantly influence what they notice about the environment and how they organize and interpret it. This, in turn, affects their abilities to remember, reason, solve problems, and acquire new knowledge.

Even young infants are active learners who bring a point of view to the learning setting. The world they enter is not a "booming, buzzing confusion" (James, 1890), where every stimulus is equally salient. Instead, an infant's brain gives precedence to certain kinds of information: language, basic concepts of number, physical properties, and the movement of animate and inanimate objects. In the most general sense, the contemporary view of learning is that people construct new knowledge and understandings based on what they already know and believe (e.g., Cobb, 1994; Piaget, 1952, 1973a,b, 1977, 1978; Vygotsky, 1962, 1978). A classic children's book illustrates this point;

A logical extension of the view that new knowledge must be constructed from existing knowledge is that teachers need to pay attention to the incomplete understandings, the false beliefs, and the naive renditions of concepts that learners bring with them to a given subject. Teachers then need to build on these ideas in ways that help each student achieve a more mature understanding. If students' initial ideas and beliefs are ignored, the understandings that they develop can be very different from what the teacher intends.

Consider the challenge of working with children who believe that the earth is flat and attempting to help them understand that it is spherical. When told it is round, children picture the earth as a pancake rather than as a sphere (Vosniadou and Brewer, 1989). If they are then told that it is round like a sphere, they interpret the new information about a spherical earth within their flat-earth view by picturing a pancake-like flat surface inside or on top of a sphere, with humans standing on top of the pancake. The children's construction of their new understandings has been guided by a model of the earth that helped them explain how they could stand or walk upon its surface, and a spherical earth did not fit their mental model. Like *Fish Is Fish*, everything the children heard was incorporated into that pre-existing view.

Fish Is Fish is relevant not only for young children, but for learners of all ages. For example, college students often have developed beliefs about physical and biological phenomena that fit their experiences but do not fit scientific accounts of these phenomena. These preconceptions must be addressed in order for them to change their beliefs (e.g., Confrey, 1990; Mestre, 1994; Minstrell, 1989; Redish, 1996).

FISH IS FISH

Fish Is Fish (Lionni, 1970) describes a fish who is keenly interested in learning about what happens on land, but the fish cannot explore land because it can only breathe in water. It befriends a tadpole who grows into a frog and eventually goes out onto the land. The frog returns to the pond a few weeks later and reports on what he has seen. The frog describes all kinds of things like birds, cows, and people. The book shows pictures of the fish's representations of each of these descriptions: each is a fish-like form that is slightly adapted to accommodate the frog's descriptions—people are imagined to be fish who walk on their tailfins, birds are fish with wings, cows are fish with udders. This tale illustrates both the creative opportunities and dangers inherent in the fact that people construct new knowledge based on their current knowledge.

A common misconception regarding "constructivist" theories of knowing (that existing knowledge is used to build new knowledge) is that teachers should never tell students anything directly but, instead, should always allow them to construct knowledge for themselves. This perspective confuses a theory of pedagogy (teaching) with a theory of knowing. Constructivists assume that all knowledge is constructed from previous knowledge, irrespective of how one is taught (e.g., Cobb, 1994)—even listening to a lecture involves active attempts to construct new knowledge. *Fish Is Fish* (Lionni, 1970) and attempts to teach children that the earth is round (Vosniadou and Brewer, 1989) show why simply providing lectures frequently does not work. Nevertheless, there are times, usually after people have first grappled with issues on their own, that "teaching by telling" can work extremely well (e.g., Schwartz and Bransford, in press). However, teachers still need to pay attention to students' interpretations and provide guidance when necessary.

There is a good deal of evidence that learning is enhanced when teachers pay attention to the knowledge and beliefs that learners bring to a learning task, use this knowledge as a starting point for new instruction, and monitor students' changing conceptions as instruction proceeds. For example, sixth graders in a suburban school who were given inquiry-based physics instruction were shown to do better on conceptual physics problems than eleventh and twelfth grade physics students taught by conventional methods in the same school system. A second study comparing seventh-ninth grade urban students with the eleventh and twelfth grade suburban physics students again showed that the younger students, taught by the inquiry-based approach, had a better grasp of the fundamental principles of physics (White and Frederickson, 1997, 1998). New curricula for young children have also demonstrated results that are extremely promising: for example, a new approach to teaching geometry helped second-grade children learn to represent and visualize three-dimensional forms in ways that exceeded the skills of a comparison group of undergraduate students at a leading university (Lehrer and Chazan, 1998). Similarly, young children have been taught to demonstrate powerful forms of early geometry generalizations (Lehrer and Chazan, 1998) and generalizations about science (Schauble et al., 1995; Warren and Rosebery, 1996).

Active Learning

New developments in the science of learning also emphasize the importance of helping people take control of their own learning. Since understanding is viewed as important, people must learn to recognize when they understand and when they need more information. What strategies might they use to assess whether they understand someone else's meaning? What kinds of evidence do they need in order to believe particular claims? How can they build their own theories of phenomena and test them effectively?

Many important activities that support active learning have been studied under the heading of "metacognition," Metacognition refers to people's abilities to predict their performances on various tasks (e.g., how well they will be able to remember various stimuli) and to monitor their current levels of mastery and understanding (e.g., Brown, 1975; Flavell, 1973). Teaching practices congruent with a metacognitive approach to learning include those that focus on sense-making, self-assessment, and reflection on what worked and what needs improving. These practices have been shown to increase the degree to which students transfer their learning to new settings and events (e.g., Palincsar and Brown, 1984; Scardamalia et al., 1984; Schoenfeld, 1983, 1985, 1991).

Imagine three teachers whose practices affect whether students learn to take control of their own learning (Scardamalia and Bereiter, 1991). Teacher A's goal is to get the students to produce work; this is accomplished by supervising and overseeing the quantity and quality of the work done by the students. The focus is on activities, which could be anything from old-style workbook activities to the trendiest of space-age projects. Teacher B assumes responsibility for what the students are learning as they carry out their activities. Teacher C does this as well, but with the added objective of continually turning more of the learning process over to the students. Walking into a classroom, you cannot immediately tell these three kinds of teachers apart. One of the things you might see is the students working in groups to produce videos or multimedia presentations. The teacher is likely to be found going from group to group, checking how things are going and responding to requests. Over the course of a few days, however, differences between Teacher A and Teacher B would become evident. Teacher A's focus is entirely on the production process and its products—whether the students are engaged, whether everyone is getting fair treatment, and whether they are turning out good pieces of work. Teacher B attends to all of this as well, but Teacher B is also attending to what the students are learning from the experience and is taking steps to ensure that the students are processing content and not just dealing with show. To see a difference between Teachers B and C, however, you might need to go back into the history of the media production project. What brought it about in the first place? Was it conceived from the start as a learning activity, or did it emerge from the students' own knowledge building efforts? In one striking example of a Teacher C classroom, the students had been studying cockroaches and had learned so much from their reading and observation that they wanted to share it with the rest of the school; the production of a video came about to achieve that purpose (Lamon et al., 1997).

The differences in what might seem to be the same learning activity are thus quite profound. In Teacher A's classroom, the students are learning something of media production, but the media production may very well be getting in the way of learning anything else. In Teacher B's classroom, the teacher is working to ensure that the original educational purposes of the activity are met, that it does not deteriorate into a mere media production exercise. In Teacher C's classroom, the media production is continuous with and a direct outgrowth of the learning that is embodied in the media production. The greater part of Teacher C's work has been done before the idea of a media production even comes up, and it remains only to help the students keep sight of their purposes as they carry out the project.

These hypothetical teachers—A, B, and C—are abstract models that of course fit real teachers only partly, and more on some days than others. Nevertheless, they provide important glimpses of connections between goals for learning and teaching practices that can affect students' abilities to accomplish these goals.

Implications for Education

Overall, the new science of learning is beginning to provide knowledge to improve significantly people's abilities to become active learners who seek to understand complex subject matter and are better prepared to transfer what they have learned to new problems and settings. Making this happen is a major challenge (e.g., Elmore et al., 1996), but it is not impossible. The emerging science of learning underscores the importance of re-thinking what is taught, how it is taught, and how learning is assessed. These ideas are developed throughout this report.

An Evolving Science

This volume synthesizes the scientific basis of learning. The scientific achievements include a fuller understanding of: (1) memory and the structure of knowledge; (2) problem solving and reasoning; (3) the early foundations of learning; (4) regulatory processes that govern learning, including meta-cognition; and (5) how symbolic thinking emerges from the culture and community of the learner.

These key characteristics of learned proficiency by no means plumb the depths of human cognition and learning. What has been learned about the principles that guide some aspects of learning do not constitute a complete picture of the principles that govern all domains of learning. The scientific bases, while not superficial in themselves, do represent only a surface level of a complete understanding of the subject. Only a few domains of learning have been examined in depth, as reflected in this book, and new, emergent areas, such as interactive technologies (Greenfield and Cocking, 1996) are challenging generalizations from older research studies.

As scientists continue to study learning, new research procedures and methodologies are emerging that are likely to alter current theoretical conceptions of learning, such as computational modeling research. The scientific work encompasses a broad range of cognitive and neuroscience issues in learning, memory, language, and cognitive development. Studies of parallel distributed processing, for example (McClelland et al., 1995; Plaut et al., 1996; Munakata et al., 1997; McClelland and Chappell, 1998) look at learning as occurring through the adaptation of connections among participating neurons. The research is designed to develop explicit computational models to refine and extend basic principles, as well as to apply the models to substantive research questions through behavioral experiments, computer simulations, functional brain imaging, and mathematical analyses. These studies are thus contributing to modification of both theory and practice. New models also encompass learning in adulthood to add an important dimension to the scientific knowledge base.

Overview of the Book

Figure 5.4 illustrates the organization of this book. This chapter (Chapter 1) represents the framework of the committee's study. We then focus on what is known about learners and learning, followed by

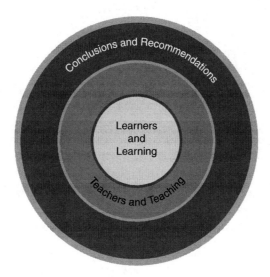

FIGURE 5.4 Report Overview

the implications of this research for the design of effective learning environments, including roles for technology, while emphasizing the key role of teachers. We end with a set of conclusions and recommendations for future research.

It is important to keep in mind that there has been a longer history of rigorous research on issues of learners and learning than on the design of learning environments and the implications of technology. Research on classroom-based learning and teacher learning (especially the many opportunities for informal learning) often use newer qualitative methodologies, such as ethnography and case-study analysis, to capture the richness of learning in context. A rigorous methodology has been developed for conducting such studies (e.g., see Erickson, 1986; Hammersly and Atkinson, 1983; Heath, 1982; Lincoln and Guba, 1985; Marshall and Rossman, 1955; Miles and Huberman, 1984; Spradley, 1979).

What is known about experts is important not because all students are expected to become experts, but because the knowledge of expertise provides valuable insights into what the results of effective learning look like.

Special emphasis is placed on understanding the kinds of learning experiences that lead to transfer—the ability to use what was learned in one setting to deal with new problems and events.

Data show that children's early competencies in areas such as causal relationships, numbers, and language are much more sophisticated than was previously believed. These competencies provide the foundations for important concepts and ideas that children build on in later learning.

Neuroscience provides converging evidence about processes of learning and development and enriches understanding of learning by explicating the mechanisms by which learning occurs.

It explores the degree to which environments are learner centered, knowledge centered, assessment centered, and community centered. These components must be brought into alignment in order for effective change to occur.

We present contrasting illustrations of effective teaching in history, mathematics, and science. Effective teaching practices vary across subjects because knowledge in different subjects is organized differently and based on different ways of knowing (epistemologies).

The science of learning has important implications for helping teachers continue to learn throughout their lives.

We discuss data on technology and learning when they exist, but we also discuss new possibilities that future research should explore.

How Experts Differ from Novices

People who have developed expertise in particular areas are, by definition, able to think effectively about problems in those areas. Understanding expertise is important because it provides insights into the nature of thinking and problem solving. Research shows that it is not simply general abilities, such as memory or intelligence, nor the use of general strategies that differentiate experts from novices. Instead, experts have acquired extensive knowledge that affects what they notice and how they organize, represent, and interpret information in their environment. This, in turn, affects their abilities to remember, reason, and solve problems.

This chapter illustrates key scientific findings that have come from the study of people who have developed expertise in areas such as chess, physics, mathematics, electronics, and history. We discuss these examples *not* because all school children are expected to become experts in these or any other areas, but because the study of expertise shows what the results of successful learning look like. In later chapters we explore what is known about processes of learning that can eventually lead to the development of expertise.

We consider several key principles of experts' knowledge and their potential implications for learning and instruction:

1. Experts notice features and meaningful patterns of information that are not noticed by novices.
2. Experts have acquired a great deal of content knowledge that is organized in ways that reflect a deep understanding of their subject matter.
3. Experts' knowledge cannot be reduced to sets of isolated facts or propositions but, instead, reflects contexts of applicability: that is, the knowledge is "conditionalized" on a set of circumstances.
4. Experts are able to flexibly retrieve important aspects of their knowledge with little attentional effort.
5. Though experts know their disciplines thoroughly, this does not guarantee that they are able to teach others.
6. Experts have varying levels of flexibility in their approach to new situations.

Meaningful Patterns of Information

One of the earliest studies of expertise demonstrated that the same stimulus is perceived and understood differently, depending on the knowledge that a person brings to the situation. DeGroot (1965) was interested in understanding how world-class chess masters are consistently able to out-think their opponents. Chess masters and less experienced but still extremely good players were shown examples of chess games and asked to think aloud as they decided on the move they would make if they were one of the players; DeGroot's hypothesis was that the chess masters would be more likely than the nonmasters to (a) think through all the possibilities before making a move (greater breadth of search) and (b) think through all the possible countermoves of the opponent for every move considered (greater depth of search). In this pioneering research, the chess masters did exhibit considerable breadth and depth to their searches, but so did the lesser ranked chess players. And none of them conducted searches that covered all the possibilities. Somehow, the chess masters considered possibilities for moves that were of higher quality than those considered by the lesser experienced players. Something other than differences in general strategies seemed to be responsible for differences in expertise.

DeGroot concluded that the knowledge acquired over tens of thousands of hours of chess playing enabled chess masters to out-play their opponents. Specifically, masters were more likely to recognize meaningful chess configurations and realize the strategic implications of these situations;

this recognition allowed them to consider sets of possible moves that were superior to others. The meaningful patterns seemed readily apparent to the masters, leading deGroot (1965:33–34) to note:

> We know that increasing experience and knowledge in a specific field (chess, for instance) has the effect that things (properties, etc.) which, at earlier stages, had to be abstracted, or even inferred are apt to be immediately perceived at later stages. To a rather large extent, abstraction is replaced by perception, but we do not know much about how this works, nor where the borderline lies. As an effect of this replacement, a so-called 'given' problem situation is not really given since it is seen differently by an expert than it is perceived by an inexperienced person . . . .

DeGroot's think-aloud method provided for a very careful analysis of the conditions of specialized learning and the kinds of conclusions one can draw from them (see Ericsson and Simon, 1993). Hypotheses generated from think-aloud protocols are usually cross-validated through the use of other methodologies.

The superior recall ability of experts, illustrated in the example in the box, has been explained in terms of how they "chunk" various elements of a configuration that are related by an underlying function or strategy. Since there are limits on the amount of information that people can hold in short-term memory, short-term memory is enhanced when people are able to chunk information into familiar patterns (Miller, 1956). Chess masters perceive chunks of meaningful information, which affects their memory for what they see. Chess masters are able to chunk together several chess pieces in a configuration that is governed by some strategic component of the game. Lacking a hierarchical, highly organized structure for the domain, novices cannot use this chunking strategy. It is noteworthy that people do not have to be world-class experts to benefit from their abilities to encode meaningful chunks of information: 10- and 11-year-olds who are experienced in chess are able to remember more chess pieces than college students who are not chess players. In contrast, when the college students were presented with other stimuli, such as strings of numbers, they were able to remember more (Chi, 1978; Schneider et al., 1993);

Skills similar to those of master chess players have been demonstrated for experts in other domains, including electronic circuitry (Egan and Schwartz, 1979), radiology (Lesgold, 1988), and computer programming (Ehrlich and Soloway, 1984). In each case, expertise in a domain helps people develop a sensitivity to patterns of meaningful information that are not available to novices. For example, electronics technicians were able to reproduce large portions of complex circuit diagrams after only a few seconds of viewing; novices could not. The expert circuit technicians chunked several individual circuit elements (e.g., resistors and capacitors) that performed the function of an amplifier. By remembering the structure and function of a typical amplifier, experts were able to recall the arrangement of many of the individual circuit elements comprising the "amplifier chunk."

Mathematics experts are also able to quickly recognize patterns of information, such as particular problem types that involve specific classes of mathematical solutions (Hinsley et al., 1977; Robinson and Hayes, 1978). For example, physicists recognize problems of river currents and problems of headwinds and tailwinds in airplanes as involving similar mathematical principles, such as relative velocities. The expert knowledge that underlies the ability to recognize problem types has been characterized as involving the development of organized conceptual structures, or schemas, that guide how problems are represented and understood (e.g., Glaser and Chi, 1988).

Expert teachers, too, have been shown to have schemas similar to those found in chess and mathematics. Expert and novice teachers were shown a videotaped classroom lesson (Sabers et al., 1991). The experimental set-up involved three screens that showed simultaneous events occurring throughout the classroom (the left, center, and right). During part of the session, the expert and novice teachers were asked to talk aloud about what they were seeing. Later, they were asked questions about classroom events. Overall, the expert teachers had very different understandings of the events they were watching than did the novice teachers;

WHAT EXPERTS SEE

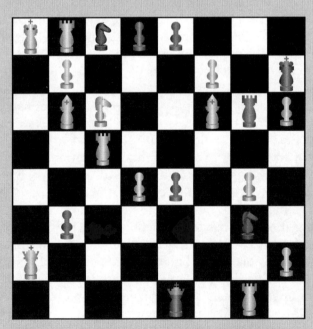

FIGURE 5.5 Chess board positions used in memory experiments.

Source: Adapted from Chase and Simon (1973).

In one study, a chess master, a Class A player (good but not a master), and a novice were given 5 seconds to view a chess board position from the middle of a chess game; see Figure 5.5. After 5 seconds the board was covered, and each participant attempted to reconstruct the board position on another board. This procedure was repeated for multiple trials until everyone received a perfect score. On the first trial, the master player correctly placed many more pieces than the Class A player, who in turn placed more than the novice: 16, 8, and 4, respectively.

However, these results occurred only when the chess pieces were arranged in configurations that conformed to meaningful games of chess. When chess pieces were randomized and presented for 5 seconds, the recall of the chess master and Class A player were the same as the novice—they placed from 2 to 3 positions correctly. Data over trials for valid and random middle games are shown in Figure 5.6.

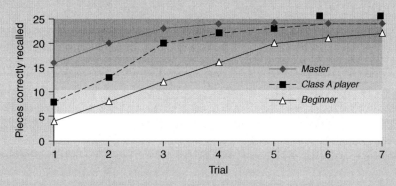

FIGURE 5.6 Recall by chess players by level of expertise.

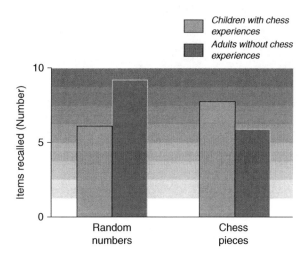

FIGURE 5.7 Recall for numbers and chess pieces.

Source: Adapted from Chi (1978).

The idea that experts recognize features and patterns that are not noticed by novices is potentially important for improving instruction. When viewing instructional texts, slides, and videotapes, for example, the information noticed by novices can be quite different from what is noticed by experts (e.g., Sabers et al., 1991; Bransford et al., 1988). One dimension of acquiring greater competence appears to be the increased ability to segment the perceptual field (learning how to see). Research on expertise suggests the importance of providing students with learning experiences that specifically enhance their abilities to recognize meaningful patterns of information (e.g., Simon, 1980; Bransford et al., 1989).

Organization of Knowledge

We turn now to the question of how experts' knowledge is organized and how this affects their abilities to understand and represent problems. Their knowledge is not simply a list of facts and formulas that are relevant to their domain; instead, their knowledge is organized around core concepts or "big ideas" that guide their thinking about their domains.

WHAT EXPERT AND NOVICE TEACHERS NOTICE

Expert and novice teachers notice very different things when viewing a videotape of a classroom lesson.

Expert 6: On the left monitor, the students' note taking indicates that they have seen sheets like this and have had presentations like this before; it's fairly efficient at this point because they're used to the format they are using.

Expert 7: I don't understand why the students can't be finding out this information on their own rather than listening to someone tell them because if you watch the faces of most of them, they start out for about the first 2 or 3 minutes sort of paying attention to what's going on and then just drift off.

Expert 2: . . . I haven't heard a bell, but the students are already at their desks and seem to be doing purposeful activity, and this is about the time that I decide they must be an accelerated group because they came into the room and started something rather than just sitting down and socializing.

Novice 1: . . . I can't tell what they are doing. They're getting ready for class, but I can't tell what they're doing.

Novice 3: She's trying to communicate with them here about something, but I sure couldn't tell what it was.

Another novice: It's a lot to watch.

In an example from physics, experts and competent beginners (college students) were asked to describe verbally the approach they would use to solve physics problems. Experts usually mentioned the major principle(s) or law(s) that were applicable to the problem, together with a rationale for why those laws applied to the problem and how one could apply them (Chi et al., 1981). In contrast, competent beginners rarely referred to major principles and laws in physics; instead, they typically described which equations they would use and how those equations would be manipulated (Larkin, 1981, 1983).

Experts' thinking seems to be organized around big ideas in physics, such as Newton's second law and how it would apply, while novices tend to perceive problem solving in physics as memorizing, recalling, and manipulating equations to get answers. When solving problems, experts in physics often pause to draw a simple qualitative diagram—they do not simply attempt to plug numbers into a formula. The diagram is often elaborated as the expert seeks to find a workable solution path (e.g., see Larkin et al., 1980; Larkin and Simon, 1987; Simon and Simon, 1978).

Differences in how physics experts and novices approach problems can also be seen when they are asked to sort problems, written on index cards, according to the approach that could be used to solve them (Chi et al., 1981). Experts' problem piles are arranged on the basis of the principles that can be applied to solve the problems; novices' piles are arranged on the basis of the problems' surface attributes. For example, in the physics sub-field of mechanics, an expert's pile might consist of problems that can be solved by conservation of energy, while a novice's pile might consist of problems that contain inclined planes; see Figure 5.8. Responding to the surface characteristics of problems is not very useful, since two problems that share the same objects and look very similar may actually be solved by entirely different approaches.

Some studies of experts and novices in physics have explored the organization of the knowledge structures that are available to these different groups of individuals (Chi et al., 1982); In representing a schema for an incline plane, the novice's schema contains primarily surface features of the incline plane. In contrast, the expert's schema immediately connects the notion of an incline plane with the laws of physics and the conditions under which laws are applicable.

Pause times have also been used to infer the structure of expert knowledge in domains such as chess and physics. Physics experts appear to evoke sets of related equations, with the recall of one equation activating related equations that are retrieved rapidly (Larkin, 1979). Novices, in contrast, retrieve equations more equally spaced in time, suggesting a sequential search in memory. Experts appear to possess an efficient organization of knowledge with meaningful relations among related elements clustered into related units that are governed by underlying concepts and principles; Within this picture of expertise, "knowing more" means having more conceptual chunks in memory, more relations or features defining each chunk, more interrelations among the chunks, and efficient methods for retrieving related chunks and procedures for applying these informational units in problem-solving contexts (Chi et al., 1981).

Differences between how experts and nonexperts organize knowledge has also been demonstrated in such fields as history (Wineburg, 1991). A group of history experts and a group of gifted, high-achieving high school seniors enrolled in an advanced placement course in history were first given a test of facts about the American Revolution. The historians with backgrounds in American history knew most of the items. However, many of the historians had specialties that lay elsewhere and they knew only one-third of the facts on the tests. Several of the students outscored several of the historians on the factual test. The study then compared how the historians and students made sense of historical documents; the result revealed dramatic differences on virtually any criterion. The historians excelled in the elaborateness of understandings they developed in their ability to pose alternative explanations for events and in their use of corroborating evidence. This depth of understanding was as true for the Asian specialists and the medievalists as it was for the Americanists.

When the two groups were asked to select one of three pictures that best reflect their understanding of the battle of Lexington, historians and students displayed the greatest differences. Historians carefully navigated back and forth between the corpus of written documents and the three images of the battlefield. For them, the picture selection task was the quint-essential epistemological exercise, a task that explored the limits of historical knowledge. They knew that no single document or picture could tell the story of history; hence, they thought very hard about their choices. In contrast, the students generally just looked at the pictures and made a selection without regard or qualification. For students, the process was similar to finding the correct answer on a multiple choice test.

In sum, although the students scored very well on facts about history, they were largely unacquainted with modes of inquiry with real historical thinking. They had no systematic way of making sense of contradictory claims. Thrust into a set of historical documents that demanded that they sort out competing claims and formulate a reasoned interpretation, the students, on the whole, were stymied. They lacked the experts' deep understanding of how to formulate reasoned interpretations of sets of historical documents. Experts in other social sciences also organize their problem solving around big ideas (see, e.g., Voss et al., 1984).

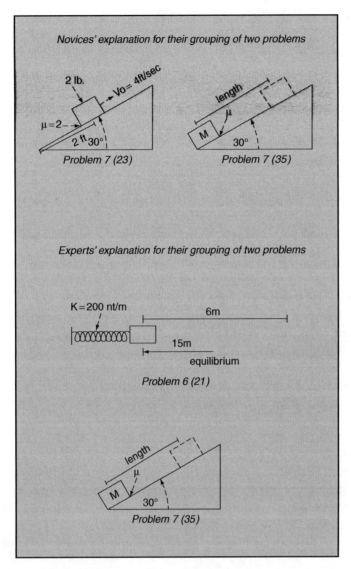

Novices' explanation for their grouping of two problems

Problem 7 (23)

Problem 7 (35)

Explanations

Novice 1: These deal with blocks on an incline plane.

Novice 5: Incline plane problems, coefficient of friction.

Novice 6: Blocks on inclined planes with angles.

Experts' explanation for their grouping of two problems

Problem 6 (21)

Problem 7 (35)

Explanations

Expert 2: Conservation of energy.

Expert 3: Work-theory theorem. They are all straight-forward problems.

Expert 4: These can be done from energy considerations. Either you should know the principle of conservation of energy, or work is lost somewhere.

FIGURE 5.8 An example of sortings of physics problems made by novices and experts. Each picture above represents a diagram that can be drawn from the storyline of a physics problem taken from on introductory physics textbook. The novices and experts in this study were asked to categorize many such problems based on similarity of solution. The two pairs show a marked contrast in the experts' and novices' categorization schemes. Novices tend to categorize physics problems as being solved similarly if they "look the same" (that is, share the same surface features), whereas experts categorize according to the major principle that could be applied to solve the problems.

Source: Adapted from Chi et al. (1981).

The fact that experts' knowledge is organized around important ideas or concepts suggests that curricula should also be organized in ways that lead to conceptual understanding. Many approaches to curriculum design make it difficult for students to organize knowledge meaningfully. Often there is only superficial coverage of facts before moving on to the next topic; there is little time to develop important, organizing ideas. History texts sometimes emphasize facts without providing support for understanding (e.g., Beck et al., 1989, 1991). Many ways of teaching science also overemphasize facts (American Association for the Advancement of Science, 1989; National Research Council, 1996).

UNDERSTANDING AND PROBLEM SOLVING

In mathematics, experts are more likely than novices to first try to understand problems, rather than simply attempt to plug numbers into formulas. Experts and students in one study (Paige and Simon, 1966) were asked to solve algebra word problems, such as:

A board was sawed into two pieces. One piece was two-thirds as long as the whole board and was exceeded in length by the second piece by four feet. How long was the board before it was cut?

The experts quickly realize that the problem as stated is logically impossible. Although some students also come to this realization, others simply apply equations, which results in the answer of a negative length.

A similar example comes from a study of adults and children (Reusser, 1993), who were asked: There are 26 sheep and 10 goats on a ship. How old is the captain?

Most adults have enough expertise to realize that this problem is unsolvable, but many school children didn't realize this at all. More than three-quarters of the children in one study attempted to provide a numerical answer to the problems. They asked themselves whether to add, subtract, multiply, or divide, rather than whether the problem made sense. As one fifth-grade child explained, after giving the answer of 36: "Well, you need to add or subtract or multiply in problems like this, and this one seemed to work best if I add" (Bransford and Stein, 1993:196).

The Third International Mathematics and Science Survey (TIMSS) (Schmidt et al., 1997) criticized curricula that were "a mile wide and an inch deep" and argued that this is much more of a problem in America than in most other countries. Research on expertise suggests that a superficial coverage of many topics in the domain may be a poor way to help students develop the competencies that will prepare them for future learning and work. The idea of helping students organize their knowledge also suggests that novices might benefit from models of how experts approach problem solving—especially if they then receive coaching in using similar strategies (e.g., Brown et al., 1989);

CONTEXT AND ACCESS TO KNOWLEDGE

Experts have a vast repertoire of knowledge that is relevant to their domain or discipline, but only a subset of that knowledge is relevant to any particular problem. Experts do not have to search through everything they know in order to find what is relevant; such an approach would overwhelm their working memory (Miller, 1956). For example, the chess masters described above considered only a subset of possible chess moves, but those moves were generally superior to the ones considered by the lesser ranked players. Experts have not only acquired knowledge, but are also good at retrieving the knowledge that is relevant to a particular task. In the language of cognitive scientists, experts' knowledge is "conditionalized"— it includes a specification of the contexts in which it is useful (Simon, 1980; Glaser, 1992). Knowledge that is not conditionalized is often "inert" because it is not activated, even though it is relevant (Whitehead, 1929).

The concept of conditionalized knowledge has implications for the design of curriculum, instruction, and assessment practices that promote effective learning. Many forms of curricula and instruction do not help students conditionalize their knowledge: "Textbooks are much more explicit in enunciating the laws of mathematics or of nature than in saying anything about when these laws may be useful in solving problems" (Simon, 1980:92). It is left largely to students to generate the condition-action pairs required for solving novel problems.

One way to help students learn about conditions of applicability is to assign word problems that require students to use appropriate concepts and formulas (Lesgold, 1984, 1988; Simon, 1980). If well designed, these problems can help students learn when, where, and why to use the knowledge they are learning. Sometimes, however, students can solve sets of practice problems but fail to conditional-ize their knowledge because they know which chapter the problems came from and so automatically use this information to decide which concepts and formulas are relevant. Practice problems that are organized into very structured worksheets can also cause this problem. Sometimes students who have done well on such assignments—and believe that they are learning—are unpleasantly surprised when they take tests in which problems from the entire course are randomly presented so there are no clues about where they appeared in a text (Bransford, 1979).

The concept of conditionalized knowledge also has important implications for assessment practices that provide feedback about learning. Many types of tests fail to help teachers and students assess the degree to which the students' knowledge is conditionalized. For example, students might be asked whether the formula that quantifies the relationship between mass and energy is $E = MC$, $E = MC^2$, or $E = MC^3$. A correct answer requires no knowledge of the conditions under which it is appropriate to use the formula. Similarly, students in a literature class might be asked to explain the meaning of familiar proverbs, such as "he who hesitates is lost" or "too many cooks spoil the broth." The ability to explain the meaning of each proverb provides no guarantee that students will know the conditions under which either proverb is useful. Such knowledge is important because, when viewed solely as proposi-tions, proverbs often contradict one another. To use them effectively, people need to know when and why it is appropriate to apply the maxim "too many cooks spoil the broth" versus "many hands make light work" or "he who hesitates is lost" versus "haste makes waste" (see Bransford and Stein, 1993).

FLUENT RETRIEVAL

People's abilities to retrieve relevant knowledge can vary from being "effortful" to "relatively effort-less" (fluent) to "automatic" (Schneider and Shiffrin, 1977). Automatic and fluent retrieval are impor-tant characteristics of expertise.

Fluent retrieval does not mean that experts always perform a task faster than novices. Because experts attempt to understand problems rather than to jump immediately to solution strategies, they sometimes take more time than novices (e.g., Getzels and Csikszentmihalyi, 1976). But within the overall process of problem solving there are a number of subprocesses that, for experts, vary from fluent to automatic. Fluency is important because effortless processing places fewer demands on conscious attention. Since the amount of information a person can attend to at any one time is limited (Miller, 1956), ease of processing some aspects of a task gives a person more capacity to attend to other aspects of the task (LaBerge and Samuels, 1974; Schneider and Shiffrin, 1985; Anderson, 1981, 1982; Lesgold et al., 1988).

Learning to drive a car provides a good example of fluency and automaticity. When first learn-ing, novices cannot drive and simultaneously carry on a conversation. With experience, it becomes easy to do so. Similarly, novice readers whose ability to decode words is not yet fluent are unable to devote attention to the task of understanding what they are reading (LaBerge and Samuels, 1974). Issues of fluency are very important for understanding learning and instruction. Many instructional environments stop short of helping all students develop the fluency needed to successfully perform cognitive tasks (Beck et al., 1989; Case, 1978; Hasselbring et al., 1987; LaBerge and Samuels, 1974).

An important aspect of learning is to become fluent at recognizing problem types in particular domains—such as problems involving Newton's second law or concepts of rate and functions—so that appropriate solutions can be easily retrieved from memory. The use of instructional procedures that speed pattern recognition are promising in this regard (e.g., Simon, 1980).

EXPERTS AND TEACHING

Expertise in a particular domain does not guarantee that one is good at helping others learn it. In fact, expertise can sometimes hurt teaching because many experts forget what is easy and what is difficult for students. Recognizing this fact, some groups who design educational materials pair content area experts with "accomplished novices" whose area of expertise lies elsewhere: their task is to continually challenge the experts until the experts' ideas for instruction begin to make sense to them (Cognition and Technology Group at Vanderbilt, 1997).

The content knowledge necessary for expertise in a discipline needs to be differentiated from the pedagogical content knowledge that underlies effective teaching (Redish, 1996; Shulman, 1986, 1987). The latter includes information about typical difficulties that students encounter as they attempt to learn about a set of topics; typical paths students must traverse in order to achieve understanding; and sets of potential strategies for helping students overcome the difficulties that they encounter. Shulman (1986, 1987) argues that pedagogical content knowledge is not equivalent to knowledge of a content domain plus a generic set of teaching strategies; instead, teaching strategies differ across disciplines. Expert teachers know the kinds of difficulties that students are likely to face; they know how to tap into students' existing knowledge in order to make new information meaningful; and they know how to assess their students' progress. Expert teachers have acquired pedagogical content knowledge as well as content knowledge; In the absence of pedagogical content knowledge, teachers often rely on textbook publishers for decisions about how to best organize subjects for students. They are therefore forced to rely on the "prescriptions of absentee curriculum developers" (Brophy, 1983), who know nothing about the particular students in each teacher's classroom. Pedagogical content knowledge is an extremely important part of what teachers need to learn to be more effective. (This topic is discussed more fully in Chapter 7.)

ADAPTIVE EXPERTISE

An important question for educators is whether some ways of organizing knowledge are better at helping people remain flexible and adaptive to new situations than others. For example, contrast two types of Japanese sushi experts (Hatano, 1990): one excels at following a fixed recipe; the other has "adaptive expertise" and is able to prepare sushi quite creatively. These appear to be examples of two very different types of expertise, one that is relatively routinized and one that is flexible and more adaptable to external demands: experts have been characterized as being "merely skilled" versus "highly competent" or more colorfully as "artisans" versus "virtuosos" (Miller, 1978). These differences apparently exist across a wide range of jobs.

One analysis looked at these differences in terms of information systems design (Miller, 1978). Information systems designers typically work with clients who specify what they want. The goal of the designer is to construct systems that allow people to efficiently store and access relevant information (usually through computers). Artisan experts seek to identify the functions that their clients want automated; they tend to accept the problem and its limits as stated by the clients. They approach new problems as opportunities to use their existing expertise to do familiar tasks more efficiently. It is important to emphasize that artisans' skills are often extensive and should not be underestimated. In contrast, however, the virtuoso experts treat the client's statement of the problem with respect, but consider it "a point for departure and exploration" (Miller, 1978). They view assignments as opportunities to explore and expand their current levels of expertise. Miller also observes that, in his experience, virtuosos exhibit their positive characteristics *despite* their training, which is usually restricted solely to technical skills.

TEACHING HAMLET

Two new English teachers, Jake and Steven, with similar subject-matter backgrounds from elite private universities, set out to teach *Hamlet* in high school (Grossman, 1990).

In his teaching, Jake spent 7 weeks leading his students through a word-by-word *explication du texte*, focusing on notions of "linguistic reflexivity," and issues of modernism. His assignments included in-depth analyses of soliloquies, memorization of long passages, and a final paper on the importance of language in *Hamlet*. Jake's model for this instruction was his own undergraduate coursework; there was little transformation of his knowledge, except to parcel it out in chunks that fit into the 50-minute containers of the school day. Jake's image for how students would respond was his own responses as a student who loved Shakespeare and delighted in close textual analysis. Consequently, when students responded in less than enthusiastic ways, Jake was ill-equipped to understand their confusion: "The biggest problem I have with teaching by far is trying to get into the mind-set of a ninth grader . . ."

Steven began his unit on *Hamlet* without ever mentioning the name of the play. To help his students grasp the initial outline of the themes and issues of the play, he asked them to imagine that their parents had recently divorced and that their mothers had taken up with a new man. This new man had replaced their father at work, and "there's some talk that he had something to do with the ousting of your dad" (Grossman, 1990:24). Steven then asked students to think about the circumstances that might drive them so mad that they would contemplate murdering another human being. Only then, after students had contemplated these issues and done some writing on them, did Steven introduce the play they would be reading.

The concept of adaptive expertise has also been explored in a study of history experts (Wineburg, 1998). Two history experts and a group of future teachers were asked to read and interpret a set of documents about Abraham Lincoln and his view of slavery. This is a complex issue that, for Lincoln, involved conflicts between enacted law (the Constitution), natural law (as encoded in the Declaration of Independence), and divine law (assumptions about basic rights). One of the historians was an expert on Lincoln; the second historian's expertise lay elsewhere. The Lincoln expert brought detailed content knowledge to the documents and easily interpreted them; the other historian was familiar with some of the broad themes in the documents but quickly became confused in the details. In fact, at the beginning of the task, the second historian reacted no differently than a group of future high school teachers who were faced with the same task (Wineburg and Fournier, 1994): attempting to harmonize discrepant information about Lincoln's position, they both appealed to an array of present social forms and institutions—such as speech writers, press conferences, and "spin doctors"— to explain why things seemed discrepant. Unlike the future teachers, however, the second historian did not stop with his initial analysis. He instead adopted a working hypothesis that assumed that the apparent contradictions might be rooted less in Lincoln's duplicity than in his own ignorance of the nineteenth century. The expert stepped back from his own initial interpretation and searched for a deeper understanding of the issues. As he read texts from this perspective, his understanding deepened, and he learned from the experience. After considerable work, the second historian was able to piece together an interpretive structure that brought him by the task's end to where his more knowledgeable colleague had begun. The future history teachers, in contrast, never moved beyond their initial interpretations of events.

An important characteristic exhibited by the history expert involves what is known as "metacognition"— the ability to monitor one's current level of understanding and decide when it is not adequate. The concept of metacognition was originally introduced in the context of studying young children (e.g., Brown, 1980; Flavell, 1985, 1991). For example, young children often erroneously believe that they can remember information and hence fail to use effective strategies, such as rehearsal. The ability to recognize the limits of one's current knowledge, then take steps to remedy the situation, is extremely important for learners at all ages. The history expert who was not a specialist in Lincoln was metacognitive in the sense that he successfully recognized the insufficiency of his initial attempts to explain Lincoln's position. As a consequence, he adopted the working hypothesis that he needed to learn more about the context of Lincoln's times before coming to a reasoned conclusion.

Beliefs about what it means to be an expert can affect the degree to which people explicitly search for what they don't know and take steps to improve the situation. In a study of researchers and veteran teachers, a common assumption was that "an expert is someone who knows all the answers" (Cognition and Technology Group at Vanderbilt, 1997). This assumption had been implicit rather than explicit and had never been questioned and discussed. But when the researchers and teachers discussed this concept, they discovered that it placed severe constraints on new learning because the tendency was to worry about looking competent rather than publicly acknowledging the need for help in certain areas (see Dweck, 1989, for similar findings with students). The researchers and the teachers found it useful to replace their previous model of "answer-filled experts" with the model of "accomplished novices." Accomplished novices are skilled in many areas and proud of their accomplishments, but they realize that what they know is minuscule compared to all that is potentially knowable. This model helps free people to continue to learn even though they may have spent 10 to 20 years as an "expert" in their field.

The concept of adaptive expertise (Hatano, 1990) provides an important model of successful learning. Adaptive experts are able to approach new situations flexibly and to learn throughout their lifetimes. They not only use what they have learned, they are metacognitive and continually question their current levels of expertise and attempt to move beyond them. They don't simply attempt to do the same things more efficiently; they attempt to do things better. A major challenge for theories of learning is to understand how particular kinds of learning experiences develop adaptive expertise or "virtuosos."

CONCLUSION

Experts' abilities to reason and solve problems depend on well-organized knowledge that affects what they notice and how they represent problems. Experts are not simply "general problem solvers" who have learned a set of strategies that operate across all domains. The fact that experts are more likely than novices to recognize meaningful patterns of information applies in all domains, whether chess, electronics, mathematics, or classroom teaching. In deGroot's (1965) words, a "given" problem situation is not really a given. Because of their ability to see patterns of meaningful information, experts begin problem solving at "a higher place" (deGroot, 1965). An emphasis on the patterns perceived by experts suggests that pattern recognition is an important strategy for helping students develop confidence and competence. These patterns provide triggering conditions for accessing knowledge that is relevant to a task.

Studies in areas such as physics, mathematics, and history also demonstrate that experts first seek to develop an understanding of problems, and this often involves thinking in terms of core concepts or big ideas, such as Newton's second law in physics. Novices' knowledge is much less likely to be organized around big ideas; they are more likely to approach problems by searching for correct formulas and pat answers that fit their everyday intuitions.

Curricula that emphasize breadth of knowledge may prevent effective organization of knowledge because there is not enough time to learn anything in depth. Instruction that enables students to see models of how experts organize and solve problems may be helpful. However, as discussed in more detail in later chapters, the level of complexity of the models must be tailored to the learners' current levels of knowledge and skills.

While experts possess a vast repertoire of knowledge, only a subset of it is relevant to any particular problem. Experts do not conduct an exhaustive search of everything they know; this would overwhelm their working memory (Miller, 1956). Instead, information that is relevant to a task tends to be selectively retrieved (e.g., Ericsson and Staszewski, 1989; deGroot, 1965).

The issue of retrieving relevant information provides clues about the nature of usable knowledge. Knowledge must be "conditionalized" in order to be retrieved when it is needed; otherwise, it remains inert (Whitehead, 1929). Many designs for curriculum instruction and assessment practices fail to emphasize the importance of conditionalized knowledge. For example, texts often present facts and formulas with little attention to helping students learn the conditions under which they are most useful. Many assessments measure only propositional (factual) knowledge and never ask whether students know when, where, and why to use that knowledge.

Another important characteristic of expertise is the ability to retrieve relevant knowledge in a manner that is relatively "effortless." This fluent retrieval does not mean that experts always accomplish tasks in less time than novices; often they take more time in order to fully understand a problem. But their ability to retrieve information effortlessly is extremely important because fluency places fewer demands on conscious attention, which is limited in capacity (Schneider and Shiffrin, 1977, 1985). Effortful retrieval, by contrast, places many demands on a learner's attention: attentional effort is being expended on remembering instead of learning. Instruction that focuses solely on accuracy does not necessarily help students develop fluency (e.g., Beck et al., 1989; Hasselbring et al., 1987; LaBerge and Samuels, 1974).

Expertise in an area does not guarantee that one can effectively teach others about that area. Expert teachers know the kinds of difficulties that students are likely to face, and they know how to tap into their students' existing knowledge in order to make new information meaningful plus assess their students' progress. In Shulman's (1986, 1987) terms, expert teachers have acquired pedagogical content knowledge and not just content knowledge.

The concept of adaptive expertise raises the question of whether some ways of organizing knowledge lead to greater flexibility in problem solving than others (Hatano, 1990; Spiro et al., 1991). Differences between the "merely skilled" (artisans) and the "highly competent" (virtuosos) can be seen in fields as disparate as sushi making and information design. Virtuosos not only apply expertise to a given problem, they also consider whether the problem as presented is the best way to begin.

The ability to monitor one's approach to problem solving—to be metacognitive—is an important aspect of the expert's competence. Experts step back from their first, oversimplistic interpretation of a problem or situation and question their own knowledge that is relevant. People's mental models of what it means to be an expert can affect the degree to which they learn throughout their lifetimes. A model that assumes that experts know all the answers is very different from a model of the accomplished novice, who is proud of his or her achievements and yet also realizes that there is much more to learn.

We close this chapter with two important cautionary notes. First, the six principles of expertise need to be considered simultaneously, as parts of an overall system. We divided our discussion into six points in order to facilitate explanation, but each point interacts with the others; this interrelationship has important educational implications. For example, the idea of promoting fluent access to knowledge (principle 4) must be approached with an eye toward helping students develop an understanding of the subject matter (principle 2), learn when, where and why to use information (principle 3), and learn to recognize meaningful patterns of information (principle 1). Furthermore, all these need to be approached from the perspective of helping students develop adaptive expertise (principle 6), which includes helping them become metacognitive about their learning so that they can assess their own progress and continually identify and pursue new learning goals. An example in mathematics is getting students to recognize when a proof is needed. Metacognition can help students develop personally relevant pedagogical content knowledge, analogous to the pedagogical content knowledge available to effective teachers (principle 5). In short, students need to develop the ability to teach themselves.

The second cautionary note is that although the study of experts provides important information about learning and instruction, it can be misleading if applied inappropriately. For example, it would be a mistake simply to expose novices to expert models and assume that the novices will learn effectively; what they will learn depends on how much they know already.

CHAPTER 6

Inclusive Practice and Learner Differentiation

Differentiated Instruction: Inclusive Strategies For Standards-Based Learning That Benefit The Whole Class

— by Diana Lawrence-Brown

INTRODUCTION

Although Jo has severe cognitive disabilities, she has been successfully included in general education classrooms for many years. While she is far behind her classmates, she is making steady progress. Jo is not required to "keep up" with the other students, or to "pass" (in the traditional sense) to be a member of general education classrooms. Instead, individualized goals are set for her by a collaborative team that includes general education teachers, the special education teacher, a speech therapist, an occupational therapist, a part-time paraprofessional, and her parents. Jo's report card reflects her progress toward these IEP (Individual Education Plan) goals.

Jo's favorite subject is science, especially labs. She also enjoys art and wants to be an artist when she leaves school. Her worst subject is social studies. Jo recognizes and can write most consonant letters; she can read a few basic sight words. She recognizes numbers up to 20, and can use manipulatives to solve simple addition and subtraction problems. Jo is one of the most motivated students in her grade. Her strengths are in spatial and interpersonal intelligences. She is outgoing and well-liked by most people she knows at school. Her speech can be difficult to understand. She needs to have changes in her routine explained in advance whenever possible, and may become upset and cry when this is not possible.

An important responsibility of the collaborative team is to identify ways for Jo to meaningfully participate in lessons that would otherwise be much too difficult for her. The team meets regularly to discuss Jo's progress and to collaborate on adaptations needed for upcoming units. For example, when other students perform math operations with large numbers, Jo participates by building models of some of these numbers using hands-on place value manipulatives; this is related to her IEP goal

From *American Secondary Education*, Vol. 32 (3) Summer 2004 by Diana Lawrence-Brown. Copyright © 2004 by Dwight Schar College of Education. Reprinted by permission.

to improve number concepts. Other examples include working on IEP goals to improve her printing and keyboarding skills while the rest of the class works on more complex writing assignments.

Andy is extremely frustrated with school. Although he makes some effort to study for tests, these are largely ineffective. The only resource materials available to him are textbooks which are significantly above his reading level, and his own woefully insufficient notes. He does not understand much of what he tries to read and is currently failing two subjects. Andy is not lacking in intelligence; he is very knowledgeable about his family's horticulture business, for example, and is entrusted to act as the cashier when the family is short-handed. Math is definitely his strong subject; although he has difficulty with memorization, he is generally able to achieve at grade level in this area. The music department considers him one of their more talented students. Whenever grade-level reading and writing are required, however, he is "sunk."

In addition, Andy has never been an easily managed student behaviorally. He is very fidgety in class, and tends to be what even his favorite teacher had labeled as "mischievous." These problems are increasing, and new ones are cropping up. He rips up or refuses to complete assignments, and is disrespectful to his special and general education teachers. He frequently comments that he does not need school, since he is counting on a job in the family business. He has been seen smoking in the parking lot across the street from the school and is increasingly involved in fights on the bus—even on the most recent class trip.

Nita's family has recently immigrated to the United States. Although she is gifted academically and artistically, her spoken English is poor and she is very quiet in class. She has good independent work skills, perhaps too good. She prefers to work alone, and both her parents and her teacher are concerned about her social adjustment. Nita prefers science over any other subject and is visibly uninterested in Social Studies, particularly history. She plans to pursue a Ph.D. in chemistry.

John is an average student academically, although he is not reliable about homework and is prone to cut corners on assignments if he can get away with it. He is also an exceptionally skilled athlete. His heroes are sports superstars, and his outlook on the world is very competitive. He is the first to cry "unfair" if someone in the class is provided with support that is not extended to him, although he does not usually need it. His family is active in local politics; John would like to be the mayor of his town when he grows up.

Classrooms increasingly are populated by students who are diverse in a variety of ways. Of course, even students traditionally found in general education classrooms were not homogeneous. Singer & Donlan (1989), for example, estimated a reading ability span in a typical classroom of two-thirds the average chronological age of the students. In a traditional class of 15-year-olds a teacher should expect a 10-year range of reading levels. Given the availability of strategies such as differentiated instruction, responsible pedagogy no longer allows us to teach as if students all learned in one way, and at the same pace. If we are to maximize achievement of general curriculum standards, we must increase our efforts to differentiate instruction. Differentiated instruction benefits students with a very wide range of ability levels (Neber, Finsterwald, & Urban, 2001), learning styles, and cultural/linguistic backgrounds (Convery & Coyle, 1993).

INCLUSION, HIGH STANDARDS, & DIFFERENTIATED INSTRUCTION

Differentiated instructional planning recognizes and supports the classroom as a community to which age peers belong, where they can and should be nourished as individual learners. According to Tomlinson & Kalbfleisch (1998) differentiated classrooms are "responsive to students' varying readiness levels, varying interests, and varying learning profiles" (p. 54). As explained by Waldron & McLeskey (2001), "differentiating instruction means that teachers will create different levels of expectations for task completion within a lesson or unit" (p. 176). They emphasize helping schools create environments in which all learners can be successful; for inclusion to be successful, all students must benefit. Differentiated instruction is as important for students who find school easy as it is for those who find it difficult. All students benefit from the availability of a variety of methods and supports and an appropriate balance of challenge and success.

The approach described in this article builds upon the work of educators such as Vaughn, Bos, & Schumm (2000), who have extended their basic, 3-level planning pyramid with a modification that allows for individualized goals for students with severe intellectual disabilities. Suggestions presented here build upon systems such as these, with specific attention to the following issues that remain troublesome for many teachers:

- Making multilevel instructional decisions (e.g., who learns at what level?) in a way that is manageable within a standards-based instructional context.
- Devising additional supports for struggling learners, especially resources that can be provided with or without additional staff assigned to the general education classroom.
- Providing an appropriate education for students with special gifts and talents and for students with severe disabilities, who both may be members of the same heterogeneous, inclusive classrooms.
- Differentiating primarily within whole-class lessons, avoiding separate, parallel tasks as much as possible.

Differentiated instruction is helpful to any teacher and critical for teachers in inclusive classrooms. Unlike mainstreaming, inclusive education does not separate students with disabilities who are unable to "keep up" without significant support. This makes differentiated instructional strategies a must, especially given the simultaneous push for all students to achieve high standards. If students with disabilities are to reach higher general curriculum standards, they need to learn in classrooms where they can both access the general curriculum, and reap the benefits of high expectations (Good, 2001; Kolb & Jussim, 1994; Lee & Smith, 1999; Rosenthal & Jacobson, 1968).

THE PROCESS OF DIFFERENTIATED INSTRUCTIONAL PLANNING

This article presents a method for bringing differentiated instruction, inclusive secondary schools, and high standards together using a manageable instructional planning strategy. An additional concern addressed in this article is the potential for reproducing tracking. Care must be taken that, in our efforts to meet the diverse needs found in heterogeneous classrooms, we do not import problems of homogeneous classrooms such as debilitating low expectations for some students.

Differentiation can be thought of as serving two broad goals. The first is to maximize attainment of the grade-level general curriculum standards (represented in Figure 6.1 as a sphere) for all students.

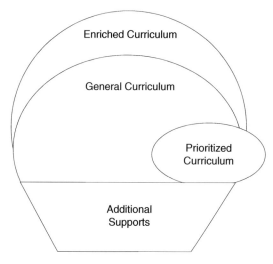

Figure 6.1 A Model of Differentiation.

As the figure shows, an important strategy for maximizing attainment of the general curriculum is providing additional supports for struggling students. The second broad goal is to provide adapted curricula for students who need it. This goal is represented in Figure 6.1 by the areas identified as Enriched and Prioritized curriculum. Each of these elements of differentiation will be discussed in the remainder of this article.

GETTING STARTED WITH DIFFERENTIATED INSTRUCTIONAL PLANNING

Not surprisingly, effective differentiated instruction starts with high-quality general education lessons; both differentiated instruction and inclusion are much more difficult and stressful within traditional, passive instruction. Desirable qualities for general education lessons include those that:

1. Promote active learning, including hands-on experiences, concrete and multi sensory representations, cooperative learning, and real life applications of concepts/skills.
2. Connect subject matter with students' interests (Warner & Cheney, 1996), communities (Gladdens, 2002), and experiences (Hollins & Oliver, 1999).
3. Incorporate multiple intelligences and I learning styles.

Given a high-quality lesson as a base, we are ready to consider differentiation within that lesson. An important strategy for maximizing attainment of the general curriculum is providing additional supports for struggling students.

ACHIEVING GENERAL CURRICULUM STANDARDS THROUGH ADDITIONAL SUPPORTS

"Additional Supports" to allow struggling students to achieve the general curriculum standards are represented in Figure 6.1 as the trapezoid-shaped foundation that supports "Grade-level General Curriculum." For these students, grade level standards are appropriate, but very challenging. Without Additional Supports, many of these students will fail.

Students in this group include those identified as having mild disabilities, those at risk for being identified as having disabilities, students for whom English is a second language, students with limited prerequisite skills, learning strategies, and background knowledge/experiences, and students with behavioral difficulties such as low motivation. These students are intellectually capable, but complex; they experience specific difficulties (e.g., processing and/or experiential differences) that prevent them from being successful without significant supports. Students with learning disabilities, for example, have intelligence within the average range (by definition), but often have reading and writing difficulties that block their ability to a) effectively access and b) demonstrate their understanding of subject matter using traditional print-based formats.

Given the push for high standards and the wealth of research documenting the importance of high expectations, it is critical to maintain the learning standard for these students; accordingly, instructional modifications need to be provided that enable them to both access the content and demonstrate what they've learned (King-Sears, 2001). This combination of high expectations and support is associated with success for students at risk of failure (Lee & Smith, 1999).

As with active learning, availability of Additional Supports benefits all students, not just struggling students. An important goal is for students to experience high rates of success, and low rates of failure. Fewer student errors result in more efficient learning, even for students with severe disabilities including autism (Heflin & Alberto, 2001). These Additional Supports can be divided into two general categories; the first category helps students access the general education curriculum, while the second category lends additional structure to the curriculum.

Access to the General Curriculum

This category targets students such as Andy (see introduction), who is capable of learning grade-level content, but is impeded by factors such as the way content is traditionally presented and tested. Andy is quite capable intellectually, but specific reading and writing disabilities make print materials inaccessible to him unless they are written at his reading level. Organizational and memory problems also interfere. Other students can effectively access information by reading the textbook, record information by taking notes, study by reviewing what is in the text and their notes, and communicate what they've learned by reading and writing traditional paper-and-pencil tests, but these print-based avenues are essentially closed to Andy. Students such as Andy are frequently placed in an untenable situation; they're smart enough to learn what is being taught, but cannot learn in the way that it is being taught. A pattern of failure over time causes these students to gradually lose faith in themselves as learners, another powerful barrier to their success. The following strategies are helpful in providing access to the general curriculum for students such as Andy, along with students for whom English is a second language, and students with limited prerequisite skills, learning strategies, or background knowledge/experiences.

Assistive Technology

In the past, nearly the only option to provide poor readers with access to grade-level subject matter was oral presentation; today however, a wide variety of assistive technology solutions is available. These include taped books, screen reading programs, software to support written expression (e.g., through webbing, speech feedback, and/or voice recognition), simulation software to illustrate science and social studies concepts, math media that illustrate real-life applications, and so forth. Increasingly, instructional software is equipped with speech capability, reducing interference from reading difficulties. (See http://www.ataccess.org for more information about assistive technology access, including an extensive list of products and vendors.)

Find vs. Guess

As noted previously, all students benefit from an appropriate balance of challenge and success; this balance is not identical from student to student. Although students who are amply capable and confident may benefit from a "trial and error" approach, students with a history of failure will require methods that structure successful experiences in order to bolster both their skills and their confidence in themselves as learners. For these students, a variety of resource materials can be provided to empower them to find answers they don't know rather than guess at them (probably incorrectly). Figure 6.2 shows examples of extra support that are structured to help struggling students successfully practice a skill/concept (and avoid practicing errors).

This "find" strategy emphasizes what Eisner (1984, p. 5) refers to as "intellectual independence," or being able to "find and use resources for dealing with tasks and problems." These are critical skills for any student in today's Information Age with its accompanying information glut. In addition to using Additional Supports in the classroom; students benefit from locating answers in the library, on the Internet, and in the community (including use of primary sources such as interviews or historical documents). This does not mean that there is no value in memorizing; however, it is overemphasized at times. Further, there is little value in requiring struggling students to continually work at a frustration level, repeatedly practicing their errors. This is the likely result in situations

Manipulatives, e.g., students can use cubes representing the base-10 number system to create models and solve problems concretely. Because they denote the base-10 system, even complex problems can be modeled using this approach. Transparent cubes are available for use with an overhead projector.

Visual aids, e.g., diagrams, models, story maps, etc. For another example, see Harmon & Hedrick's (2000) visual representation of vocabulary related to Harriet Tubman.

Charts, e.g., when memorization is needed, students create their own charts to allow them to look up facts that they've not yet memorized (again, as opposed to practicing incorrect answers).

Outlines (partially completed when appropriate), summaries, organizers, & reading guides (see Gianuzzi & Hudson, 1998). For example, when the textbook is beyond the student's reading level, 1–2 page chapter summaries that highlight the most important information and are written at the student's reading level can be provided. To help ensure a match between students' reading levels and reading materials, word processing programs can provide reading level estimates of text (e.g., using the Spelling & Grammar checking tool). For nonreaders, summaries can be audio taped or accessed using screen reading software (e.g., go to www.ReadPlease.com for a free text-to-speech software download).

Picture cues, e.g., combining vocabulary words with graphics and other illustrations.

Audio taped books, instructions, etc.

Figure 6.2 Types of Resources for Extra Support.

where students do not know the correct answer and have no means of finding it (especially when traditional resources, such as textbooks, are inaccessible to them). Under such circumstances, students are left with few alternatives to random guessing.

Personal Assistance

Personal assistance, including both peer tutoring and help from adults, can also serve the purpose of providing access to grade-level curriculum but should be used with caution to avoid unnecessary dependencies.

Additional Supports are most effective when they provide the least assistance necessary to allow the student to practice successfully. They are particularly useful during practice and study sessions, since they allow struggling students to avoid practicing errors. Of course, use of Additional Supports should be limited to those who need them; students able to practice with reasonable levels of accuracy without such supports (such as John, see introduction) should not be allowed to depend upon them.

Adding Structure

Students such as Andy also benefit from strategies that add structure to the general curriculum. These students may lack learning and study strategies that seem to come naturally to more successful students. The following section includes both instructional strategies for the teacher, and learning strategies for the student.

Emphasize the most important concepts and skills

Not all aspects of the curriculum are equally important; a characteristic of successful students is that they are able to hone in on main ideas, and discount minor details. However, students in need of Additional Supports often require assistance in prioritizing the most important content on which to focus their efforts. This strategy also helps the class as a whole, since it helps focus their efforts on the most critical information. For example, Mrs. Green makes available a one-page summary of the "key concepts," a study guide, and a concept map in both paper and electronic format in her 11th-grade social studies class (See Figure 6.3). Andy relies heavily on these to help him concentrate on the most important ideas and connections. A screen reading program allows the classroom computer to read electronic versions aloud for students who are auditory learners or poor readers.

Provide clear expectations and examples

This advice is most often heard in relation to behavior management; however, it also applies to instruction. This strategy may be especially important for students whose background differs from that of the teacher. Students who have more school experience and those from cultures and backgrounds similar to the teacher's (including race/ethnicity, socioeconomic status, etc.) will have an easier time interpreting the expectations of the teacher, given their common histories. However, even these students will benefit from greater explicitness, more precise instructions, and examples of past student work. Examples (with names removed) can serve to point out both exemplary features and mistakes to be avoided. If your students tend to model too closely, limit their access to examples once the point being illustrated has been made. Students with reading and memory difficulties will need an accessible record of instructions to use as they work (e.g., a checklist at the student's reading level, audio taped instructions, and a word processing file to which the student can listen using a screen reading program, etc.). These need not always be prepared in advance, e.g., instructions can be audio taped (by the teacher, or by a student) as they are given verbally to the large group.

Systematic breakdown of specific strategies, skills, and concepts

Readers with special education background will recognize in this suggestion familiar concepts such as cognitive strategy training and task analysis; however, students without disabilities also benefit from this approach. Desirable student performance is analyzed and recorded in step-by-step format, as in the following example for math problem-solving (adapted from Polya's four-stage problem solving model in Pressley & Woloshyn, 1995):

    a. Describe problem in your own words.
    b. Decide if the answer should be more or less than what you started with.
    c. Represent the problem concretely (e.g., use manipulatives or draw pictures).
    d. Write the problem and the answer.
    e. Check the answer.
    f. Self-evaluate (did I complete all the steps?).

Warner & Cheney (1996) teach strategies such as how to get important information from oral or print sources, how to communicate information gathered/learned to others (including to teachers for assessment purposes), and how to approach assignments in an organized way. These skills apply to future academic and occupational situations as well as to the current school setting.

Lesson Example	Additional Supports	Goal Adaptations
Social Studies: Mr. Green's 11th graders are learning about the Homestead Act. He is using paintings and folk songs from the period to illustrate various concepts. In addition, Mr. Green has greatly reduced the time that he spends lecturing about the reading assignments; instead, students are creating a variety of hands-on projects to develop their understanding of key concepts. These include the purpose of the Act, cost of and eligibility to purchase land under the Act, guidelines for land usage, and the relationships of the Act to the concept of "manifest destiny," to Native American treaties, and to current land usage. He uses a holistic rubric to evaluate the projects, insuring that key concepts are included in each.	With the help of the librarian, Mr. Green and his class have assembled a variety of resource materials related to the Homestead Act. These include paper and electronic texts at various reading difficulty levels, a video, websites, etc. Also available are a one-page summary of the "key concepts," a study guide, and a concept map, in both paper and electronic format. Some materials were created by a part-time paraprofessional, under the direction of Mr. Green and special education teacher. **Andy (Grade-level Curriculum):** Andy works on improving independent reading and writing skills in the context of shorter assignments, while utilizing technology that allows him to both access and demonstrate his understanding of general curriculum content. He relies heavily on the summary, study guide, and concept map to help him focus on the most important ideas and connections. He also uses assistive technology designated on his IEP, including a screen reading program that reads electronic text aloud, books-on-tape, and word processing and voice recognition programs (to allow him to produce longer written assignments). The IEP team has identified use of these programs as job skills for the transition component of his IEP, as well as strategies for current content-area assignments.	**Jo (Prioritized Curriculum):** Jo also uses taped books, the summary, and concept map to gain access grade-level curriculum (and sometimes learns things that surprise her teachers). However, the content priority for her is current land usage (e.g., the role of the Midwest in providing food for the nation). She also works on her IEP goals to improve articulation, printing and keyboarding skills. **Nita (Enriched Curriculum):** In addition to being responsible to demonstrate mastery of general curriculum, Nita's project responsibilities include more detailed exploration of immigrants' perspectives toward the concept of "manifest destiny."

Figure 6.3 An Example of Additional Structure.

Make specific connections with prior knowledge and experiences

This strategy helps students to create a space for new information/skills within their existing cognitive schema, an essential aspect of learning and retention. Harmon & Hedrick (2000), for example, extend conventional concept teaching (describing prototypes and characteristics, providing examples and non-examples) to include such strategies as rank ordering important information related to the concept, brainstorming a list of unrelated or improbable ideas, and situating the current concept in relation to other important concepts. Connections with students' interests, communities, and experiences should of course incorporate students' cultures, a strategy also supported by research on reducing school violence (Gladdens, 2002).

Work toward increased independence by fading assistance systematically

Traditionally, systematic fading of assistance has utilized a graduated guidance sequence structured on a continuum from greatest to least amounts/types of assistance. For example, in learning to perform manual tasks, a student may gradually progress from needing physical guidance, to following a model, to verbal feedback, to independence. Fading is also used to promote independence in cognitive strategy training. In the math problem-solving strategy (above), a student may initially rely upon specific verbal instructions provided by the teacher (perhaps on audiotape), followed by talking himself through the steps (e.g., by whispering), followed by silent self-monitoring (and perhaps self-recording) of strategy use.

Use of additional supports such as those described above will better enable struggling students to achieve in the general curriculum (King-Sears, 2001). Because they rely largely upon use of resource materials and group instructional strategies, they minimize the danger of creating dependencies on support personnel. Differentiated instructional strategies for students requiring more extensive adaptations (to content and expectations) are described in the next section.

GOAL ADAPTATIONS TO THE GENERAL CURRICULUM

If secondary schools are to achieve the vision of inclusive education as a community that supports all learners, the needs of another broad group of students also must be considered when planning multi-level instruction—those who need Goal Adaptations. These students benefit from the instructional supports described above, but also need adapted instructional goals. For students such as Jo and Nita (described in the introduction), only parts of the grade-level general curriculum constitute appropriate instructional goals. In Nita's case, more advanced goals are needed because much of the content has already been mastered (or will be mastered much more quickly than by most students); in Jo's case, less advanced and/or functional curriculum goals are needed. Goal Adaptations for both groups are explained in the next section, with Enriched Curriculum for students with special gifts and talents, and Prioritized Curriculum for students with significant disabilities.

Both groups of students have been served in pull-out programs, either for the gifted, or in self-contained special education classrooms. For gifted students, services are often not required by law, and may be nonexistent, neglected, or subject to inconsistent funding. Yet, as argued by Tomlinson (1994–1995), differentiated instruction is at least as important for students with significantly higher ability as for students with significantly lower ability. For these students, differentiated instruction in general education classrooms provides a means to better meet their needs even in the absence of a comprehensive "Gifted & Talented" program. Further, the sense of isolation sometimes experienced by students in pull-out programs can be avoided when differentiated instruction is provided for them within the general education classroom.

ENRICHED CURRICULUM

Enriched Curriculum for students with special gifts and talents is represented in Figure 6.1 by the large oval, indicating that opportunities for more challenging and/or creative work are provided above and beyond grade-level curriculum standards. The goal of Enriched Curriculum is to provide a more appropriate education for students with special gifts and talents within the general education classroom program. An additional advantage to providing enriched opportunities within the general education classroom is that they can be available even to students from traditionally marginalized groups that have often been underrepresented in gifted and talented programs, including students from diverse racial/ethnic groups, students with disabilities, and girls (Vaughn, Bos, & Schumm, 2000). Teachers are encouraged to think in broad terms when considering students in their classrooms who may be in need of enriched curricula. While these students would certainly include those who are academically gifted, others in need of enriched curricula include students who are talented in a variety of other ways (e.g., mechanically, interpersonally, and artistically including the visual arts, drama, dance, and music).

A practical way of providing differentiated instruction for students with special gifts and talents is using cooperative groups with individualized roles. In math, Nita participates in a small-group math game with age peers but is responsible for more advanced problems (see Sapon-Shevin, 1990 for additional suggestions for using cooperative groups in heterogeneous, inclusive classrooms). For students whose strengths are artistic (including those who may not be academically gifted), Goal Adaptations can provide additional opportunities for creative work. In the Social Studies example (see Figure 6.2), students express their understanding of important concepts in American history (in this case, the Homestead Act) by creating a variety of hands-on projects. These projects could include paintings, sculptures, dioramas, songs, dance, drama, etc. (Goldberg, 1997); given the variety of forms that such projects take, it is important that the evaluation system is structured to ensure that key concepts are included. For example, a holistic rubric can be devised that addresses the same key concepts that would be included on a paper-and-pencil test, but allows them to be expressed in a variety of ways. Of course, students generally will benefit from these opportunities; for some, the opportunity to express their learning using the arts may mitigate written language difficulties.

Some students may also be able to pursue independent study involving higher-level concepts and skills. In the Social Studies example (see Figure 6.2), all students are involved in creating a variety of projects; Nita's responsibilities include critique of concepts such as "manifest destiny." In some cases, the first step may be teaching (or refining) independent work skills. Teaching these skills initially using grade-level content (rather than enriched curricula) may not only make providing this instruction more manageable, but can also provide access to such instruction for the entire class. School and community librarians are natural allies in this effort; classroom volunteers (including senior citizens, cross-age tutors, and student interns) may also find it enjoyable to assist a talented student in pursuing projects related to his/her interests. (For additional suggestions, see "Making It Manageable," Figure 6.4.) Caution should be exercised in the use of independent projects that are not connected with the work of the class as a whole; they may detract from the culture of the classroom as a community, or function to further isolate students such as Nita (who already tends to be somewhat reclusive).

Prioritized Curriculum

The goal of Prioritized Curriculum is to allow students with severe disabilities to reap the benefits of general class placement while addressing individual needs. As noted by King-Sears (2001), adaptations can be made that will enable such a student to participate in general curriculum "while accomplishing very different content or curriculum goals" (p. 75). Educators are understandably likely to be uncomfortable with inclusion when the needs of students with severe disabilities for functional skills instruction are neglected (Lawrence-Brown, 2000a). ("Functional" skills are those that

Subject	Modifications	IEP Goals
English	• Taped books (from National Library Service for the Blind & Physically Handicapped); screen reading program. • Can use personal spelling list (e.g., from community signs goal), or work on regular list emphasizing comprehension of vocabulary vs. spelling. • Use word processing program for written assignments. Composes using velcro word/picture card system or by dictating to aide or peer, then types into computer. Needs assistance with sentence structure. Loves to compose and share dictated stories with the class.	• Articulate target sounds (s, z, f). • Request information/assistance. • Use velcro word/picture card communication system. • Improve knowledge of word meanings. • Improve keyboarding skills.
Social Studies	Taped textbooks (from Recordings for the Blind & Dyslexic). Creating picture timeline in lieu of worksheet assignments. Takes modified (multiple-choice) tests on main ideas. Needs processing time for answering questions in large-group discussions.	
Science	Taped textbooks (from Recordings for the Blind & Dyslexic). Emphasize functional applications of content. Use word processing program for modified written assignments. Takes modified (multiple-choice) tests on functional applications. Needs processing time for answering questions in large-group discussions.	• Improve fine motor dexterity (open containers, use hand-held implements). • Improve counting skills. • Improve calculator use. • Articulate target sounds (s and, z, f). • Request information/assistance. • Use velcro word/picture card system. • Improve knowledge of word meanings. • Improve keyboarding skills.
Math	Uses talking calculator. Emphasize functional applications of math operations. Takes modified (multiple-choice) tests using calculator to solve problems utilizing functional applications. May substitute community-based and/or vocational instruction for some units (as prioritized by the collaborative team).	Improve calculator use. Improve counting skills. Request information/assistance.

Figure 6.4 IEP Goals & Schedule Matrix Example.

directly make the student less dependent upon others, e.g., communication, motor, interpersonal, independent living skills, job skills, and so forth.) IEP's for students with severe disabilities will often need to balance these goals with academics at the student's level; a frequent mistake in inclusive settings is overemphasis on one or the other for these students. Either the general curriculum is emphasized to the near exclusion of functional skills instruction, or functional skills instruction is emphasized to the near exclusion of general curriculum. Often, the latter results in over-reliance upon parallel tasks; "inclusion" takes place only in the sense of being physically present. A vital support for students with severe disabilities in general education classrooms is addressing their IEP goals within the context of large-group lessons. By addressing goals that have been prioritized for the individual student by a knowledgeable and caring IEP team, general and special educators can feel confident that they are taking a major step toward providing an appropriate education for the student.

Contrary to long-held assumptions, students with disabilities do not usually learn more in self-contained special education classrooms; equal or superior results are obtained when appropriate supports are provided in general education classrooms (Affleck, Madge, Adams, & Lowenbraun, 1988; Banerji & Dailey, 1995; Bunch & Valeo, 1997; Cole & Meyer, 1991; Freeman & Alkin, 2000; Fryxell & Kennedy, 1995; Hunt & Goetz, 1997; Ingraham & Daugherty, 1995; Logan & Keefe, 1997; Lipsky & Gartner, 1995; Madden, Slavin, Karweit, Dolan & Wasik, 1993; McGregor & Vogelsberg, 1998; Schulte, Osborne, & McKinney, 1990; Wang & Birch, 1984; Waldron & McLeskey, 1998; Willrodt & Claybrook, 1995). This evidence, along with a presumptive legal right to general class placement (Individuals with Disabilities Education Act of 1997), suggests that students with disabilities should ordinarily be included unless good-faith efforts to support a particular student in general education classrooms have indicated that s/he cannot receive an appropriate education there.

It is unacceptable to place students in special education classrooms simply based on labels indicating a particular level or type of disability (e.g., severe mental retardation), without measuring the student's progress in appropriately supported general education classrooms (Individuals with Disabilities Education Act of 1997). Of course, teachers are concerned about the progress of students without disabilities as well; in this case the outcomes research is equally reassuring, with equal or superior academic, social, and behavioral outcomes for students without disabilities in inclusive general education classrooms compared to non-inclusive classrooms (Holloway, Salisbury, Rainforth, & Palombar, 1995; Peck, Donaldson, & Pezzoli, 1990; Salend, 1999; Sasso & Rude, 1988; Sharpe, York, & Knight, 1994).

Prioritized Curriculum for students with severe disabilities is represented in Figure 6.1 by the small oval. Students with severe disabilities can learn of course, but at a much slower pace. This makes setting priorities a must. When the number of things that can be learned is limited due to length of time needed to learn any one thing, it is essential that students' and teachers' time is invested in those that are most critical. What is "most critical" will vary from student to student; central to the IEP process is determining and communicating those individualized priorities. They must be determined based upon the individual strengths, needs, interests, and preferences of a particular student, not by the setting in which s/he is placed. Teachers in both general and special education settings have been criticized for failure to individualize instruction for struggling students (Kauffman, 1993; Tomlinson & Kalbfleisch, 1998).

For most students with severe disabilities, Prioritized Curriculum will include a mixture of academic and functional skills goals. As shown in Figure 6.1, Prioritized Curriculum includes material that falls within the general curriculum sphere, but also includes goals such as functional daily living skills that fall outside of it. The amount and proportion of general curriculum content to functional skills goals will vary from student to student. Again, priorities for an individual student will be determined by the specific strengths, needs, interests, and preferences of that student. Person-centered planning approaches can be helpful in determining these individualized priorities (e.g., see Dennis, Williams, Giangreco, & Cloninger, 1993 for further information).

Priorities for students with severe disabilities are likely to include communication, interpersonal, and motor skills. Ongoing opportunities to learn prioritized skills must be provided as part of special education services (Warner & Cheney, 1996). Fortunately for practitioners of differentiated instruction, these are among the easiest Prioritized Curriculum goals to address in general education settings because they are natural parts of most active lessons. We tend not to focus on them, of course, because most general education students have already mastered these skills (and thus provide good models for students who have not) but communicating, moving, and getting along with others are parts of nearly all active lessons. Examples include asking for help/materials, answering questions intelligibly, moving materials and themselves from place to place, sharing materials, taking turns, working cooperatively, and so forth.

Generalization difficulties common to students with severe disabilities (e.g., transfer of skills from the training setting to the natural setting) are significantly reduced when skills are taught directly in the natural environment. The general education class, with nondisabled peers, provides a more natural environment for learning these critical skills than special education classrooms; if students with severe disabilities are to relate effectively in integrated settings (now and as adults), they need to be taught in integrated settings. This will normally require the collaborative efforts of both the general education teacher and a special education teacher who "pushes in" to the general education classroom on a frequent basis to provide direct support to the student and the general education teacher.

IEP goals for Jo (see introduction) are sufficiently different from the general curriculum that they may be difficult to schedule without a specific strategy for doing so. A simple strategy is construction of an individual matrix that connects Jo's schedule in the general education classroom with her IEP goals (see Figure 6.4).

A matrix not only illustrates how IEP goals connect to general curriculum subjects, but also provides a means of facilitating other important outcomes. It helps ensure that IEP goals can be addressed regularly, and provides a starting point for discussions during regular collaborative team meetings of adaptations needed for upcoming units of instruction. When necessary, matrices can provide direction for impromptu adaptations that are inevitably needed in classrooms (e.g., when changes arise in the classroom schedule, or in the event that time does not permit the team to discuss all adaptations on the team meeting agenda).

As noted previously, addressing these skills will require additional personnel at times (e.g., some push-in special education teacher time, possibly also a paraprofessional on a full or part-time basis), but general education teachers and students who are knowledgeable about the student also can address them. This can take place in a natural and unobtrusive manner that does not detract from the lesson. Jo's special education teacher provides "push-in" support that rotates among various classes, but she also has taught other team members and students how to respond in helpful ways in her absence.

An additional benefit of her frequent presence in the general education classroom is that Jo's special education teacher has become familiar with the needs of students without disabilities. This has enabled her to effectively collaborate with Jo's teacher when concerns have arisen about the skills of other students in the class. Similar benefits accrue when therapists "push-in" to the general education classroom, along with avoiding difficulties generalizing from "pull-out" settings back to the classroom.

Communication, motor, and interpersonal skills have been referred to as "embedded" skills (Schnorr, Ford, Davern, Park-Lee, & Meyer, 1989), because they are embedded in other tasks. The concept of embedded skills can also be applied to lower-level academic skills, for example, Jo's IEP goals for improved printing skills and improved understanding of number concepts. While these would not be part of the general curriculum past elementary school, they can be viewed at the secondary level as skills embedded within more complex tasks. Examples relevant to Figure 6.4 include working on beginning reading skills during the same lesson in which other students work on more advanced English objectives such as analysis of literature, or working on counting and number identification as part of more complex math lessons. The alternative is pulling the student aside to work on parallel tasks; this needs to be avoided as much as possible.

As noted in the Enriched Curriculum section, cooperative learning with individualized roles is an effective way to provide differentiated instruction for students with special gifts and talents; the same is true for students with significant disabilities. When students are responsible to assist each other in accomplishing goals set for them, both academic skills and interpersonal relationships improve (Johnson & Johnson, 1999). In math, for example, a heterogeneous, small-group game format can provide opportunities for some students to work on grade-level problems, for Jo to work on basic number concepts, and for Nita to work on more advanced problems.

Authentic Instruction

Additional goals for students with severe disabilities can be addressed with relatively minor changes in emphasis and presentation of large-group lessons, focusing on real-life applications of general curriculum content. This is known today as authentic instruction or applied curriculum. Again, this strategy benefits the class as a whole. General educators as far back as John Dewey (1916/1944) have advocated its use, and it is still being recommended today in both the general and special education literature (Christ, 1995; Cox & Firpo, 1993; Gladdens, 2002; Hamill & Everington, 2002; Kluth, 2000; Miller, Shambaugh, Robinson, & Wimberly, 1995; Moore, 1996; Newmann & Wehlage, 1995; Perkins, 1993; Yager, 1987).

Miller, et al, (1995), for example, describe authentic instruction in middle school science. Students learned required science content through a partnership with a local botanic garden. Students created self-sustaining ecosystems, propagated plants for landscaping their campus, and created brochures and trail maps for the botanic garden. Project-based learning such as this has a number of benefits for a wide range of students. It provides a motivating, authentic, real-life context for all students to learn academic content, and it allows students to see and apply interdisciplinary connections. For example, note the connections above between science, technology, and English. For additional examples in math, history, and English see Christ (1995), Cox and Firpo (1993), and Kluth (2000).

Authentic instruction is not an add-on, but a means of teaching the same general curriculum content and skills that would be taught in traditional, passive lessons. The botanic garden partnership was developed as a way of teaching required subject matter (sustaining life and balanced ecosystems) in a way that was both more motivating to students and increased the complexity of their learning. In addition to life science content, students also acquired research skills such as using multiple resources (botanical texts, the Internet, and government resources such as the local county extension agent), collecting and analyzing data, drawing conclusions, and disseminating their results.

For students with significant disabilities, authentic instruction provides opportunities for learning various skills that are likely to have been prioritized on their IEP's, including functional academics and communication, interpersonal, and motor skills. Functional academics refers to academic skills applied in functional, everyday situations. Examples include applying number recognition skills in the context of finding the correct room or bus number, applying reading skills to finding the correct restroom, applying writing skills to labeling personal items with one's name or filling out a job application. These opportunities are important because students with severe disabilities are unlikely to automatically transfer skills learned in isolation to natural settings in which the skills are needed.

Authentic instruction provides many opportunities to teach functional academics. For example, while many educators would find it challenging to include Jo in a secondary science unit heavily dependent upon text and worksheet tasks, it becomes much easier in the botanic garden project described above. She has many opportunities to work on IEP goals such as printing and keyboarding skills while helping to develop brochures and trail maps, etc.

In addition, classmates John, Nita, and Andy have a motivating, authentic, real-life context for learning academic content, including interdisciplinary connections. As in the Social Studies example

(Figure 6.3), Andy will still need summaries and concept maps for text-based information. Several other students benefit from these as well, including Jo (although she is not responsible for all of the information contained in these documents). Nita has opportunities for working on both her spoken English and more advanced content through interviewing a botanic garden staff person. See "Making It Manageable" (Figure 6.5) for tips on getting started without becoming overwhelmed.

The emphasis in the Prioritized Curriculum discussion so far has been on IEP goals. However, general education classrooms provide much more for students with disabilities than integrated environments for learning IEP goals; they also provide important opportunities to learn from the general curriculum in ways that may not be specifically addressed in the IEP. In the Social Studies example (Figure 6.3), Jo works on her IEP goals to improve articulation, printing and keyboarding skills; however, the team has also identified current land usage in the region affected by the Homestead Act (e.g., the role of the Midwest in providing food for the nation) as a general curriculum focus for her in this unit. In determining these foci for particular units, the team looks for aspects of the general curriculum that seem relevant to Jo's daily life, including her interests, increased independence, and general understanding of the world around her. As another example, a focus for Jo in a general curriculum unit about the requirements for sustaining life and balanced ecosystems (whether in the context of the botanic garden project, or a more traditional presentation) might relate basic concepts from this unit to daily living concerns such as care of house plants, gardens, and pets.

Don't panic—not all of these supports will be needed for every lesson; the team will decide which supports are needed for individual students of concern. For example, while Andy needs oral and/or hand-on methods to learn and demonstrate his learning in Science and Social Studies, these supports are not usually needed in math.

Don't try to do everything at once—making changes in your classroom is something like remodeling a house. If you let yourself get overwhelmed with everything you'd like to do, you'll never get anything done. If you have help (e.g., from a collaborative team), progress will be faster; however, even teams need to prioritize. Start with the highest priority, and work your way down the list.

Address issues of fairness as needed, with students and/or your team. Redirect students who may prefer to rely on Additional Supports, but do not need them (see John example).

Gradually build a collection of materials for Additional Supports and Enriched Curricula, enlisting support within your department, building/district, local professional association, etc. Potential resources include your librarian, paraprofessionals, teachers in grade levels above and below yours, special area teachers, special education teachers, etc. (see Social Studies example). Consider enlisting the assistance of your PTA or curriculum personnel to provide such materials in a common area available to any teacher. Include availability to teachers of materials and resources to diversify instruction as part of the district's curriculum/program evaluation criteria (King-Sears, 2001).

Build upon your own strengths and talents. For example, one teacher may have a special interest in horticulture, leading him to develop projects such as those associated with the botanic garden project, above. Other teachers will develop projects more in line with their own interests, e.g., in sports, the arts, etc. Student interests may also be reflected in such projects; older students can be enlisted as co-developers of authentic instructional projects.

Figure 6.5 *Making It Manageable.*

In addition to acquiring IEP goals and general curriculum foci identified in advance by the collaborative team, students with significant disabilities may surprise their teachers by revealing additional, unanticipated strengths related to the general curriculum. For example, Jo (who is based on a real student), not only progressed in her IEP goals for printing, keyboarding, and articulation skills through her participation in a general education English class, but showed a real gift and delight for composing and sharing short stories with her class. The curricula for students in the special education class in which Jo would have been placed had she not been included was almost entirely focused upon functional skills and readiness-level academics (Lawrence-Brown, 2000b). This is an incidental but important benefit of exposure to general curriculum for students with significant disabilities that is not available to them in special education curricula. Special education curricula are of necessity directed by educators' perceptions of students' disabilities, and are unlikely to include opportunities to learn at levels significantly above that. The power and importance of high expectations for students with disabilities is once again illustrated.

Community-based Instruction

Although the general classroom provides the most appropriate integrated, natural environment for learning most IEP goals for students with significant disabilities, some goals will need to be addressed outside of the general education classroom. For example, Jo's goal to improve street safety skills (cross only when cars are not approaching) must be implemented in the community to be learned effectively. Other goals, e.g., hygiene skills, eating skills, and so forth are most properly addressed outside of the classroom, in areas such as restrooms, locker rooms, lunch-rooms, etc. Here a teacher with extensive experience supporting students with severe disabilities in inclusive programs explains:

> [We have a] simple model. Essentially, no special ed room. We'd have like a little kind of, resource room kind of thing, where you could do private therapy, where the therapists and I could have our team meetings, where you could do parent meetings, where you could store stuff, where you could take a kid if they were having, like, an outburst of some sort that was really disruptive. . . .
>
> Because you look at, like, Ryndak's model [cf. Ryndak & Alper, 1996] . . . taking the goals that the kids really need. . . . These are, like, 10, or 15 things this kid really needs to learn this year, and when can we do them? Well, we can do these in a regular environment, we can do these in the community, and surrounding the school, or we can do these in alternate sites within the school. . . . Anyplace else, but not in a special ed. room. (Lawrence-Brown, 2000a, pp. 55–56)

The benefits of community-based instruction are not limited to students with disabilities. It is increasingly recommended for students without disabilities as well, often in the form of school-to-work or service learning (Alleman & Brophy, 1994; Schukar, 1997; Wade & Saxe, 1996).

Evaluating Effectiveness

In judging the effectiveness of these efforts, teachers need usable data about students' learning. For most students, existing classroom assessment data will serve this purpose. For students whose performance falls either above or below the range of existing classroom assessment data, additional data that is specific to their adapted goals will be needed. For IEP goals (the primary means of evaluating progress for students with severe disabilities), these data collection systems should already be in place (e.g., Individuals with the Disabilities Education Act of 1997). Halverson & Neary (2001) emphasize that record-keeping systems must be simple and convenient enough to be practical for consistent classroom use, and provide examples such as self-graphing data collection forms (see p. 107).

CAUTIONS

As with any other school change effort, care must be taken to avoid unintended consequences of the change. For differentiated instruction, these include the following:

1. Reproducing tracking within the classroom. Always consider active participation in the lesson as an objective for students who traditionally have been served in segregated settings (whether special education or programs for the gifted and talented). Parallel tasks should be considered a last resort, when no other way can be devised to meet the student's needs. Actively avoid fixed groups, especially those based on ability; as an alternative, consider interest-based groups. Interest-based groups can avoid problems associated with low expectations for students in the "low group" while still providing the benefits of small group instruction.

2. Keep in mind that needs vary from lesson to lesson, even for the same student. Some students may need Additional Supports in some lessons and Enriched or Prioritized Curriculum in other lessons. For example, Andy may need Prioritized Curriculum for reading (focusing on decoding and comprehension skills at his level, while other students work on more advanced skills), but only Additional Supports for social studies when reading disabilities are mitigated using assistive technology to provide oral presentation of content. In the botanic garden project described previously, Andy may need Enriched Curriculum due to his extensive knowledge of horticulture, e.g., more advanced topics such as genetics and fungi that attack plants. It is particularly important to recognize, even seek out, such strengths in students like Andy, whose experiences in school are likely to have been dominated by failure and frustration.

3. Conceptualize differentiated instruction broadly do not merely focus on ability levels, but also consider learning styles and multiple intelligences, cultural/linguistic backgrounds, and creative abilities. Students with special talents in art, music, or movement. need opportunities to develop these gifts at least as much as students with academic gifts (Goldberg, 1997). By using the arts as a vehicle to present content and by allowing students to express their learning using the arts, teachers not only provide important opportunities to develop these skills, but open doors for students to acquire and express their learning in ways that are closed off by traditional text-based approaches. Instructional applications of the arts can also help teachers to identify special gift and talents that may otherwise not be recognized, especially in students who also are identified as having disabilities.

4. Seek out professional development for the team in specific collaboration skills. Ongoing and effective team collaboration (involving general and special education teachers, therapists, paraprofessionals, and parents) is critical to successful inclusion. Yet effective collaborators are made, not born. Most teams will benefit from professional development in specific teaming skills, such as active listening, group problem solving, conflict management, etc.

5. Keep it manageable (see Figure 6.5).

CONCLUSION

Discussion of legal issues related to inclusion has deliberately been minimized here. Although the law has had an important role in opening doors for students with disabilities, it is not the most important reason for including students with disabilities, and can be overemphasized. More important than the law is the spirit in which the law was designed. The Education of All Handicapped Children Act of 1975 was an outgrowth of widespread civil rights efforts of the 1960s and 1970s; it employs the same legal foundations as the Civil Rights Act of 1964, including the 5th and 14th Amendments to the Constitution and the landmark 1954 Supreme Court case, Brown vs. the Board of Education. Separate is not equal; we now know, as noted previously, that students with disabilities generally learn as much or more in appropriately supported general education classrooms as they do in special education classrooms. A teacher with extensive experience supporting students with disabilities in inclusive classrooms comments:

> It's a statement of one's outlook on life. . . . What do you think in your life about people who are different?. . . . Because this isn't, like, what did I learn in teacher's college. This is, like, what do I think about life, and where should people be (Lawrence-Brown, 2000a, p. 84).

Segregation harms not only those who are segregated, but society in general. According to Martin Luther King, Jr., "All life is interrelated. All . . . are caught in an inescapable network of mutuality, tied in a single garment of destiny. Whatever affects one directly, affects all indirectly." Differentiated instruction supports the classroom as a community to which age peers belong and can/should be nourished as individuals. With differentiated instruction and appropriate supports, intended benefits of inclusion for both sudents with and without disabilities can be realized.

REFERENCES

Affleck, J., Madge, S., Adams, A., & Lowenbraun, S. (1988). Integrated classroom vs. resource model: Academic liability and effectiveness. *Exceptional Children, 54,* 339–348.

Alleman, J. & Brophy, J. (1994, November/December). Taking advantage of out-of-school opportunities for meaningful social studies learning. *The Social Studies,* 262–267.

Banerji, M., & Dailey, R. (1995). A study of the effects of inclusion model on students with specific learning disabilities. *Journal of Learning Disabilities, 28,* 511–522.

Bunch, G., & Valeo, A. (1997). *Inclusion: Recent research.* Toronto: Inclusion Press.

Christ, G. (1995, May). Curriculums with real-world connections. *Educational Leadership,* 32–35.

Cole, D., & Meyer, L. (1991). Social integration and severe disabilities: A longitudinal analysis of child outcomes. *The Journal of Special Education, 25*(3), 340–351.

Convery, A., & Coyle, D. (1993). Differentiation-Taking the Initiative. London: Centre for Information on Language Teaching and Research. (Eric Document Reproduction Service No. ED382025).

Cox, M., & Firpo, C. (1993, March). What would they be doing if we gave them worksheets? *English Journal,* 42–45.

Dennis, R., Williams, W., Giangreco, M., & Cloninger, C. (1993). Quality of life as context for planning and evaluation of services for people with disabilities. *Exceptional Children, 59*(6), 499-.

Dewey, J. (1916/1944). Thinking in education. In Democracy and education. New York: MacMillan. Retrieved from http://www.ILT.Columbia.edu/publications/projects/Digitexts/Dewey/d_e/Chapter12.HTML on October 2, 2003.

Eisner, E. (1984). The kind of schools we need. *Interchange, 15*(2), 1–12.

Freeman, S., & Alkin, M. (2000). Academic and social attainment of children with mental retardation in general education and special education settings. *Remedial and Special Education, 21*(1), 3–18.

Fryxell D., & Kennedy, C. (1995). Placement along the continuum of services and its impact on students' social relationships. *Journal of the Association for Persons with Severe Handicaps, 20,* 259–269.

Gianuzzi, M., & Hudson, F. (1998). A cognitive reading guide: Equalizing instruction for [title] Where the Red Fern Grows. *Intervention in School & Clinic, 33*(3), 169-.

Gladdens, R.M. (2002). *Reducing school violence: Strengthening student programs and addressing the role of school organizations.* Secada, W. (Ed.), Review of Research and Education, (Vol. 26). Washington, DC: American Educational Research Association.

Goldberg, M. (1997). *Arts and learning: An integrated approach to teaching and learning in multicultural and multilingual settings.* White Plains, NY: Longman.

Good, T. (2001). Expectancy effects in the classroom: A special focus on improving the reading performance of minority students in first-grade classrooms. *Educational Psychologist, 36*(3), 113-.

Halverson, A., & Neary, T. (2001). *Building inclusive schools: Tools and strategies for success.* Needham Heights, MA: Allyn & Bacon.

Hamill, L., & Everington, C. (2002). *Teaching students with moderate to severe disabilities: An applied approach for inclusive environments.* Upper Saddle River, NJ: Merrill Prentice Hall.

Harmon, J., & Hedrick, W. (2000). Zooming in and zooming out: Enhancing vocabulary and conceptual learning in social studies. *Reading Teacher, 54*(2), 155–159.

Heflin, L.J., & Alberto, P.A. (2001). Establishing a behavioral context for learning for students with autism. *Focus on Autism and Other Developmental Disabilities, 16*(2), 93–101.

Hollins, E., & Oliver, E. (1999). *Pathways to success in school: Culturally responsive teaching.* Mahwah, NJ: Erlbaum.

Holloway, T., Salisbury, C., Rainforth, B., & Palombar, M. (1995). Use of instructional time in classrooms serving students with and without severe disabilities. *Exceptional Children, 61*(3), 242–253.

Hunt, P., & Goetz, L. (1997). Research on inclusive educational programs, practices, and outcomes for students with severe disabilities. *Journal of Special Education, 31*(1), 3–29.

Individuals with Disabilities Education Act of 1997 Pub. (1999) L. No. 105–17, §300.347(a)7 .Ingraham, C.L., & Daugherty, K.M. (1995). The success of three gifted deaf-blind students in inclusive educational programs. *Journal of Visual Impairment & Blindness, 89*(3), 257.

Johnson, D., & Johnson, R. (1999). Making cooperative learning work. *Theory into Practice, 38*(2), 67–73.

Kauffman, J. (1993). How we might achieve the radical reform of special education. *Exceptional Children, 60*(1), 6–16.

King-Sears, M. (2001). Three steps for gaining access to the general education curriculum for learners with disabilities. *Intervention in School & Clinic, 37*(2), 67-.

Kluth, P. (2000). Community-referenced learning and the inclusive classroom. *Remedial and Special Education, 21*(1), 19–26.

Kolb, K., & Jussim, L. (1994). Teacher expectations and underachieving gifted children. *Roeper Review, 17*(1), 26-.

Lawrence-Brown, D. (2000a). *The nature and sources of educators' comfort and/or concerns with inclusion of students with significant intellectual disabilities in general education classrooms.* Unpublished doctoral dissertation, University at Buffalo, Buffalo, NY.

Lawrence-Brown, D. (2000b). The segregation of Stephen. In Cornbleth, C. (Ed.), *Curriculum politics, policy, practice: Cases in comparative context.* Albany, NY: State University of New York Press.

Lee, V., & Smith, J. (1999). Social support and achievement: For young adolescents in Chicago: The role of school academic press. *American Educational Research Journal, 36*, 907–945.

Logan, K., & Keefe, E. (1997). A comparison of instructional context, teacher behavior, and engaged behavior for students with severe disabilities in general education and self-contained elementary classrooms. *Journal of the Association for Persons with Severe Handicaps, 22*(1), 16–27.

Lipsky, D. K., & Gartner, A. (1995). The evaluation of inclusive education programs. *National Center on Restructuring and Inclusion Bulletin, 2*(2), 1–6.

Madden, N., Slavin, R., Karweit, N., Dolan, L., & Wasik, B. (1993). Success for all: Longitudinal effects of a restructuring program for inner-city elementary schools. *American Educational Research Journal, 30*, 123–148.

McGregor, G., & Vogelsberg, R.T. (1998). *Inclusive schooling practices: Pedagogical and research foundations: A synthesis of the literature that informs best practices about inclusive schooling.* Baltimore: Brookes.

Miller, P., Shambaugh, K., Robinson, C., & Wimberly, J. (1995, May). Applied learning for middle schoolers. *Educational Leadership*, 22–25.

Moore, R. (1996, April 11–13). *Creating a culture of learning for diverse school populations.* Paper presented at the Annual Meeting of the Reading Association of Kansas, Salina, KS. (Eric Document Reproduction Service No. ED396043).

Neber, H., Finsterwald, M.,& Urban, N. (2001). Cooperative learning with gifted and high-achieving students: a review and meta-analysis of 12 studies. *High Ability Studies, 12*(1), 199–214.

Newmann, F., & Wehlage, G. (1995). *Successful school restructuring.* Madison: Center on Organization Restructuring of Schools, University of Wisconsin-Madison.

Peck, C., Donaldson, J., & Pezzoli, M. (1990). Some benefits nonhandicapped adolescents perceive for themselves from their social relationships with peers who have severe handicaps. *Journal of the Association for Persons with Severe Handicaps, 15*(4), 241–249.

Perkins, D. (1993, Fall). *Teaching for understanding. American Educator*, 27–35.

Pressley, M., & Woloshyn, V. (1995). *Cognitive strategy instruction (2nd ed.).* Cambridge, MA: Brookline Books.

Rosenthal, R., & Jacobson, L. (1968). *Pygmalion in the classroom: Teacher expectation and pupils' intellectual development.* New York: Holt.

Ryndak, D., & Alper, S. (1996). *Curriculum content for students with moderate and severe disabilities in inclusive settings.* Boston: Allyn and Bacon.

Salend, S., & Duhaney, L. (1999). The impact of inclusion on students with and without disabilities and their educators. *Remedial & Special Education, 20*(2), 114-.

Sapon-Shevin, M. (1990). Student support through cooperative learning. In W. Stainback, & S. Stainback (Eds.), *Support networks for inclusive schooling.* (pp. 67–78). Baltimore: Brookes.

Sasso, G., & Rude, H. (1988, March). The social effects of integration on nonhandicapped children. *Education and Training and Mental Retardation*, 18–23.

Schnorr, R., Ford, A., Davern, L., Park-Lee, S., & Meyer, L. (1989). *The Syracuse curriculum revision manual.* Baltimore: Brooks.

Schukar, R. (1997). *Enhancing the middle school curriculum through service learning. Theory Into Practice, 36*(3), 176–183.

Schulte, A., Osborne, S., & McKinney, J. (1990). Academic outcomes for students with learning disabilities in consultation and resource programs. *Exceptional Children, 57*, 162–172.

Sharpe, M., York, J., & Knight, J. (1994). Effects of inclusion on the academic performance of classmates without disabilities: A preliminary study. *Remedial and Special Education, 15*, 281–87.

Singer, H., & Donlan, D. (1989). *Reading and learning from text.* Hillsdale, NJ: Erlbaum.

Tomlinson, C. (1994–95). Gifted learners too: A possible dream? *Educational Leadership, 52*(4).

Tomlinson, C., & Kalbfleisch, M.L. (1998, November). Teach me, teach my brain: A call for differentiated classrooms. *Educational Leadership*, 52–55.

Vaughn, S., Bos, C., & Schumm, J. (2000). *Teaching exceptional, diverse, and at-risk students in the general education classroom (2nd ed.).* Boston: Allyn and Bacon.

Wade, R., & Saxe, D. (1996). Community service-learning in the social studies: Historical roots, empirical evidence, critical issues. *Theory and Research in Social Education, 24*(4), 331–359.

Waldron, N., & McLeskey, J. (1998). The effects of an inclusive school program on students with mild and severe learning disabilities. *Exceptional Children, 64*, 395–405.

Waldron, N. & McLeskey, J. (2001). An interview with Nancy Waldron and James McLeskey. *Intervention and School & Clinic, 36*(3), 175-.

Wang, M. ,& Birch, J. (1984). Comparison of a full-time mainstreaming program and a resource room approach. *Exceptional Children, 5*, 33–40.

Warner, M., & Cheney, C. (1996). Guidelines for developing and evaluating programs for secondary students with mild disabilities. *Intervention and School & Clinic, 31*(5), 276-.

Willrodt, K., & Claybrook, S. (1995). *Effects of inclusion on academic outcomes.* Unpublished dissertation, Sam Houston State University. (Eric Document Reproduction Service No. ED 389102).

Yager, R. (1987). Assess all five domains of science. *The Science Teacher, October 1987*, 33–37.

The Culturally Responsive Teacher
— by Ana Maria Villegas and Tamara Lucas

To engage students from diverse cultural and linguistic backgrounds, we must see them as capable learners.

Belki Alvarez, a young girl one of us knows, arrived in New York from the Dominican Republic several years ago with her parents and two siblings. After a difficult start in the United States, both parents found jobs; their minimum-wage earnings were barely enough for a family of five to scrape by month to month. As the oldest child in the family, Belki soon had to assume caretaking responsibilities for her younger brother and sister. At only 8 years old, she was responsible for getting her siblings ready for school, taking them there each morning, bringing them back home at the end of the school day, and caring for them until her parents came home from work.

On weekends, she worked with her mother at the community street fair to make extra money for the family by selling products prepared at home. She astutely negotiated prices with customers and expertly handled financial transactions. Belki often spoke enthusiastically about having her own business in the future. She spoke Spanish fluently at home and in the community, and she often served as the English language translator for her parents.

Belki's teachers, however, did not know this competent, responsible, enthusiastic girl. They perceived her as lacking in language and math skills, having little initiative, and being generally disinterested in learning.

Such profound dissonance between her in-school and out-of-school experiences is not unique to Belki. Sadly, this is typical for an increasing number of students in U.S. schools today

Over the past three decades, the racial, ethnic, and linguistic demographics of the K-12 student population in the United States have changed dramatically. In 1972, 22 percent of all students enrolled in elementary and secondary public schools were of racial/ethnic minority backgrounds (National Center for Education Statistics [NCES], 2002). By 2003, racial/ethnic minority students accounted for 41 percent of total enrollments in U.S. public schools. In six states and the District of Columbia, students of color are already in the majority (NCES, 2005). The immigrant student population has also grown significantly in the past 30 years. Currently, one in five students speaks a language other than English at home, and the majority of these students are learning English as a second language in school (Center on Education Policy, 2006).

A Framework and a Vision

Successfully teaching students from culturally and linguistically diverse backgrounds—especially students from historically marginalized groups—involves more than just applying specialized teaching techniques. It demands a new way of looking at teaching that is grounded in an understanding of the role of culture and language in learning. Six salient qualities (see Villegas & Lucas, 2002) can serve as a coherent framework for professional development initiatives in schools seeking to respond effectively to an increasingly diverse student population.

UNDERSTANDING HOW LEARNERS CONSTRUCT KNOWLEDGE

Our conception of culturally and linguistically responsive teaching is grounded in constructivist views of learning (National Research Council, 2000). From this perspective, learners use their prior knowledge and beliefs to make sense of the new ideas and experiences they encounter in school. A central role of the culturally and linguistically responsive teacher is to support students' learning by helping them build bridges between what they already know about a topic and what they need to learn about it.

For example, Belki will learn more from a social studies unit on immigration if her teacher draws on her very real experience as a newcomer to the United States. The teacher might ask her and other immigrant students in the class to describe their experiences learning a new language and compare living in the United States to living in their native countries. The teacher could build on those narratives to introduce relevant concepts, such as factors that lead people to immigrate and phases in the immigration process. The teacher could invite immigrant parents to the class to share their experiences. By involving the students and their parents in these ways, the teacher would not only help students build bridges to learning but also strengthen the connections between home and school. If the teacher does not tap into the experiences of students in the class and instead teaches the unit by focusing solely on the experiences of earlier immigrant groups coming to the United States—such as the Germans and Irish—the material will be much less relevant and engaging.

Learning also involves questioning, interpreting, and analyzing ideas in the context of meaningful issues. With this in mind, an English teacher in a community in the U.S. Southwest that had a large Latino population designed a unit on immigration to the United States. The students were asked to write a letter to the editor of a local newspaper expressing their views on the topic. To write the letter, the students realized that they needed to understand the issues more deeply So they summarized relevant newspaper articles and developed and administered a questionnaire in their neighborhoods to learn about the community's views on immigration. They debated in class the proposal to build a fence along the United States/Mexico border. Working in groups, they wrote letters to the editor and then assessed their drafts using a rubric that focused on grammar, clarity of position taken, and development of supporting arguments. After receiving the teacher's feedback, the students revised and sent their letters. The students were deeply engaged in a process that helped improve their writing skills.

In embracing constructivist views of learning, we do not mean to suggest that there is no place in schools for direct instruction, memorization, and basic skills instruction. When such transmission-oriented strategies predominate, however, their pedagogical value diminishes, much to the students' disadvantage. Such an approach to teaching does not give students opportunities to actively engage in learning and integrate new ideas and frameworks into their own ways of thinking. Therefore, students are less likely to learn to think critically, become creative problem solvers, and develop skills for working collaboratively—all qualities that are essential for success in life and work.

LEARNING ABOUT STUDENTS' LIVES

To teach subject matter in meaningful ways and engage students in learning, teachers need to know about their students' lives. We are not suggesting that teachers learn generic information about specific cultural or social groups. Such thinking leads to stereotypes that do not apply to individual students.

Instead, teachers need to know something about their students' family makeup, immigration history, favorite activities, concerns, and strengths. Teachers should also be aware of their students' perceptions of the value of school knowledge, their experiences with the different subject matters in their everyday settings, and their prior knowledge of and experience with specific topics in the curriculum. For example, Belki's teachers would benefit from knowing that she and her family are immigrants, that she often serves as the English language translator for her parents, that she aspires to own a business some day, and that she expertly manages financial transactions at the weekend street fair.

Effective strategies for learning about students' lives outside school include conducting home visits, creating opportunities in the classroom for students to discuss their aspirations for the future, posing problems for students to solve and noting how each student goes about solving them, and talking with parents and other community members. For instance, Belki's teacher might have asked her to give examples of how she uses math outside school. The teacher could have learned even more by visiting the street fair. By observing her animated interactions with customers, the teacher would have seen that Belki is a fluent Spanish speaker with sophisticated negotiation skills and some important math skills.

The vast majority of teachers in the United States are white, middle class, and monolingual English speaking. In most cases, their lives differ profoundly from the lives of their students. Although information-gathering strategies are simple enough to develop, it is more challenging for teachers to learn how to interpret what they discover about students through their data gathering. To make productive instructional use of this information, teachers must possess two fundamental qualities: They must have sociocultural consciousness and hold affirming views toward diversity (Nieto, 1996).

BEING SOCIOCULTURALLY CONSCIOUS

We define sociocultural consciousness as the awareness that a person's worldview is not universal but is profoundly influenced by life experiences, as mediated by a variety of factors, including race, ethnicity, gender, and social class. Teachers who lack sociocultural consciousness will unconsciously and inevitably rely on their own personal experiences to make sense of students' lives—an unreflective habit that often results in misinterpretations of those students' experiences and leads to miscommunication. For example, students from cultures with a less individualistic and more collectivist worldview than that of mainstream U.S. culture may be overlooked in class and assumed to be less capable than their mainstream peers because, in general, they do not seek individual attention and praise.

To develop sociocultural consciousness, teachers need to look beyond individual students and families to understand inequities in society. In all social systems, some positions are accorded greater status than others, and such status differentiation gives rise to differential access to power. Teachers need to be aware of the role that schools play in both perpetuating and challenging those inequities. Professional development carried out in groups and guided by an experienced facilitator who is knowledgeable about multicultural issues can be instructive. Activities might involve reading about the differential distribution of wealth and income in the United States or reflecting on the well-documented fact that a person's social class is the best predictor of academic success and future social standing (Natriello, McDill, & Pallas, 1990). To see the powerful connections between social and education inequities, participants could read The Shame of the Nation: The Restoration of Apartheid Schooling in America, by Jonathan Kozol (2006). By reading and discussing accounts of successful teaching and learning in diverse settings (see Garcia, 1999; Ladson-Billings, 1994; Nieto & Rolón, 1997), teachers can develop a vision of how schools can challenge such inequities.

HOLDING AFFIRMING VIEWS ABOUT DIVERSITY

Unfortunately, evidence suggests that many teachers see students from socially subordinated groups from a deficit perspective (Nieto, 1996). Lacking faith in the students' ability to achieve, these teachers are more likely to have low academic expectations for the students and ultimately treat them in ways that stifle their learning. They are more apt to use drill, practice, and rote-learning activities at the expense of more challenging work that demands the use of higher-order thinking skills. They are also less likely to call on the students in class, give them sufficient wait time to respond thoughtfully to questions, or probe incomplete answers for clarity.

By contrast, teachers who see students from an affirming perspective and truly respect cultural differences are more apt to believe that students from nondominant groups are capable learners, even when these students enter school with ways of thinking, talking, and behaving that differ from the dominant cultural norms. Teachers who hold these affirming views about diversity will convey this confidence by providing students with an intellectually rigorous curriculum, teaching students strategies for monitoring their own learning, setting high performance standards and consistently holding students accountable to those standards, and building on the individual and cultural resources that students bring to school. For example, instead of setting out to "correct" students' language through the use of decontextualized drill and worksheet activities, the English teacher who asked her students to write to the newspaper editor helped her students develop their writing skills by involving them in purposeful and intellectually stimulating tasks.

USING APPROPRIATE INSTRUCTIONAL STRATEGIES

Teachers can activate students' prior knowledge by asking them to discuss what they know about a given topic, as Belki's teacher could have done by having the immigrant students in the class share their personal experiences with immigration. Teachers can embed new ideas and skills in projects that are meaningful to the students, as the English teacher who helped students improve their writing skills through researching immigration did.

Teachers can also give English language learners access to the curriculum by drawing on the student's native language resources. They can provide students who are literate in their native language with material to read in that language to help them build background knowledge for specific content. They can encourage students to use bilingual dictionaries. They can prepare study guides for instructional units that define relevant vocabulary and outline key concepts in English, using simplified language. They can also use more visual cues and graphic organizers and incorporate more hands-on activities into their lessons.

Using pertinent examples and analogies from students' lives is another instructional strategy that helps students build bridges to learning. For example, one of us recently observed a teacher introducing the concept of rhythm in poetry by having students analyze the rhythm in a well-known hip-hop recording and then engaging the students in a similar analysis of a poem by Robert Frost. In U.S. history classes, teachers can help engage students from historically marginalized groups by having them examine the curriculum to determine whose perspectives are and are not presented. This would work well, for example, with a textbook treatment of slavery. If the students determine through an analysis of the text that they are learning little about the real experiences of slaves, they can read one of the many published slave narratives to deepen their understanding. As these examples suggest, the job of the culturally and linguistically responsive teacher involves engaging all students in learning for understanding.

ADVOCATING FOR ALL STUDENTS

Numerous practices embedded in the fabric of everyday schooling put students from nonmainstream groups at a disadvantage. These include a school culture of low expectations for students from low-status groups, inadequate general and multicultural learning materials, large class sizes, assignment of the least-experienced teachers to classes in which students need the most help, insensitivity toward cultural differences, questionable testing practices, and a curriculum that does not reflect diverse student perspectives.

To continue to move toward greater cultural and linguistic responsiveness in schools, teachers must see themselves as part of a community of educators working to make schools more equitable for all students. Teaching is an ethical activity, and teachers have an ethical obligation to help all students learn. To meet this obligation, teachers need to serve as advocates for their students, especially those who have been traditionally marginalized in schools.

For example, teachers involved in school- or district-level textbook review committees could ensure that selected textbooks and supplemental materials appropriately reflect the diversity of experiences and perspectives in the student population. Those who have input into the design of professional development activities could identify specific areas in which the faculty might need professional growth. Topics might include how to implement strategies for learning about students' lives, become socioculturally conscious, build on students' interests outside school to advance curriculum goals, and tap community resources in teaching. Responsive classroom teachers could also request common planning time with the English as a second language teacher to coordinate instruction in ways that maximize content learning for their English language learners.

Just Imagine

Certainly, individual teachers can enhance their success with students from diverse backgrounds by working on their own to cultivate these qualities of responsive teaching. However, the framework that we have presented here will have the greatest effect on a school if teachers and school leaders develop a shared vision of the culturally and linguistically responsive teacher.

Imagine Belki Alvarez's school life if her teachers had explored these six qualities and shared ideas for applying them in their teaching. They could have capitalized on her entrepreneurial skills to help her learn mathematical concepts. They would have seen her as a capable learner and understood the relevance of her life experiences for her school learning. They might have tapped her experience as the English translator for her family by having her translate for other Spanish-speaking students in the class who spoke minimal English. Approaching a student's education in these culturally and linguistically responsive ways—rather than emphasizing deficits—has the potential to truly engage all students in learning, both in school and beyond.

References

Center on Education Policy. (2006). A public education primer: Basic (and sometimes surprising) facts about the U.S. education system. Washington, DC: Author. Garcia, E. E. (1999). Student cultural diversity: Understanding and meeting the challenge. Boston: Houghton Mifflin.

Kozol, J. (2006). The shame of the nation: The restoration of apartheid schooling in America. New York: Three Rivers Press.

Ladson-Billings, G. (1994). The dreamkeepers: Successful teachers of African American children. San Francisco: Jossey-Bass.

National Center for Education Statistics. (2002). Digest for education statistics tables and figures. Washington, DC: U.S. Government Printing Office. Available: http://nces.ed.gov/programs/digest/d02/dt066.asp

National Center for Education Statistics. (2005). Digest for education statistics tables and figures. Washington, DC: U.S. Government Printing Office. Available: http://nces.edu.gov/programs/d05/tables/dt05%5f038.asp

National Research Council. (2000). How people learn. Washington, DC: National Academies Press.

Natriello, G., McDill, E. L., & Pallas, A. M. (1990). Schooling disadvantaged children: Racing against catastrophe. New York: Teachers College Press.

Nieto, S. (1996). Affirming diversity: The sociopolitical context of education. White Plains, NY: Longman.

Nieto, S., & Rolón, C. (1997). Preparation and professional development of teachers: A perspective from two Latinas. In. J. J. Irvine (Ed.), Critical knowledge for diverse teachers and learners (pp. 89–123). Washington, DC: American Association of Colleges for Teacher Education.

Villegas, A. M., & Lucas, T. (2002). Educating culturally responsive teachers: A coherent approach. Albany, NY: SUNY Press.

CHAPTER 7

Teaching English Language Learners

Unlocking the Research on English Learners

—by Claude Goldenberg

WHAT WE KNOW—AND DON'T YET KNOW—ABOUT EFFECTIVE INSTRUCTION

The number of professional publications aimed at improving instruction for English learners has exploded since the early 2000s. Dozens of books, articles, and reports were published in the space of a few years following the appearance of two major research reviews in 2006. According to one count, nearly 15 books on the topic of English learners were published in 2010 alone, most aimed at professional audiences. Since then, the pace has only accelerated, with new and specialized books on assessment, literacy, English language development, and content instruction for English learners (ELs) seeming to appear continuously.

Yet there is surprisingly little research on common practices or recommendations for practice with the more than 5 million ELs in our nation's schools, many of whom come from families in poverty and attend lower-resourced schools. This absence of adequate research applies to all areas, including promoting English language development and instruction in content areas such as math and history. One of the 2006 research reviews noted "a dearth of empirical research on instructional strategies or approaches to teaching content" for ELs. A subsequent review of research on content area instruction for ELs echoed the same theme. Rather than providing a list of instructional practices specifically validated by research as effective with ELs—which would be a short list—I instead identify three important principles based in the research. These are:

   I. Generally effective practices are likely to be effective with ELs.
   II. ELs require additional instructional supports.
   III. The home language can be used to promote academic development.

Reprinted with permission from the Summer 2013 issue of the American Educator, the quarterly journal of the American Federation of Teachers, AFL-CIO.

There is also a fourth principle: ELs need early and ample opportunities to develop proficiency in English (see page 13 for an article devoted to that topic). For each of the three principles listed above, I provide specific examples from research on ELs.

This serious look at the research comes at an opportune time. The new Common Core State Standards (CCSS) for English Language Arts and Literacy in History/Social Studies, Science, and Technical Subjects, which have been adopted by the vast majority of states and the District of Columbia, are now in the process of being implemented. In calling for students to study and understand complex texts in English language arts and other academic subjects, these new standards place an even greater emphasis on content knowledge and language and literacy skills than the previous standards of many states. Indeed, large numbers of ELs had difficulty meeting states' prior standards. In California, for example, data from the past several years indicate that approximately 40–50 percent of originally classified ELs performed well below criteria established for the previous English language arts standards. To meet the demands of the CCSS, ELs clearly need additional help, and teachers need a great deal of support. Meeting the Common Core standards constitutes an enormous challenge we should not underestimate.

I. Generally Effective Practices Are Likely to Be Effective with ELs

There is a vast literature on effective teaching practices. Educational research over more than a half century has yielded a number of reasonably consistent findings about the features of teaching likely to result in improved student learning. These include:

- Clear goals and objectives;
- Appropriate and challenging material;
- Well-designed instruction and instructional routines;
- Clear instructions and supportive guidance as learners engage with new skills;
- Effective modeling of skills, strategies, and procedures;
- Active student engagement and participation;
- Informative feedback to learners;
- Application of new learning and transfer to new situations;
- Practice and periodic review;
- Structured, focused interactions with other students;
- Frequent assessments, with reteaching as needed; and
- Well-established classroom routines and behavior norms.

All published studies with which I am familiar that have demonstrated positive effects on ELs' achievement incorporate at least several of these features into the instructional procedures. For example, one found that structured writing instruction—including teacher instruction, error correction and feedback, and a focus on building writing skills—had more positive effects on fifth-grade ELs' writing than did a free writing approach with no explicit instruction or error correction. Both groups were allowed to write in either Spanish or English. Another writing study with native Cantonese speakers in Hong Kong reported similar findings— explicit teaching of revision strategies helped improve the quality of student writing and helped students learn to write so that readers could understand them.

Many other studies illustrate the value of well-known elements of effective instruction to promote the learning of ELs, whether in vocabulary instruction, early reading interventions, English language development, or science education. In fact, several studies have shown similar effects on both ELs and non-ELs, again suggesting that there is considerable overlap between what is effective instruction for ELs and what is effective for students already proficient in English.

Two researchers reviewed many of the same studies as the National Literacy Panel on Language-Minority Children and Youth* and concluded that "the programs with the strongest evidence of effectiveness in this review are all programs that have also been found to be effective with students in general" and modified for ELs (see the next section on instructional supports and modifications). These programs include various versions of Success for All (a school-wide program that involves far more than classroom instruction), Direct Instruction,* and phonics instruction programs. Other programs with at least some evidence of effectiveness include vocabulary instruction programs, a comprehensive language arts program combining direct teaching and literature study, a program that promotes reading between parents and kindergarten children, a Spanish version of Reading Recovery, an English tutoring program, and programs that incorporate cooperative learning.

The key message is that what we know about effective instruction in general is the foundation of effective instruction for ELs. However, as we'll see in the next section, although "generic" effective instruction is almost certainly a necessary base, it is probably not sufficient to promote accelerated learning among ELs.

II. ELs Require Additional Instructional Supports

ELs in an English instructional environment will almost certainly need additional supports so that instruction is meaningful and productive. Aside from the pedagogical need, there is also the legal requirement mandated by the Supreme Court's decision in *Lau v. Nichols* (1974) that classroom instruction must be meaningful to students even if their English language proficiency is limited. The need for additional supports is particularly true for instruction aimed at higher-level content and comprehension of academic texts. Because the Common Core standards focus more on academic literacy skills than do prior state standards, teachers will certainly need to bolster ELs' efforts to understand more challenging content in English language arts and all academic subjects. One of the most important findings of the National Literacy Panel on Language-Minority Children and Youth was that the effects of reading instruction on ELs' reading comprehension were uneven and often nonexistent even when comprehension skills were taught directly. This is in contrast to studies with English-proficient students, for whom reading instruction helps improve reading comprehension. Why does improving reading comprehension for English learners instructed in English appear so elusive? A likely explanation is that lower levels of English proficiency interfere with comprehension and can blunt the effects of otherwise sound instruction. William Saunders and I conducted a study that suggests this possibility. We randomly assigned a group of ELs either to an instructional conversation group (interactive teacher-led discussions designed to promote better understanding of what students read) or to a control condition, where the teacher used comprehension questions in the teacher's guide. We found that instructional conversations had no overall effect on ELs' story comprehension—students in both groups understood the story about equally. We did find that instructional conversations produced deeper understandings of a complex concept at the heart of a story the students read, but this is different from story comprehension.

However, when we looked at the results for students with different English proficiency levels, we found something striking: for the students with the highest English proficiency, participation in instructional conversations did have an impact on story comprehension—91 percent accuracy versus 73 percent accuracy for students in the comparison group. The middle-level students also did better with instructional conversations, but the results were not statistically significant. The lowest-level English speakers did worse with instructional conversations, although also not to a statistically significant degree. These results suggest that instruction aimed at improving ELs' comprehension is likely to be more effective when ELs have relatively higher English skills, but less effective, *in*effective, or even possibly counterproductive when their English skills are lower.

One obvious implication is that we need to focus on English language development for ELs, particularly those least proficient in English. (Along with William Saunders and David Marcelletti, I address that topic in a companion article that begins on page 13.) But what can teachers do to help

ELs who are developing their English skills as they simultaneously learn advanced academic content and skills in English?

Sheltered Instruction

To meet this challenge, educators and researchers have proposed a set of instructional supports or modifications that are sometimes referred to as *sheltered instruction*. The goal of sheltered strategies is to facilitate the learning of grade-level academic content and skills for students being instructed in English but who have limited proficiency in the language. Sheltered instruction can be expected to contribute to English language development, but its real focus is academic content and skills.

Some of the supports and modifications that have been proposed for instructing ELs include:

- Building on student experiences and familiar content (then adding on material that will broaden and deepen students' knowledge);
- Providing students with necessary background knowledge;
- Using graphic organizers (tables, web diagrams, Venn diagrams) to organize information and clarify concepts;
- Making instruction and learning tasks extremely clear;
- Using pictures, demonstrations, and real-life objects;
- Providing hands-on, interactive learning activities;
- Providing redundant information (gestures, visual cues);
- Giving additional practice and time for discussion of key concepts;
- Designating language *and* content objectives for each lesson;
- Using sentence frames and models to help students talk about academic content; and
- Providing instruction differentiated by students' English language proficiency.

There are also sheltered strategies that involve strategic use of students' home language—for example, cognates and other home language support. These will be discussed in the third section on use of the home language for classroom instruction.

The problem, however, is that there is not much evidence that these strategies actually help English learners overcome the challenges they face in learning advanced academic content and skills, as they will be required to do with the implementation of the CCSS for English language arts. There are virtually no data to suggest that sheltered instruction or any of these modifications and supports help ELs keep up with non-ELs or help close the achievement gap between them. For some of the items on the list, such as the use of content and language objectives, sentence frames, and differentiating instruction by English proficiency levels, there are no published data at all about their effects on ELs' learning.

Even the most popular sheltered model in existence and one that brings together many disparate elements into a useful and coherent instructional model—the Sheltered Instruction Observation Protocol (SIOP)—has yet to demonstrate more than a very modest effect on student learning. A recent study showed stronger effects than did prior research, but unfortunately researchers excluded from the analysis classrooms with lower implementation levels. The most recent study found modest effects that were *not* statistically significant. Another professional development model designed to help teachers of ELs accomplish high-level language and content goals with students, Quality Teaching for English Learners, produced no significant effects on student achievement in language arts or English language proficiency and no effects on teacher attitudes, knowledge, or classroom practice. Other popular programs, such as Project GLAD (Guided Language Acquisition Design), have never even been evaluated.

We also have compelling portraits of teachers who incorporate many of the supports included in the SIOP into their teaching in order to make instruction more meaningful for English learners and to promote academic language skills. One researcher, for example, describes high school biology teachers who integrate language and content instruction; use hands-on activities, pictures, and diagrams; build on student background and experiences; and provide opportunities and time for discussion and language use. But we do not know the extent to which these supports actually compensate for students' lack of proficiency in English, particularly in the sort of English language skills required for academic success.

Some Evidence of Benefits

There is some evidence that these supports and modifications do benefit ELs. For example, studies reviewed by the National Literacy Panel on Language-Minority Children and Youth find that building on students' experiences and using material with familiar content can facilitate ELs' literacy development and reading comprehension. One ethnographic study found that young English learners' writing development is helped when the teacher incorporates literacy activities and materials from home and the community into classroom activities. Another set of studies showed that second-language learners' reading comprehension improves when they read material with familiar content.

It is generally true that what we know and are already familiar with can influence new learning and the comprehension of what we read. Teachers should therefore use materials with some degree of familiarity to students. If students are expected to read material with unfamiliar content, it is important to help them acquire the necessary background knowledge. Building background knowledge or building on prior experience and familiar content might be especially important for ELs, since they face the double challenge of learning academic content and skills as they learn the language of instruction. However, like all students, ELs must learn to read and comprehend unfamiliar material—important objectives of the CCSS for English language arts.

There is also a substantial literature on graphic displays and organizers, which facilitate and support learning by clarifying content and making explicit the relationships among concepts. One study found that graphic representations helped improve seventh-grade Canadian ESL (English as a second language) students' comprehension and academic language, but this appears to be the only study of its kind with second-language learners. Another researcher also described the use of graphic organizers to help sixth-grade ELs write a historical argument, although he concluded that students would have benefited from additional explicit instruction in historical writing.

Perhaps these and other instructional supports, which are applicable to learners generally, are especially important or helpful for ELs. That certainly makes intuitive sense, but we have scant evidence either way. In fact, there is some evidence that these supports are equally effective for ELs and non-ELs. One team of researchers taught students explicitly about the science inquiry method by using pictures to illustrate the process, employing multiple modes of representation (for example, verbal, gestural, graphic, or written), and incorporating students' prior linguistic and cultural knowledge into the instruction. Another team built its intervention around the topic of immigration, which presumably had considerable resonance for the ELs, who were themselves immigrants or whose parents were immigrants from Latin America or the Caribbean. This team also used supports in the home language. While both programs showed positive effects on student learning, neither study found any difference in learning outcomes for ELs and non-ELs.

One recent study represents a new development. The researchers found that "multimedia-enhanced instruction" (videos used as part of lessons) helped make read-aloud vocabulary instruction more effective for ELs in preschool to second grade but had no effect on the learning of non-ELs. Teachers used videos related to the topics in books they read aloud to their students as part of the science curriculum on habitats (for example, coral reefs or deserts). The ELs who saw the videos as part of the vocabulary instruction learned more of the target words and made greater gains on a general vocabulary measure than those who did not. The videos helped either greatly diminish or eliminate the gap between ELs and non-ELs on the target words. This suggests a potentially very effective strategy that improves ELs' vocabulary learning while not compromising the learning of students already proficient in English.

In short, we have many promising leads but not a very good understanding of how to help ELs learn high-level academic content and skills despite limited English proficiency. What one researcher wrote about instruction focusing on language in addition to academic content—"the published research is at an early stage"—is equally true for other supports intended to help ELs achieve at high academic levels.

III. The Home Language Can Be Used to Promote Academic Development

We turn, finally, to the most controversial topic in instructing ELs—the role of the home language. There are two aspects to the issue: teaching academic content and skills, such as reading and mathematics, in the home language, and using the home language as support in an otherwise all-English instructional environment—for example, providing definitions or brief explanations in the home language, but keeping instruction overwhelmingly in English.

Teaching academic skills in the home language is at the core of the great "bilingual education" debate. Proponents of bilingual education have long argued that students should be taught in their home language (although certainly not exclusively) and that doing so strengthens the home language and creates a more solid foundation for acquiring academic skills in English. Opponents of bilingual education argue that instruction in a student's home language is a waste of time, depresses achievement in English, and simply delays an EL's entrance into the academic (and social) mainstream.

These debates over bilingual education are typically framed in terms of outcomes in English. English outcomes are without a doubt important, but there is an additional reason to consider primary language instruction for English learners, and that is the inherent advantage of knowing and being literate in two languages. No one should be surprised to learn that all studies of bilingual education have found that teaching children in their primary language promotes achievement in the primary language. This should be seen as a value in and of itself. Of course, if primary language achievement comes at the expense of achievement in English, this might not be a worthwhile tradeoff. As we will see, however, bilingual education tends to produce better outcomes in English; at worst, it produces outcomes in English equivalent to those produced by English immersion. In other words, bilingual education helps students become bilingual—something that is valuable for anyone, not just ELs. This should not be lost amid the controversy over bilingual education and English immersion.

What the Research Tells Us

Although bilingual education continues to be a politically charged issue, we can draw some conclusions from the research.

Reading Instruction in the Home Language Can Be Beneficial.   Numerous experimental studies have been conducted over the past 40 years, and the consensus—although it is by no means unanimous—is that learning to read in their home language helps ELs boost reading skills in English. Learning to read in the home language also maintains home language literacy skills; there is no controversy over this. To date, there have been five meta-analyses conducted since 1985 by researchers from different perspectives. All five reached the same conclusion—namely, that bilingual education produced superior reading outcomes in English compared with English immersion.

A more recent study, and probably the strongest methodologically, reached a different conclusion. Researchers randomly assigned Spanish-speaking ELs to either transitional bilingual education or English immersion. All students were in the Success for All program. This is very important, since previous studies of bilingual education had not controlled for instruction, curriculum, or other factors that could have compromised the findings. The authors found that in first grade, children in English immersion did significantly better on English achievement measures than did children in bilingual education. By fourth grade, English immersion students' scores were somewhat higher than that of the bilingual education students, but the differences were not significant. The researchers contend that these results support neither side in the bilingual education controversy. Instead, they argue, quality of instruction and curriculum and the school supports needed to support them are more important determinants of ELs' achievement than language of instruction.

Effects Are Small to Moderate.   The effects of home language instruction on English achievement are fairly modest, even if we disregard the findings of the recent study just discussed. The five meta-analyses mentioned in the previous section found that, on average, teaching reading in the home language could boost children's English literacy scores by approximately 12 to 15 percentile points in comparison with children in the control conditions. This is not a trivial effect, but neither is it as large as many proponents of bilingual education suggest. Of course, if we add in the results of the new study, the average effect would be reduced. But we should keep in mind that there is no controversy over the positive effects of home language instruction *on home language skills*. This should be seen as an important outcome in itself, given the many possible advantages—intellectual, cultural, and economic—of bilingualism and biliteracy.

Insufficient Data on Length of Time in Primary Language Instruction.   The soundest studies methodologically focus on relatively short-term transitional bilingual education. In transitional programs, children generally receive instruction in the home language from one to three years and then transition to all-English instruction. Among this group of studies, there is no evidence that more or less time spent in bilingual education is related to higher or lower student achievement.

Another type of bilingual education is two-way or dual-language. The goal of two-way bilingual education is bilingualism and biliteracy, in contrast to transitional bilingual education, which uses the home language only to help students transition to all-English instruction and then stops instruction in the home language. Two-way programs use the home language for far longer, at least through elementary school and often into middle school and beyond (K–12 two-way programs are rare). Two-way programs were virtually excluded from the five meta-analyses. The reason is that these longer-term studies do not meet the methodological requirements set by the meta-analyses. For example, they do not control for possible differences in the types of students in different programs, who vary considerably in terms of language, literacy, and parents' education levels. If we don't control for these factors, we are likely to get misleading results.

Our knowledge about the effects of two-way programs is unfortunately very limited. Nonetheless, two-way bilingual education offers a promising model for the education of ELs. It also offers a way to promote bilingualism and biliteracy for non-English learners, since two-way programs include English-speaking students as well as students from language-minority backgrounds (for example, Spanish speakers). This is an area in great need of additional research and rigorous evaluation.

Virtually No Data Exist on Bilingual Education in Other Curriculum Areas.   Reading is by far the curriculum area that has received the most attention in studies of bilingual education. A small number have found positive effects in math. We know very little about the effects of bilingual education in other areas of the curriculum.

Instructional Support in the Home Language

Students' home language can play a role even in an all-English instructional program. This is referred to as home (or primary) language support. There is no teaching of content and academic skills in the home language; instead, the home language is used to help facilitate learning content and skills in English. The home language can be used to support learning in an English instructional environment in the following ways:

- Cognates (words with shared meanings that have common etymological roots, such as *geography* and *geografía*);
- Brief explanations in the home language (not direct concurrent translations, which can cause students to "tune out" while English is being spoken);
- Lesson preview and review (lesson content is previewed in students' home language to provide some degree of familiarity when the lesson is taught; following the lesson, there is a review in the home language to solidify and check for understanding); and
- Strategies taught in the home language (reading, writing, and study strategies are taught in the home language but then applied to academic content in English).

Cognates have been used with a number of vocabulary and reading programs. No study has ever isolated the specific effects of cognate instruction, but more successful second-language learners do use cognates when trying to understand material in the second language.

In one study, teachers previewed difficult vocabulary in Spanish before reading a book in English; the teachers then reviewed the material in Spanish afterward. This produced better comprehension and recall than either reading the book in English or doing a simultaneous Spanish translation while reading. The program described above that was based on the topic of immigration made use of a similar technique. Before the class read a written passage, Spanish speakers were given written and audio-taped versions to preview in Spanish.

We also have evidence that reading strategies can be taught in students' home language, then applied in English. One study found that teaching comprehension strategies in students' primary language improved reading comprehension when students afterward read in English.

It should be clear that despite progress in understanding how to improve teaching and learning for the millions of ELs in our schools, many gaps remain. The challenges posed by the Common Core State Standards make those gaps glaring. Two Berkeley researchers put it squarely:

> What will the more demanding complex texts implied by the Common Core State Standards (CCSS) mean for those students who are already having trouble with existing standards? This group includes English learners (ELs), and also the language minority students (LMs) who speak English only, but not the variety that is valued and promoted in the society's schools. What will the CCSS mean for the educators who work with these students? . . . [Teachers] are worried. How can they be expected to help their students handle materials that are more demanding than what already seems difficult enough?
> This worry is justified.

The researchers then outline an approach to studying complex texts that holds promise for helping ELs meet the Common Core challenge but for which, they acknowledge, there is no real supporting evidence. As we've seen over the course of this article, this is a familiar refrain. And even when there is evidence of effects, they are modest—far too modest to make major inroads on the very large achievement gaps ELs face. It is an inconvenient truth: we lack the knowledge base to fully prepare teachers to help many of their English learner and language-minority students overcome this gap.

So what is to be done? Clearly, educators cannot wait until researchers have adequately solidified our understanding of how to help ELs meet the content and language challenges they face. They'll be waiting a long time. Maybe forever. But if policymakers and the public wish to create a high-stakes environment where teachers and students are expected to do what we do not fully know how to do, at the very least we must provide all possible supports. A good place to begin in thinking about these supports is with famed psychology professor Seymour Sarason's admonition from more than 20 years ago: "Teachers cannot create and sustain the conditions for the productive development of children if those conditions do not exist for teachers." What this means in practice is that we must create settings in schools where teachers have the time and space to:

- Systematically study with colleagues the CCSS or whatever standards or learning goals teachers are expected to follow;
- Specify and articulate what these standards and goals mean for curriculum and instruction *in their classrooms*;
- Implement curriculum, and plan and carry out instruction, based on these understandings;
- Systematically collect student work indicating student progress toward desired outcomes;
- Analyze and evaluate student work with colleagues to help determine what is working and what is not; and
- Repeat the above continuously and systematically, throughout and across school years.

Putting the above in place is no simple matter. It will require school-wide, concerted, and coherent efforts made possible by leadership, accountability, support, and assistance.* Even with all this in place, there are no guarantees that we can accomplish the very ambitious and worthwhile goals we have set for ourselves and our students. However, without creating these conditions in schools, these goals will remain a pipe dream.

I am cautiously optimistic. The current interest in developing, studying, and evaluating effective practices for ELs promises increased understanding of how to help these students succeed, even thrive, in our schools. But evaluating effective practices will not suffice. Schools must become places, in Sarason's words, for teachers' "productive development." In the end, progress will require creating these conditions in schools, continued research, and thoughtful practice to see what works in classrooms. Practitioners have an extraordinary opportunity to contribute to our knowledge base for educating ELs. We should put aside the ideological debates that have defined this field for too long and work as a profession to seek approaches that will enable all students to succeed in school and beyond. The millions of EL children and youth represent a vast and largely untapped source of social, economic, cultural, and linguistic vitality. Our job is to make sure this vitality is not squandered.

CHAPTER 8

Best Practices of Assessment

Types of Assessments

—by Steven R. Banks

CASE STUDY

Late in the summer. Mr. Sampson was hired in his first full-time teaching job as a high school history teacher in a large southwestern city. Like other recent teacher education graduates. Mr. Sampson had completed some assessment and grading activities during his time as a student teacher. Nevertheless, he had usually evaluated students only with his supervising teacher's guidance and had used only the grading policies developed by his supervising teacher.

Now, Mr. Sampson must develop his own system in a very short time. His school district requires a written classroom assessment policy to be ready by the first day of school. It must be reviewed by both the principal and the curriculum supervisor. Mr. Sampson has a wide array of assessment practices from which to choose. He wants answers to the following questions:

1. What types of assessments are available?
2. What types of assessments are appropriate for teaching history?
3. What types of assessments will provide positive feedback to his students?
4. What types of assessments will satisfy state and school district criteria for educational accountability?
5. How does a teacher determine the quality of an assessment—in effect. what is a good assessment and what is not a good assessment?

INTRODUCTION

In the last two decades, teachers have seen an increase in their assessment options. Performance-based assessments such as portfolios have become more common (Salmani-Nodoushan, 2008). Other assessments, including formative assessments, peer assessments, and self-assessments, also have become integrated into instructional practices (Buhagiar, 2007). These developments have led some experts to promote a change in how we conceptualize assessment—shifting away from viewing an assessment as simply "measuring learning and towards assessment that is explicitly designed to promote learning" (ibid., p. 40). In effect, the idea is to view assessments (or at least some assessments) as a method to help students learn, rather than only as a way of judging them.

Such changes offer you a greater variety of assessment choices and a better way to help integrate them into your teaching. The array of choices is almost bewildering. To help you sort through these choices, this chapter provides a classification system for assessments, including recently developed assessment procedures as well as more traditional methods of assessment. This classification scheme serves as an advance organizer for the more detailed presentations of each assessment procedure covered in later chapters.

Accompanying this assessment typology is an examination of the quality control procedures to use with your assessments. These procedures include a discussion of *reliability* and *validity* as well as a procedure called *item analysis* that can increase the quality of your assessments.

ASSESSMENT DEFINITIONS AND DISTINCTIONS

As mentioned in Chapter 1, *assessment* is the total set of information gathered about the students in your classroom. It is the most all-encompassing concept in the field. Other categories are subsumed under assessment. A flowchart indicating the relationship among the various concepts used in assessment practices is provided in Figure 8.1. As you can see, classroom assessment practices are divided into two basic types. One type is developed to make judgments about students. This category is used to determine grades and make placement decisions. The second type of assessments includes nonjudgmental assessments, which are used for instructional feedback, student growth, and development.

In Figure 8.1, the first category listed under *Assessments* is evaluations. **Evaluation** is the specific process of describing and making judgments about assessments. It is important to reemphasize that not all assessments are evaluative. Some assessments, such as informal assessments, are used as an aid in your instruction. Evaluations of formal assessments, such as classroom tests and papers, are used to determine student outcomes and assign grades.

Several studies indicate that there is considerable uniformity in grading practices. McMillan, Myran, and Workman (2002) found that elementary teachers use three predominant types of

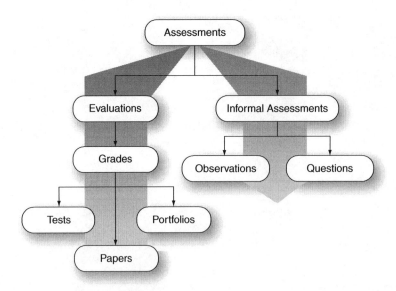

Figure 8.1 Assessment.

teacher-made assessments to assign grades: constructed-response assessments (e.g., essays, projects, and presentations), objective assessments (e.g., multiple-choice items in quizzes), and major summative examinations, such as midterms and final exams that included both essays and objective assessments. Of the three types of assessments, objective assessments were used most frequently. Ohlsen (2007) found that secondary classroom teachers also used two types of teacher-made assessment: major exams, such as midterm and final exams, and quizzes to account for most of students' overall course grades. In Ohlsen's study it was noted that performance assessments and essay tests accounted for a much smaller fraction of assessments. Kirtman (2002) also found that a majority of teachers preferred the use of traditional assessments to assign overall grades.

Grades are the measurement of student progress in a way that can be communicated to others. Grades are the aggregate of the formal assessments and evaluations used in your classroom. Since grading is partly a communicative process, you should make it as interactive as possible. In effect, grades should be used as an opportunity for the kind of feedback that enables your students to increase their classroom achievement level. Thus, grading should be seen as a chance for growth and development, not just as a judgmental activity at the end of the semester.

For beginning teachers, this sometimes is difficult. Some new teachers tend to be more controlling and judgmental about students than more seasoned teachers. As indicated by Wilson and Cameron (1996), in the early stages of their teaching beginning teachers often see control as an end in itself. This includes the control that they exercise in determining grades. Winger (2005) notes, "As a young teacher. I found the authority to give grades empowering. The grade was my ace in the hole, providing the leverage needed to entice students to cooperate" (p. 61). Winger goes on to say that in time he realized that this need for control conflicted with the need to educate; to help students truly learn and understand.

Tests are a type of assessment procedure that provides you with an estimate, often with a quantitative aspect, of your students' achievement or ability. Classroom tests constructed by the teacher are one way of measuring student achievement. When used with other assessment procedures, such as performance-based assessments and essays, these tests may form the basis for determining your classroom grades.

The second assessment category in Figure 8.1 represents assessments that are generally non-evaluative. These include informal assessments and sometimes formative assessments (discussed in Chapters 5 and 2, respectively). Since these assessments may not be used for evaluation purposes such as grades, they offer a nonthreatening way to provide feedback to your students about their classroom performance. They also offer a way for you to get feedback about the effectiveness of your instruction. Informal assessments might include informal observations of students during classroom activities, or questions and probes during classroom discussions.

CATEGORIZING ASSESSMENT PROCEDURES

A number of different viewpoints exist about how to categorize assessments. One such viewpoint focuses on categorizing assessments by their purpose. This idea was first presented by Gipps and Stobart (1993) and elaborated by Buhagiar (2007) in Box 8.1.

In addition to the list in Box 8.1, Buhaglar (2007) also includes two other purposes for assessments: motivation and control. Assessments can be used as a motivational tool to encourage students to learn. For instance, teachers can use a final exam as an incentive—doing well on this exam will help students graduate, and graduating will help them get good jobs. However, as Buhagiar notes, this type of assessment is sometimes inappropriately used as a method of coercion and control over students.

One important distinction about assessments is who is responsible for developing the them. As the classroom teacher, do you develop your own assessments or are they developed for you? Although many standardized assessments are available, these usually are too general to use in your own classroom. Certain programmed instructional packages for reading and arithmetic also offer assessment items. However, these tend to be limited in scope, measuring only those areas that are specific to the part of the programmed instruction for which the student is studying.

For instance, some phonics-based programs such as the Open Court reading series provide detailed instructional methods and assessments, but they are explicitly tailored to the program or based on specific parts of an instructional module.

BOX 8.1 CATEGORIZING ASSESSMENT PROCEDURES

1. *Screening* refers to the process of testing groups of students, normally at primary level, to identify individuals who are in need of special help.
2. *Diagnosis* involves the use of tests to identify children's strengths and (more usually) weaknesses.
3. *Record keeping* involves entering test scores and teacher assessments into student records for the purpose of assisting in the transfer process from one school level to the next.
4. *Feedback* is the transmission of results in the form of information about the progress of individual students as well as the teacher's success. Results of assessments also can provide information to the school administration about level of progress and success across the school, and school results can be used by outsiders to "evaluate" schools and teachers.
5. *Certification* provides students with a qualification that signifies that they have reached a certain level of competence or knowledge.
6. *Selection* is a process by which students are accepted into different institutions for further and higher education."

Source: Adapted from Buhagiar 2007, p. 46.

In assessing the ability to decode a sound such as *th* or *oi*, for example, the teacher uses oral dictation of various sounds. Students then copy into an instructional workbook the correct letters or words. For the most part, standardized assessments are not applicable to other areas. Thus, as with other parts of your lesson plans, you develop your own assessment materials just as you develop your own instructional methods. Assessment instruments constructed by the classroom teacher usually best address the particular needs of each instructional module.

When properly designed, quality assessments can increase student motivation. Appropriate assessment practices also can provide you with a good defense against possible grade challenges. The front-end time you spend in making good assessments will save you some time later (or at least save you a lot of grief and headaches).

Six types of assessment procedures are summarized in Table 8.1. Some overlap occurs among the categories in any system of making assessment classifications. Educators have proposed a number of alternative assessments in the last two decades in an attempt to develop more realistic or effective assessments. One result of this trend is to increase the variety of assessments available in public schools.

By Method of Development: Teacher-Constructed versus Standardized Assessments

Teacher-constructed or standardized assessments are categorized by method of development. As the name indicates, **teacher-constructed assessments** are created by the classroom teacher for a specific instructional purpose. These assessments may involve a variety of activities, such as a spelling

Table 8.1 Categorizing Assessments

By method of development:	teacher-constructed or standardized
By level of formality:	informal or formal
By instructional purpose:	formative or summative
By type of grading standard:	criterion-referenced or norm-referenced
By item format:	objective or constructed-response
By degree of authenticity:	performance or traditional

quiz, an art class portfolio, or a performance assessment in physical education. As previously stated, teacher-constructed assessments should be directly tied to the individual lesson plans created for a specific classroom. Therefore, they are tailored for a particular classroom and may not be useful beyond that given classroom.

In contrast, standardized assessments are used across any number of different classrooms. The use of the term **standardized assessment** means that all students answer the same questions, complete the assessment under similar conditions, are scored the same way, and are compared with a uniform reference group. It is with this comparison group that individual scores are compared. Standardized assessments are distinguished from teacher-constructed assessments by at least two other features:

- They use extensive pretesting on sample groups to provide statistical norms.
- They purport to assess a much larger, more general knowledge base.

For instance, a standardized achievement test for the ninth grade attempts to assess the knowledge base acquired by all ninth-grade students. In this sense, the test measures relatively global aspects of what would typically be expected of a ninth-grade student. The result is that a standardized measure provides a fair amount of comparative data in the form of test scores that can be compared with those of other schools, school districts, or states. But by increasing the domain to be assessed, a standardized assessment may sacrifice the ability to assess specific instructional outcomes in your classroom.

POINT/COUNTERPOINT: STANDARDIZED ASSESSMENTS

Point

Supporters of standardized assessments state that these tests offer an external, objective view of student achievement. Since these assessments are not developed by the classroom teacher or the school district, they provide an unbiased outside view of student performance. Supporters also claim that standardized assessments generally are able to offer a more valid and reliable measure of overall achievement than classroom assessments.

Although supporters of standardized assessments note that aligning these tests with the curriculum can be a challenge, this problem tends to be true about specific tests but not standardized assessments in general. In effect, standardized assessments can easily be devised that are aligned with a specific curriculum. In terms of measuring curriculum, appropriate standardized assessments can be just as effective as teacher-constructed assessments. The problem is that states and school systems simply make inappropriate choices about which tests to use.

Supporters of standardized assessments also note that these types of tests should be used in conjunction with other assessments. By using these assessments with teacher-constructed measures, teachers have the benefit of another viewpoint about their students. Supporters claim that, if correctly used, standardized assessments can offer an important piece of information about a classroom. It is the misuse or misinterpretation of the assessment that is the problem, not the fact that it is standardized.

Counterpoint

Critics of standardized assessments point out that teacher-constructed tests ensure a more direct connection between instruction and assessment. The classroom teacher constructs these assessments and is accountable for aligning them with the instructional objectives and the curriculum. These critics state that these teacher-constructed tests have served public schools quite well and that there is no good reason to change the policy.

According to critics of standardized assessments, the change from teacher-constructed tests to high-stakes standardized testing was *not* completed for sound educational reasons: instead, the reasons were political and social. As part of this change, the public became convinced that teachers could not appropriately assess their students. As a result, public stakeholders demanded that other methods of assessment be used to evaluate students. Therefore, externally created standardized assessments were developed to ensure teacher accountability.

Critics of standardized assessments state that these assessments often are not aligned with the mandated curriculum. They claim that such tests simply measure a somewhat nebulous, general level of achievement that is typically expected of a specific grade level. Since these tests are not directly connected with the curriculum, they cannot actually gauge student performance on that curriculum. Critics also note that these tests also are not an accurate gauge of teaching performance, which is dependent on a specified curriculum that these tests do not measure.

Despite the criticisms of standardized assessments, there are some positive uses of these assessments beyond just for teacher accountability. The following teacher application offers one example of a positive use of these tests.

TEACHER APPLICATION

Using Standardized Assessment with Teacher-Constructed Assessments

Ms. Webb teaches third grade. Recently a student transferred to her classroom from another school district. Ms. Webb has noticed that the student has a reading problem. On Ms. Webb's classroom reading assessments the child scored significantly below average. However, in all other academic areas the student scored above average.

A cross-check of scores on the state standardized exam indicates the same score pattern: above-average scores by this student in all areas except for reading. Ms. Webb knows that this type of pattern may indicate more than a reading problem, possibly even a reading learning disability such as dyslexia. Ms. Webb begins the process for a possible referral for a psychoeducational assessment by contacting the school intervention specialist who will, in turn, contact the child's parents.

By Level of Formality: Informal versus Formal Assessments

A second assessment category consists of the continuum formed by informal and formal assessments. Teachers begin making informal assessments of students from the first day of class. **Informal assessments** determine the developmental level of students—how far they have progressed in their mastery of a particular subject. Informal assessments are based on a variety of unofficial activities.

For example, Mr. Sampson, the new teacher introduced in the case study, now includes informal observations of class performance or student interactions during group discussion as part of his informal assessments. He also employs a series of diagnostic questions or probes when he first meets with his history class. He asks:

- What did the Founding Fathers mean by a Constitutional balance of power between the executive, legislative, and judicial branches of government?
- What is meant by the separation of church and state?

These types of questions give Mr. Sampson an idea of the knowledge level and thinking level of his students. By using informal assessments, he can tailor his instruction to the level of his students. Informal assessments can be used in a variety of fields, including mathematics (Allsopp, Kyger, & Lovin, 2007). Informal assessments are also becoming increasingly sophisticated and can be adapted for use with both regular and special education students (Allsopp, Kyger, Lovin Gerretson, Carson, & Ray, 2008).

In contrast, **formal assessments** are preplanned, structured assessments developed for evaluative purposes. In your classroom formal assessments can range from a weekly quiz to a standardized state exam. Formal assessments generally make judgments about student achievement and are used as the basis for student grades.

Another distinction between informal and formal assessments is that informal assessments are used solely as an aid in the teacher's instructional process while formal assessments are constructed to evaluate learning outcomes and student achievement. Based on informal assessments, many teachers adjust the difficulty of their presentation level to adapt to the cognitive level of their students. While such adjustments also may be made after formal assessments, only formal assessments are used to measure student outcomes and to determine grades.

By Instructional Purpose: Formative versus Summative Assessments

Another major categorization of assessment procedures makes the distinction between formative and summative assessments. **Formative assessments** are planned assessments that provide a guide and a direction for both teacher and student *during* an instructional program or course. Formative assessments may or may not be used as part of course grades. An example of a formative assessment that might be graded is a checklist of completed steps in a chemistry lab assignment. A self-assessment, such as those used with computer-assisted instructional programs, is an example of a formative assessment that might not be used to determine grades.

Summative assessments are a type of formal assessment used to measure student outcomes *at the end* of the instructional program of course. They may be used to determine if the student achieved mastery of an instructional segment or an academic program. Summative assessments can be used in a number of other ways, such as to determine whether a student has passed a course or whether a student should receive a high school diploma. A final exam and a minimum competency test are examples of summative assessments.

By Type of Grading Standard: Criterion-Referenced versus Norm-Referenced Assessments

Among the major issues regarding classroom assessments, two questions concern overall standards for assessments and grades:

- Should teachers grade students on the basis of how they perform on a specific standard?
- Should teachers grade students on the basis of how they compare with other students?

When students are graded on the basis of a specific performance standard. It is called a **criterion-referenced assessment** (Hambleton, 1990). For example, Mr. Sampson sets the performance criterion for an assessment at 40 correct responses out of 50 items. Regardless of how many students reach or surpass the criterion of 40 correct responses, all such students will have met the performance standard on that measure. Therefore, all the students who meet or surpass this standard will have successfully completed the activity.

A similar system can be applied to Mr. Sampson's letter grades. All students who achieve 90 out of 100 possible correct responses receive a grade of *A*. All students who achieve 80 to 89 of possible correct responses receive a *B*. Other cutoff scores may be used for *C. D.* and *F*. Regardless of how many students achieve a certain level, they still receive the same letter grade.

In contrast, a **norm-referenced assessment** is based on a student's standing in class—on how well a student does in comparison to other students. The top-scoring students receive the highest grades and the lowest scoring students receive the lowest grades, regardless of how many tests items are correct. For instance, in Mr. Sampson's history class a student achieved a correct-response rate of 90 out of 100 on an exam. However, many other students had even higher scores. The student with a 90 might be given a *B* or even a *C*, since so many other students did better.

Norm-referenced assessments are sometimes called *grading on the curve*. In effect, the assignment of grades is based on certain reference points on the normal curve. But in the typical classroom this term is frequently a misnomer. There should be the same number of *F*s as *A*s and the same number of *D*s as *B*s when a teacher grades strictly on the normal curve. (This is hardly what my students want when they ask if test grades will be curved. With my students, "curving the grades" means to raise the low scores—never to lower those "inflated" high scores.)

Norm-referenced assessments usually require some sort of transformation procedure to convert the actual test scores to grades. Teachers can use normal curve statistics or some other type of scoring system to transform student scores. In using norm-referenced assessment procedures, teachers compare students' scores and then transform them into grades. This can be used to ensure a given number of *A, B, C,* and even *D* and *F* grades.

By Item Format: Objective versus Constructed-Response Assessments

Assessments also can be categorized as objective assessments and constructed-response assessments. **Objective assessments** are based on structured items from which your students are required to choose an answer from among a number of alternatives, or fill in words that will correctly complete a statement. Multiple-choice items, true/false items, and matching items are used in objective assessments.

It is generally agreed that multiple-choice items are both the most popular and most appropriate type of objective item (Banks & Thompson, 1995). Nearly all standardized tests predominantly use the multiple-choice format. In judging the quality of objective assessments, most researchers in the field maintain that multiple-choice items offer better quality control than any other objective item.

In contrast, **constructed-response assessments** use items that require the student to make a detailed written or oral narrative. In general, constructed-response assessments use written essay items. A possible alternative is to use an oral exam format.

Constructed-response assessments have certain benefits for your classroom. If presented in a written essay format, they may increase writing skills by requiring your students to write in an organized and coherent manner. They also may increase higher-level cognitive skills by encouraging your students to synthesize and defend their ideas. When the structure of the essay item is appropriate, the ability to apply and integrate ideas into a coherent whole can be increased.

Some critics of constructed-response assessments note that they are prone to certain problems. For example, the grade assigned to such assessments is often dependent on who is doing the grading. There may be little consistency from one person to another in determining essay grades. For instance, one social studies teacher might emphasize content over format, while another might do the opposite.

By Degree of Authenticity: Traditional versus Performance-Based Assessments

A number of alternatives to traditional assessment procedures have been proposed in recent years. The focus of these alternatives has been on the development of more realistic assessments—that is, assessments that more directly relate to the performance of activities they assess than traditional assessments do. These alternative assessments led to a trend in teacher education called the *Authentic Assessment Movement* (Wiggins, 1989). This movement emphasizes the use of performance measures, including portfolios, exhibitions, and simulations, as alternatives to the more traditional assessments of classroom tests and research papers.

Performance-based assessments often measure skills that involve some type of observable activity. In many teacher education programs performance-based assessments are used to evaluate student teachers during field experiences and student teaching. Performance-based assessments may include the evaluation of skills used in a science lab or a special project. They are also frequently used in such areas as assessing public speaking. In his review of performance assessments Carey (1988) states, "They enable teachers to analyze students' performances and to comment on such aspects as timing, speed, precision, sequence, and appearance" (pp. 220–221).

Another example of a performance test is the driver's test required by each state for a driver's license. The keyboarding or data-entry speed test required by many companies for hiring employees in word-processing positions is another example. Physical education teachers increasingly use performance-based assessments in measuring physical performance activities.

Flynn (2008) noted that performance-based assessments offer students an opportunity to more fully communicate what they know. Such assessments also provide students with a kind of assessment that can sharpen their critical thinking skills.

Portfolios (discussed in further detail in Chapter 8) are an accumulated record of a student's performances or of performance-based assessments in a particular academic discipline. They usually contain the "best work" of the student. In journalism, for example, a portfolio is the repository for the best articles that a student has written for the school newspaper or for journalism classes. The portfolio may contain items for just a semester or it may contain material needed to complete graduation requirements. Wiggins (1989) provides the following example of a general portfolio developed for graduation requirements: "The requirements include a written autobiography, a reflection on work (including a résumé), an essay on ethics, a written summary of coursework in science, and an artistic product or a written report on art (including an essay on artistic standards used in judging artwork)" (p. 42).

Exhibitions tend to be a more summative type of performance-based assessment that indicates the mastery of a subject area (Wiggins, 1989). In this sense, exhibitions are like a performance test. However, exhibitions also are used to determine whether the course of study is now completed. Some examples of exhibitions are the oral defense of a doctoral dissertation and the final recital performance at a music school.

In summary, an increasing variety of assessment practices are available to teachers. There also is considerable debate about what types of assessments are best to use. As previously stated, the first law of assessments applies: *A variety of assessments is the best practice.*

Because of the many types of assessments available now, there is some degree of overlap among the categories of assessment practices. For instance, a multiple-choice, final exam in a math class could be classified as teacher-constructed, summative, objective, and criterion-referenced. Thus, categorizing assessments into a single category may not always be appropriate.

POINT/COUNTERPOINT: PERFORMANCE OR TRADITIONAL ASSESSMENTS

Point

Proponents of performance-based assessments claim that these assessments can be more effectively aligned with instruction than traditional assessments— that performance assessments may be more directly related to instruction than traditional assessments. This claim is made because of the apparently more realistic nature of performance assessments as compared to traditional assessments. For example, in a physical education class or a driver's training class, performance assessments can directly involve observations of specific skills linked to instruction. In the physical education class, completing a particular skill such as rope climbing can be easily documented. In a driver's training class, the ability to parallel park also can be readily observed and documented.

Even with typically academic subject areas, supporters of performance assessments claim that they can be more authentic than traditional assessments. For example, with performance-based curriculum and assessment, students complete a science project on amphibians. This project includes a portfolio that illustrates a sequence of skills that were completed during the project. Using a performance rubric that evaluates each skill, the teacher then completes a performance-based assessment of the project that is directly linked to each skill.

Supporters of performance-based assessments say this measurement can be more closely aligned with standards-based instruction, because the student must display work and be assessed on work that is tied to a specific standard for learning. Not only is the activity linked to a standard, but it is also tied to an idea or an experience. The activity and the assessment of the activity allow the student to plan and implement a solution to an authentic problem. This type of performance-based assessment may provide a better way of measuring performance abilities, higher-level cognitive skills, and creative abilities than more traditional assessments.

Counterpoint

Critics of performance-based assessments state that the degree of subjective judgment involved in grading some forms of performance assessments may produce a number of problems. Because some performance assessments require a high degree of judgment, grading problems may be similar to those found with grading essays. In effect, the reliability or consistency of grading performance-based assessments may be questionable. Critics point out that objective assessments with quantifiable numbers are much more reliable. They are easier to explain and defend to parents and students. They also do not require the teacher to make subjective judgments, since the answers are generally clear-cut.

In addition, according to critics of performance assessments, such assessments take time and planning. For example, devising a portfolio assignment, creating a grading rubric, and then grading the portfolio are very time consuming. Teachers' time may be better spent in creating more efficient traditional assessments. Critics also point out that the trend at the federal and state levels is to emphasize traditional standardized assessments. Teachers need to create assessments that focus on the same skills and tests required by the federal and state regulations.

QUALITY CONTROL WITH ASSESSMENTS

To judge the quality of assessments, two basic methods are used: reliability and validity. These methods apply both to standardized assessments and to teacher-constructed assessments. In general, these measures of quality control are applied to performance-based assessments as well as to traditional assessments. In addition, item analysis of individual test questions is used to assist in increasing the quality of an assessment. By analyzing each individual test question, the overall reliability and validity of an assessment may be increased. This section examines reliability and validity, as well as reviewing the role of item analysis.

Reliability

Reliability measures the consistency of an assessment. In understanding reliability, think of measuring the quality of a classroom assessment as similar to judging the quality of any other measurement instrument. For instance, in measuring the reliability of a thermometer, the consistency of the temperature readings is determined by multiple examinations of the instrument under similar conditions. A similar procedure is completed with the bathroom weight scale. When you get on the bathroom scale in the morning, you weigh yourself two or three times to see if the readings are consistent. (Maybe five times if you don't like what you see.)

The same basic principle is used with assessments. One of the most common forms of reliability is *test-retest reliability*. This type of reliability addresses the question: When the same students take an assessment and then retake this same assessment after an appropriate interval, do they score approximately the same?

If students score approximately the same in comparison with each other, the assessment scores are consistent. For example, the students who had the higher test scores and those who had the lower scores on the first test administration maintained their relative class rankings on the subsequent test administration. If rankings are relatively maintained across test administrations, the assessment is judged to have appropriate test-retest reliability.

There are many types of reliability. *Alternate forms reliability*, for example, uses two equivalent forms of the same assessment. The same students take the two alternate forms of a test. If students score approximately the same in comparison with each other on the two forms, then the test is considered to have reliability. In effect, if student rankings are generally the same when the alternate forms are compared, the assessment is judged to have acceptable alternate forms reliability.

In contrast, *internal consistency reliability* examines one single administration of an assessment. In this case, the consistency of students' scores across items is measured within that one assessment. This type of reliability addresses the question: Are students' scores consistent across the different sections of a single assessment? If students' scores are consistent across the different sections, then the assessment is considered to be reliable.

Validity

Validity is used to determine whether the test measures what it claims to measure. The analogy of the thermometer or the weight scale also applies with the concept of validity. To determine if a thermometer or a scale measures what it claims to measure, the instrument is calibrated with another similar instrument. In effect, a new thermometer is compared with an established thermometer under similar conditions. If their readings are the same, then the new thermometer has established its validity. A new scale is compared with an established scale. If the weights registered by the two scales are the same, then the new scale has established its validity. (If the weights are different, of course, you go with the lowest reading.)

A common form of assessment validity is called *criterion-related validity*. With this type of validity an assessment is given to a group of students. Their assessment scores are then compared to their scores on an external criterion appropriately related to what the test claims to measure.

With a new standardized achievement test, criterion-related validity may be measured by comparing the students' scores on the test with an older, already established achievement test. If the new test scores are closely related to the established test, then the new test is considered valid. As with reliability, the key statistical aspect is in terms of student rankings. Likewise, students who had higher scores on the new test also should have higher scores on the older test. Students with lower scores on the new test should also have lower scores on the old test. If this pattern holds true when the tests are compared, then the new test has good validity.

A second type of validity is called *content validity*. This type of validity usually is based on whether the assessment appropriately measures or samples the domain of instructional material presented to the student. For instance, given the state standards and benchmarks for a seventh-grade history class, does the assessment fully assess the range of objectives and knowledge included in these standards? The measurement of content validity may involve a degree of subjective opinion. To minimize possible subjective biases, some researchers use a panel of expert judges to review the test content and then compare it with the instructional content.

Construct validity is another form of validity that is used when a new assessment is developed that attempts to measure some type of educational or psychological construct or ability. Construct validity is the process of analyzing and relating the assessment to a particular construct. For example, let's say you want to create an assessment that measures the construct of job stress. The scores on the job stress assessment should relate to various predictions indicated by theories about job stress. For example, job stress test theories indicate a relationship between job stress and the variables of absenteeism, job turnover, or peer ratings of job stress. If the job stress test is able to predict these variables, then the test is considered to have construct validity.

Validity is the most important type of quality control procedure for measuring assessments (Thorndike, 1997). If a test is not valid, if it does not measure what it claims to measure, then the test has no meaningful use. Procedures similar to those discussed here can be used to determine validity with teacher-constructed assessments. Student scores on a classroom assessment can be related directly to their scores on standardized achievement tests. Scores on different exams can be compared. Stobart (2009) notes that establishing validity is an increasingly multifaceted procedure, particularly when applied to state assessments.

While noting the central importance of validity in determining quality control, Stobart indicates that a careful review of all quality control procedures, including reliability, is necessary in determining the use of state assessments.

Item Analysis

Item analysis is an in-depth examination of individual assessment items after an assessment has been given. Item analysis reviews the pattern of scores and answers to the assessment items. By reviewing these items, the teacher may want to discard certain items and modify other items. By doing so, the teacher will increase the reliability and validity of the assessment.

According to Hopkins, Stanley, and Hopkins (1990), there are two fundamental aspects involved in conducting an item analysis for classroom assessments: item difficulty and item discrimination. **Item difficulty** is determined by the percentage of individuals who correctly answered a given test item. When reviewing the results of a classroom assessment, this is one of the first questions that should be answered. Although there is no hard and fast rule for item difficulty on classroom assessments, there are some general guidelines. Hopkins, Stanley, and Hopkins (1990) note two aspects about item difficulty on objective assessments:

- An item correctly answered by fewer than 25 percent of students may be a questionable item.
- An item correctly answered by more than 75 percent of students may be a questionable item.

On criterion-referenced assessments or performance tests, the level of item difficulty may be set in a different manner. In effect, a teacher would expect students to correctly answer more items on these types of assessments. Therefore, the number of items that are answered correctly (item difficulty level) could be substantially different for criterion-referenced assessments than for other types of assessments. Clearly, item difficulty must take into account the type of assessment procedure.

Another reason for conducting an analysis of item difficulty is for instructional decisions and student feedback. If certain test items are missed by nearly everyone, then an instructional change may be in order. It may be that the classroom instruction did not appropriately cover the information. Or the item may have been incorrectly worded or inappropriate for the developmental level of the students. Another way of determining the efficacy of the item is to compare those who missed very few items on the assessment with those who missed many items.

Item discrimination is the ability of each separate item to differentiate between the high scorers and the low scorers on the assessment. An item that successfully discriminates is an item that is answered correctly by students who have high scores on the assessment, whereas students who have low scores answer it incorrectly. The better an item differentiates between the high scorers and the low scorers, the better the level of item discrimination.

Who is a high-scoring student and who is a low-scoring student? Hopkins, Stanley, and Hopkins (1990) state that the optimum division is the top-scoring 27 percent versus the lowest-scoring 27 percent. They also say that for classroom assessments it makes little difference whether the teacher uses a figure as low as 21 percent or as high as 33 percent. Therefore, depending on the classroom circumstances, a teacher may want to compare the top 25 percent versus the lowest 25 percent on each item to determine the item discrimination. Box 8.2 provides an application for using item discrimination with classroom tests.

Using Reliability, Validity, and Item Analysis

Reliability, validity, and item analysis offer methods for you to examine different aspects of your own teacher-constructed assessments. When effectively used, these techniques can increase the quality of your classroom assessments. For instance, one frequently asked question is: How many test items should one have on a formal classroom assessment?

Although there is no specific right answer to this question, the general answer is, the more the merrier. In effect, if the items are good questions, then the longer a test is, the more it will meet the reliability, validity, and item analysis standards. Think of it this way: The more samples or measurements that one takes of any phenomenon, the more reliable and valid is one's final evaluation of the phenomenon. This is true of political polling. This is true of earthquakes. It is even true of middle-school boys.

This section presents two ways of using these measures of quality control:

1. *Informal analysis.* It is relatively easy to complete an informal analysis of quality control procedures. However, you sacrifice some accuracy and precision by an informal analysis. The first thing to do is to transform test scores into class rankings. You can then compare students' class rankings and get an approximation of reliability and validity scores. For instance, with reliability, the questions are:
   - Do the same students have the same or similar rankings on different sections of the same test? Are the top-scoring students still the top-scoring students?
   - Are the lower-scoring students still the lower-scoring students?

   With validity, the procedure is essentially the same. You want to determine the validity of a new chemistry exam. You obtain the test scores on the new exam and the overall chemistry grades. You rank both the exam scores and the grades. You then compare the rankings on both measures to see if the students have approximately the same rankings on both the test and the grades.

   An informal item analysis can be easily completed by examining the test scores of the top 21 to 33 percent of your students. If the test items are appropriate, your top students should be missing different items. If they miss different items, this would indicate that the items are not the problem. If the top group consistently misses the same items, this indicates a problem. These are the items that need to be closely reviewed and may need to be discarded.

BOX 8.2 APPLYING ITEM DISCRIMINATION

Mr. Sampson's history class of 32 students just completed a midterm exam. He wants to use item discrimination to analyze the results of the multiple-choice part of the exam. He decides to examine the top 25 percent of students on the test versus the lowest scoring 25 percent.

Question 9	Item-Response Alternatives			
	A	**B**	**C**	**D**
Top-scoring group	0	8	0	0
Low-scoring group	0	0	4	4

The correct answer for Question 9 was B. As shown, all eight members of the top-scoring group answered this item correctly. None of the eight members of the low-scoring group answered the item correctly. Thus, this item perfectly discriminated between the top group and the low group.

Question 12	Item-Response Alternatives			
	A	**B**	**C**	**D**
Top-scoring group	4	0	4	0
Low-scoring group	0	2	4	2

The correct answer for Question 12 was C. Equal numbers of the top-scoring group and the low-scoring group answered this item correctly. Thus, this question has zero item discrimination and would be considered inappropriate. Mr. Sampson decides to review and change item-response alternative A. This item was answered by a large number of the top group. When a significant number of the top group lists the same incorrect answer, careful scrutiny should be given to that item alternative.

Question 17	Item-Response Alternatives			
	A	B	C	D
Top-scoring group	1	1	0	6
Low-scoring group	2	2	2	2

The correct answer for Question 17 is D. Six members of the top group answered this item correctly, and two members of the low group answered this item successfully. This item successfully discriminated between the two groups and therefore should be retained.

2. *Formal analysis.* Many statistical programs are available that will examine and report reliability, validity, and item analysis. Although these programs require training for individual use, some school systems may offer assistance through their technology specialists or their research bureau. Other computer programs offer applications that are much easier to learn. For instance, some machine scoring programs that use bubble sheets (computer-scored answer sheets) will also offer reliability and item analysis. Some spreadsheet programs, such as Excel, also provide the ability to complete some types of reliability and validity analysis.

By carefully applying reliability, validity, and item analysis procedures, you can discard inappropriate assessment items (or even entire assessments). You then retain those items that are appropriate. This increases the quality of your assessments. You will be a happier teacher, and your students will reinforce that happiness.

SUMMARY

Assessment Definitions and Distinctions

The variety of assessments has markedly increased in the last two decades. As a result, a teacher can create myriad alternatives to traditional assessments, and it is important to distinguish between assessments and evaluations. Assessments may be evaluative in nature and lead to formal grades or academic judgments. However, certain assessments, such as informal assessments, are nonevaluative and are used simply to provide feedback.

Categorizing Assessment Procedures

To help conceptualize assessment practices, a classification system for assessments is presented. The different classifications of assessments are based on the following aspects: who constructs the tests, the degree of formality, how they are graded, how they are used, and how authentic they are. Assessments range from informal observations to standardized state exams.

Quality Control with Assessments

Reliability, validity, and item analysis are used to measure quality control with assessments. Reliability measures the consistency of an assessment. Validity measures the degree to which the assessment measures what it claims to measure. Item analysis reviews individual items after the assessment has been administered in order to examine the quality of the items.

CASE STUDY EPILOGUE

Mr. Sampson has decided to use a variety of assessments as part of his assessment policy in his history classes. He begins his first fall term with a series of informal assessments. These assessments use question-and-answer discussion sessions with the whole class. Mr. Sampson begins these sessions by asking a series of questions that initiate the discussion. He then informally observes the knowledge and ability level of his students.

After two weeks of informal assessments. Mr. Sampson gives bi-monthly formal assessments in the form of tests that use both objective and essay items. After these assessments, he reviews each of his new formal assessments. He completes an item analysis of each assessment. He then examines and discards a number of items that appear to have problems. Next he checks the internal consistency reliability of his new assessments. Along with two other teachers. Mr. Sampson reviews the construct validity of his formal assessments.

In addition to these assessments, Mr. Sampson also requires his students to complete a journal that documents and analyzes current news stories. At least twice a week students must document a news story by describing it. Then they must analyze the different aspects of the news story and analyze the relationship of the news story to the history course. At the end of the term, each student is required to write a research paper on one of these news stories.

CHAPTER ACTIVITIES

Websites

http://www.unl.edu/buros/ The online version of the *Mental Measurements Yearbook* developed by the Buros Center for Testing. The website has perhaps the most complete index on published tests. It also includes an index for test reviews.

http://www.cse.ucla.edu/ Funded by the National Center for Research on Evaluation, Standards, and Student Testing, this website is created by UCLA. The site includes a variety of information and research on assessment practices.

www.nytimes.com This website for the *New York Times* provides some of the most current information on educational issues. The site also provides an archive for previous newspaper articles on educational issues.

Portfolio Activities

1. Review Mr. Sampson's situation as listed in the chapter case study. In your portfolio try to answer the questions that Mr. Sampson has about his teaching. Here are some of the questions:
   - What types of assessments are appropriate for teaching history?
   - What types of assessments will provide appropriate feedback to students?

- What types of assessments will satisfy state and school district criteria for educational accountability?
- How can a teacher determine what is good assessment and what is not good assessment?

2. Visit this website: http://www.unl.edu/buros/ (As indicated above, this website features nearly all published standardized assessments.) Once there, use the search engine: Test Reviews Online. Find a test that you have taken at some point. This might include the ACT, the SAT, a state standardized assessment for your state, or a nationally standardized test such as the Comprehensive Test of Basic Skills (CTBS) or the Stanford-10 Achievement Test. In three sentences summarize the basic aspects of this test. Include statements about the test's validity and reliability.

3. Using the examples provided in this chapter on item analysis, complete an examination of both item difficulty and item discrimination with material from your own class. (If you do not have your own students, borrow some test data. There are plenty of teachers who need to make their assessments better.) With item difficulty, review items that were correctly answered by fewer than 25 percent of students or items that were correctly answered by more than 75 percent of students. These are items that may need to be changed or discarded. With item discrimination first determine which students were in the top 25 percent on the assessment and which students were in the bottom 25 percent. Then for each question, devise a grid like the one provided below.

Question _____	Item-Response Alternatives			
	A	B	C	D
Top-scoring group				
Low-scoring group				

Review each item on the test to see which questions effectively discriminate between the top and low groups. (The top group answers them correctly and the low group does not answer them correctly.) Again, those items that produce the greatest response difference between the two groups are generally the best items.

KEY CONCEPTS

authentic assessment movement
constructed-response assessments
criterion-referenced assessment
evaluation
exhibitions
formal assessments
formative assessments
informal assessments
item analysis
item difficulty

item discrimination
norm-referenced assessment
objective assessments
performance-based assessments
portfolios
reliability
standardized assessment
summative assessments
teacher-constructed assessment
validity

Assessment as Learning

—by Lorna M. Earl

Classroom assessment should not be abandoned nor replaced because of its difficulties, instead, it should be transformed, strengthened, and focused so that it becomes a powerful instrument of learning for students and also for teachers.

Historically, tests, quizzes, projects, and so on have occurred at or near the end of instruction, as a basis for reporting to parents and making selection or placement decisions. Assessments differentiated or sorted students into groups and, in the process, set or confirmed their future schooling, their likely employment, and the course of their lives. This process worked well enough for most students and largely went unchallenged, as long as there were plenty of places for the majority of students to lead productive and worthwhile lives, many of which did not depend directly on passing or failing in school (e.g., agriculture, manufacturing, trades). As the world has changed, this approach is proving to be inadequate. High school graduation is a minimum prerequisite for almost all jobs; students and their parents are refusing to accept the judgment of educators as fair, especially when the criteria for the judgments are vague or kept secret and the result is that some receive status and opportunity and are valued, while others are excluded or diminished. At the same time, we are learning a great deal about how people learn. The human mind is a fascinating but mysterious organ. So much about how it works is still unknown. Teachers, as the guides of the mind, have a responsibility to remain ever vigilant for new knowledge about learning and to continually rethink their approach to teaching and their assessment practices in relation to learning theory.

Imagine a different conception of assessment, one that is rooted in the far past, one that holds assessment as an inextricable part of learning. It is ironic that the word *assessment* is derived form the Latin word *assidere*— "to sit with" (Wiggins, 1993). Its very origin implies more than marks, percentiles, grade point averages, and cut scores. It also suggests a perspective that eschews efficiency and economy as assessment hallmarks. Instead, it conjures up images of teachers observing students, talking with them, and working with them to unravel their understandings and misunderstandings— making assessment an integral part of learning that offers detailed feedback to the teacher and the student (Earl & LeMahieu, 1997).

This notion of *assessment as learning* is deeply rooted in a constructivist theory that learning is a process of taking in information; interpreting it; connecting it to existing knowledge or beliefs; and, if necessary, reorganizing understanding to accommodate the new information (Shepard, 1991). If people learn by constructing their own understanding from their experiences, assessment is not only part of learning, it is the critical component that allows learners (and teachers) to check their understanding against the views of others and against the collective wisdom of the culture as it has been recorded in the knowledge, theories, models, formulas, solutions, and stories that make up the curriculum and the disciplines. The notion that assessment is inextricably tied to learning challenges the very core of many educational practices and raises the specter for teachers of fundamentally changing much of what they do. This challenge is daunting but seductive, especially for teachers who see teaching as a moral enterprise and the moral purpose of teachers as enhancing or enriching the lives of their students (Fullan, 1993). There is no "one right way" to assess students; rather, teachers have to create their own understanding and make their own professional decisions moment by moment. And there are many exciting approaches emerging in classrooms.

The Keys to Effective Schools: Educational Reform as Continuous Improvement edited by Hawley, Willis D.; Rollie, Donald L.
Reproduced with permission of Sage Publications, Inc. in the format Republish in a book via Copyright Clearance Center.

GETTING THERE

It won't be a simple task to change assessment in schools. In fact, there will be many vocal opponents to the views that I have described in this chapter. But opposition is not a sufficient reason for refusing to try. The ideas in this section are ones that have been observed, proposed, tried, and adapted by teachers working in all kinds of schools, at all grade levels, and in a variety of places around the world. I offer them here as starting points for some and touchstones for others. Use them for discussion and for action as you venture along or continue on the pathway of assessment as learning.

- *Declare Your Purpose.* If you are using assessment as learning, tell your students. Show them in your actions and your words that this is an exercise in self-discovery for them and that you are their guide, their mentor, and their mirror. Make them participants in their own learning and provide them with many, many opportunities to use assessment to challenge their own knowledge and beliefs, without the interference of anxiety about marks and class standing.
- *No Surprises.* When students and parents, as well as teachers, understand what is expected of them, they have a much better chance of reaching the expectations. Learning targets should be clear, and descriptions and examples of good work should not only be visible to students and parents but also be open for negotiation and adjustment. Reporting to students and parents should be continuous, reciprocal conversations about progress and about learning, not merely information giving. Judgments should not arrive suddenly, by surprise, when the time for action is far past, but as shared decisions heralding the next steps in learning.
- *Self-Assessment Should Be the Ultimate Goal.* Stiggins (1993) said it all:
  If you want to appear accountable, test your students.
  If you want to improve schools, teach teachers to assess their students.
  If you want to maximize learning, teach students to assess themselves.

Students need to become their own best assessors. A participatory democracy depends on citizens who can make informed and defensible decisions. If students are to become critical thinkers and problem solvers who can bring their talents and knowledge to bear on unanticipated problems, they have to develop high-level skills of self-assessment and self-adjustment. Broadfoot (1994) describes a study in Great Britain in which teachers came to realize that the things that really made a difference in students' motivation and the quality of their learning were (a) sharing and discussing curriculum goals with students, (b) encouraging students to set their own learning targets and make "learning plans," (c) involving students in assessing their own work so that they were more willing and able to monitor their own learning and took greater responsibility for doing so, and (d) teachers and students reviewing progress together and revising "learning plans" based on information from classroom assessments. Effective assessment empowers learners to ask reflective questions and consider many strategies. It is not likely that students will become competent, realistic self-evaluators on their own. They need to be taught skills of self-evaluation and have routine and challenging opportunities to practice and validate their own judgments (Earl & Cousins, 1995).

- *Making Connections.* The essence of assessment as learning for teachers lies in being talented conductors with the complete musical score in their head and a flair for improvisation. They must hear the nuances of each instrument, intuit the emotions of the players, allow them the freedom to experiment, and subtly guide and extend the talent and virtuosity of each of them in personal ways by providing feedback and encouragement moment by moment.
- *Working Together.* As teachers engage in classroom assessment, they are plagued with questions: How sure am I that I'm right? Is this really an accurate and fair picture of this student's learning? These questions become particularly important when teachers' judgments carry serious consequences for students. In measurement terms, these are issues of *reliability* and

validity. Teachers don't need to know the nuances of these concepts, but they do need to be able to ensure that their assessments are both reliable and valid. One of the most powerful ways to increase confidence in assessments is for teachers to work together and share decision making. When teachers work together to establish criteria for judging their students' work, set standards, locate examples of quality work, and make group decisions, the collaboration has many spin-offs. At the very least, it gives teachers some confidence in their decisions because they did not come to them in isolation. In the long run, they develop agreement about the nature and quality of their assessment and of the students' work. When teachers share the decisions about how to assess, there will be fewer discrepancies in student assessment standards and procedures between grades or classes; they will develop a deeper understanding of curriculum and of individual students; and they will engage in the intense discussions about standards and evidence that lead to a shared understanding of expectations for students, more refined language about children and learning, and consistent procedures for making and communicating judgments. This exercise becomes even more powerful when students are involved in the practice of setting and internalizing standards for their own work.

Classroom assessment matters. I can imagine a time, in the not too, too distant future when it is not viewed with foreboding and terror; not separated from teaching and learning; not used to punish or prohibit access to important information; and not seen as a private, mystical ceremony. Instead, assessment and teaching and learning will be reciprocal, each contributing to the other in ways that enhance both. I believe as Haney (1991) does:

> Once teachers begin such efforts, the difficulties fall away and their work becomes, in a sense, easier. They become thoughtful observers, documenters and organizers of evaluation. In the end, these fresh directions are not as complex as they appear. They call upon us to ask, in relation to purpose, what would cause us to say that our students are thinkers, readers, writers and comprehenders of knowledge, and to then work out systematic processes to follow up such questions. In doing so, we make assessment a more powerful educational tool and return credibility to school practice. Most important, though, we improve the quality of student learning. (p. 166)

REFERENCES AND RESOURCES

Broadfoot, P. (1994, October). *Assessment and evaluation: To measure or to learn?* Paper presented at the International Conference on Evaluation, Toronto.

Brown, R. (1989). Testing and thoughtfulness. *Educational Leadership, 46*(7), 31–33.

Darling-Hammond, L. (1994). Performance-based assessment and educational equity. *Harvard Educational Review, 64*(1), 25.

Earl, L., & Cousins, B. (1995). *Classroom assessment: Changing the face; facing the change.* Toronto: Ontario Public School Teachers' Federation.

Earl, L., & LeMahieu, P. (1997). Rethinking assessment and accountability. In A. Hargreaves (Ed.), *Rethinking educational change with heart and mind.* Alexandria, VA: Association for Supervision and Curriculum Development.

Fullan, M. (1993). *Change forces: Probing the depths of educational reform.* London: Falmer.

Haney, W. (1991). We must take care: Fitting assessments to function. In V. Perrone (Ed.), *Expanding student assessment.* Alexandria, VA: Association for Supervision and Curriculum Development.

Hargreaves, A. (1994). *Changing teachers, changing times.* Toronto: Ontario Institute for Studies in Education Press.

McLean, L. (1985). *The craft of student evaluation in Canada.* Toronto: Canadian Education Association.

Natriello, G. (1987). The impact of evaluation processes on students. *Educational Psychologist, 22*(2), 155–175.

Rogers, T. (1991). Educational assessment in Canada. *Alberta Journal of Educational Research, 36*(2), 179–192.

Shepard, L. (1991). Psychometricians' beliefs about learning. *Educational Research, 36*(2), 179–192.

Stiggins, R. (1990). *Understanding the meaning and importance of quality classroom assessment.* Portland, OR: Northwest Regional Laboratory.

Stiggins, R. (1991, March). Assessment illiteracy. *Phi Delta Kappan,* pp. 534–539.

Stiggins, R. (1993, May). *Student-centered assessment.* Workshop sponsored by the Association of Educational Research Officers of Toronto.

Stiggins, R. (1994). *Student-centered classroom assessment.* New York: Merrill.

Wiggins, G. (1993). *Assessing student performance.* San Francisco: Jossey-Bass.

Wilson, R. (1990). Classroom processes in evaluation student achievement. *Alberta Journal of Educational Research, 36*(2), 134–144.

Wilson, R. (1994, May). *Back to basics: A revisionist model of classroom-based assessment.* Paper presented at the annual meeting of the Canadian Educational Research Association, Calgary, Alberta.

The Fundamentals of Formative Assessment

—by Laura Greenstein

This chapter looks at the essential principles of formative assessment and provides a preview of best practice. Our focus here is both the content and context of formative assessment: its basic elements and some of the reasons it has risen to prominence and gained support as an effective means of improving student learning.

Essential Principles

The information in this section has been gathered from numerous sources and aligned around three significant concepts: (1) formative assessment is student focused, (2) formative assessment is instructionally informative, and (3) formative assessment is outcomes based.

In an effort not to duplicate information available in other resources, I have condensed the elements and their definitions quite a bit. If you would like to read more about the fundamentals of formative assessment, I recommend "Working Inside the Black Box" (Black, Harrison, Lee, Marshall, & Wiliam, 2004); *Classroom Assessment for Student Learning: Doing It Right— Using It Well* (Stiggins, Arter, Chappuis, & Chappuis, 2004); and *Classroom Assessment and Grading That Work* (Marzano, 2006).

Formative Assessment Is Student Focused

Formative assessment is purposefully directed toward the student. It does not emphasize how teachers deliver information but, rather, how students receive that information, how well they understand it, and how they can apply it. With formative assessment, teachers gather information about their students' progress and learning needs and use this information to make instructional adjustments. They also show students how to accurately and honestly use self-assessments to improve their own learning. Instructional flexibility and student-focused feedback work together to build confident and motivated learners.

In brief: Formative assessment helps teachers

- Consider each student's learning needs and styles and adapt instruction accordingly
- Track individual student achievement
- Provide appropriately challenging and motivational instructional activities
- Design intentional and objective student self-assessments
- Offer all students opportunities for improvement

In practice: Students in Mrs. Chavez's English class are studying character development. They have read about Scout in *To Kill a Mockingbird* and Holden Caulfield in *The Catcher in the Rye*.

Early in the unit, Mrs. Chavez asks her students to define a character trait and give an example of someone in literature or in real life who demonstrates that trait. She gathers their examples in a list, which she posts in the classroom. This is valuable information about the starting point for the unit: in this case, it helps the teacher determine whether she needs to clarify the concept of character traits or can move on with the application of character traits to literature.

Based on the data her students provide, Mrs. Chavez decides to move forward. She arranges the class into random groups and asks each group to write all the character traits of Scout that they can think of on individual yellow sticky notes—one trait per note—and then do the same for Holden Caulfield, this time using blue sticky notes. Then each group posts their responses on the original list of traits, alongside each character trait. Areas of agreement and disagreement are discussed. Mrs. Chavez uses a questioning strategy to elicit information and to clarify any lingering gaps in understanding or accuracy. Following this, students work on their own to create a T chart for each character, using the left side of the T to list life experiences and challenges and the right side to list how these factors have influenced traits and behaviors. Note that Mrs. Chavez has done very little lecturing or whole-class teaching to this point, making for a very student-focused lesson.

Formative Assessment Is Instructionally Informative

During instruction, teachers assess student understanding and progress toward standards mastery in order to evaluate the effectiveness of their instructional design. Both teachers and students, individually and together, review and reflect on assessment outcomes. As teachers gather information from formative assessment, they adjust their instruction to further student learning.

In brief: Formative assessment

- Provides a way to align standards, content, and assessment
- Allows for the purposeful selection of strategies
- Embeds assessment in instruction
- Guides instructional decisions

In practice: During a high school social studies unit on the development of American nationalism after the War of 1812, Mr. Sandusky uses a series of assessments to monitor his students' developing understanding of the presented material. Mr. Sandusky begins with a pre-assessment focused on content similar to what students will encounter in the final selected-response test. After reviewing the pre-assessment data, he concludes that his students either remember little of their prior learning about the material or haven't been exposed to these topics before. He had intended to begin the unit with a discussion of how the popularity of "The Star-Spangled Banner" fueled nationalistic spirit but decides to alter those plans somewhat by having students read articles about the War of 1812, grouping them by readiness and assigning purposefully selected readings. One group reads about the reasons the United States and Britain went to war, another reads about specific events that occurred during the war, and a third reads about Francis Scott Key. Each group reports out, sharing information with the rest of the class.

As the unit progresses, students keep track of their learning and assignments on a work-along, turning it in to Mr. Sandusky every day for a quick check. For example, they describe causes of the war, answer a question about Key's motivation to write "The Star-Spangled Banner," and note the location of the battle he observed (Baltimore's Fort McHenry). This is followed by a Corners activity where students pick different lines of the song to analyze and respond to in terms of relevance to current events. Later, after a discussion of the diverse opinions on the War of 1812, the teacher asks students to report one pro and one con viewpoint. To probe students' understanding of the significant outcomes of the war, he asks the class to describe three specific changes in the power of the U.S. government that resulted from the war. In these activities, Mr. Sandusky works to align his formative assessment questions with the lesson's specific objectives, incorporate the questions into instruction, and use the information to guide future instruction.

Formative Assessment Is Outcomes Based

Formative assessment focuses on achieving goals rather than determining if a goal was or was not met, and one of the ways it does so is by helping to clarify learning goals and standards for both teachers and students. Teaching and learning are based on these standards. Students know the criteria for meeting the standards and are frequently shown exemplars. Teachers give frequent and substantive feedback to students about their progress, pointing out both strengths and areas that need improvement. Teachers plan steps to move students closer to learning goals. Work is assessed primarily on quality in relation to standards rather than student attitude or effort.

In brief: Formative assessment

- Emphasizes learning outcomes
- Makes goals and standards transparent to students
- Provides clear assessment criteria
- Closes the gap between what students know and desired outcomes
- Provides feedback that is comprehensible, actionable, and relevant
- Provides valuable diagnostic information by generating informative data

In practice: A curricular standard for 10th grade Biology requires that students understand the chemical basis of all living things. In her classroom, Ms. Jefferson asks students to track their progress toward the specific objective of describing, comparing, and contrasting the molecular structure of proteins, carbohydrates, and fats. The applied learning comes from explaining how these differences are exhibited by foods that students eat every day. Ms. Jefferson uses a signaling activity to get a baseline assessment of where her students stand; afterward, she delivers a traditional lecture, beginning the lesson (as she will all lessons) by stating the specific learning outcome students are expected to master and then focusing on transitioning students from what they know to what they need to know. Students keep a record of their learning by recording specific content knowledge in lab report notebooks. In one section, they draw the molecular structure of proteins, carbohydrates, and fats. Later in the unit, they watch a video and fill in a provided empty outline and then complete a lab in which they test a variety of foods for the presence of proteins, carbohydrates, and fats and report their findings in their lab notebooks. Ms. Jefferson reviews these notebooks regularly to monitor student progress and understanding, provide specific feedback, and inform her instructional decisions. Other formative assessment strategies she uses include Bump in the Road and Feathers and Salt.

A Brief History of Formative Assessment

As with most effective teaching methods and practices, individual teachers have probably used formative assessment throughout history. Indeed, we could claim Socrates as an early practitioner. Peppering his students with questions that probed and provoked, he used their responses to measure their learning and guide his instruction; this is the primary attribute of formative assessment.

Although teachers have long used strategies like the Socratic method and other forms of meaningful questioning, the term "formative assessment" is a relatively new one. Its contemporary use is often traced to Michael Scriven (1967), who used "formative" and "summative" to indicate differences in both the goals for collecting evaluation information and how that information is then used. Scriven explained that while a program is in the planning and developmental stages, it is still malleable, and the information gathered from evaluation can therefore contribute to change in the program. He called evaluation for this purpose of improving "formative." Once a program has been created and implemented, Scriven argued, evaluations can only yield information to determine whether the program has met its intended goals. Scriven called this final gathering of information a "summative evaluation."

Benjamin Bloom was one of the first to apply the concepts of formative versus summative to educational assessment, helping to lay the foundations for the concept of mastery learning (Bloom,

Hastings, & Madaus, 1971). The purpose of mastery learning was to ensure that students didn't move forward to the next level of learning until they had demonstrated mastery of the learning objectives set for the current level. This concept, in turn, became the basis for modular instruction, widespread in the 1970s, in which students learned from self-directed packets, or modules of instruction. When a student successfully completed one packet, he or she could move on to the next packet, proceeding through modules until all objectives were met. In theory, mastery learning resembles today's scaffolding, but in practice, students worked mostly in isolation without much teacher support or peer interaction.

In the decades following, formative assessment began to be more widely explored. States considered ways to embed it in standardized tests. Bloom continued his theoretical work, examining several issues relating to formative assessment. He identified two essential elements of formative learning: feedback for students and corrective conditions for all important components of learning (Bloom, 1977). He also argued that formative information could be used to divide the class into cooperative groups based on the corrections required. From this point, teachers could differentiate instruction to meet the needs of individual students through selected teaching strategies and corrective responses (Bloom, 1976).

In New Zealand, Terry Crooks studied the effect of classroom assessment practices on students and reported on their potential to emphasize what is important to learn and positively affect student motivation. Crooks (1988) asserted that classroom assessment "appears to be one of the most potent forces influencing education. Accordingly it deserves very careful planning and considerable investment of time from educators" (p. 476). Around the same time, Sadler (1989) reasoned that assessment is most effective when students can monitor the quality of their own work through specific provisions that are incorporated directly into instruction.

Perhaps the biggest step forward in the embrace of formative assessment came in 1998, when Paul Black and Dylan Wiliam completed a meta-analysis of more than 250 research studies on the topic. Their findings, published as "Inside the Black Box," make a compelling case for formative assessment. Black and Wiliam's review concluded that "there is no other way of raising standards for which such a strong prima facie case can be made" (1998, p. 148).

"Inside the Black Box" led the way for many educational leaders to define and apply formative assessment in classrooms, not just in the United States but throughout the world. New Zealand, Australia, and Great Britain have been especially strong leaders in this movement. The recent groundswell in interest and information is creating an imperative to change how we think about and use assessment.

Evidence for Formative Assessment

The 1998 Black and Wiliam study provided evidence that formative assessment can make a difference in learning outcomes at all grade levels. This review of research studies, journal articles, and book excerpts concluded that "formative assessment shows an effect size of between .4 and .7, the equivalent of going from the 50th percentile to the 65th" (p. 141). An effect size is a comparison of a range of scores of students exposed to a specific practice to those of students who were not exposed to the practice. Black and Wiliam drew additional conclusions, each of which is worthy of further research:

- The success of formative assessment is highly related to how teachers use it to adjust teaching and learning practices.
- Effective learning is based on active student involvement.
- Enhanced feedback is crucial to improved outcomes.
- There is a link between formative assessment and self-assessment.

More information about the Black and Wiliam study is available through the Web site of Kings College London (www.kcl.ac.uk/schools/sspp/education/research/groups/assess.html).

At the National Research Council, Bransford, Brown, and Cocking's work *How People Learn* (1999) became the basis for the book *Knowing What Students Know* (Pellegrino, Chudowsky, & Glaser, 2001) and drew the following conclusions:

- An assessment plan must come first, not last, in the educational process.
- Assessment, by necessity, integrates knowledge, skills, procedures, and dispositions.
- Assessment as a diagnosis of student progress shifts the emphasis from summative to formative.

In a follow-up to "Inside the Black Box," Wiliam, Lee, Harrison, and Black (2004) examined the achievement of secondary students in math and science who were exposed and not exposed to formative assessment. Teachers involved in the study were trained and supported in their use of classroom-based formative assessment. The research team measured the effects of formative assessment on learning outcomes and found a mean effect size of 0.32 when exposed to the intervention. Also in 2004, Ruiz-Primo and Furtak measured the effect of three formative assessment strategies—eliciting, recognizing, and using information—in the science classroom. They found that the quality of teachers' formative assessment practices was positively linked to the students' level of learning.

The research base for formative assessment will continue to grow, and we look forward to additional data that can strengthen the case for assessing formatively, help confirm best practices for teachers, and pinpoint the most effective strategies for responding to data and for measuring formative assessment's effect on learning outcomes.

Moving Forward with Formative Assessment

In recent years, recommendations for including high-quality formative assessment as an integral part of a larger and more balanced assessment system has come from many groups and organizations, among them the Joint Committee on Standards for Educational Evaluation (2002) and the National Council on Measurement in Education (1995). Content- and level-specific organizations, such as the National Council of Teachers of Mathematics, the National Science Teachers Association, and the National Middle School Association, have also endorsed formative assessment as a way to advance learning.

Although influential organizations and education thought-leaders have reached a general consensus about the benefits of formative assessment, teacher education and training efforts lag behind. As research has shown, teachers get little training or support in assessment and often turn to their untrained peers for information (Black & Wiliam, 1998; Shepard, 2000; Stiggins, 2001, 2002), and we are left with a gap between what we know is effective assessment practice and how most teachers use assessment in the classroom. This deficit in teacher knowledge and practice was the basis of my own doctoral dissertation, in which I concluded that secondary teachers continue to use traditional summative assessment that infrequently aligns with recommended strategies. Shepard (2000) summed it up well when she quoted this observation by Graue (1993): "Assessment and instruction are often conceived as curiously separate in both time and purpose" (p. 4). The key to high-quality formative assessment is to intertwine the two. What teachers and students need is assessment and instruction that are conceived as a unit, employed as a unit, and applied as a unit.

The most important thing you can take away from this discussion of formative assessment is the understanding that no single principle makes assessment formative. It is through the weaving together of all the principles that high-quality formative assessment arises and the blending of assessment and teaching occurs. For a quick overview of what these components look like woven together, see Figure 8.2, which shows the general flow of formative assessment principles.

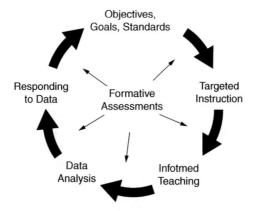

Figure 8.2   The Cycle of Instruction with Formative Assessment.

Now let's consider what the cycle of instruction might look like in practice. A teacher preparing for a discussion of current events in an English, social studies, or other class might produce the following plan. (You may not be familiar with some of the plan's strategies, but I will present these in more detail in Part 2 of the book and in the lexicon of strategies in Appendix B.)

Objective, Goal, Standard: Differentiate fact from opinion in written text.

Formative Strategy: Signaling in response to simple sentences read aloud by the teacher.

Targeted Instruction: Identify points of fact as contrasted with expression of the author's opinion in a newspaper editorial.

Formative Strategy: A Corners activity in which the teacher reads more complex sentences and students express their response by going to Fact or Opinion corners. One student in each group presents the group's opinion, and the teacher leads a follow-up discussion.

Informed Teaching: The teacher gives examples of how writers extend fact into opinion along with guidelines for distinguishing fact from opinion. Students read selected text, color-code examples of fact and opinion, and record their responses in their work-alongs.

Formative Strategy: A Think–Pair–Share activity in which students create a color-coded T chart with facts on the left and opinions on the right. This is followed by a whole-class review of the charts to reach consensus.

Data Analysis: The teacher uses data gathered to chart individual and group learning outcomes and target areas of misunderstanding and areas where students need additional challenge.

Formative Strategy: A chart of students' progress, capturing and reflecting on data gathered during Signaling, Corners, the work-along, and the T chart.

Responding to Data: The teacher adjusts instruction and assessment as needed to readdress the objective more effectively.

Formative Strategy: Adjustment to content/resource level of difficulty, grouping students for additional practice or expanded learning, and differentiating the final assessment.

Finding the Balance in Assessment Systems

Large-scale accountability measures have been and will continue to be with us for a long time. The use of formative assessment does not preclude standardized testing but, rather, contributes to a balanced assessment system. Summative assessment has traditionally asked students to definitively express what they know. It's akin to asking, "Are we there yet?" or, "Have we arrived at the intended learning destination?" In comparison, formative assessment asks what route we are taking to reach the goal and in what way the teacher can assist in the journey.

Formative assessment gives teachers continual information on student progress—information that supports decisions about how much and what kind of learning, support, and practice students need to reach the goal. In this model, assessment data come from a variety of activities, rather than from a single assessment at the end. While formative assessment and summative assessment serve the same learning goals, the former is an ongoing process and the latter is a finale: the finish line at the end of the race.

The use of standardized tests alone as the measure of knowledge does not typically lead to improved learning. There is little evidence that standardized tests have raised student achievement except in a few narrow areas, primarily at the elementary level. SAT scores have been generally consistent for many years, and most state standardized test results have flattened out during the past few years. If we want better standardized scores or higher final achievement for our students, we must begin at the classroom level. Research shows that the pathways to school improvement are lined with formative assessment. Students need constructive feedback on how to achieve the targets and guidepost measures along the way, not simply feedback on whether they reached the targets or not. It is formative assessment rather than summative assessment that will make the greatest difference.

As you come to the end of this chapter, please take a moment to consider the questions you may have about the fundamentals of formative assessment. You may want to review any section of this chapter that was not clear to you or move on to Chapter 2, which answers many frequently asked questions about using assessment formatively. Your question may be addressed there.

CHAPTER 9

Preparing for the Teaching Practicum and Field Observations

Bringing the World to Your Students

—by Edward S. Ebert, Christine Ebert, and Michael Lee Bentley

The essence of teaching is arranging opportunities for experiences from which students can learn. Though a lecture may seem a rather dry and passive approach to some, it nonetheless can be an experience that a teacher decided would be the most appropriate means of conveying information in that particular situation. Another teacher may choose to use DVDs (CD-ROMs, Document Cameras, electronic presentation boards, PowerPoint, etc.) to present information. Yet another teacher favors some approach that more actively engages the students. There are merits to each, but all are a matter of the teacher trying to engage students in learning situations.

The section that follows will discuss four broad categories of experiences: classroom lessons, multi-media, guest speakers, and field trips (see Figure III.4 on page 129). As you consider each category notice the progression from the specialized atmosphere of the typical classroom, which metaphorically brings the world to the students, all the way to the opportunities for experiences provided in a real-world context, in essence taking the students to the world.

> The essence of teaching is arranging opportunities for experiences from which students can learn.

Classroom Lessons

Classroom lessons are those experiences most typically associated with teaching school. As states and school districts struggle to bring class sizes to a manageable level, a typical classroom today will have twenty to thirty students. Depending on the district's policy with regard to ability grouping, it could be the case that all students in your classroom are classified on the same grade level (which does not mean the same thing as being *on* the same grade level academically). Some districts use regrouping plans that bring students from other grade levels to your room for instruction in particular subjects such as reading or math. In any case, classroom lessons represent a format in which teachers bring information, culture, and the world at large to the students. The contributions of scientists, mathematicians, authors, composers, artists, and all the rest are represented as passages in books, class discussions, activities, and discrete assignments to be completed. It is no wonder that students, elementary students in particular, think of their teachers as knowing everything. There is a certain mystique associated with being the individual who brings new ideas to the classroom day in and day out. That, of course, is the romantic aspect of being a teacher. The responsibilities that come along with this are formidable.

Everything that will be necessary for the presentation of a lesson must be accounted for by the teacher. If special skills are required for any aspect of the presentation (e.g., working with hazardous materials in a science demonstration or operating electronic equipment), they are skills that the teacher needs to possess. The autonomy of working with your own classroom can be empowering, and the sense of accomplishment for completing a well-presented lesson is what leads to pride in a job well done. However, even the best teacher can become tired of hauling the world (let alone the universe!) into class every day, and so there are other ways that teachers can augment some of these classroom lessons.

Multimedia Presentations

Technology is a ubiquitous term in our new millennium. Increasingly there are **multimedia presentations** available that make use of a wide range of electronic media. Books and encyclopedias on CD-ROM allow whole-text searching of documents and files. Television (broadcast, satellite, and closed-circuit), VCRs, DVDs, and the Internet not only bring high quality presentations into the classroom but also allow students to engage in interactive projects that can collect information from all around the world. Even so, the teacher remains as the ringmaster.

A key difference between high tech of today and high tech of days gone by is the heavy reliance on computer-based systems. While this brings with it the requirement that teachers be better versed than ever in the use of technology in the classroom, it is also the case that most students, and first-year teachers, come to the classroom with a significant amount of computer literacy. To avail yourself of the benefits of educational technology, you may simply have to move from the basic skills of word processing to computer-based record keeping, spreadsheets, interactive investigations, recording grades, and so forth.

The effective use of multimedia allows the teacher to bring a more accurate representation of the real world to the classroom setting. It also allows students to interact with the sights and sounds of historic events, scientific inquiry, and self-expression in matters academic or artistic.

Guest Speakers

In terms of the continuum moving from representations of the real world to the real world itself, next on the scale would be bringing **guest speakers** to the classroom. Having a real person in the classroom is bringing life outside of the school inside. However, guest speakers don't come with all of the bells and whistles that a slick multimedia presentation typically has. Nonetheless, it is valuable in our increasingly electronic and interactive age that children have the opportunity to speak with people.

Many guest speakers are well versed in the requirements of being teacher for a day and come prepared to inform and dazzle. Others may be flattered by your request to address the class and are full of good intentions, but are understandably lacking in what is required to seize and hold the attention of a classroom full of students. They may need your assistance to carry off the presentation successfully. In either case, a teacher wants to seek out organizations and individuals who can offer significant insights about a topic under consideration in the class. Note, however, that it will *always* be a good idea to have something else planned for when the speaker finishes early or at the last minute calls to say he just can't be there. Being prepared for that contingency is part of the strategy. And it is just as important to prepare your students for the guest who will be speaking with them. Your students should understand why this person is in the room and how it relates to what you have been teaching. Requiring older students to take notes or to listen for particular information will also increase attentiveness.

Field Trips

There comes a time when no amount of pushing and shoving will fit the real world into a classroom. At this point, the only alternative if the experience is to occur, is to take the students to the world. **Field trips** to a museum, an assembly plant, nature study areas, or other specialized environments can provide students with rich experiences that simply could not be duplicated in the classroom.

Field trips have fallen into disfavor in recent years. This is not because of the efficacy of the experience but rather is due to the logistics, expense, and liability involved when moving large numbers of students away from the relatively safe confines of the school. Such concerns have given rise to the explosion of multimedia presentations available to educators. Those multimedia products can also serve a role in making field trips more plausible by preparing students for what is going to occur.

There is another perspective to be taken, however. That is, the real world is not far away. In fact, it waits just beyond the classroom door. This might not do much for you if what you want is to have your students sit down in front of the local philharmonic orchestra, but keep in mind that sometimes the "field" you need is just outside the building. That is, try to overcome the feeling that all things educational must happen within the walls of your classroom. Science, art, mathematics, and even history can be found just outside of the school building, and still on school grounds, in the "real world."

As a teacher conceptualizes a lesson, it tends to emerge as one form or another of the four situations just described (classroom lesson, multimedia presentation, guest speaker, field trip). It is interesting to note the inverse relationship between the frequency of each type of experience and exposure to the real world. Thinking back over your own classroom situations, you will find that the vast majority of your educational experiences were presented in terms of classroom lessons. To a lesser degree your teachers incorporated various multimedia presentations and activities to enhance the experience. To an even lesser degree, people from the community and specialized services were brought in to speak with you. And you can probably count the number of field trips that you ever took. Since school is all about preparing students for the world in which they will live, it is an intriguing paradox that the most basic practice within organized education (classroom lessons) is the furthest removed from that world. Many factors play into this, not the least of which are matters of efficiency and economy. That is what makes this a very specialized challenge of the classroom teacher: arranging opportunities for educational experiences within the classroom that students can find relevant outside of the classroom.

INSTRUCTIONAL TECHNIQUES

Having decided which of the basic formats a lesson will involve, you must next decide which of many instructional techniques would be most appropriate for the particular situation. Issues such as the developmental level of the students, the instructional venue (indoors, outdoors, individual desks,

Classroom Lessons	Bring experiences and knowledge to the students
Multimedia Presentations	Bring depictions of people and events to the classroom: can also provide instructional experiences
Guest Speakers	Bring expertise, knowledge, and insight from people who represent particular skills, abilities, and responsibilities (e.g., local political figures)
Field Trips	Take students to the real-world experience in its natural environment (i.e., away from the classroom)

Figure 9.1 The General Categories of Instructional Experiences

tables and chairs for group work, etc.), and the subject matter to be presented must be considered. Generally speaking, there are eight categories of techniques from which a teacher might choose. As has previously been the case, the teacher may well determine that a combination of techniques would be most appropriate.

As you read through the techniques, consider that we have arranged them in terms of increasing sophistication of the thinking required of students. This is not to say that any one of the techniques is inappropriate for particular ages. After all, you can probably remember being lectured to by your parents at one time or another in your life, and you likely discovered some things on your own even as a young child. However, when planning for educational experiences, teachers need to identify the level of cognitive processing they want to engage and select the technique that best encourages that level of thinking (Lasley, Matczynski, & Rowley, 2002). Our list of techniques parallels Bloom's Taxonomy, the *Taxonomy of Educational Objectives Handbook I: Cognitive Domain* (Bloom, Englehart, Furst, Hill, & Krathwohl, 1956). The taxonomy begins with the least sophisticated level of processing, that being the recall of knowledge and facts, and progresses to the highest level, thinking that involves evaluative processes.

Direct Instruction

We list **direct instruction** in the teaching of skills as the lowest level of our taxonomy of instructional techniques because in this case the teacher decides what is important for the students to know and specifically explains or demonstrates a skill, and the student attempts to replicate it. There is very little abstraction involved here, though that is by no means intended to imply that the task is a simple one. As children struggle to reproduce the letters of the alphabet, they need all the concentration and control they can muster. Similarly, the high school student performing the steps of an experiment can be very focused and intent. Nonetheless, the demands for deep understanding and recombining of information on the part of the student are minimal in a direct instruction format. The emphasis is clearly on the acquiring of information or procedural skills.

Drill and Practice

One level up from direct instruction is **drill and practice.** Though it might seem that this technique is even more rote in nature than direct instruction, the implication is that something has already been learned, or at the very least been presented, and now the emphasis is on repetition to hone the skill or provide a strong link to the information to improve remembering it.

With this particular technique there is not a great emphasis on abstraction or on the synthesis of new understanding. Your own experience with multiplication tables would be an example of drill

Cognitive Skill	Verbs that characterize the skill
Knowledge	Label, list, match, recall, select, state, underline
Comprehension	Describe, explain, interpret, summarize, paraphrase
Application	Complete, organize, solve, calculate, compute, use
Analysis	Categorize, classify, find patterns and relationships, compare
Synthesis	Compose, create, formulate, hypothesize, write
Evaluation	Judge based on criteria, support, conclude

Figure 9.2 The Taxonomy of Educational Objectives: Cognitive Domain

and practice. There was not much mathematical theory being taught when you were required to memorize those products.

Lecture

The mainstay of a traditional college education, the **lecture,** shows up third in our instructional technique hierarchy. What does that tell you about the thinking that lectures require of a student? We are by no means denigrating the lecture approach, but the simple fact is that lectures in their pure form serve only to offer information from one person to another in a one-way verbal transaction.

It needs to be mentioned that many times teachers will follow up a lecture with some sort of discussion session. However, lectures can be, and often are, presented without any opportunity for an intellectual exchange between student and teacher. Its strength is that a large amount of information can be conveyed to a large group of people in a short amount of time with a concomitant personal touch.

Question and Answer

At this point we begin considering techniques that actually require *reflection* on the part of the student and thus involve evaluation and the synthesis of new information, the two highest levels of Bloom's Taxonomy. Reflection requires that a student receive information and then consider it with regard to his or her own experiences and interpretations. The **question-and-answer** technique supposes that to one degree or another the teacher and the student share a common body of knowledge. This does not mean that the student has the same depth of knowledge or understanding, but there are sufficient elements to the common core that allow the student and teacher to make consideration of the topic a two-way exchange.

There are several approaches to using the question-and-answer technique. In one approach, the students may question the teacher. The teacher needs to be sufficiently knowledgeable of the subject matter to provide appropriate responses without knowing the questions in advance or having the opportunity to look things up. A teacher cannot have all of the answers, but *being prepared to deal with the unexpected is part of being a teacher,* not something that happens once in awhile. Children come to school thinking about the same questions that they have heard their parents discuss at home. They may not always understand those questions, but the idea of asking the teacher for an answer is typically considered to be a good one.

> Being prepared to deal with the unexpected is part of being a teacher.

The other side of question and answer is the situation in which the teacher asks questions of the students. You are certainly familiar with this approach! However, our concern now is with the reason for those questions. One purpose would be for giving the students practice with the recall (and perhaps application) of particular information. Another would be for assessing the students' acquisition of particular information. In either of these cases, techniques such as providing think-time (Gambrell, 1983) and challenging initial responses will be valuable skills to improve the use of question-and-answer sessions. Indeed, in her classic study of the effects of wait time, Mary Budd Rowe (1978) found that providing students additional time to think increased the number and quality of responses and decreased discipline situations.

Yet a third purpose for the use of this instructional technique is to stimulate thought and encourage *divergent thinking* (as opposed to the *convergent thinking* of the previous two examples). In this situation the teacher is challenging students to apply prior knowledge and then use that as a basis for synthesizing new knowledge. The challenge presented to the teacher is that when such questions are asked, a wide range of answers is possible. The teacher must be prepared for whatever might come along, and this involves finding ways to identify merit in virtually any response. If a teacher is willing to open up the classroom to divergent thinking and the opinions of the students, then he or she must be ready to help students formulate and reformulate their ideas without diminishing the value of the original idea. Asking students for their opinions and then telling them they are wrong is one of the surest ways to bring original thinking in the classroom to a halt. The amount of innovative and creative thinking that a teacher can initiate, in virtually any subject area, is empowering both for students and teachers.

Discussion

A step higher on our taxonomy of instructional techniques is **discussion.** This differs from the previous level in that neither the teacher nor the student holds the upper hand. In this situation the teacher is concerned with a very different treatment of information than possible using the previous methods. Discussions involve the exchange of ideas. With this approach a teacher hopes to develop greater depth of thinking and perhaps to foster the manipulation of information for solving problems rather than just the acquisition of knowledge.

Some might argue that discussion is not the most appropriate term for what teachers wish to accomplish. In fact, discussion does refer more to the arguing of points of view whereas *dialogue* refers to an exchange of ideas. In either case, the instructional intent is to take students beyond "just the facts" and to engage them in a more poignant treatment of the subject matter.

Mental Modeling

Mental Modeling (Culyer, 1987) and a variation of it, the "I wonder . . ." model (Bentley, Ebert, & Ebert, 2000), are techniques specifically intended to enhance students' ability to direct their own learning by modeling the use of cognitive processes in the solving of some problem. This might sound "elementary" at first, and it is quite effective when working with young children, but it is a process that you may well have been exposed to in your secondary and now higher education experiences.

For example, during an elementary school lesson about using maps a teacher might say,

> I'd like to find my way to Sarah's house. I know the address, but I don't know how to get there from the school. I think I'll use the map of our city to find the way there. First I'll check the street index to find out where to look on the map. Then I'll use the numbers from the index to find the street.

In this way a teacher demonstrates how to sequence steps and put information to work in solving a problem. Students are then able to practice the same procedure.

The "I wonder . . ." model uses the same approach, though in the context of science education. Bentley, Ebert, and Ebert (2000) consider this to be one of the best ways of initiating the information-seeking process. An otherwise unobservable process, this technique attempts to *verbalize* the thinking that goes on. Here's an example from *The Natural Investigator* that a teacher might use with elementary level children:

> This morning I looked outside and noticed that it wasn't very sunny. I observed lots of gray clouds. I wondered if it was going to rain today. I could have just carried an umbrella in case it did rain and not thought about it anymore. However, I was planning to wear my new shoes, and I really didn't want to get them wet and dirty the first time I wore them. So I checked the newspaper and the weather channel. The paper predicted . . . (p. 127)

In this scenario, the children are exposed to the steps of listing observations, formulating a question, and identifying possible sources of information. These steps are not confined to elementary instruction. For instance, in college-level science courses you are encouraged to go through the same three steps. Your chemistry professor probably will talk you through conducting an experiment to prepare you for what might occur.

Mental modeling is a powerful technique that is on a high cognitive level. Precisely for that reason, it is something that you should try to use with your students at every opportunity. But practice first! The keys to using this technique are modeling thinking that your students can understand and then providing them with immediate opportunities to apply what they have learned. Having your students explain their own mental models or "I wonder . . ." models aloud will help clarify the process for them and allow you to assess their understanding.

Discovery Learning

Discovery learning is an approach to instruction that focuses on students' personal experiences as the foundation for conceptual development. It is unlikely that children will walk into your classroom with all of the necessary experiences that relate to the concepts you want to teach, so the challenge is to *provide* your students with the opportunities for experiences they need in the context of discovery. That is, allowing students to find the information for themselves by virtue of some activity you have provided. The students in your class will then share a common experience that you can develop as it relates to the concept under consideration. In essence, we are cheating just a bit because, from an instructional perspective the idea is to have children discover what we *want* them to discover. It's new to them, of course, but it is all part of the strategy for the teacher.

Discovery learning channels the natural inquisitiveness of children (and the natural inquisitiveness that remains in adults) by providing structure to the experience without imposing unnecessary structure on the *thinking*. That is, unlike the science experiments that you did in high school that were "wrong" if they didn't come out the way the book said they should, discovery learning encourages children to engage in the activity and document what does happen.

Even with structured activities in the classroom, twenty students will experience the activity in twenty different ways. Because of that, for discovery learning to be pedagogically sound it must be accompanied by a structure that goes beyond the discovery phase of the exercise. Such a structure, or framework, is intended to clarify the experience in terms of the concept being taught. The four-phase learning cycle (from Atkins & Karplus, 1962), a simpler version of the 7E Learning Cycle discussed in Unit I, offers one such framework.

FOUR-PHASE LEARNING CYCLE

1. **Introduction:** a question, challenge, or interesting event that captures the students' curiosity.
2. **Exploration:** the opportunity for students to manipulate materials, to explore, and to gather information.
3. **Concept Development:** With a common experience to relate to, terminology is introduced and concepts developed in class discussion.
4. **Application:** This could take the form of an enrichment activity, an opportunity to apply what has been learned, or a test to assess learning.

An example might be packaging an egg to withstand being dropped from a height of ten feet or so. After posing the question to the students about how this might be done (Introduction), students are provided time to devise various packaging strategies (Exploration). Instruction about packaging is not provided before the egg is dropped; the students are on their own at this stage. Discussions of forces, mass, acceleration, and so forth do not yet enter into the picture. It is only after the eggs have been packaged, dropped, and checked for survival that the lesson moves to a discussion of what has been found. With the common experience of this trial-and-error activity, students are prepared to have a meaningful lesson about the topics relating to forces and motion (Concept Development). Finally, the students might be challenged to package another egg (or something else) to apply what they have learned (Application). You can see that this entire lesson, though arranged by the teacher, is centered on the students' thinking. In fact, the students' thinking will drive the lesson as the teacher assesses and accommodates the various perspectives that the students will have.

Inquiry

We have placed **inquiry** at the highest level of our taxonomy not only because it involves the use of prior knowledge and the discovery of new knowledge, but because it also involves *generating the question* to be answered. It is no coincidence that the tendency to ask questions is characteristic of children as well as of adults at the top of their professions. Scientists, professors, writers, politicians, and others are people who frame questions and then go about finding solutions. Children, with their natural curiosity, are compelled to ask questions and take delight in finding answers. The task for professional educators is to channel that inquisitiveness in ways that are beneficial to the individual and perhaps even to the world at large. Suddenly our discussion has come a very long way from rudimentary direct instruction. Teaching changes lives, and it changes the world!

The teacher who uses an inquiry approach has a considerable amount of preparation to do and also must be prepared to teach the students how to use inquiry. Foremost among the concerns would be helping the student frame a question in a manner that can be investigated. For example, what would your response be if a child were to ask, "Why do birds fly?" Would you say that birds fly because it's faster than walking? Because they enjoy being in the air? Just *because? Why* birds fly is a legitimate question, but likely one to be addressed by theologians or philosophers. A more appropriate question might be "How do birds fly?" This is a question that can be investigated in the context of school. Students could even investigate what factors allow one type of bird to fly faster or higher than another or, in the case of ostriches and chickens, not at all. Helping to frame an appropriate question, without diminishing the validity of the initial question, is a primary challenge the teacher faces.

A chief strength of the inquiry approach is that it can integrate the curriculum by involving many disciplines in meaningful ways. Children can read, write, calculate, engage in scientific investigations, address social concerns, and use the arts, all in the context of answering their own questions. While the amount of lecturing that a teacher does is significantly reduced, the intellectual challenge for a teacher preparing and conducting such activities is considerable, and considerably rewarding.

A teacher may use combinations of all of the techniques we have discussed in the course of a single lesson. A lesson plan may begin with a question-and-answer session that stimulates student interest and thinking and then proceed to a discovery-learning experience that will be followed by a discussion of what was learned. It is important for you to understand that teaching is a task that requires considerable instructional flexibility, and we still have not even considered the topic of knowing the subject matter!

If you were an astute observer of the nature of each technique that we have discussed, you may have already noticed that the first three levels represent approaches in which the teacher does the most talking or directing of student activity. The middle two levels transition to a dialogic approach in which the teacher and student share more of a partnership. The teacher continues to direct the activity, if only by virtue of having planned the whole experience, but the exchange of ideas is of central concern with these levels.

But notice what happens as we move to mental modeling and the levels beyond. See how the emphasis changes now to the thinking that students will do? At these levels students are not only investigating academic topics but ultimately are also asking their own questions and finding ways to

	Teacher Focused
Direct Instruction	Teacher explains or demonstrates
Drill and Practice	Repetition to hone a skill or memorize information
Lecture	Teacher provides information to students in a one-way verbal presentation
	Dialogue Oriented
Question and Answer	Requires reflection as information is exchanged in response to a question
Discussion	An exchange of opinions and perspectives
	Student Focused
Mental Modeling	Assists students in managing their own learning by modeling a problem-solving technique
Discovery Learning	Uses students' personal experiences as the foundation for building concepts
Inquiry	Allows students to generate the questions that they will then investigate and answer

Figure 9.3 The Taxonomy of Instructional Techniques

seek answers and solve problems. You have probably heard that education is a process that seeks to develop lifelong learners. The teacher who uses all levels of the taxonomy with an eye toward leading students to these highest levels and allowing them to develop their critical and creative thinking abilities will be the teacher whose students develop that love of learning that we all wish to impart.

MONITORING AND FLEXIBILITY

Deciding on a format for presenting opportunities for educational experiences and selecting the most appropriate technique(s) for presenting the lesson constitute the foundation work that any teacher must do to present a lesson. In the course of your own educational experiences you have been in classes with teachers who have prepared this foundation to greater or lesser degrees, and no doubt you have been able to tell the difference. We would suggest to you that a key to developing expertise as an effective teacher will be your ability to make the concerns we have discussed here a part of your typical routine for planning for educational experiences.

It would be foolish for us to suggest, however, that you can put together a plan that simply could not fail. There's no way to deny the fact that teaching is an interpersonal concern, and you simply cannot know for certain the attitudes, moods, and recent experiences that your students will bring to the classroom on any given day. Therefore, as you implement the plan that you've developed, it will also be necessary to *monitor* the progress of that lesson. Is it going smoothly? Are the students receptive? Does learning appear to be occurring? Is this experience appropriate? Is this technique working? Are there student needs that you did not account for adequately? And all of this, of course, is something you do while also teaching the lesson.

Whether or not the monitoring you do is effective will be represented in terms of the adjustments *you* make. Flexibility is a virtue that all effective teachers have cultivated to a high degree. For example, if you get into a car and turn the key, only to be met by that dreaded silence of a dead battery, no amount of turning the key will overcome the basic facts. You'll have to do something else to start the car, or find alternative transportation, or cancel your plans. So too with teaching. If the information you receive from monitoring indicates that changes need to be made, it is imperative that (a) you are willing to make them and (b) you are capable of making them. A lesson that isn't working is lost time. It's that simple.

Flexibility is what saves the day. You may even find yourself in a situation in which discontinuing the lesson and moving on to something else will be an appropriate course of action. Put that instructional time to efficient use and then devise another strategy for teaching the lesson that just couldn't take off. Monitoring and flexibility are the tools a teacher uses to maintain the momentum of learning.

TOMORROW: PUTTING IT ALL TOGETHER

Now that you have conceptualized a plan, a strategy for the presentation of lessons, let's discuss what happens when you walk into the classroom tomorrow. Our peek into the future (tomorrow) considers modeling, questioning, listening, and demonstrating, directing, and orchestrating. Doesn't this sound more descriptive of what teachers actually do rather than to just say "first tell the students to open their books, have everybody turn to page . . . blah, blah, blah"? Instead, these four teacher behaviors describe what teachers really do in the classroom. Let's begin with modeling.

Modeling

Modeling? How does that figure into a strategy for teaching? Well, that's a good question. Think back for a moment to one or two of your best teachers. Did you ever notice that they never seemed to have a bad day? Their dogs never died. Stress was not a problem. They never had sour milk in their breakfast cereal. And though you may have come to class a time or two with tales of woe explaining why your homework wasn't done, you got the feeling that those calamities never seemed to befall those teachers. Well, it just wasn't true. Teachers are people, and they have the same problems that other people have. However, as with folks in show business, when it's time for class to begin, personal problems, concerns, sadnesses (and sometimes gladnesses) are left outside. The class must go on!

Are Teachers Role Models?

What is really happening here involves an undeniable aspect of teaching: teachers are **role models.** At the very least they model an attitude toward learning that includes the joy of discovery as well as an understanding of how difficult discovery can be. They model the idea that learning is worthwhile. Your best teachers made dull subjects (were there any dull subjects?) come alive by virtue of their own enthusiasm for what they were doing. It is likely that very few, if any, of your really good teachers modeled despair, discontent, and disinterest. And that left an impression on you, didn't it? You will teach lessons to students simply as a function of who you are. Students, to varying degrees, will want to be like you. Those desires will be based on the model that you provide every time you interact with them in school or away from the classroom.

Your actions as a teacher, beliefs, sense of humor, self-discipline, bearing, and demeanor are all lessons that are presented to students throughout the educational experience. Albert Bandura's (1986) landmark work with social learning theory places great emphasis on the impact of observing and imitating a model in the development of behaviors. We can expect that children will imitate and internalize those behaviors that they observe as being valued and rewarded.

As a teacher in a public or private school, you can anticipate that the school will expect you to model behaviors such as self-control, good grooming, a good work ethic (valuing work, punctuality, preparedness, following the rules, etc.), and placing a value on learning. But you may also expect that the school wants you to model ideologies such as being prodemocracy, accepting of cultural diversity, and maintaining a high moral standard. Whether or not explicitly stated within the curriculum, these are lessons that schools bring to the students. The teacher who encourages students not to recite the Pledge of Allegiance, albeit on defensible grounds, will likely be at odds with the district and the community. The teacher who habitually arrives late for work probably will not have a contract renewed. Teachers are not expected to be surrogate parents, but they are—without question—role models of one sort or another to their students.

Are Teachers Role Models Away From School?

There is another compelling side to the role-model issue: Are teachers role models *away* from school? Based on what has been presented thus far, the obvious answer is "yes." Students—and this applies to students anywhere along the educational continuum—delight in seeing their teachers away from school. Their expectations, however, remain the same. Seeing the teacher who is always neatly dressed at school now loading bags of mulch into the car at the local gardening shop will be a cognitive stretch for the child. Since gardening is not something on the list of improper behaviors in a child's mind, the experience will likely just require a cognitive assimilation. This could actually be a good expansion of the child's view of the world.

However, seeing their teacher purchase alcoholic beverages at the local grocery store or appearing somewhat inebriated at a community function will leave a very different impression. The question, therefore, is whether teachers are *responsible* for modeling particular behaviors even when away from school? Is this a fair expectation?

Whether or not it is fair, you will find that the expectation is widely held. This is a delicate issue that involves one's personal rights as well as the concerns of a community (society) that has entrusted its children to the influence of the teachers it has hired. Keep in mind, as you consider this issue, that children typically do not get involved in the philosophical and political aspects of these deliberations. The teacher is "the teacher."

Questioning

Just as teachers are role models for learning, they are role models for asking questions. Think of it this way: Statements, with that period right at the end, bring thinking to a halt. Questions, on the other hand, are what initiate and encourage thinking. And that, of course, is what teachers are trying to do. Imagine how many questions a teacher asks in just one day. The questions range from "How are you?" or "How was the [game, performance, play, concert, etc.] last night?" to "Who will show us how to balance this equation?" At times you may hear questions related to safety and the learning environment, such as "Does everyone understand why you should wash your hands with soap?" or "Do you need to move so you can see the SMART Board?" Typically you hear lots of questions about the application of concepts that are the focus for the day's lessons, such as "What is the answer to the third problem?" or "What is the next word in the sequence?" or "Which strategy did you use to solve the problem?" Occasionally there are reflective or philosophical questions, such as "What did you learn today that surprised you, or that interested you, that you want to talk about when you get home?" While these reflective questions are the least often asked, they may be the most important. What kind of questions do you frequently ask? As we have said, it is the asking of questions—of ourselves or as teachers—that initiates thinking.

> Statements, with a period at the end, typically bring thinking to a halt. Questions, on the other hand, with that thought-provoking question mark at the end, initiate and foster thinking. Which do you suppose is the powerful tool for teachers?

Lower-Level and Higher-Level Questions

There are various ways of classifying questions, with the two most frequent ones being in terms of Bloom's Taxonomy and convergent vs. divergent thinking. As we have seen, Bloom's taxonomy has six distinct levels and questions can be made to match those levels quite easily. For example,

1. **Knowledge** — What is the word for a group of turkeys?
2. **Comprehension** — What is the purpose of a topic sentence when writing paragraphs?
3. **Application** — Using our numerical code rather than the alphabet, how would you write your name?
4. **Analysis** — In what ways are deciduous trees and evergreen trees similar?
5. **Synthesis** — How could you use a barometer to determine the height of a building?
6. **Evaluation** — What do you think will be the most significant change that individuals can make to offset global warming? Why?

Perhaps more frequently, questions are classified into two subdivisions of the taxonomy: higher-level thinking questions (often referred to as *higher-order thinking*, or H.O.T.) and lower-level thinking questions. Lower-level questions are those on the Knowledge level. Using this system it is easier because identifying questions for specific higher-level questions, especially application and analysis, sometimes depends on the context or setting. For example: What is the nutritional value of mushrooms? For this question the level of thinking depends on the situation. Did the lesson on nutrition state the value of mushrooms? If so, the answer would require recall. If the lesson provided a list of foods but did not include mushrooms, the thinking involved in answering the question would be more challenging. The following are other examples of low-level vs. high-level thinking questions:

Lower Level

What is photosynthesis?
What is the name of the main character in the story?
$9 \times 3 = \rightarrow$?

Higher Level

How is the formula for photosynthesis similar to respiration?
Who is your favorite character in the story? Why?
How could you simplify this equation: $9x + 27y = 153$?

Convergent and Divergent Questions

Convergent questions are those that typically have one correct answer, while **divergent questions**, also called open-ended questions, are used to encourage many answers and generate greater participation of students. Besides engaging students' memory through recall, convergent questions can be used to guide students' observations, perhaps during a demonstration. Divergent questions, on the other hand, stimulate student creative or critical thinking, encouraging students to be better observers. These open-ended questions can guide students as they discover information for themselves, analyze data, make inferences, and identify relationships.

Examples of convergent questions:

- How many of the pilgrims who sailed on the Mayflower survived the first winter?
- Which is smaller, 5/16 or 3/8?
- Is saltwater denser than freshwater?

Examples of divergent questions:

- What do you predict will happen?
- What can you tell me about shadows?
- What sacrifices made by settlers traveling west by covered wagon would be most difficult for you?
- What different strategies can we use to solve the problem?

Questions That Can Derail Thinking

Teachers typically ask many more convergent questions, perhaps 85 percent of the time. A more balanced frequency will assure a value of and an emphasis on student thinking. By making audio recordings of your instructional time, you can determine the level and frequency of your question types.

Sometime teachers ask the *wrong* question. For instance, does a teacher really want to know the answer to the question, "Who can tell me how a sundial works?" "My dad" is probably not the answer the teacher was expecting. What about questions such as this: "Using information in the data table, can you construct a graph comparing the size of the fish in the aquarium?" There is great potential for H.O.T., but the way the question is worded, the answer is either "yes" or "no." In each case, however, there is potentially a good question that will encourage students to think.

Another category of questions that you will want to use sparingly includes those that employ guesswork. For example,

1. Only women have femoral arteries. True or False
2. The average number of times college students change majors is _____.
   a) 2 times   b) 4 times   c) 6 times

There is a 50 percent chance of guessing the answer to the first question, and a 1:3 chance with the second one. If the students' answers are correct, *you are not going to know whether they guessed correctly or actually knew the information.*

Of course, there are times when you, as teacher, must ask convergent questions. They are an appropriate part of the curriculum as long as you avoid limiting your questions to convergent ones.

> There are times when you, as teacher, must ask convergent questions. They are an appropriate part of the curriculum as long as you avoid limiting your questions to convergent ones.

Why? Questions

The "why?" question is a wonderful question. It can stimulate one's thinking, encourage creative and critical thinking, and open up a whole realm of possibilities. It is a question that typifies four-year-olds but engages adolescents and adults as well. Why does thunder have to be so loud? Why don't I understand algebra? Such questions are asking for explanations (inferences) from someone perceived to be wise or at least more experienced, or are pointing the way toward further understanding.

But why stop there? Yes, four-year-olds ask those questions that sometimes challenge adults to really think about something. Rather than stifling the questions of young people as they continue their efforts to understand the world around them, teachers can capitalize on their natural curiosity. By encouraging children to develop their own questions related to the topic of study, the search for answers becomes a great motivation for meaningful learning. Ultimately, the teacher can help the student to change those "why?" questions into questions more suited for investigation: What causes thunder to be so loud? What is preventing me from understanding algebra?

Taking their cue from the teacher, students place value on the types of questions asked most frequently or those questions that dominate the lessons. If you want to value a particular level of thinking, consider the amount of time or frequency with which you encourage that level.

Listening

Good communication depends on three essential components: (1) someone willing to share, (2) someone willing to receive, and (3) a common language. Sometimes teachers listen for what they want to hear. For example, if the question is asking for students to recall the three types of rock and a student says, "Igneous, sedimentary, and metamorphosis," the teacher may respond, "Yes, igneous, sedimentary, and metamorphic" and proceed to the next question. What happens when the answer is, "sedimentary, metamorphic, and granite"? In this situation, the teacher may say, "Yes, sedimentary, metamorphic and granite is an example of igneous." In both cases, the teacher was listening for the three important words and accepting the answers without giving thought to the reasons behind the actual responses given and clarifying the misunderstandings. The emphasis was on recalling information at the expense of comprehension.

Good communication requires three elements:

1. A willing sender of information
2. A willing recipient of information
3. A common language between sender and receiver

In some situations there are multiple answers to a question, but in the given context the teacher has one answer in mind. For example, when a geometry teacher asks, "How can you determine the height of a tree?" At the end of a lesson she most likely is expecting an answer that uses the information about determining the sides of a right triangle. However, students may respond with other ways that would be useful in determining the height of a tree. What would you do as a teacher when a student says to chop it down and then measure it?

A student teacher, a few years ago, reported that during a third-grade science lesson on plants, she asked the question, "Where do seeds come from?" With confidence and sincerity a little girl said, "From Walmart!" As a teacher how would you respond to that child? That is, would you simply dismiss this answer as incorrect (from the perspective you were pursuing) or would you give it merit—which values her thinking—and *then* redirect your students to the idea you were trying to develop? One approach fails to "hear" the student and the other one empowers the student as a thinker. Talking *with* students, rather than *at* them, requires good listening on the part of the teacher.

> Good listening skills will help you avoid talking at your students and focus on talking with your students.

Suggestions for Improving Your Listening Skills

There are several things you can do, and do right away, to begin improving your listening skills. With each of the following suggestions you will see that there are two parts: listening to what is said and then handling what has been said. Let's take a look.

A Correct Response Is Not a Stopping Point

Teachers are sometimes so focused on identifying the correct answer that little attention is given to the thinking on the part of the student. For example, a teacher assigns math questions that require students to apply the new problem-solving strategy just presented. The teacher then calls on individuals for answers. When a student gives a correct answer, the teacher asks another individual to answer the next question. When a student responds incorrectly, the teacher asks others to respond until the response is correct. In both cases, it appears that the answer is important.

What would happen, however, if you ask a question and, when a student provides a correct answer, you *don't* stop there? Ask follow-up questions such as, "How did you get that answer?" or "How do you know that is correct?" How will the students react? Well, the first time you do that the student is going to think that the answer was incorrect. After all, what is the purpose of talking about the answer?

Try Writing Down the Students' Answers Verbatim

By using a marker board or a projected computer screen, write students' responses, being as careful as possible not to change the wording. If the teacher is listening for the correct answer or proper use of terminology, the temptation will be to reword the answer to fit. Instead, by listening carefully and writing down the exact words used by the students, you advance two important outcomes of teaching. First, it sends a message saying you value the individual and the thoughts that student has to share. That is an important step in empowering the thinking of students. And second, as you listen to several students' responses or explanations and you capture their words on the board, you will actually be able to hear the diversity of understanding within your class.

Try Providing Time to Think

This is popularly referred to as allowing wait-time. Before calling on a student to respond to the question, allow some silent time for thinking. Most often, teachers wait only 0.6 second before calling on someone to answer. If the question is "Who's hungry?" perhaps 0.6 second is plenty of time. However, if the purpose of the question is to have students apply something learned in class to situations outside of school, it will take time. The typical recommendation is to allow three to five seconds of thinking time before taking responses.

There is another dimension to this that most any classroom teacher is familiar with. Some students, for whatever reason, cannot wait three to five seconds before responding. Rather than sending students to the principal day in and day out (and likely the same students) simply due to wait-time violations, consider what we refer to as *dynamic wait-time.*

In this case, when a student blurts out an answer, correct or otherwise, don't look dismayed because the surprise has been spoiled. And certainly don't accept the answer right away and move on. Instead, ask something like, "Does everybody agree with that?" or "Is that the answer the rest of you found?" Notice that in this situation several things are occurring. First, you have not told the student that the initial answer is incorrect. Second, you have put everyone on notice that they are still expected to compose a response. And third, rather than asking the answering student to consider the response

> Dynamic wait-time, asking students if they agree or if there is another possibility, extends thinking time even when a student blurts out an answer.

further (which is not a bad idea), you are allowing the rest of the class to continue considering the question with the additional information provided by the student. Very dynamic, it extends thinking time and includes no hidden costs or fees.

Always Provide Feedback

The encouragement and confidence that comes from hearing a teacher say things like "Great idea!" or "Very well organized" makes students want to try harder . . . *unless it is overdone.* Have you been in classrooms where teachers say "yes," "good," or "nice answer" time after time? Teachers will sometimes automatically say positive responses without really listening to the students. On more than one occasion, we have seen preservice teachers walking around the room monitoring student work and making positive, encouraging remarks without actually reading the answers carefully. The feedback was meant to compliment the child for completing as many of the items on the page in a short amount of time. In one case, if the teacher actually looked at the answers, it would have been seen that the responses to the first two questions were reversed.

DEMONSTRATING, DIRECTING, AND ORCHESTRATING

Demonstrating is an active instructional approach to teaching that is strongly teacher oriented. The teacher is the one who touches the materials and manipulates the objects while students observe the demonstration. Because it is so strongly teacher oriented, the number of times demonstrating is the preferred approach are few. However, there are three circumstances in which demonstrating is a necessary instructional strategy:

1. When the activity involves special precautions or working with hazardous materials, ensure the safety of everyone by conducting the activity.
2. When expensive pieces of equipment are involved, a demonstration may be warranted. Under these circumstances, provide special directions and demonstrate the appropriate use of such equipment before students use it (e.g., the first time microscopes are used).
3. Sometimes things happen so quickly or subtly that students would miss key observations unless the teacher did the demonstration. You can facilitate those observations by conducting the demonstration and stopping when appropriate to ask pertinent questions or tell students what to look for.

Directing is an instructional approach that is more student oriented than demonstrating. The teacher may present a new concept, provide examples on the board, direct students to read in the appropriate book, and then have students participate in an activity that clarifies the concept or reinforces understanding. For example, you might plan a lesson that involves introducing a new method for determining the volume of irregular shapes. You write examples on the board, and your students are then directed to work with math manipulatives to achieve a better understanding of the concept for the day. Being able to provide clear, meaningful directions either orally or in writing is essential to this instructional approach. The success of activities depends on students following directions.

While designing activities, make sure everybody has something to do at all times. Classroom management becomes a problem when children don't know what to do or they think that they don't have something to do. When your students work in small groups, provide directions that assign specific roles for each student. For example, there might be

- a procurement officer who collects and distributes materials needed to complete assignments,
- a spokesperson (aka reporter) who is the first person from the small group to share the group's findings or report results,
- an encourager who provides positive feedback when others are working well and encourages teammates when there is a lull in activity,
- a worrier who makes sure everyone on the team knows the answers to questions or solutions to problems, or has collected and recorded appropriate information.

The ones we mention here are merely examples. Your imagination can generate other roles and responsibilities throughout the year. Keep in mind that directions are key to this instructional approach. If you provide the information, making sure the students know what to do and how to do it, the students are quite likely to be successful.

Orchestrating is the most student-centered instructional approach. Students are not only actively engaged in the learning; they are encouraged to assume responsibility for their own learning. In this situation the teacher is not determining the questions and making decisions about seeking answers to the questions. The students start with their own curiosity to pose a problem or identify the initial questions and determine the ways to solve the problem or answer the questions. Much as the orchestral leader relates to the musicians, the teacher is there to facilitate the learning of the many individuals involved in the activity. Just because the students have more responsibility for the learning, the teacher does not have less work. More anticipation and preparation are involved not only before the lesson begins but also throughout the unit of study as it evolves.

FINALLY: THIS IS A PEOPLE PROFESSION

Everything involved in the work of a teacher is all about people. You will work with students, parents, other teachers, administrators, the community at large, and then there's . . . you. The needs of all of these constituencies (you included) are to be met through the work you do. So as we conclude this unit on instruction, let's consider two people-oriented topics: preparation and taking time to enjoy your work.

Preparation, Preparation, Preparation

In real estate it's location, location, location. In higher education, we once heard a professor say, "At Cornell it's all about three things: research, research, and research." Well, for the classroom teacher it comes down to preparation, preparation, preparation. This will be the key to a successful lesson.

Understand Your Constituents

You will work with many constituencies. Each one needs a different sort of preparation. Your students come to you to learn the identified curriculum (OK, they don't look at it that way, but that's what is happening). Administrators, however, are concerned with the degree of success you are having in presenting that curriculum. Parents are concerned with the performance, and happiness, of their particular children. And *you* need to be able to meet the needs of all of these folks while preserving your mental health and enjoying the work you do.

Life as a professional educator can be both overwhelming and deeply gratifying. Preparing appropriately for each constituency is what will breed confidence and success through your career as an educator. Do not take any constituency for granted! They each have their specific needs.

Understand the Curriculum You Enact

The specific curriculum where you teach is what you now need to study. Read the background information. Review the textbooks and instructional materials that your school has adopted. Be as prepared for *planning* a lesson as you wish to be for presenting a lesson. Really, would you feel comfortable sitting in an examination room at a medical office knowing that the physician was in the next room studying up before seeing you? Of course not; you expect that person to know what they are talking about before they come in to assist with whatever ails you.

You need to know what you will be teaching. Think about the questions provided in the textbook or teacher's edition of the curriculum materials. Do you want to use any of the questions or add your own questions? Try to anticipate questions your students might ask. If you are going to do a demonstration or have the students do an activity, practice ahead of time. If something can go wrong, you don't want that to happen during the lesson. Practice is a necessary part of learning.

Make Learning Relevant

With all this preparation and understanding of teaching, it is to be hoped that the children see connections between lessons in school and the world in which they live. Though you will find various ways to help make learning relevant for students, keep in mind that the student is the only one who can actually establish relevancy. The teacher can create opportunities and design experiences that are more likely to be seen by the students as relevant through connections to the world in which they live.

Homework typically has been used to provide students with opportunities to practice newly acquired concepts, principles, skills, and vocabulary. Most homework assignments involve contrived situations that do not make direct connections to the world outside of school. This approach to practice perpetuates what Moravcsik (1981) calls the sterile manipulation of a set of rules. Instead, you might conceptualize homework as the academic bridge between the lessons at school and the relevance of those lessons to the world of the student. With a little bit of effort, you can create assignments having students apply their new learning within the context of their own environments. You will find great satisfaction in hearing a student explain how he or she used what had been done in class or recognized in a nonschool activity something that had been discussed in class.

TAKE TIME TO ENJOY YOUR PROFESSION

And finally, take time to enjoy your work. It will be far too easy to let the paperwork, planning, and preparation occupy all of your concern. It is the interaction with children, and with colleagues, that has brought you to this profession. If you follow the suggestions presented in this unit so that you understand what you are going to do and plan well to do it, then get in there and have fun! Your enthusiasm, particularly during the presentation of difficult topics, will influence the performance of your students as well.

> Remember that you are the one who is controlling the attitude, the atmosphere, in your classroom. That alone is an empowering statement for the work of a professional educator.

Reflective teaching is a term you will hear quite a bit these days. This means to take time to consider what works, what didn't work so well, and how you might make changes. But you don't always have to wait until it's a rainy Saturday afternoon to do this reflecting. As you work with your students, consider what is happening and whether you need to change pace or direction. And certainly ask yourself whether you are smiling enough. If the answer is "no," then take a breath, adjust your perspective a bit, and remember that *you* are the one who is controlling the attitude, the atmosphere, in your classroom. That alone is an empowering statement for the work of a professional educator.

What to Look for in a Classroom

—by Alfie Kohn

An earlier version of this chart was published in the September 1996 issue of Educational Leadership, and reprinted as the title essay in the anthology *What to Look for in a Classroom . . . And Other Essays.*

This revised version appeared as Appendix B of *The Schools Our Children Deserve.*

	GOOD SIGNS	POSSIBLE REASONS TO WORRY
FURNITURE	Chairs around tables to facilitate interaction Comfortable areas for learning, including multiple "activity centers" Open space for gathering	Chairs all facing forward or (even worse) desks in rows
ON THE WALLS	Covered with students' projects Evidence of student collaboration Signs, exhibits, or lists obviously created by students rather than by the teacher Information about, and personal mementos of, the people who spend time together in this classroom	Nothing Commercial posters Students' assignments displayed, but they are (a) suspiciously flawless, (b) only from "the best" students, or (c) virtually all alike List of rules created by an adult and/or list of punitive consequences for misbehavior Sticker (or star) chart—or other evidence that students are rewarded or ranked
STUDENTS' FACES	Eager, engaged	Blank, bored
SOUNDS	Frequent hum of activity and ideas being exchanged	Frequent periods of silence The teacher's voice is the loudest or most often heard
LOCATION OF TEACHER	Typically working with students so it takes a few seconds to find her	Typically front and center
TEACHER'S VOICE	Respectful, genuine, warm	Controlling and imperious Condescending and saccharine-sweet

STUDENTS' REACTION TO VISITOR	Welcoming; eager to explain or demonstrate what they're doing or to use visitor as a resource	Either unresponsive or hoping to be distracted from what they're doing
CLASS DISCUSSION	Students often address one another directly Emphasis on thoughtful exploration of complicated issues Students ask questions at least as often as the teacher does	All exchanges involve (or are directed by) the teacher; students wait to be called on Emphasis on facts and right answers Students race to be first to answer teacher's "Who can tell me . . . ?" queries
STUFF	Room overflowing with good books, art supplies, animals and plants, science apparatus; "sense of purposeful clutter"	Textbooks, worksheets, and other packaged instructional materials predominate; sense of enforced orderliness
TASKS	Different activities often take place simultaneously Activities frequently completed by pairs or groups of students	All students usually doing the same thing When students aren't listening to the teacher, they're working alone
AROUND THE SCHOOL	Appealing atmosphere: a place where people would want to spend time Students' projects fill the hallways Library well-stocked and comfortable Bathrooms in good condition Faculty lounge warm and inviting Office staff welcoming toward visitors and students Students helping in lunchroom, library, and with other school functions	Stark, institutional feel Awards, trophies, and prizes displayed, suggesting an emphasis on triumph rather than community

A Synthesis of Ethnographic Research

—by Michael Genzuk, PH.D.

An Ethnography

"When used as a method, ethnography typically refers to fieldwork (alternatively, participant-observation) conducted by a single investigator who 'lives with and lives like' those who are studied, usually for a year or more." —John Van Maanen, 1996.

"Ethnography literally means 'a portrait of a people.' An ethnography is a written description of a particular culture–the customs, beliefs, and behavior–based on information collected through fieldwork." —Marvin Harris and Orna Johnson, 2000.

"Ethnography is the art and science of describing a group or culture. The description may be of a small tribal group in an exotic land or a classroom in middle-class suburbia." —David M. Fetterman, 1998.

Ethnography is a social science research method. It relies heavily on up-close, personal experience and possible participation, not just observation, by researchers trained in the art of ethnography. These ethnographers often work in multidisciplinary teams. The ethnographic focal point may include intensive language and culture learning, intensive study of a single field or domain, and a blend of historical, observational, and interview methods. Typical ethnographic research employs three kinds of data collection: interviews, observation, and documents. This in turn produces three kinds of data: quotations, descriptions, and excerpts of documents, resulting in one product: narrative description. This narrative often includes charts, diagrams and additional artifacts that help to tell "the story" (Hammersley, 1990). Ethnographic methods can give shape to new constructs or paradigms, and new variables, for further empirical testing in the field or through traditional, quantitative social science methods.

Ethnography has it roots planted in the fields of anthropology and sociology. Present-day practitioners conduct ethnographies in organizations and communities of all kinds. Ethnographers study schooling, public health, rural and urban development, consumers and consumer goods, any human arena. While particularly suited to exploratory research, ethnography draws on a wide range of both qualitative and quantitative methodologies, moving from "learning" to "testing" (Agar, 1996) while research problems, perspectives, and theories emerge and shift.

Ethnographic methods are a means of tapping local points of view, households and community "funds of knowledge" (Moll & Greenberg, 1990), a means of identifying significant categories of human experience up close and personal. Ethnography enhances and widens top down views and enriches the inquiry process, taps both bottom-up insights and perspectives of powerful policy-makers "at the top," and generates new analytic insights by engaging in interactive, team exploration of often subtle arenas of human difference and similarity. Through such findings ethnographers may inform others of their findings with an attempt to derive, for example, policy decisions or instructional innovations from such an analysis.

Variations in Observational Methods

Observational research is not a single thing. The decision to employ field methods in gathering informational data is only the first step in a decision process that involves a large number of options and possibilities. Making the choice to employ field methods involves a commitment to get close to the subject being observed in its natural setting, to be factual and descriptive in reporting what is observed, and to find out the points of view of participants in the domain observed. Once these fundamental commitments have been made, it is necessary to make additional decisions about which particular observational approaches are appropriate for the research situation at hand.

Variations In Observer Involvement: Participant or Onlooker?

The first and most fundamental distinction among observational strategies concerns the extent to which the observer is also a participant in the program activities being studied. This is not really a simple choice between participation and nonparticipation. The extent of participation is a continuum which varies from complete immersion in the program as full participant to complete separation from the activities observed, taking on a role as spectator; there is a great deal of variation along the continuum between these two extremes.

Participant observation is an omnibus field strategy in that it "simultaneously combines document analysis, interviewing of respondents and informants, direct participation and observation, and introspection. In participant observation the researcher shares as intimately as possible in the life and activities of the people in the observed setting. The purpose of such participation is to develop an insider's view of what is happening. This means that the researcher not only sees what is happening but "feels" what it is like to be part of the group.

Experiencing an environment as an insider is what necessitates the participant part of participant observation. At the same time, however, there is clearly an observer side to this process. The challenge is to combine participation and observation so as to become capable of understanding the experience as an insider while describing the experience for outsiders.

The extent to which it is possible for a researcher to become a full participant in an experience will depend partly on the nature of the setting being observed. For example, in human service and education programs that serve children, it is not possible for the researcher to become a student and therefore experience the setting as a child; it may be possible, however, for the research observer to participate as a volunteer, parent, or staff person in such a setting and thereby develop the perspective of an insider in one of these adult roles.

It should be said, though, that many ethnographers do not believe that understanding requires that they become full members of the group(s) being studied. Indeed, many believe that this must not occur if a valid and useful account is to be produced. These researchers believe the ethnographer must try to be both outsider and insider, staying on the margins of the group both socially and intellectually. This is because what is required is both an outside and an inside view. For this reason it is sometimes emphasized that, besides seeking to "understand", the ethnographer must also try to see familiar settings as "anthropologically strange", as they would be seen by someone from another society, adopting what we might call the Martian perspective.

Methodological Principles

Following are three methodological principles that are used to provide the rationale for the specific features of the ethnographic method. They are also the basis for much of the criticism of quantitative research for failing to capture the true nature of human social behavior; because it relies on the study of artificial settings and/or on what people say rather than what they do; because it seeks to reduce meanings to what is observable; and because it reifies social phenomena by treating them as more clearly defined and static than they are, and as mechanical products of social and psychological factors (M. Hammersley, 1990). The three principles can be summarized under the headings of naturalism, understanding and discovery:

1. **Naturalism.** This is the view that the aim of social research is to capture the character of naturally occurring human behavior, and that this can only be achieved by first-hand contact with it, not by inferences from what people do in artificial settings like experiments or from what they say in interviews about what they do elsewhere. This is the reason that ethnographers carry out their research in "natural" settings, settings that exist independently of the research process, rather than in those set up specifically for the purposes of research. Another important implication of naturalism is that in studying natural settings the researcher should seek to minimize her or his effects on the behavior of the people being studied. The aim of this is to increase the chances that what is discovered in the setting will be generalizable to other similar settings that have not been researched. Finally, the notion of naturalism implies that social events and processes must be explained in terms of their relationship to the context in which they occur.

2. **Understanding.** Central here is the argument that human actions differ from the behavior of physical objects, and even from that of other animals: they do not consist simply of fixed responses or even of learned responses to stimuli, but involve interpretation of stimuli and the construction of responses. Sometimes this argument reflects a complete rejection of the concept of causality as inapplicable to the social world, and an insistence on the freely constructed character of human actions and institutions. Others argue that causal relations are to be found in the social world, but that they differ from the "mechanical" causality typical of physical phenomena. From this point of view, if we are to be able to explain human actions effectively we must gain an understanding of the cultural perspectives on which they are based. That this is necessary is obvious when we are studying a society that is alien to us, since we shall find much of what we see and hear puzzling. However, ethnographers argue that it is just as important when we are studying more familiar settings. Indeed, when a setting is familiar the danger of misunderstanding is especially great. It is argued that we cannot assume that we already know others' perspectives, even in our own society, because particular groups and individuals develop distinctive worldviews. This is especially true in large complex societies. Ethnic, occupational, and small informal groups (even individual families or school classes) develop distinctive ways of orienting to the world that may need to be understood if their behavior is to be explained. Ethnographers argue, then, that it is necessary to learn the culture of the group one is studying before one can produce valid explanations for the behavior of its members. This is the reason for the centrality of participant observation and unstructured interviewing to ethnographic method.

3. **Discovery.** Another feature of ethnographic thinking is a conception of the research process as inductive or discovery-based; rather than as being limited to the testing of explicit hypotheses. It is argued that if one approaches a phenomenon with a set of hypotheses one may fail to discover the true nature of that phenomenon, being blinded by the assumptions built into the hypotheses. Rather, they have a general interest in some types of social phenomena and/ or in some theoretical issue or practical problem. The focus of the research is narrowed and sharpened, and perhaps even changed substantially, as it proceeds. Similarly, and in parallel, theoretical ideas that frame descriptions and explanations of what is observed are developed over the course of the research. Such ideas are regarded as a valuable outcome of, not a precondition for, research.

Ethnography as Method

In terms of method, generally speaking, the term "ethnography" refers to social research that has most of the following features (M. Hammersley, 1990).

(a) People's behavior is studied in everyday contexts, rather than under experimental conditions created by the researcher.

(b) Data are gathered from a range of sources, but observation and/or relatively informal conversations are usually the main ones.

(c) The approach to data collection is "unstructured in the sense that it does not involve following through a detailed plan set up at the beginning; nor are the categories used for interpreting what people say and do pre-given or fixed. This does not mean that the research is unsystematic; simply that initially the data are collected in as raw a form, and on as wide a front, as feasible.

(d) The focus is usually a single setting or group, of relatively small scale. In life history research the focus may even be a single individual.

(e) The analysis of the data involves interpretation of the meanings and functions of human actions and mainly takes the form of verbal descriptions and explanations, with quantification and statistical analysis playing a subordinate role at most.

As a set of methods, ethnography is not far removed from the sort of approach that we all use in everyday life to make sense of our surroundings. It is less specialized and less technically sophisticated than approaches like the experiment or the social survey; though all social research methods have their historical origins in the ways in which human beings gain information about their world in everyday life.

Summary Guidelines for Fieldwork

It is difficult, if not impossible, to provide a precise set of rules and procedures for conducting fieldwork. What you do depends on the situation, the purpose of the study, the nature of the setting, and the skills, interests, needs, and point of view of the observer. Following are some generic guidelines for conducting fieldwork:

1. Be descriptive in taking field notes.
2. Gather a variety of information from different perspectives.
3. Cross-validate and triangulate by gathering different kinds of data. Example: observations, interviews, program documentation, recordings, and photographs.
4. Use quotations; represent program participants in their own terms. Capture participants' views of their own experiences in their own words.
5. Select key informants wisely and use them carefully. Draw on the wisdom of their informed perspectives, but keep in mind that their perspectives are limited.
6. Be aware of and sensitive to the different stages of fieldwork.
   (a) Build trust and rapport at the entry stage. Remember that the researcher-observer is also being observed and evaluated.
   (b) Stay alert and disciplined during the more routine middle-phase of fieldwork.
   (c) Focus on pulling together a useful synthesis as fieldwork draws to a close.
   (d) Be disciplined and conscientious in taking detailed field notes at all stages of fieldwork.
   (e) Be as involved as possible in experiencing the observed setting as fully as possible while maintaining an analytical perspective grounded in the purpose of the fieldwork: to conduct research.

(f) Clearly separate description from interpretation and judgment.

(g) Provide formative feedback as part of the verification process of fieldwork. Time that feedback carefully. Observe its impact.

(h) Include in your field notes and observations reports of your own experiences, thoughts, and feelings. These are also field data.

Fieldwork is a highly personal experience. The meshing of fieldwork procedures with individual capabilities and situational variation is what makes fieldwork a highly personal experience. The validity and meaningfulness of the results obtained depend directly on the observer's skill, discipline, and perspective. This is both the strength and weakness of observational methods.

Summary Guidelines for Interviewing

There is no one right way of interviewing, no single correct format that is appropriate for all situations, and no single way of wording questions that will always work. The particular evaluation situation, the needs of the interviewee, and the personal style of the interviewer all come together to create a unique situation for each interview. Therein lie the challenges of depth interviewing: situational responsiveness and sensitivity to get the best data possible.

There is no recipe for effective interviewing, but there are some useful guidelines that can be considered. These guidelines are summarized below (Patton, 1987).

1. Throughout all phases of interviewing, from planning through data collection to analysis, keep centered on the purpose of the research endeavor. Let that purpose guide the interviewing process.

2. The fundamental principle of qualitative interviewing is to provide a framework within which respondents can express their own understandings in their own terms.

3. Understand the strengths and weaknesses of different types of interviews: the informal conversational interview; the interview guide approach; and the standardized open-ended interview.

4. Select the type of interview (or combination of types) that is most appropriate to the purposes of the research effort.

5. Understand the different kinds of information one can collect through interviews: behavioral data; opinions; feelings; knowledge; sensory data; and background information.

6. Think about and plan how these different kinds of questions can be most appropriately sequenced for each interview topic, including past, present, and future questions.

7. Ask truly open-ended questions.

8. Ask clear questions, using understandable and appropriate language.

9. Ask one question at a time.

10. Use probes and follow-up questions to solicit depth and detail.

11. Communicate clearly what information is desired, why that information is important, and let the interviewee know how the interview is progressing.

12. Listen attentively and respond appropriately to let the person know he or she is being heard.

13. Avoid leading questions.

14. Understand the difference between a depth interview and an interrogation. Qualitative evaluators conduct depth interviews; police investigators and tax auditors conduct interrogations.

15. Establish personal rapport and a sense of mutual interest.

16. Maintain neutrality toward the specific content of responses. You are there to collect information not to make judgments about that person.

17. Observe while interviewing. Be aware of and sensitive to how the person is affected by and responds to different questions.

18. Maintain control of the interview.
19. Tape record whenever possible to capture full and exact quotations for analysis and reporting.
20. Take notes to capture and highlight major points as the interview progresses.
21. As soon as possible after the interview check the recording for malfunctions; review notes for clarity; elaborate where necessary; and record observations.
22. Take whatever steps are appropriate and necessary to gather valid and reliable information.
23. Treat the person being interviewed with respect. Keep in mind that it is a privilege and responsibility to peer into another person's experience.
24. Practice interviewing. Develop your skills.
25. Enjoy interviewing. Take the time along the way to stop and "hear" the roses.

Site Documents

In addition to participant observation and interviews, ethnographers may also make use of various documents in answering guiding questions. When available, these documents can add additional insight or information to projects. Because ethnographic attention has been and continues to be focused on both literate and non-literate peoples, not all research projects will have site documents available. It is also possible that even research among a literate group will not have relevant site documents to consider; this could vary depending on the focus of the research. Thinking carefully about your participants and how they function and asking questions of your informants helps to decide what kinds of documents might be available.

Possible documents include: budgets, advertisements, work descriptions, annual reports, memos, school records, correspondence, informational brochures, teaching materials, newsletters, websites, recruitment or orientation packets, contracts, records of court proceedings, posters, minutes of meetings, menus, and many other kinds of written items.

For example, an ethnographer studying how limited-English proficient elementary school students learn to acquire English in a classroom setting might want to collect such things as the state or school mandated Bilingual/ESL curriculum for students in the school(s) where he or she does research, and examples of student work. Local school budget allocations to language minority education, specific teachers' lesson plans, and copies of age-appropriate ESL textbooks could also be relevant. It might also be useful to try finding subgroups of professional educators organizations which focus on teaching elementary school language arts and join their listservs, attend their meetings, or get copies of their newsletters. Review cumulative student records and school district policies for language minority education. All of these things could greatly enrich the participant observation and the interviews that an ethnographer does.

Privacy or copyright issues may apply to the documents gathered, so it is important to inquire about this when you find or are given documents. If you are given permission to include what you learn from these documents in your final paper, the documents should be cited appropriately and included in the bibliography of the final paper. If you are not given permission, do not use them in any way.

Ethics in Ethnographic Research

Since ethnographic research takes place among real human beings, there are a number of special ethical concerns to be aware of before beginning. In a nutshell, researchers must make their research goals clear to the members of the community where they undertake their research and gain the informed consent of their consultants to the research beforehand. It is also important to learn whether the group would prefer to be named in the written report of the research or given a pseudonym and to offer the results of the research if informants would like to read it. Most of all, researchers must be sure that the research does not harm or exploit those among whom the research is done.

Analyzing, Interpreting and Reporting Findings

Remember that the researcher is the detective looking for trends and patterns that occur across the various groups or within individuals (Krueger, 1994). The process of analysis and interpretation involve disciplined examination, creative insight, and careful attention to the purposes of the research study. Analysis and interpretation are conceptually separate processes. The analysis process begins with assembling the raw materials and getting an overview or total picture of the entire process. The researcher's role in analysis covers a continuum with assembly of raw data on one extreme and interpretative comments on the other. Analysis is the process of bringing order to the data, organizing what is there into patterns, categories, and basic descriptive units. The analysis process involves consideration of words, tone, context, non-verbals, internal consistency, frequency, extensiveness, intensity, specificity of responses and big ideas. Data reduction strategies are essential in the analysis (Krueger, 1994).

Interpretation involves attaching meaning and significance to the analysis, explaining descriptive patterns, and looking for relationships and linkages among descriptive dimensions. Once these processes have been completed the researcher must report his or her interpretations and conclusions

Qualitative Description

Reports based on qualitative methods will include a great deal of pure description of the program and/or the experiences of people in the research environment. The purpose of this description is to let the reader know what happened in the environment under observation, what it was like from the participants' point of view to be in the setting, and what particular events or activities in the setting were like. In reading through field notes and interviews the researcher begins to look for those parts of the data that will be polished for presentation as pure description in the research report. What is included by way of description will depend on what questions the researcher is attempting to answer. Often an entire activity will be reported in detail and depth because it represents a typical experience. These descriptions are written in narrative form to provide a holistic picture of what has happened in the reported activity or event.

Reporting Findings

The actual content and format of a qualitative report will depend on the information needs of primary stakeholders and the purpose of the research. Even a comprehensive report will have to omit a great deal of the data collected by the researcher. Focus is essential. Analysts who try to include everything risk losing their readers in the sheer volume of the presentation. This process has been referred to as "the agony of omitting". The agony of omitting on the part of the researcher is matched only by the readers' agony in having to read those things that were not omitted, but should have been.

Balance Between Description and Analysis

In considering what to omit, a decision has to be made about how much description to include. Detailed description and in-depth quotations are the essential qualities of qualitative accounts. Sufficient description and direct quotations should be included to allow readers to understand fully the research setting and the thoughts of the people represented in the narrative. Description should stop short, however, of becoming trivial and mundane. The reader does not have to know absolutely everything that was done or said. Again the problem of focus arises.

Description is balanced by analysis and interpretation. Endless description becomes its own muddle. The purpose of analysis is to organize the description in a way that makes it manageable. Description is balanced by analysis and leads into interpretation. An interesting and readable final account provides sufficient description to allow the reader to understand the analysis and sufficient analysis to allow the reader to understand the interpretations and explanations presented.

REFERENCES AND SUGGESTED READINGS

Agar, M. (1996). <u>Professional Stranger: An Informal Introduction To Ethnography,</u> (2nd ed.). Academic Press.

Fetterman, (1998). <u>Ethnography,</u> 2nd ed., Thousand Oaks, CA: Sage Publications.

Hammersley, M. (1990). <u>Reading Ethnographic Research: A Critical Guide</u>. London: Longman.

Harris, M. & Johnson, O. (2000). <u>Cultural Anthropology,</u> (5th ed.), Needham Heights, MA: Allyn and Bacon.

Krueger, A. R. (1994). <u>Focus Groups: A Practical guide for Applied Research,</u> Thousand Oaks, CA: Sage Publications.

Moll, L.C. & Greenberg, J.M. (1990). Creating Zones of Possibilities: Combining Social Constructs for Instruction. In: L.C. Moll (ed.) <u>Vygotsky and Education: Instructional Implications and Applications of Sociohistorical Psychology,</u> New York, NY: Cambridge University Press.

Patton, M.Q. (1987). How to Use Qualitative Methods in Evaluation. Newberry Park, CA: Sage Publications.

Spradley, J. (1980). <u>Participant Observation</u>. New York: Holt, Rinehart and Winston.

Spradley, J. (1979). <u>The Ethnographic Interview</u>. New York: Holt, Rinehart and Winston.

Van Maanen, J. (1996). Ethnography. In: A. Kuper and J. Kuper (eds.) <u>The Social Science Encyclopedia, 2nd ed.,</u> pages 263-265. London: Routledge.

Yin, R.K. (1989). <u>Case Study Research: Design and Methods</u>. Newberry Park, CA: Sage Publications.

Re-printed with permission.

Original: Genzuk, M. (1999). Tapping Into Community Funds of Knowledge. In: Effective Strategies for English Language Acquisition: A Curriculum Guide for the Development of Teachers, Grades Kindergarten through Eight. Los Angeles Annenberg Metropolitian Project/ARCO Foundation. Los Angeles.

Re-printed: Genzuk, M. (Fall, 2003): A Synthesis of Ethnographic Research. Occasional Papers Series. Center for Multilingual, Multicultural Research (Eds.). Center for Multilingual, Multicultural Research, Rossier School of Education, University of Southern California. Los Angeles.

CHAPTER 10

Preparing to Enter the Profession

Beginning:
The Challenge of Teaching

—by William Ayers

School—take out the "sh" and it's cool. —John O'Connor

The Words *teaching and teacher* evoke in almost everyone particular memories and images. For some, these memories are dull, even fearful—they include boredom, routine, and worse. For those of us who construct lives in teaching, these images are necessarily changing and growing, and while they are sometimes vivid and concrete, they can as often be characterized by wonder. In either case, images of teaching can fill us with awe, and we can choose to see within them an abiding sense of challenge.

Education for what?

> At this time when teaching, schooling, and any attempt to support students' efforts to really learn something of value have fallen under brutal political attack [we must note] the ways education can be deployed to create moments of liberation for seemingly despairing young people. Today's education-policy questions about social promotion, standardized testing, and even school uniforms are beside the more fundamental point of what we are preparing students for and how such preparation leads to a more just and equitable society.
> *—Gloria Ladson-Billings*

A life in teaching is a stitched-together affair, a crazy quilt of odd pieces and scrounged materials, equal parts invention and imposition. To make a life in teaching is largely to find your own way; to follow this or that thread; to work until your fingers ache, your mind feels as if it will unravel, and your eyes give out; and to make mistakes and then to rework large pieces again and again. It is sometimes tedious and demanding, sometimes confusing and uncertain, and yet it is as often creative and dazzling: Surprising splashes of color can suddenly appear at its center; unexpected patterns can emerge and lend the whole affair a sense of grace and purpose and possibility.

I find fragments of my own teaching everywhere, sections of a large and growing quilt now filling my house, cluttering my mind. I remember Kelyn, a poor, five-year-old African-American child I taught years ago. One day, Kelyn and I, with a half a dozen other kids on a trip from school, were playing the I Spy game. "I spy something red and white with the letters S-T-O-P on it," I said. (My choices tend to be the easiest ones and, when too self-consciously geared toward "learning," the most boring as well.) "Stop sign!" cried seven voices in unison.

A big brown truck pulled up to the stop sign opposite us. Darlene eagerly offered the next challenge: "I spy something brown." Kelyn's eyes lit up and a broad smile crossed his face. He sat up as tall as he could and, with his right hand spread-fingered and flat across his chest and his left hand pulling excitedly on his cheek, he shouted, "Hey! That's me! That's me!"

No one sensed anything peculiar or taboo or funny in Kelyn's response. After all, Darlene had asked for something brown, and Kelyn is brown. But for me there was something more. In that classroom we had spent a lot of energy on self-respect and affirmation and on exploring differences. Kelyn's father was active in the civil rights movement, and his parents were conscious of developing self-esteem in their children. Kelyn was expressing some of that energy, and so he responded with gusto.

Once another child, Duke, asked me to sit with him while he did a portrait in crayon of the two of us. As he drew, he talked about what he saw and how he would draw it. "You have yellow, curly hair," he said, "and mine's black and curlier." He didn't draw any noses, and he used two straight lines for our mouths. On another day, Duke suddenly broke out laughing and, pointing at my nose, said, "Your nose is so pointy and straight!" Everyone joined in laughing as I felt it, and I guessed that they were right. "And your nose is flat and short," I said. Everyone started describing their own or someone else's nose: Renee's was straight, Mona's short, Cory's like a button—all different, each a new discovery.

I found a poem that moved me at that time by an eleven-year-old named Carolyn Jackson (1966), and here is a fragment:

> When I ride the train and sit next to a person of the opposite race/ I feel like a crow in a robin's nest/ And I feel dirty.

Carolyn has a powerful interpretation of what it means to be black in America: to be not wanted; to be "dirty"; to be a "a crow in a robin's nest." This was what I was trying to teach against, and Kelyn had accomplished a small victory.

I remember another classroom years later and José La Luz, abused and neglected, a posturing thirteen-year-old wise guy whose friends called him "Joey the Light." School failure fit José and followed him around like a shadow. Since he hated school and felt hurt and humiliated there, José made himself a one-man wrecking crew—the path to the principal's office was a deep rut he walked many times.

My struggle was to find something of value in José that we might build his classroom life upon, something he knew how to do, something he cared about or longed for. In March, I saw a knot of kids skateboarding over and around some huge drain pipes at a construction site near school, and in the middle of it all, king of the mountain, was José La Luz. I asked José some days later if he could teach a mini-course on skateboarding to the class. He agreed. Soon we were having insignia design contests, subscribing to *Thrasher* magazine, and repairing skateboards on Friday mornings in a shop designed by José in one corner of the classroom. No one lived happily ever after—there was no sudden or perfect turnaround for José—but a moment of possibility, a glimmer of what could be for him, has remained in my mind.

And, finally, I remember a college seminar I taught on curriculum and instruction. The class was based on the notion that learning is a process of active discovery and that learning depends on concrete experiences and contact with primary sources if it is to be lasting, meaningful, and, most important, if it is to lead to further growth and learning.

In that class we had seen films, read articles, and talked about schools where hands-on learning with children is the norm, not the exception. We had also experimented with discovery learning at our own adult level. I felt then, as I do now, that it would be virtually impossible to teach in this way if you had never experienced the power of this approach as a learner. One assignment, for example, asked each student to develop an authentic question about the world, a question of some urgency or personal meaning, and then to go out and find the answer to that question by getting close to it, by touching it, by exploring primary sources, and then to document the whole process in a variety of ways. Later, students would use the question and the process as a model to develop curriculum with youngsters. While all students—schooled as most of us are in passivity and conformity—had a painful time finding a question ("I don't know what you want us to do." "Would 'the jury system' be an OK question?" "I'm not interested in anything."), some students eventually asked burning questions and were able to pursue sustained inquiries with astonishing results. One student, for example, whose sister was anorexia, investigated anorexia and became involved in an innovative support project for families. Another asked what life was like for the children of alcoholics and discovered what she had always denied but suspected: that her own mild-mannered, "normal" father was a quiet alcoholic. A hearing-impaired student looked into the reactions of a residential neighborhood when a live-in facility for mildly disabled adults was established.

What I remember particularly about that seminar was one student—Elaine. Her first attempts at an authentic question had been "What is the meaning of the Constitution?" and "How are race relations going in Chicago?" Finally she asked, "Where does the woman in the green shoes whom I see every day outside Sam Marcy's Restaurant sleep at night?" This question led her beyond a statistical and distanced view of homelessness and into a consciousness-expanding personal journey with Irene, the woman with the green shoes. She discovered a thriving shantytown within half a mile of the university, a place of community and collectivity as well as of pain and poverty. She traveled to soup kitchens and to church basements, scrounged trash outside restaurants, panhandled at the train station. She uncovered personal histories: Irene's story of the closing of a mental hospital where she was being treated for schizophrenia; John's story of losing his job as a security guard when his firm lost a contract at the airport; Sharon's story of an abusive husband and an ongoing struggle with alcohol. Elaine took pictures and recorded and transcribed interviews. She later developed a dazzling curriculum project filled with energy, experimentation, creativity, and open-endedness. It included an oral history component; a service project at a food pantry; an investigation of government policies and their impact on homeless people; and a weekend with the Mad Housers of Chicago, a group of housing activists who construct simple and livable (but not licensable) structures for the homeless. And it all began with that seemingly mundane question.

Before i stepped into my first classroom as a teacher, I thought teaching was mainly instruction, partly performing, certainly being in the front and at the center of the classroom. Later, with much chaos and some pain, I learned that this is the least of it—teaching includes a more splendorous range of actions. Teaching is questioning, instructing, advising, counseling, organizing, assessing, guiding, goading, showing, managing, modeling, coaching, disciplining, prodding, preaching, persuading, proselytizing, listening, interacting, nursing, doing and making, discovering and inspiring. Teachers must be experts and generalists, psychologists and cops, rabbis and priests, judges and gurus, and, paradoxically, students of our students. And that's not all. When we face ourselves, we face memories of our own triumphs and humiliations, our cowardice and bravery, our breakthroughs and breakdowns, our betrayals as well as our fidelity. When we characterize our work—even partially, even incompletely—straightforward images and one-dimensional definitions dissolve, and teaching becomes elusive, problematic, often impossibly opaque.

One thing becomes clear enough. Teaching as the direct delivery of some preplanned curriculum, teaching as the orderly and scripted conveyance of information, teaching as clerking, is simply a myth. Teaching is much larger and much more alive than that; it contains more pain and conflict, more joy and intelligence, more uncertainty and ambiguity. It requires more judgment and energy and intensity than, on some days, seem humanly possible. Teaching is spectacularly unlimited.

When students describe us, the picture becomes even denser and more layered. Teachers are good and bad, kind and mean, unjust and fair, arbitrary and even-handed, thoughtful and stupid. For our students, we embody the adult world and we are, next to parents, among the strongest representatives of and guides into that world. The hopes and dreams of youth are in our hands; their goals and aspirations are shaped through their encounters with us. Positive memories of teachers are reserved for particular and special people: the teacher who touched your heart, the teacher who understood you or who cared about you as a person, the teacher whose passion for something—music, math, Latin, kites—was infectious and energizing. In any case, teachers are a large presence in the lives of students; we take up a lot of space and we have a powerful impact. This is why I chose teaching: to share in the lives of young people, to engage and touch the future.

Teachers are asked hundreds, perhaps thousands of times why they choose teaching. The question often means: "Why teach, when you could do something more profitable?" "Why teach, since teaching is beneath your skill and intelligence?" The question can be filled with contempt and cynicism or it can be simply a request for understanding and knowledge: "What is there in teaching to attract and keep you?" Either way, it is a question worth pursuing, for there are good reasons to teach and equally good reasons not to teach. Teaching is, after all, different in character from any other profession or job or occupation, and teaching, like anything else, is not for everyone.

There are many reasons not to teach, and they cannot be easily dismissed, especially by those of us who love teaching. Teachers are badly paid, so badly that it is a national disgrace. We earn on average a quarter of what lawyers are paid, half of what accountants make, less than truck drivers and shipyard workers. Romantic appeals aside, wages and salaries are one reflection of relative social value—a collective, community assessment of worth. There is no other profession that demands so much and receives so little in financial compensation; none in which the state stipulates such extensive and specific educational requirements, for example, and then financially rewards people so sparingly. Slight improvements in pay and benefits in some districts serve only to highlight how out of step we really are when it comes to valuing and rewarding teaching.

Teachers also suffer low status in many communities, in part as a legacy of sexism: Teaching is largely women's work, and it is constantly being deskilled, made into something to be performed mechanically, without much thought or care, covered over with layers of supervision and accountability and bureaucracy, and held in low esteem. Low pay is part of that dynamic. So is the paradox of holding teachers up as paragons of virtue (the traditional pedestal) while constraining real choices and growth.

Teachers often work in difficult situations, under impossible conditions. We are usually isolated from other adults and yet have no privacy and no time for ourselves. We teach youngsters who are compelled by law to attend school, many of whom have no deep motivation or desire to be there. We sometimes work in schools that are large, impersonal, and factory-like; sometimes in schools that resemble war zones. We are subject to the endless and arbitrary demands of bureaucracies and distant politicians. Teachers are expected to cover everything without neglecting anything, to teach reading and arithmetic, for example, but also good citizenship, basic values, drug and alcohol awareness, AIDS prevention, dating, mating, and relating, sexuality, how to drive, parenting skills, and whatever else comes up.

The complexity of teaching can be excruciating, and for some that may be a sufficient reason not to teach (for others, it is one of teaching's most compelling allures). Teachers must face a large number of students: thirty or more for typical elementary school teachers, a hundred and fifty for high school teachers. Each youngster comes to us with a specific background, with unique desires, abilities, intentions, and needs. Somehow, we must reach out to each student; we must meet each one. A common experience of teachers is to feel the pain of opportunities missed, potential unrealized, students untouched. Add to this the constancy of change and the press of time, the lack of support and the scarcity of resources, and some of the intensity and difficulty of teaching becomes apparent. It is no wonder that many of us retreat into something certain and solid, something reliable, something we can see and get our hands around—lesson plans, say, or assertive discipline workshops—because we fear burning out altogether.

These are some of the reasons not to teach, and, for me at least, they add up to a compelling case. So, why teach? My own pathway to teaching began long ago in a large, uniquely nurturing family, a place where I experienced the ecstasy of intimacy and the irritation of being known, the power of will and the boundary of freedom, both the safety and the constraints of family living. I was the middle child of five, and I had opportunities to learn as well as opportunities to teach. In my family, I learned to balance self-respect with respect for others, assertiveness with compromise, individual choice with group consciousness.

I began teaching in an alternative school in Ann Arbor, Michigan, called the Children's Community. It was a small school with large purposes; a school that, we hoped, would change the world. One of our goals was to provide an outstanding, experience-based education for the young people we taught. Another was to develop a potent model of freedom and racial integration, a model that would have wide impact on other schools and on all of society. We thought of ourselves as an insurgent, experimental counterinstitution; one part of a larger movement for social change.

The year was 1965, and I was twenty years old. For many young people, teaching was not only respectable, it was one of the meaningful, relevant things a person could choose to do. Many schools then, as now, were inhumane, lifeless places. But we were crusading teachers. We felt that we could save the schools, create life spaces and islands of compassion for children, and, through our work, help create a new social order. We were intent on living lives that did not make a mockery of our values, and teaching seemed a way to do just that. We were hopeful and altruistic, and we were on a mission of change.

Today, teaching may not seem so attractive, nor so compelling in quite the same way. Not only are many schools in terrible shape, burdened with seemingly intractable problems, but there is still a narrow, selfish spirit loose in the land. Idealists are "suckers" from that perspective, and the notion that schools should be decent, accessible, and responsive places for all children is just more pie-in-the-sky. With a combative social Darwinism setting the pace, and a cynical sense that morality has no place in our public lives, teaching today can seem a fool's errand.

But it is not. Teaching is still a powerful calling for many people, and powerful for the same reasons that it has always been so. There are still young people who need a thoughtful, caring adult in their lives; someone who can nurture and challenge them, who can coach and guide, understand and care about them. There are still injustices and deficiencies in society, in even more desperate need of repair. There are still worlds to change—including specific, individual worlds, one by one—and classrooms can be places of possibility and transformation for youngsters, certainly, but also for teachers. Teaching can still be world-changing work, and in the contested space of schools and classrooms, our voices must be heard. Crusading teachers are still needed—in fact, we are needed now more than ever.

And this, I believe, is finally the reason to teach. People are called to teaching because they love children and youth or because they love being with them, watching them open up and grow and become more able, more competent, more powerful in their worlds. They may love what happens to themselves when they are with children, the ways in which they become better, more human, more generous and thoughtful and caring. Or they become teachers because they love the world or some piece of the world enough that they want to show that love to others. In either case, people teach as an act of construction and reconstruction, as a gift of oneself to others. I teach in the hope of making the world a better place.

While practically every teacher I have known over many years came to teaching in part with this hope, only a few outstanding teachers are able to carry it fully into a life in teaching. What happens? To begin with, most of us attend colleges or preparation programs that neither acknowledge nor honor our larger and deeper purposes—places that turn our attention to research on teaching or methods of teaching and away from a serious encounter with the reality of teaching, the art and craft of teaching, the morality of teaching, or the ecology of childhood. Our love of children, out idealism, is made to seem quaint in these places. Later, we find ourselves struggling to survive in schools structured in ways that make our purposes seem hopeless and inaccessible. We may have longed for youth-centered communities of shared values and common goals, but mostly we settle for institutions, procedure-centered places characterized by hierarchy, control, and efficiency. We may have imagined the kind of wonderful teachers we could become in an ideal world, but we had no idea of the obstacles that would be scattered along our pathways into teaching.

One common obstacle is the pressure not to teach. Family and friends question the choice to teach, and even experienced teachers advise young people to search somewhere else. One elementary school teacher I know, while in graduate school, worked as an assistant to a prominent education professor who told her repeatedly that she was too bright and too able to be a teacher. She found herself defending her choice against a person she thought would be an obvious ally but was not, and she learned an important lesson: The profession is full of people who don't respect its purposes. If teaching is to become vital and honorable, it is teachers who will have to make it so. It is the voice of the teacher that must at last be heard.

Another obstacle is the chorus of references to the "real world," as in, "Now this school is the real world." The point is to tell you that you are naive and foolish and that this school is immutable, that it has always been as it is and that it can never be changed. School, in this view, is not an institution of society or history, not something created by people, but rather something outside of history, agency, and choice. Teachers and students alike are supposed to compromise, accommodate, and adjust; to be compliant, conformist, and obedient.

There is a related, even more subtle sapping of your energy and mind as you submit to the structure of schooling. I observed a principal recently welcoming a group of new teachers to his school. Indoctrinating may be a more accurate word. He began by praising these teachers, by admiring their commitment and acknowledging their youthful energy and idealism. They should have known that when anyone praises your youthful idealism, it's time to duck, but instead there were smiles and a sense of worth and pride all around. Then, without changing tone or expression, he began to caution them about the families and the children they would encounter, warning them that they should not expect too much from these youngsters. "Your idealism is wonderful, just what our school needs," he concluded. "But don't blame yourselves if you can't teach these kids to read. It will be enough if you can get them to listen."

All the praise of youth and admiration of idealism turned out to be a cover for cynicism. These teachers were being told to accept something that is really unacceptable, to "grow up," to lower their expectations for learners. It's true that no one is wise before innocent, competent before clumsy. It is also true that teachers need to grow in experience, skill, and judgment. But that growth does not need to be based on narrowing goals, aspirations, or ideals, as this principal would have it. It is true that teaching is the kind of activity that develops and flowers over time, that there is no way to be an experienced teacher without first being a new teacher. But that development can be constructed on the basis of high and seriously considered ideals, hope, realism, and compassion for others. Teachers do, indeed, need to be forgiving of their own inevitable shortcomings, but always in the context of being critical and demanding of themselves as well.

Finally, a major obstacle on the pathway to teaching is the notion that teaching is essentially technical, that it is easily learned, simply assessed, and quickly remediated. Students of teaching spend an inordinate amount of time learning how to make lesson plans (an astonishingly simple, entirely overblown, and not very useful skill) or reading the research on classroom management. We are encouraged to attend to the voice of the supervisor and the administrator, the academic and the researcher, not to the more immediate and important voices of children and youth, their parents and community. This is, perhaps, the most difficult obstacle to overcome, and resistance and reconciliation are major themes in the act of effective teaching.

I know that i celebrate a kind of teaching that is exceedingly rare. I know that becoming an outstanding teacher is a heroic quest: Like Odysseus, one must navigate turbulent and troubled waters, overcome a seemingly endless sea of obstacles, and face danger and challenge (often alone) on the way toward an uncertain reward. Teaching is not for the weak or the faint-hearted; courage and imagination are needed to move from myth to reality.

Teaching is entombed in myth—there are literally thousands of tiny ones clinging like barnacles to teaching, while others perch on it like giant, fire-breathing creatures. These myths are available in every film about teaching, in all the popular literature, and in the common sense passed across the generations. Here is a sample:

MYTH 1: Good Classroom Management is an Essential First Step Toward Becoming a Good Teacher

This myth is central to the everyday lore of teaching. It is the old "don't-smile-until-Christmas" wisdom. Some teachers say, "I get tough in September to gain their respect, and then I can ease up without losing control." Others say, "I play 'bad cop' first so they know who's boss, and then I can afford to be 'good cop.'" Others describe teaching as trench warfare and claim that control of the trenches is a primary goal.

There is a sleight-of-hand involved here, for it is true that an out-of-control classroom is dysfunctional for everyone. But what makes this a myth is its linearity, the assumption that classroom management precedes teaching in time, and its insularity, the notion that classroom management can sensibly be understood as an event separated from the whole of teaching. The classroom management myth represents, in a sense, the triumph of narrow behaviorism and manipulation over teaching as a moral craft and an intellectual enterprise.

The ability to work productively with a large group of students is a skill that only comes with experience. The development of that skill is not aided by focusing on techniques from the pantheon of classroom management: "positive reinforcement," "anticipatory set," "wait time," and all the rest. Those simply turn a teacher's attention in the wrong direction. Nor is it useful to assume that once in control, teaching can begin. There are a lot of quiet, passive classrooms where not much learning is taking place, and others where children's hearts, souls, and minds are being silently destroyed in the name of good management.

Working well with a group of youngsters is something learned in practice. And it is best learned not as a set of techniques to shape behavior without regard to persons or values, but while attempting to accomplish larger goals and purposes. This means focusing on three essentials: youngsters (Are they active? Are they pursuing questions and concerns of importance to them and us?), the environment (Is it appropriate? Does it offer sufficient challenge? Are there multiple opportunities to succeed?), and curriculum (Is it engaging? Does it connect the known to the unknown?). While this will not yield instant "results," it will allow for the emergence of more authentic and productive teachers and teaching relationships, and questions of group coherence and standards of behavior can then be worked out in context.

MYTH 2: Teachers Learn to Teach in Colleges of Education

Teachers know that they learned to teach on the job (and, unfortunately, some of what is learned on the job is never subjected to serious scrutiny and is, in fact, a mass of conflict and contradiction) and that their journey through teacher education was painfully dull, occasionally malevolent, and mostly beside the point. Some teachers believe that a few college courses could have been useful if they had been offered during the first years of actual classroom experience, instead of being dished out as "truth" disconnected from the messy reality of schools.

A related myth is that a smart kid from a good college with a backpack full of good intentions is all we need to rescue failing schools from the sewers of their circumstances. It's always wonderful when a young person chooses teaching, but there are serious work, heavy lifting, deep intellectual and practical hurdles ahead. This is no job for a voyeur or an accidental tourist in search of an exotic interlude

When teacher education structures the separation of theory and practice, this message alone is enough to degrade teaching. When we imply that teaching is quickly learned and easily fixed (like learning the fox trot), that it is based on methods and techniques or on little formulas, that it is generic, in the sense that learning to teach in Hannibal equips a teacher for teaching in Harlem—then teaching can be killed off entirely.

Teaching is an eminently practical activity, best learned in the exercise of it and in the thoughtful, disciplined, and sustained reflection that must accompany that. Best when structured into the teaching day, this deep consideration and rethinking should be conducted with peers and with more experienced people who can act as coaches or guides and can direct a probingly critical eye at every detail of school life. The complexity of real teaching can then be grasped, and the intellectual and ethical heart of teaching can be kept in its center.

MYTH 3: Good Teachers are Always Fun

Fun is distracting, amusing, diverting. Clowns are fun. Jokes can be fun. Learning can be engaging, engrossing, amazing, disorienting, involving, and often deeply pleasurable. If it's delightful, joyful, or festive, even better. But it doesn't need to be fun. Imagine falling in love, connecting with your loved one in intimate embrace, making love, and finding yourself for the first time really known and understood, transported and transformed. If, as you looked deeply into those beloved eyes, your lover said, "That was fun," it would utterly destroy the moment. Good teachers are not always fun; good teachers should aim always for authentic engagement with students.

MYTH 4: Good Teachers Always Know the Materials

This is tricky. On the one hand, teachers need to know a lot, and good teachers are always reading, wondering, exploring—always expanding their interests and their knowledge. Who would argue for knowing less? On the other hand, since the universe is expanding and knowledge is infinite, there is simply no way for any teacher to know everything. The game some teachers play of trying to stay one step ahead in the text in order to teach the material is ludicrous. That game assumes that knowledge is finite and that teaching is a matter of conveying the same limited stuff to students, who are themselves beneath respect, incapable of thinking outside the informational realm of "one step forward at a time."

Many fine teachers plunge into the unknown alongside their students, simultaneously enacting productive approaches to learning and demonstrating desirable dispositions of mind, like courage and curiosity. A unit on machines in elementary school might involve bringing in broken house-hold appliances and working together to understand how they function. A unit on Asian immigration in high school might involve a collective search through newspaper archives or interviews in the community. Learning with students can be a powerful approach to teaching. Good teachers often teach precisely so that they can learn.

MYTH 5: Good Teachers Begin With the Curriculum They are Given and Find Clever Ways to Enhance It

Good teachers begin with high hopes and deep expectations for learners and struggle to meet those expectations in every instance. Too often the question is "Is it practical?" when the question ought to be "Is it passionate!" The given curriculum can be a guide or an obstacle, a framework or a hindrance, a resource or a barrier. The point is to get the job done, and sometimes that means starting elsewhere and circling back to the official curriculum simply to satisfy administrators.

For example, my brother teaches English at Berkeley High School. In a class in which he was required to teach Shakespeare's *The Tempest*, he decided to surround that reading with Bertold Brecht, William Golding, Kenzaburo Oe, and much more. The syllabus he wrote began in an interestingly original place:

> *Do you ever wonder why the world is so messed up? Do you ever think to yourself what kind of society you would create if you could just start over? Plenty of people have tried just that, either in writing stories or in actually remaking governments. This year we are going to spend a long time considering our society and many alternatives. We will always be looking to answer the question: What are the characteristics of a just society? We will begin with* The Tempest . . . *a play about a strange magical land . . . .On this island an exile from Milan has created his world, a regime of secret followers and spirits. Would you like to live there? Of course, everything depends on your point of view: The world looks different through the eyes of the master and of the slave. In Brecht's poem "A Worker Reads History," he asks: Who built the pyramids? Not the Pharaoh—who did the actual work?*

And so on.

MYTH 6: Good teachers are Good Performers

Sometimes. But just as often, good teachers are not charismatic and are not exhibitionists. Certainly they are not "center stage," because that place is reserved for students.

When I taught preschool, much of my work was behind the scenes, quiet, unobtrusive. One year, a student teacher paid me a high compliment: "For two months, I didn't think you were doing anything. Your teaching was indirect, seamless, and subtle, and the kids' work was all that I could see."

This myth of teachers as performers strips teaching of much of its depth and texture and is linked to the idea that teaching is telling, that teaching is delivering lessons or dispensing knowledge. This is a tiny part of teaching, and yet in myth it is elevated to the whole of it.

MYTH 7: Good Teachers Treat All Students Alike

It is important for teachers to be fair, to be thoughtful, and to be caring in relation to all students. If all students were, the same then a good teacher would treat them all the same. But here is Sonia, with an explosive anger that can take over the room, and she needs more; here is James, whose mother died recently, and he needs more; here is Angel, who cannot speak English, and he needs more. Needs shift and change. When I was a new teacher and Kevin showed up one day without lunch money, I gave him the necessary 50 cents; several colleagues encouraged me to let him go hungry or I'd "be buying every kid's lunch every day." It never happened.

In a family, the nighttime fears of one child might take considerable focus and energy for a time, and then the struggle of another child to read takes over. Helping the two children in kindergarten who are having difficulty separating from their mothers assures all children that this is a safe and friendly place. Good teachers spend time and energy where they must and expect that positive results will spread laterally among the group.

MYTH 8: Students Today are Different From Ever Before

Every generation of adults tells of a golden age of teaching or parenting when youngsters were well behaved and capable. This misty-eyed view is typically a highly edited version of their own youth. Some teachers claim to have been outstanding early in their careers but now assert: "I can't teach these kids." Today, the justifications for this are put in terms of "cocaine babies" and "households headed by women," where once it was the "culture of poverty" and "cultural deprivation," and before that, "immigrants who didn't care about their children." That last one may be making a comeback.

The fact is that kids come to school with a range of difficult backgrounds and troubling experiences. They come from families, each of which has strengths and weaknesses. Teachers, as always, must resist the idea that there is some ideal child with whom they would be brilliant; they must reject the notion that a child's school experience or relative success is determined exclusively by family background or social circumstance; they must respond to the real children coming through the door and find ways to teach each and every one of them. That has always been a complex and difficult goal, and it will always be so.

MYTH 9: Good Teaching Can Be Measured By How Well Students Do On Tests

Besides the many problems related to standardized testing, there are also problems that revolve around the connection of teaching to learning. Learning is not linear; it does not occur as a straight line, gradually inclined, formally and incrementally constructed. Learning is dynamic and explosive, and a lot of it is informal; much of it builds up over time and connects suddenly. This means that teachers have an awesome responsibility, as we shall see, to keep their teaching robust and energetic, for learning is vast and forward-charging and irreducible.

MYTH 10: A Good Teacher Knows What's Going On in the Classroom

Teachers sometimes assume that there is one true story of classroom life and then thirty misinterpretations. In reality, teachers know one story of what's going on, but not the only story or even the "true story." True stories are multitudinous because there are thirty-some true stories. Kids are active interpreters of classroom reality, and their interpretations are only sometimes synonymous with their teacher's interpretations. Classrooms are yeasty places, where an entire group comes together and creates a distinctive and dynamic culture; sometimes things bubble and rise; sometimes they are punched down or killed off.

MYTH 11: All Children are Above Average

There is a pervasive "myth of third grade," as in, "He's reading at the third-grade level." It's as if there is an "ideal" third grader somewhere on Mt. Olympus, and everyone else is just a shadow or a pretender. This explains why every fourth-grade teacher is angry at every third-grade teacher, every high school teacher unhappy with every elementary teacher, and college teachers miserable with the whole lot—the kids didn't come "ready." The truth is that third graders are various, and the teacher's job is to teach to that variety, that diversity.

MYTH 12: Kids Today are Worse Than Ever Before

The children now love luxury. They have bad manners, contempt for authority, they show disrespect for adults, and love to talk rather than work or exercise. They no longer rise when adults enter the room. They contradict their parents, chatter in front of company, gobble down food at the table, and intimidate their teachers.

This version of the myth was written by Socrates about 2,400 years ago. Shakespeare (2002) added: "I would there were no age between ten and three-and-twenty, or that youth would sleep out the rest: for there is nothing in the between but getting wenches with child, wronging the ancientry, stealing, fighting" (p. 52). Kids today are kids nonetheless, and they need caring and connected adults to engage and encourage them—even if we have conveniently forgotten our own youthfulness.

Teaching is a human activity, constrained and made possible by all the limits and potential that characterize any other human activity. Teaching depends on people—people who choose to teach and other people who become students, by choice or not. There are these two sides to teaching, and on each side there are human beings, whole people with their own unique thoughts, hopes, dreams, aspirations, needs, experiences, contexts, agendas, and priorities. Teaching is relational and interactive. It requires dialogue, give-and-take, back-and-forth. It is multidirectional. This explains in part why every teaching encounter is particular, each unique in its details.

When Jakob learned to read, for example, he was five years old, a student in my class, and he accomplished this feat without formal instruction. He felt strong and independent and important as a person, and he approached most things with courage and confidence. Reading was no different. He loved hearing stories read, and he had many favorites. He dictated his own stories to accompany pictures he painted. And he could read bits and pieces from his environment: "stop," "pizza," "fruit." One day, he announced he could read. He read a couple of familiar stories, moved on with occasional help, and never looked back. He was reading.

Molly read at six. She watched from a distance when she was in my class as others learned to read, and she looked hard at her own books. She never asked for help, and when help was offered, she pushed it away. And then she apparently made a decision that she could do it, that the time had come. She asked me to teach her to read. We sat down and read for two hours. We recognized easy words together and then more difficult ones. We discussed letter sounds and the mystery of phonics. Within a few days she felt like she, too, was a reader.

Shawn learned to read independently at eight, some years after he had been my student. Reading had been a goal for years, but it seemed out of reach to him. He struggled hard to get it, and I struggled to help, both by making him comfortable and by offering a range of reading strategies and opportunities. He found phonics both an incredibly helpful aid and a consistent betrayer. Slowly, painstakingly, he broke the code in the second grade, and read. When he was nine, he was as sophisticated a reader as any of his classmates, and the early frustration was a distant memory.

Each of these learners was different; each had his or her own specific talents, styles, obstacles, and needs. Each demanded a teacher who could invent an appropriate response to a unique encounter.

A powerful, perhaps dominant, view of teaching holds that teaching is nothing more than the simple and efficient delivery of a package called curriculum. There is little need for adjustment, no need for dialogue. In this model, teachers are glorified clerks or line employees, functionaries whose job it is to pass along the wisdom and the thinking of some expert, academic, or policy maker: Here is the literary canon; here is the truth of history; here is the skill of reading. The teacher is near the base of the educational hierarchy, just above the student, who is the very bottom of the barrel. Years ago, there was serious talk of making the curriculum "teacher-proof," creating bundles of knowledge that even thoughtless, careless people could pass along. The idea behind "new math," for example, was that teachers would transmit something they neither experienced nor understood and that a generation of brilliant mathematicians would somehow emerge, bypassing teachers altogether. This was, of course, a monumental failure, and such talk has been largely discredited. Today teachers are expected to develop "critical thinking" and "ethical reflection" in youngsters, too often without opportunities to think critically or reflect on values in their own lives. These approaches to reform are folly. The current enthusiasm for some imagined artificial intelligence that will replace the need for thinking, warm-blooded, and committed teachers in classrooms is only the most recent high-tech version of the old idea of teacher-as-clerk.

I have been a teacher for over forty years. In that time, I have taught at every level, from preschool to graduate school; I have taught reading, math, and social studies, research methodology and philosophy. I have cared for infants in a day-care center and for juvenile "delinquents" in a residential home. In every instance, there have been discovery and surprise, for me as much as for my students. Human relationships are always that way: surprising, idiosyncratic, unique, and marked by variety. Over time, a basic understanding about teaching has emerged and become deeply etched in my own consciousness: Good teaching requires most of all a thoughtful, caring teacher committed to the lives of students. So simple and, in turn, somehow so complicated and so elegant. Like mothering or parenting, good teaching is not a matter of specific techniques or styles, plans or actions. Like friendship, good teaching is not something that can be entirely scripted, preplanned, or prespecified. If a person is thoughtful, caring, and committed, mistakes will be made, but they will not be disastrous; if a person lacks commitment, compassion, or thought, outstanding technique and style will never really compensate. Teaching is primarily a matter of love. The rest is, at best, ornamentation, nice to look at but not of the essence; at worst it is obfuscating—it pulls our attention in the wrong direction and turns us away from the heart of the matter.

Of course, we cannot love what we neither know nor understand. Nor can we teach someone entirely outside our capacity for empathy or comprehension. No one can teach someone they hate, or despise, or find unworthy; someone completely alien or apart from some sense of a shared humanity. On the other hand, sustained interest in and deep knowledge of another person is in itself an act of love—and a good preparation for teaching.

M y teacher, maxine greene (1973), argues that "the teacher who wishes to be more than a functionary cannot escape the value problem or the difficult matter of moral choice" (p. 181). We recognize, in the first place, how routinely we are made into functionaries. Even as society occasionally ??? a romanticized view of the dedicated, caring, inspiring teacher— brilliant, creative, self-sacrificing—we know that the harsh reality in many schools is a structure that disempowers and de-skills, a system that pre-specifies each teacher's thoughts and oversees and constrains our activities. In large, impersonal systems, teachers are expected to become obedient, to uniform and to follow all the rules—we are expected to deliver the curriculum without much thought and to control the students without much feeling. Students are expected, in turn, to follow the rules and go along with whatever is put before them. The key lessons for everyone in such a school system, top to bottom, are about hierarchy and one's place in it, convention and one's obligation to it, and unquestioning passivity in the face of authority.

We become party to our own depersonalization, then, and to the thoughtlessness of our students; we see ourselves as merely placeholders and low-level bureaucrats, filling out forms and completing procedures. When I visited a classroom recently, a teacher welcomed me and added proudly, "We're on page 257 of the math text, exactly where we're supposed to be according to board guidelines." She was, indeed, on page 257, but several students were clearly lost, a few were actually sleeping, and virtually every student in that class was failing math. For this teacher, the received curriculum— certainly not the children and certainly not her own ideas and ideals and worthwhile projects— had become the central thing: powerful, wise, and unchallenged. She was marching through it as instructed, herself a victim of this approach. Everyone was losing—the children through a narrowing of life chances and possibilities; the teacher through a degraded sense of her calling and her work.

Teachers, then, too often implement the initiatives of others; we pass on someone else's ideas of what is valuable to know or experience, and we cultivate a sense of "objectivity" as the greatest good. We become passionless, nonthinking, uninvolved, and we hand over important considerations to "the experts," evading our deepest responsibility and marooning ourselves with the merely technical. As we separate means from ends, we begin to see our students as objects for manipulation.

Moral considerations become irrelevant; in the banal language of our time, we are each merely discharging our duties, following orders, simply doing our jobs.

Becoming more than this, resisting this view of teaching is what Greene has in mind when she talks about "the difficult matter of moral choice." She is thinking in part of the ways in which teachers become representatives of adult culture and society to the young, the ways in which we are engaged, sometimes consciously, sometimes unwittingly, in a larger project of inculcating youngsters into a particular social world, a specific set of relationships, "a distinctive way of life." Teachers may have more down-to-earth goals, and the words *socialization* and *acculturation* may seem lofty, alien, or inappropriate to describe classroom reality, but perceived through a larger historical lens, teachers are indeed part of a society's attempt to reproduce itself and stay alive. Teaching is more than transmitting skills; it is a living act, and it involves preference and value, obligation and choice, trust and care, commitment and justification.

Hannah Arendt (2006) was Maxine Greene's teacher, and she sums it up this way:

> Education is the point at which we decide whether we love the world enough to assume responsibility for it and by the same token save it from that ruin which except for renewal, except for the coming of the new and the young, would be inevitable. And education, too, is where we decide whether we love our children enough not to expel them from our world and leave them to their own devices, nor to strike from their hands their chance of undertaking something new, something unforeseen by us, but to prepare them in advance for the task of renewing a common world. (p. 196)

Not long ago, for example, a teacher in South Africa would have to consider her own classroom experience, the math and science or language arts, her own teaching, but she would also need to be aware of the school system with its strict racial categories and restrictions. The schools, of course, were a part of the system of apartheid, they mirrored it and reproduced it, and so the teacher thought about the larger society outside her school or classroom and about how it impacted her teaching. If she taught in a school for white children, there was one set of requirements and expectations— a higher set—and if she taught in a school for "colored" or African children, there were different requirements and expectations. The schools passed along the received conventions of the society, and they sorted children according to that particular wisdom. There was in the old South Africa a harsh division in all things, and that division rested on an educational system that offered a small group of white people an education for privilege and power, and the great mass of non-white people an education that would, it was hoped, fit them for lives of exploitation and control. Each South African teacher was expected to pass along the culture's goals and attitudes and aims; each was to play a small part in keeping South African society as it was. Aware of this, each teacher had to wrestle somehow with the problem of values and justifications.

Perhaps this is an extreme example. But if we turn to China or to Poland, Germany, Nicaragua, Saudi Arabia, or Peru, the same problem presents itself. Schools serve societies in all kinds of direct and indirect ways. Societies set up schools as institutional forms for the re-creation of specific values and norms, dispositions and assumptions. Teachers must somehow warrant these larger social goals and values in order to teach easily and comfortably; if they cannot, then they must discover how to teach in an alternative way, perhaps as an act of resistance. This is one reason why the schools in South Africa, and elsewhere, are such pivotal points of struggle; why students and teachers have been so active and public in their opposition to government policies; and why school reform is such a regular part of our own landscape. Schools are one important place where we fight out notions of the good and the right.

There is no American exception, and the problem is as real in the United States as it is anywhere. Of course, this is a time of intense doubt and confusion in our own society, of fundamental questioning and serious reconsideration. It is a time of changing roles and expectations and a time of conflicting demands on schools and teachers. While uncertainty and upheaval may encourage a tendency to seek solace in easy answers, those answers—those references to convention or precedent or higher authority—in many instances simply will not hold. The teacher must find ways to choose and to act in a shifting, uncertain world. She must find ways to take responsibility for her teaching without guarantees. This, as we shall see, requires a teacher to be wide-awake and fully present in her teaching; it requires a kind of heroism in the classroom.

The teacher who embraces the "difficult matter of moral choice" is thrust face to face with students in a classroom. At some level she has already addressed a fundamental ethical question, for she has chosen the task of encouraging and empowering others. This is so because whatever subject or discipline or approach she follows, she is engaged in an activity designed (by someone's definition) to improve or enable or endow others. All teaching, consciously or unconsciously, explicitly or implicitly, deals, therefore, with two questions: What knowledge and experiences are most worthwhile? And what are the means to strengthen, invigorate, and enable each person to take full advantage of those worthwhile experiences and that valuable knowledge?

Of course, neither question has an easy, straightforward, or universal answer for every individual in every situation. The dizzying diversity of human experience and capacity alone demands that teachers look deeply at our students, that we see them as creatures like ourselves and yet unique in important ways. This is a central challenge of teaching, and it is essentially a moral challenge; it cannot be resolved by referring to fact or to empirical data alone. There is no single, provable answer. There are several possible answers and infinite possible courses of action to follow. We are left to think about what ought to be and what ought not to be; we are left to investigate and inquire into and with our students, and to interrogate the larger contexts of our teaching; we are left to choose among conflicting claims, and this requires thinking critically and intensely about possible courses and outcomes. If we teachers want our students to acquire the knowledge, skills, and dispositions of mind that will allow them to live fully and well, to be strong and capable and competent, and to have the capacity to shape their individual and collective destinies, then we must struggle to figure out how to realize these lofty goals in specific situations with particular students. When do we focus our efforts on teaching what we consider necessary skills, and when do we allow students to act and to initiate? When do we nurture and hold close, and when do we let go? How do we know when we are doing the right thing?

For Greene, the answer lies in teachers learning how to "do philosophy." She means that teachers can approach teaching and learning critically and deliberately. They can struggle to stay conscious and alive, resisting the merely routine. They can use the findings of social scientists, for example, not as universal truths, but as something to be examined, considered, and contemplated. It means they can hold even their own experiences as tentative, contingent, and open to question. "Doing philosophy" means being self-aware and highly conscious of the world around us. And it means attending again and again to a fundamental teaching question: "Given what I now know (about the world, about this class, about this student before me), what should I do?" As Greene (1973) says:

> Involved individuals have to make the moral choices which are ordinarily specific. The more sensitive teachers are to the demands of the process of justification, the more explicit they are about the norms that govern their actions, the more personally engaged they are in assessing surrounding circumstances and potential consequences, the more "ethical" they will be; and we cannot ask much more. (p. 221)

Nel Noddings (1986) helps, too, by arguing that teachers can be aided in the "difficult matter of moral choice" if they can adopt an "ethic of caring." For Noddings, the central issue is not following a specific duty or principle, but rather being true in a direct, immediate sense to people with whom one has a relationship:

> Natural caring—the sort of response made when we want to care for another [a loved one, a baby, a sick friend] establishes the ideal for ethical caring, and ethical caring imitates the ideal in its efforts to institute, maintain or reestablish natural caring. . . . Persons guided by an ethic of caring do not ask whether it is their duty to be faithful . . . rather, for them fidelity to persons is fidelity; indeed, fidelity is a quality of the relation and not merely an attribute of an individual moral agent's behavior or character. (p. 497)

This points us in the direction of the whole person. From the perspective of an ethic of caring, it is the person before us who becomes our central concern. This in no way implies a lack of concern for academic rigor or excellence, or for teaching basic skills, but it does mean that skills are taught, for example, as a result of concern for the person, that is, that "the one is undertaken in light of the other" (p. 499). I insist that my students learn algebra because of my love of them, not of it.

A generative challenge in teaching is to decide who you want to be as a teacher, what you care about and what you value, and how you will conduct yourself in classrooms with students. It is to name yourself as a teacher, knowing that institutional realities will only enable that goal in part (if at all) and that the rest is up to you. It is to choose the rocky road of change. It is to move beyond the world as we find it with its conventional patterns and its received wisdom in pursuit of a world and a reality that could be, but is not yet.

It is, furthermore, to choose to do something that enables the choices of others and that supports the human impulse to grow. In this sense it is to choose teaching not as a job only, not even as a career or a profession. It is to choose teaching as a project or a vocation, something one is called to do. In a vocation like teaching there is a vital link between private and public worlds, between personal fulfillment and social responsibility. There is also a sense of commitment and purpose that rejects the measured calculation that pervades so much of work today. Teaching is the vocation of vocations, because to choose teaching is to choose to enable the choices of others. It is to be about the business of empowerment, the business of enabling others to choose well. There are all kinds of skills, tools, dispositions, and opportunities required for these broad choices to be made, and teachers must somehow become responsible for all of it.

Because society is indifferent and because we as members of society are floating in a kind of purposelessness, it is easy to dismiss talk of ethical action as romantic, foolish, or even quaint. This image of quaintness is intensified in schools increasingly bent toward a narrow agenda of efficiency and control. But we need to talk of values—of what ought to be—if we are ever to really understand ourselves, our situations, and our options, and if we are ever to undertake meaningful action toward improvement in schools or in society. The problems we face today are not essentially technical or material problems; they are, at their heart, moral problems.

Teaching is at its heart an act of hope for a better future. The rewards of teaching are neither ostentatious nor obvious—they are often internal, invisible, and of the moment. But paradoxically, they can be deeper, more lasting, and less illusory than the cut of your clothes or the size of your home. The rewards of teaching might include watching a youngster make a connection and come alive to a particular literacy, discipline, or way of thinking, or seeing another child begin to care about something or someone in a way that he never cared before, or observing a kid become a person of values because you treated her as a valuable person. There is a particularly powerful satisfaction in caring in a time of carelessness and of thinking for yourself in a time of thoughtlessness. The reward of teaching is knowing that your life can still make a difference.